T0153863

ANALECTA BIBLICA

INVESTIGATIONES SCIENTIFICAE IN RES BIBLICAS

— 101 —

Somatic Comprehension of Unity:
The Church in Ephesus

ROMAE
E PONTIFICIO INSTITUTO BIBLICO
1983

KŌSHI USAMI, S.J.

Sophia University, Tokyo

Somatic Comprehension of Unity:
The Church in Ephesus

ROME
BIBLICAL INSTITUTE PRESS
1983

Preface

The author of this book has tried to read the letter to the Ephesians *as a Japanese Christian*. In this, he has been influenced by certain realities. In Japan, many non-Christian people read the New Testament. They come to respect Jesus of Nazareth and even claim to be Christians. But, because of historical factors and the lack of unity among Christians, they do not join a church. They also realize that there is a gap between "western" theological expression of Christian faith-conviction and their own cultural background.

The Apostle Paul and his collaborators seem to have had similar problems in the ancient Mediterranean World. Some of the issues dealt with in the letter to the Ephesians are comparable to the problems of a Christian community in a modern metropolis like Tokyo or Hongkong, Singapore or Seoul. The letter to the Ephesians, with its description of a Hellenistic urban society, provides a model for Christian life even today.

In the church of Ephesus, there were tensions between older Christians and newcomers. While many commentaries identify the two groups indicated in Ephesians with Jews and Gentiles, our examination of the text of the letter does not allow us to follow such a simple identification. There were tensions between different races, as well as between people who clung to local customs and missionaries coming from outside. In Ephesians chapter 2, the apostle teaches a message of unity and shows the way to achieve it. How can we not read this chapter in a new light today? From their cultural soil, the Japanese have an inherent sense of harmony (*wa*), of the unity between man and man, and between man and *Nature*.

The first part of this book, therefore, studies the meaning and quality of the unity taught in the letter to the Ephesians.

People in Asia have a deep appreciation for real spiritual leadership when it is based upon *experience*. The concept and image of a way or path which is shared by many Asian religions plays an important role in relation to such leadership. In the letter to the Ephesians, the apostle presents himself as a spiritual master, *a mystagogus*. With this intent, he sets forth instructions, admonitions and ways of preceeding which are meant to encourage and help new Christians along the way toward becoming full members of the Body of Christ. The "hymnic" section at the beginning of the epistle is a sign of its mystagogical literary genre.

The epistle contains a key notion which leads to the mystery of the Church. Christian communities, immersed in modern civilisation and surrounded by other religions, need a deeper understanding of the meaning of the Church. The apostle, preaching the Gospel together with his collaborators, founded Christian communities (i.e. local churches) in Asia Minor. Through this missionary activity, he came to perceive profound meaning in Christian community (i.e. the church). Through use of the image of "Body", he explains and develops his perception in order to express the dynamic character of Christian community in relation to both its members and its surroundings. The apostle, therefore, conveys a new understanding of the Body of Christ. This understanding is of great significance when considered in the light of what can be called the "somatic comprehension" found in Asian cultures. Is there a bridge between the description of the Church in the letter to the Ephesians and the cultural and connatural appreciation of what leads to a good and spiritual community? Can the epistle give outlines and serve as a guide for an ecclesiology which is at once genuinely Christian but also Asian? To answer these questions it seems necessary first to describe the conception of the Church found in Ephesians as it was.

The letter to the Ephesians reveals the situation of Christians 2000 years ago, in which the structures of family and society were different from those of the present which is dominated by the "nuclear family unit". The people of the ancient world were familiar with suffering from natural disasters, as well as from famine, political turmoil, and foreign oppression. The apostle's teaching penetrates a radically human situation, in a time when family and society in the ancient Mediterranean world were still held intact through close *forms of human interrelation*. Man in our own day suffers from isolation, dehumanization, alienation, and from unilateral value claims which are often fabricated and imposed by consumer societies.

The task of this study has not been so much to examine the differences between cultures and attempt to construct bridges between various forms and expressions, but to discover *the common human*—and therefore "*in Christ*" (i.e. Christian)—*reality*. Because man is, according to the apostle, ONE, Greeks and Barbarians can understand each other. When faced with the real needs of human life, they may hate each other, or they may help each other. But man's vocation, the call of God, is clear: mutual help because of the hope that lies in man.

The letter to the Ephesians gives outlines for a common human, "bodily" level of understanding, mutual respect, and comprehension, as opposed to uniformity of doctrine, ideology or religion. Understanding between different cultures becomes possible on this level of a common human and Christian ("somatic") experience. New concepts may be useful, but an ever growing understanding at this common level, the innermost level of common human nature which can be shared through "body," is of far greater importance. What is of the greatest concern to us, then, in our study is the *quality or nature of unity*.

This book itself originated in and depended upon mutual understanding and help from many people. The main body of the work was defended at the Pontifical Gregorian University in Rome December 10, 1980.

Expressing one's thought in foreign language is an impossible effort when the matter in question is deeply rooted in different cultural soils. In this regard, I wish to express my sincere thanks to Rev. Fr. R. Dressman, who corrected the manuscript of this dissertation with great patience, and to Prof. M. Grosvenor of the Pontifical Biblical Institute, who kindly undertook the tiring work of reading through the entire text, polishing and improving the English for publication.

To Prof. F. Lentzen-Deis of the Pontifical Biblical Institute, I will always owe the deepest gratitude. As first reader of this dissertation he made unfailing efforts to understand differences of culture and mentality and encouraged me continually to overcome innumerable difficulties. Without his direction and Christian spirit, I could never have completed this work. I am very grateful to Prof. E. Rasco of the Pontifical Gregorian University, the second reader of this dissertation, who provided much in the way of valuable criticism and suggestions. I am indebted to all the professors of the Pontifical Biblical Institute who formed and guided me to become what I now am, especially to Prof. J. Swetnam, Managing Editor of "Analecta Biblica".

Finally, I cannot fail to express my thanks to Sister M. L. Mendizábal of San Sebastian, Spain, who in her Christian generosity typed the manuscript of this work, to Rev. E. Schellhoff of Köln and the German benefactors who supported my studies, and to the many people in Japan, who though they cannot be named, supported and encouraged me during my years in Rome.

Tokyo, 1981 Kōshi Usami, S.J.

Table of Contents

Abbreviations

References to books of the *Bible* are given according to the abbreviations used in the *Revised Standard Version*.

References to books and journals are given according to the abbreviations of Siegfried Schwertner, *International Glossary of Abbreviations for Theology and Related Subjects* (de Gruyter 1974).

ANET	=	Ancient Near Eastern Texts
AnBib	=	Analecta Biblica (Rome)
AngThR	=	Anglican Theological Review
BHTh	=	Beiträge zur historischen Theologie
Bib	=	Biblica
BZ	=	Biblische Zeitschrift
BZNW	=	Beihefte zur Zeitschrift für die Neutestamentliche Wissenschaft
ChQ	=	Church Quarterly Review
EvTh	=	Evangelische Theologie
Exp	=	The Expositor Times (London)
JAC	=	Jahrbuch für Antike und Christentum
JBL	=	Journal of Biblical Literature
JThS	=	Journal of Theological Studies
NTS	=	New Testament Studies (London)
NRTh	=	Nouvelle Revue Theologique
NT	=	Novum Testamentum (Leiden)
RE	=	Real-Encyclopädie der classischen Altertumswissenschaft
RSR	=	Recherches de Science Religieuse
RSV	=	The Holy Bible, Revised Standard Version (1973)
SJTh	=	Scottish Journal of Theology
StEv	=	Studia Evangelica
TDNT	=	Theological Dictionary of the New Testament
ThRv	=	Theologische Revue
ThR	=	Theologische Rundschau
ThTo	=	Theology Today
TU	=	Texte und Untersuchungen zur Geschichte der altchristlichen Literatur

Transliteration of Greek

a$_i$	=	ᾳ		ō	=	ω
ē	=	η		ō$_i$	=	ῳ
ē$_i$	=	η		ou	=	ου
eu	=	ευ		ᶜ	=	h
au	=	αυ				
th	=	ϑ				
y	=	υ				
ph	=	φ				
ch	=	χ				
ps	=	ψ				

CHAPTER 1

Introduction

This work has a double purpose: it tries firstly to understand a message given in the Letter to the Ephesians, and secondly, to apply the message to the modern Christian community in a situation such as in Japan and similar countries where Christianity is still a religion for "foreigners" and alien to the peoples.

After carefully reading the text of the letter to the Ephesians (in the following pages we abbreviate it Eph) and comparing the text with the archeological and historical evidence about the city of Ephesus in Asia Minor, we became aware of the problems confronting the letter's author. It became clear that, in fact, the problems approached in the letter had to do with the problems typical of a community in a metropolis such as Ephesus in antiquity. And we came to realize that one of the serious dangers of such a community was a human tendency to look for exclusiveness and disunity. The achievement of unity between different groups in a community is always an important task.

Starting from this insight, we found that the letter was not only attempting to solve a like problem, but was also cultivating a deeper understanding of the question in the right terms. The author gives a new and strikingly profound answer to a possible disunity and even split in a community. It is not easy to see and to discern the danger of disunity when groups, each seeming to have their right, are claiming this and that for their own sake, to fulfill the need of their own way of life as a condition of remaining in the community. The Ephesians were in great need of wisdom and spiritual experience in order to be able to discern the problem rightly. According to our proposal in the following pages, the author of Eph was just such a spiritual leader. But the new solution which he was giving to a general and obviously common problem reveals itself as the deepest insight into Christian faith and its realization. "Somatic consciousness" of a Christian community seems to be an answer which could also fascinate a people living on the "other shore" of the Asiatic continent.

Problems of a Metropolis

This general outlook includes several preliminary points best presented as questions. Taking account of modern exegesis and historical method, what do we know about the "Setting" ("Sitz im Leben") of Eph? Was Ephesus a "metropolis" in so far as we can make use of a sociological and topographical term in reference to the era between 1st century B.C. and 1st century A.D.? Does Eph describe a disunity and possible split between the groups in the city to which it was addressed? We will reserve our answer for Chapter 2, to continue with the question of how Eph conceived the main difference among the Christians. The letter makes this clear: this community consisted of "you" and "we" groups of people.

Two Groups

From the recognition of the two existing groups in the community, we start to investigate who they were. Can it be that the author of Eph meant with these two groups (i.e. the "you" and the "we" group) the classical Pauline distinction between Jews and Pagans? We find that the apostle was teaching them about the "way" of conducting a Christian life. Consequently, we have to reflect on the real meaning of "being heathen" and "being Christians" and have to study the real sense of "old" and "new"-comers in Christianity. Possibly we can apply the results of our investigation to similar situations in a church and in a society today. It is important that the problem be posed in terms which refer to "Christian" reality, and at the same time that we avoid a purely psychological form of solution and any solution which involves the use of power on the part of a totalitarian, inhuman authority.

In the light of the community that this letter describes, we shall try to give some answers to the questions mentioned above, by interpreting the second chapter of Eph and by developing the theological ideas which Eph expresses.

The Mystery of the Unity - The Mystery of the Body

To these problems, the answer of the apostle who wrote this letter to his community, is not only a theoretical one. The apostle wanted and took measures to lead his addressees to a common conduct and action. We have to ask: what is the sense of the "hymnic" exordium (beginning) of Eph? To answer this question, the style and language, literary genre, and the structure of the first part of this letter are important. The specific manner in which the author of Eph wrote belongs to the content he wanted to communicate to his readers.

We find in this letter a Christian master giving a solution to life.

All the expressions which deal with the secret of the Christian community have to be investigated. We choose especially the expression
*en Christō*ᵢ ("in Christ") trying to describe the dynamics which issue
from the use of prepositions, tenses and other grammatical and structural
relations.

Then we come to study the core of the message of Eph regarding our
problems. The author of Eph speaks about a mystery of Christ. He
explains its origin, its arrival, its initiatory effect among believers, its
rooting in a community. He speaks about the "Christ-event" which has
its presupposition, its object and its subject. He explains how the spiritual dynamism of the risen Lord becomes a glorious and active reality
in the community. "Christ is the Head of the community." We shall
have to follow the teaching of the author of Eph through the corresponding parts of the letter. The answers will result in a deeper insight into
the mystery of the "Body of Christ." We have to open our minds to new
dimensions of "comprehension" in order to understand a bit better what
Eph has to teach about the role of the Body of Christ in this world. It is
helpful to compare the concepts of Eph with the spiritual experience of
Far-Eastern people and we shall try to describe the dynamism of the
"Body" in this way.

Apostle - Master

It is very clear that this message mainly depends upon the spiritual
master who taught it. Therefore, we should like to dedicate the following chapter to the role of the apostle and of every follower of Christ
who is called to preach this message. What is the role of the group of
Christians? What is the role of the "church," a "structured" community
communicating this mystery to the hearers?

Following the letter to the Ephesians, our paper has to give a strong
emphasis on the divine gift of "somatic" dynamism. This aspect is very
feebly expressed by translations of Eph into English by the simple word
"hope." Its final fulfilment will be found — according to Eph — in a life
of comprehension and unity with the "four" dimensions of the Body of
Christ with the world.

What we have described above, however, already contains too many
technical terms taken from the letter itself. We shall have to study the
letter step by step in order to make understandable what this letter
wanted to say.

The Method

We follow the "classical" exegetical methods of textual analysis, of
comparison of each part with others of the same literary work. We seek
to incorporate in our study recent insights into the structure of language,

at least in so far as basic features are concerned.[1] We try to confirm
results complementarily from one part of the investigation (e.g. analysis
of single forms, expressions, of the whole "word field" with a semantically
similar meaning) with the other parts (e.g. the convergence of the "disposition" or "structure" of the text with the other data), and also the
correspondence between the total literary form and with the "genre".[2]

Study of the Letter to the Ephesians

This study is favoured by many decades of intensive research on Eph,
on the cognate letter to the Colossians and on the background of phil-
osophical-theological and popular religions.[3] The full information about
this research is available and cannot be repeated here, but we should
like to give an outline of opinions reflected in the writings most often
quoted in our study, in order to show our place in the discussions and
to clarify the state of the question stated above.

First, we wish to affirm that we fundamentally disagree with the
viewpoint under which two authors especially approach the intention and
the literary genre of the letter to the Ephesians: *Wolfgang Speyer* and
Norbert Brox. The title of the *Handbuch der Altertumswissenschaften*,
1. Abteilung, 2. Teil, München 1971: "Die literarische Fälschung im heidnischen und christlichen Altertum. Ein Versuch ihrer Deutung" by W.
Speyer, indicated that a kind of *literary forgery* determines the line of
thought in which this author sees the intention of Eph. *Norbert Brox*
wrote several studies from a similar attitude; one of the chief being:
*Falsche Verfasserangaben. Zur Erklärung der frühchristliche Pseudepigra-
phie* (SBS 79; Stuttgart 1975).[4] The whole writing of Eph, seen as a

---

[1] We developed our method in dialogue with reflections discussed by the follow-
ing authors: A. Vanhoye, *La structure littéraire de l'épître aux Hébreux* (Paris 1976²);
L. Alonso Schökel, *Estudios de poética hebrea* (Barcelona 1963); F. Lentzen-Deis, in:
Bib 60 (1979) 286-91.

[2] For the literary genre, see F. Lentzen-Deis, "Methodische Überlegungen zur
Bestimmung literarischer Gattungen im Neuen Testament": *Bib* 62 (1981) 1-20.

[3] See bibliographies and surveys especially in the following works: H. Schlier,
Der Brief an die Epheser. Ein Kommentar (Düsseldorf 1963³); J. Gnilka, *Der Epheserbrief* (Herders Theol. Komm X/2; Freiburg 1971); M. Barth, *Ephesians* (2 vols) (Anchor
Bible; Garden City, N.Y. 1974); S. Hanson, *The Unity of the Church in the New Testament. Colossians and Ephesians* (ASNU 14; Uppsala 1946); E. Percy, *Die Probleme
der Kolosser- und Epheserbriefe* (Lund 1946); C. Colpe, "Zur Leib-Christi-Vorstellung
im Epheserbrief", in: *Judentum-Urchristentum-Kirche* (Festschrift für J. Jeremias)
(BZW 26; Berlin 1964²) 172-87; F. Mussner, *Christus, das All und die Kirche. Studien
zur Theologie des Epheserbriefes* (TrThSt 5; Trier 1968²); G. Wagner (ed.), *An Exegetical
Bibliography on the Letter to the Ephesians ...* (Zürich 1977). Cf. H. J. Gabathuler,
*Jesus Christus, Haupt der Kirche Haupt der Welt. Der Christushymnus Colosser 1,15-
20.* (AThANT 45; 1965).

[4] N. Brox, "Zum Problemstand in der Erforschung der altchristlichen Pseudepigraphie", in: N. Brox (ed.), *Pseudepigraphie in der heidnischen und jüdisch-christlichen Antike* (Darmstadt 1977) 311-34. The whole volume is most instructive. Cf. on
the problem also: J. A. Sint, *Pseudonymität im Altertum. Ihre Formen und ihre
Gründe* (Innsbruck 1960).

literary unity and a literary work and compared with the contemporary literature of the first century, clearly can not be conceived in such terms. The early Christian literature is anonymous or pseudepigraphic because *of its nature,* not because of an intention of forgery. Speyer enumerates a great amount of evidence, and in this respect his work is most welcome and useful, but he does not define the full reasons why these religious authors in Jewish and Christian circles around the beginning of the Christian era suppressed their own names and submitted their works as common property to an existing community, so that they either ascribed their works to great personalities of the constitutive past (pseudepigraphy) or simply witheld their own names (anonymity). In the reactions to these studies, the many differences are pointed out so that we distinguish Christian (and partly Jewish) pseudepigraphy and anonymity from real literary forgery.

It is methodologically wrong to compare these works with later or with very special falsifications.[5] We shall try to explain our own reasons, taken from another cultural background, as to how we understand the attitude of these authors. The reason is — or seems to be — a special kind of authors' identification with the forces and powers (of God) which influence the (Jewish or) Christian community. These anonymous or pseudepigraphic authors find their place in the process of communication between themselves and their readers or hearers precisely when they did not intend to speak in their own names. This preoccupation is so strong, — it was respected by the whole community — that they were prevented from giving their names as authors.

On the other hand, this identification with the role of the ancient leaders of the community, with the way God's revelation was designed to influence the chosen community "today," is not simply a relation of a "master to his disciples." The critics whom we instanced above as contesting the concept of literary forgery as a key to the understanding of Eph are confirmed by the developing studies on early Christian literature. The recent monography of A. Lindemann, *Paulus im ältesten Christentum. Das Bild des Apostels und die Rezeption der paulinischen Theologie in der frühchristlichen Literatur bis Marcion* (BHTh 58; Tübingen 1979) gives a survey of the research.[6] His methodological remarks can only be affirmed.[7] In our opinion Lindemann sums up very carefully what can be said at the present moment of research about the character and the background of Eph. We should like to do more than simply take over the more general statement that Eph is a "revised and en-

---

[5] Cf. already the review by W. G. Kümmel, on W. Speyer's "Die literarische Fälschung", in: *ThR* 38 (1973) 64f.; and again: K. Aland, "Falsche Verfasserangaben? Zur Pseudonymität im frühchristlichen Schrifttum", in: *ThRv* 75 (1979) 1-10; see also H. Quecke: *Bib* 58 (1977) 292f.

[6] Op. cit. 1-10.

[7] Op. cit. 11-19.

larged" version of Col [8] and to express the intention of the author of Eph
more precisely.   By stressing a literary dependence on Col, Lindemann
is seeking to determine the development of Pauline thought, doctrine
and moral instruction "after Paul."   With this in view he traces back
possible other relations of Eph to Pauline letters.   But his final conclusions are very careful: there are discernible allusions to Rom, the first
and second Cor, also to Phil, but only in the case of 1 Cor are there
enough reasons for a "probable" literary relation.[9]

Lindemann thinks that the author of Eph had the intention of reaching a theological synthesis between Col and the "beginning gnosis." [10]   Eph
is considered as a document created under the continuing influence of
Pauline thought.   This general treatment of the growth of "Pauline
theology" in Lindemann's recent book shows well how all the characteristics and all the ramifications of such a "doctrine" must be seen in their
mutual connection and interrelation, in order to assess the degree to
which a piece of writing is "influenced" by Paul.   The proper intention of
such a letter can be discerned only by a consideration of all the data
present in the text of the letter itself and available from its setting and its
historical background.   A former study of A. Lindemann was dedicated
to Eph: *Die Aufhebung der Zeit. Geschichtsverständnis und Eschatologie
im Epheserbrief* (StNT 12; Gütersloh 1975).[11]

It treats of the special conception of "time" [12] in the letter and, we
can say, the ecclesiology of Eph.   Lindemann sees the life of the community of Eph determined by (present) resurrection.   Many of the single
analyses and many results of Lindemann seem to us convincingly proved.
Some of his conclusions, especially his understanding of the exclusively
present "resurrection," are not relevant to our study.   And we think that
our concept of the influence of the "Master"—whom we conceive as the
author of Eph—is not in contrast to Lindemann's polemic against a
"Pauline school".[13]

Directly concerned with our work, and worthy of mention even though
not written in recent years, is the book of K. M. Fischer, *Tendenz und
Absicht des Epheserbriefes* (FRLANT 111; Göttingen 1973).[14]   Here, like-

---

[8] Op. cit. 122, characterised as corresponding to the great majority of opinions
about Eph.   Lindemann treats Eph more precisely on pp. 122-30.

[9] Op. cit. 129.

[10] Op. cit. 130.   Lindemann agrees on this point with the judgement of K. M.
Fischer.

[11] See also his article: A. Lindemann, "Bemerkungen zu den Adressaten und zum
Anlaß des Epheserbriefes", in: *ZNW* 67 (1976) 235-51.

[12] Cf. F. J. Steinmetz, *Protologische Heils-Zuversicht. Die Strukturer des soteriologischen und christologischen Denkens im Kolosser- und Epheserbrief* (Frankfurt
ThSt 2; Frankfurt/M 1969).

[13] Lindemann, *Die Aufhebung*, 253f.

[14] This work brings also many summaries of opinions and gives short surveys
of research.

wise, we not only find many analyses of parts of Eph itself, but also
excursuses on the religious background, on the "conceptions" of popular
and more systematized philosophic and theological circles. Fischer often
interprets sections of Eph in a valuable and interesting manner together
with other post-apostolic writings, though his conclusions do not always
appear to result from the evidence he adduces. The general placing of
Eph "between apostolic and post-apostolic time" [15] is further determined
by characteristics of that time and of Eph. We enumerate only some of
the characteristics which he takes over from previous research on that
period: the organization of the community became more institutionalized,
it saw the end of the charismatic ministry, the separation between "her-
etics" and "orthodox" became more and more of an urgent problem, etc.[16]
According to Fischer, the main intention of the author of Eph is to
maintain the "Pauline" structure of the "mission" against all the other
writings of that time which wanted to introduce an "episcopal" organization of the communities. We shall quote Fischer's opinion where we
discuss other problems treated by him.

The partly exaggerated theses of Fischer are to a certain extent rectifi-
ed by a monograph which appeared at the same time: H. Merklein, *Das
kirchliche Amt nach dem Epheserbrief* (StANT 33; München 1973). Merklein evaluated carefully the arguments for and against Pauline authorship
of Eph.[17] He treats extensively all the texts of Eph which can elucidate
the character of the ministry and of the ministries according to the letter.
He describes the theological meaning and importance of the ministry.[18]
The book itself is helpful, also the sphere of its research. We liked the
impulse given by a book which does not treat directly of Eph, but of the
development of Paul's ministry. W.-H. Ollrog, *Paulus und seine Mitarbeiter. Untersuchungen zu Theorie und Praxis der paulinischen Mission*
(WMANT 50; Neukirchen 1979) gives a new and very well documented
outline of what we could describe as the "team work" of Paul and his collaborators in preaching the gospel. The phenomenon as such has never
up to now been treated in a monograph. One of the more important
results seems to be the new insight into the possible origin of the letter
to the Colossians. Ollrog—according to our opinion—does give reasons
and arguments such as to renew reflection on the "deutero-Pauline"
character of Col.[19] The "Pauline school" is vividly described and the

---

[15] Fischer, *Tendenz*, 201. The results are listed in short sentences on pp. 201-03.
[16] Ibid.
[17] Merklein, *Amt*, 19-54. Cf. the results on p. 53f.
[18] The "central theological idea" of the ministry can be expressed, according to
Merklein, as follows: "the ministry is the function of the gospel (Evangelium) and
its tradition", see pp. 398ff. These considerations form a theological foundation for
the reflections on the role and function of "the apostle" in Chapter 4 of our book.
Some aspects are differently posed.
[19] For Ollrog this is an "excursus", op. cit., 236-242. We recommend also the
following outline of the chronology of Paul's mission. See pp. 243ff.

evidence from the Pauline letters, from Acts, and from other writings of the N.T. seems to be very well evaluated. Here we find the necessary sociological considerations which render understandable why and how Paul could have such an influence in early Christianity. If scholars review the presupposition that Eph is nothing but a revised version of Col, the relation of Eph to Paul takes on a new light. It does not necessarily imply that Paul was still alive when Eph was written. But the character of the "Pauline" spirit in Eph can be understood better if we admit the existence of circles which started in the way described by Ollrog.[20]

Our study is very much concerned with the "liturgical" character, that is, with the characteristics of "prayer" and of "mystagogy" in Eph. Since the beginning of this century, this feature, especially regarding the exordium of Eph (the "hymn" of Eph 1,3-14 seen as a crystallization and representative [typical] part of the "hymnic" language of Eph) has been treated in many studies.[21] The growing interest in the prayer and liturgical nature of many parts of the Pauline literature lead to new insights into the spiritual aspect of the communication between the apostle and his communities. The main part of these studies was concerned with the "reconstruction" of "original" hymns. The literary analysis was made in consideration of the parallels and of possible comparisons with evidence from the cultural and religious "background." Recently this subject has been investigated stylistically and linguistically. It is not necessary here for us to repeat the whole history of this research, because most of these studies have given an outline of its development. We refer only to a few recent monographs which give further information.

Constant reference to the totality of the letter considered as a literary and also stylistic unity, and the analysis of the style[22] in contrast to concentrating on single expressions, were first applied to the letter to the Colossians by W. Bujard, *Stilanalytische Untersuchungen zum Kolosserbrief als Beitrag zur Methodik von Sprachvergleichen* (StUNT 11; Göttingen 1973). Because of the relationship between Col and Eph, there are many data, and some of the conclusions about the character of the style, that make sense not only for Col but also for Eph. Especially the method of Bujard, with more recent necessary emendations, should be applied to Eph—and to the letter as a whole—as well.

Bujard was mainly interested in the Pauline or deutero-Pauline authorship and aimed at a conclusion in this regard. But his study is helpful also to a better understanding of the sequence of thought, the

---

[20] The many references and balanced judgements about recent and older literature dealing with problems which also concern our work, make this book most valuable.

[21] T. Innitzer, "Der Hymnus in Eph 1,3-14", in: *ZKT* 28 (1904) 612-21 is looked at as the beginning of these studies. We will discuss these authors when we treat of the verses 2,14ff., on pp. 78ff. and 1,3-14 on pp. 115ff.

[22] We discuss stylistic questions in Chapter 3-2, pp. 75ff.

"rhetorical emphasis" and of many single characteristics of the style used in Col.

F. Zeilinger attempted to explain the "theology" of Col, basing his study also on the letter as a whole. He investigated the "formal structure," that is the disposition and inner coherence of the letter. With a new general view taken from there, he tried to make a fresh approach to the results of former studies which had collected many items and references from contemporary religious literature and from "history of religion" (see *Der Erstgeborene der Schöpfung. Untersuchengen zur Formalstruktur und Theologie des Kolosserbriefes* [Wien 1974]). These books are—in our judgement—based upon a more solid method than the many investigations which separate single texts and smaller units from the context of the letter as a whole, especially when they claim that a "hymnic style" or a "liturgical wording" allows of such an operation.

Gottfried Schille [23] and most recently C. Burger, *Schöpfung und Versöhnung. Studien zum liturgischen Gut im Kolosser- und Epheserbrief* (WMANT 46; Neukirchen 1975) brought the exercise of "reconstruction of an original hymn" to a certain culmination. We are more sceptical towards the attempts to separate "strata" of tradition, additions and glosses to an original pagan or early Christian "hymn," especially with regard to Eph 1,3-14 and Eph 2,14-18 (also to Col 1,15-20). It is perfectly true that these parts of the letters are not "totally coherent" or "from one and the same mould," but the differences may not necessarily point to different sources and subsequent versions of the same original. In any event, the results of the authors who claim to have found such original hymns or parts of hymns do not agree with one other. It seems impossible to find sane criteria which can prove, without reasonable doubt, earlier strata of tradition. It may well be that different "theologies" between parts of the same text do not exist, but that the text simply continues to develop one and the same line of thought with more than one application. We use and quote the recent investigations about these important parts of Ephesians and carefully refer to the efforts made by these authors.

An aspect which comes close to our theme, the meaning of the term "mystery" and many terms related to it, was studied by C. C. Caragounis, *The Ephesian "Mysterion". Meaning and Content* (Coniectanea Biblica, NTSer 8; Lund 1977). The author gives abundant and well structured information about the background of the word *Mysterion* since ancient times, about the language of the Mystery Religions and about similar phenomena in philosophy, in medicine, in the Septuagint, in the Jewish pseudepigraphical books. He investigates the word-field and the relations of the single expressions in Eph and compares them with similar data

---

[23] G. Schille, "Liturgisches Gut im Epheserbrief" (Göttingen 1953), and: *Frühchristliche Hymnen* (Berlin 1965).

of the Old Testament, of the Qumran literature, and apocalyptic texts. This book illustrates the background of history of religions and certain linguistic phenomena, which also influence our investigation.

Again and again, since Schlier wrote his commentary on Ephesians,[24] authors have argued, sometimes passionately, for or against the "gnostic" character of Eph. The term *gnōsis* itself and the interpretation of what should be counted as "essentially" gnostic, is much disputed. To indicate in general terms our position we should like to adopt views very close to the proposals made by Robert Haardt,[25] Sasagu Arai [26] and the descriptions of Kurt Rudolph,[27] knowing well how varied and diverse gnostic ideas and conceptions are. We are convinced that not only scholars of history of religion but also exegetes should try not to look at Paul's writings only under the aspect of "anti-gnostic polemics." [28] It seems to us that the discussion about "pre" or "proto-gnostic" [29] shows clearly to what extent the terminology of scholars is dependent upon suppositions as to when and where an attitude should be called gnostic. If we look at the repeated attempts of man everywhere in the world to advance, to be enlightened, to acquire a knowledge by more than purely "intellectual" or "rational" cognition, we find phenomena which come close to those from the end of Mediterranean antiquity which by our scholars are called "gnostic." We find affinities to such an attitude and to this vocabulary also in religions of the "East coast" of the Asiatic continent. In this study, we prefer to describe simply what we find in Eph and what we feel important, when we seek an application to our time, without a special effort to relate it explicitly to ancient *gnōsis*.

We wanted to make these very short remarks about recent works on Eph and related problems in order to give some sources for further bibliographic references and a very general outline of our own position. These works will be quoted again and more references to the present discussion will be given in the following chapters where we treat special questions and problems in relation to the exegesis of the text of Eph.

---

[24] Schlier himself shows by many notes to his special studies that he develops a line of research started before him.

[25] The following authors are quoted esp. because we find their summaries and "definitions" useful. In the book of R. Haardt, *Die Gnosis. Wesen und Zeugnisse* (Salzburg 1967) can be found enough warnings against over-simplification.

[26] More easily accessible for a wider public may be: S. Arai, "Zur Definition der Gnosis in Rücksicht auf die Frage nach ihrem Ursprung" (1967), in: K. Rudolph (ed.), *Gnosis und Gnostizismus* (Wege der Forschung 262, Darmstadt 1975) 646-53. This collection of articles can give an insight into the variation of opinions and into the diversity and variety of evidence.

[27] K. Rudolph, "Gnosis und Gnostizismus. Ein Forschungsbericht", in: *ThR* 38 (1974) 1-25; K. Rudolph, *Die Gnosis. Wesen und Geschichte einer spätiken Religion* (Leipzig 1977). Cf. *Altes Testament - Frühjudentum - Gnosis Neue Studien zu "Gnosis und Bibel"*, edited by K. W. Tröger (Berlin 1980).

[28] See recently E. H. Pagels, *The Gnostic Paul. Gnostic Exegesis of the Pauline letters* (Philadelphia 1975).

[29] Cf. R. McL. Wilson, *Gnosis and the New Testament* (Oxford 1968) 17, 57.

CHAPTER 2

Unity of "Old" and "New" Christians

Eph 2,11-22 carries great appeal for a church which is composed of two groups, namely, "old Christians" and "new Christians," or those who have been converted to the faith. The community to which the letter is addressed is composed of two such groups. And the situation of this community resembles very much the modern situation of a church in which one group, consisting of the descendants of those who had been drawn to the faith by the first Euro-American missionaries, co-exists with another group composed of recent converts to the faith. The former group has fought and suffered for the faith; the neophyte has only just arrived on the scene. This type of community is typical of that of a "mission-country" which is formed mainly of newly converted christians.

Eph 2,11ff. has a very important message for those churches existing in a non-Christian cultural sphere.

Missionaries "from thousands of miles away come bringing the good news" to pagans. In the past they braved the rough seas to reach these pagan shores but today they come by air. Their identities are as before firmly rooted in their native soil and their ancient cultures—cultures that have long been permeated with Christianity—and they come to a pagan world and another culture. Face to face with this "pagan" culture they become aware of their own cultural relativity. These pagans to whom they preach have a very ancient culture with other philosophies and religions.

They ask themselves, "Why should these people who are far removed from a Christian culture accept a foreign religion? What have we missionaries come to teach them? Have not these pagans their own self-sufficient technology, culture and religion? What are we doing risking our lives in these foreign lands far from our native soil and our loved ones? Are these people really in need of something? Have we come "to sell" our own traditions and cultures? If not, why have we set foot in a foreign land?"

It is of great interest to find in the letter to the Ephesians a hymn of a church which is also composed of old and newcomers, a joyful hymn created by the communion of old "Jewish" Christians and new "pagan" converts.

For the author of the letter to the Ephesians, the fact that the good news was preached by an obscure Jew from a Roman colony, perhaps, to an urban people which enjoyed a proud and prominent Greco-Roman culture was not a disadvantage. The message of salvation was proclaimed by a small and oppressed race. More, the old "Jewish" Christians accepted the converts into their community without any preconceptions. No bitterness or discrimination was shown them.[1] Indeed, the new Christians were welcomed into the "old" communion.

The apostle was even able to sing a song about the new situation through his encounter and communion with these "pagans." The apostle's attitude in this situation is important for the relationship of our present Christian churches, composed mainly of pagan Christians, to the non-Christians with whom they live.

The recalling of the pagan way of life has a positive meaning for the apostle who tells all of us "pagan Christians" a truth which finds an echo and a response in our inmost hearts (cf. 2,1ff.). There is still a great deal of discussion about the writer and the addressees of the so-called "Letter to the Ephesians." [2] This question will be left open for the present until the text and content of the letter has been examined.

Despite the textual uncertainty surrounding the phrase *en Ephesōi* in Eph 1,1,[3] we presume that a city in Asia Minor where St. Paul stayed for some time during his journeying,[4] and more precisely, Ephesus, is the right addressee. To begin with, a brief description of the city of Ephesus will help to understand the background of the letter in which sense and feeling of unity and community existed. Thus a specific comprehension of the church grew in such an urban atmosphere. Ephesus was really an international city. She had a sense of unity in pluralistic societies.

2-1: Artemis (Diana), the Symbol of Unity

2-1-1: *Ephesus — An "Industrialized" City*

The author of the letter to the Ephesians does not appear to be dealing with a nomadic or a rural people. On the contrary, this man who lived in a pagan world and had a sense of urban life appears to be con-

---

[1] Here we are describing the setting of the letter to the Ephesians. The situation in this city is not the same as in Antioch, where Peter took the part of the Jewish Christians of Jerusalem and discriminated against the "pagan" Christians, as can be found in Gal 2 and Acts 15. In any event, when the letter to the Ephesians was written, such discussions belonged to the past.

[2] See J. Gnilka, *Der Epheserbrief* (Freiburg 1971) 1ff.

[3] B. M. Metzger, *A Textual Commentary on the Greek New Testament* (London 1971) 601. Cf. the major commentaries. Also, cf. the comprehensive study of A. Van Roon, *The Authenticity of Ephesians* (Leiden 1974), esp. 3, 72ff., 439.

[4] Cf. Acts 18-20; 1 Cor 15,32; 16,8; 1 Tim 1,3; 2 Tim 4,12; 1,18.

ducting a dialogue with a community which lives in a pluralistic society, a community to which he himself belongs and within which he speaks.

Characteristic of the city in the pagan world were the division and organization of handicraft, economic interdependence, the international character of religion, a trading port, and so on. Life in the city differed greatly from that of the rural or nomadic communities in which the family formed a self sufficient economic unit which could provide for itself within a bond of blood.

The city of Ephesus, where the Roman proconsul had his seat,[5] had been the capital of Asia Minor since 133 B.C. This Hellenistic city was built by the genius Lysimachus who called it "Arisinoeia" after his wife (289/288 B.C.).[6] The city was well endowed by nature.[7] Its excellent geographical position led to its becoming the commercial centre of Asia Minor in ancient times. A port at the mouth of the river Kaystros, the west wind carried hither the sails from the Aegean Sea. Ships came from Thessalonika in the north, from Athens, Corinth and even from Rome in the west and from Alexandria in the south and Antioch in Syria.

All the goods of the Mediterranean area passed through here. Land and sea routes met at this great cross-roads: corn came from the Black Sea and Prussian amber from the mouth of the Danube. Wool came from Phrygia, woven goods from Sardis, spices from Mesopotamia. Goods from India made their way here as well as precious stones, pearls, and ivories from Egypt; silk and purple dyes came from Syria and the Far East. Important trade routes went north to Smyrna and Pergamon, south along the river Maeander to Phrygia and inland along the river Kaystros to the Persian king's highway which led to the Eastern world and the silk road to China.

Various industries flourished in Ephesus itself. Best known, perhaps, are its famous silversmiths, but here also textiles were manufactured, carpets were produced, and handicrafts flourished. Large shipping companies had their main offices and shipyards in Ephesus and there were many local fisherman.[8]

2-1-2: *Artemis, Symbol of Unity*

The temple of Artemis was antiquity's largest bank.[9] The Goddess of the temple which was the symbol of the city was called "Artemis" by

[5] W. Alzinger - S. Karwiesse - D. Knibbe, "Ephesos", in: *Pauly-Wissowa, Suppl.* vol. XII (Stuttgart 1970), col. 263f. (Henceforward we abbreviate *RE*.)

[6] *RE*, Suppl. vol. XII, col. 258f.; D. Magie, *Roman Rule in Asia Minor*, vol. I, *Text*, (Princeton 1950) 75f.

[7] L. Bürchner, "Ephesus", in: *RE* V, col. 2778ff.; D. Magie, *Roman Rule ...*, vol. I, *Text* (Princeton 1950) 74f.; id., vol. II, 885f.; R. Oster, "The Ephesian Artemis as an Opponent of Early Christianity": *Jahrbuch für Antike und Christentum*, 19 (1976) 24-44, esp. 24.

[8] *RE*, ibid., v. col. 2783f.

[9] Cf. *RE*, Suppl. XII, col. 271; *RE*, ibid., col. 2802f.; Dio Chrysostom, *The Thirty-*

the Greeks and "Diana" by the Romans.[10] The Goddess Artemis was worshipped as a fertility goddess and a nursing mother. She was at the same time virgin.[11] Her abundance of vitality is symbolised by the many breasts of her statue. This is also the significance of the sacred animal, the bee, which is found on her garment and on her coins. Originally, she was a goddess of the hunt and so the deer is also associated with her.[12] The Goddess Artemis was very popular not only in Ephesus and in the surrounding areas but also throughout the whole Ionian world, and her shrine remained a place of pilgrimage even in Christian times.[13]

"Artemis dwelt neither in the vast temple nor in the tiny terra-cotta: she was implicit in the life of nature; she was the reproductive power that kept the great world ever the same amid the constant flux of things. Mother of all and nurse of all, she was most really present wherever the unrestrained life of nature was most freely manifested, in the woods, on the mountains, among the wild beasts. Her worshippers expressed their devotion and their belief in her omnipresence by offering shrines to her, and doubtless by keeping shrines of the same kind in their own homes, certainly also by placing such shrines in graves beside the corpse, as a sign that the dead had once more gone back to the mother who bore them." [14]

2-1-3: *Ionian Federation*

The sense of "communion" which existed between Ephesus and many cities and islands in that part of the Aegean Sea, cannot be accounted for solely by the cult of Diana. One must also take cognizance of the sense and feeling of the ancient Ionian federation which perdured through the centuries.[15] The Greek tribes who came in early historical times from Attica and Euboea and who took possession of long stretches of seaboard on the Asiatic coast between Phocaea and Miletus called themselves Ionians. Their dialects can be ascertained from inscriptions found in the cities of Ephesus, Miletus, Priene, Samos, and many other cities of the so-called Ionian federation. These cities are listed by Vitruv.[16]

---

first discourse: The Rhodian Oration, 54-55 (Loeb Classical Library; translated by J. W. Cohoon,; 1951; reprint 1961); R. Oster, art. cit., 32f.

[10] O. Jessen, "Ephesia", in: *RE*, V, 2754; D. Magie, *Roman Rule* ..., vol. II, 887, note 86. R. Oster, art. cit., 30f.

[11] Jessen, art. cit., 2760.

[12] *RE*, Suppl., XII, col. 297ff.; R. Fleischer, *Artemis von Ephesos und Verwandte Kultstatuen aus Anatolien und Syrien* (Leiden 1973) 46ff.

[13] *RE*, Suppl., XII, col. 263-69.

[14] W. M. Ramsay, *The Church in the Roman Empire before A.D. 170* (London 1892) 126.

[15] Cf. D. Magie, *Roman Rule* ..., vol. I (Princeton 1950) 53ff. esp. 65ff.; vol. II, 819ff.; Th. Lenschau, "Die Gründung Ioniens und der Bund am Panionion", in: *Klio* 36, N.F. 18 (1944) 201-37; D. Knibbe, "Ephesos und der Ionische Städtebund", in: *RE*, Suppl. XII (1970), col. 256f.

[16] See the text of Vitruv, *de arch.* IV, 1, 4-6 and the explanation in: P. Hommel,

The immigrants, who brought with them to Asia their religious beliefs and their civic organisations, intermingled with the native population and absorbed its culture. They quickly developed trade relations between the cities and the hinterlands and attained a high degree of prosperity. They had to protect themselves against the Carians and Lydians, however, and for this reason they founded a confederation of cities and islands. The religious centre of this federation was the sanctuary of the cult of Poseidon Helikonios in Panionion, which was situated on the peninsula Mykele close to the city of Melie.[17] Here every year the federation celebrated a feast. Sacrifices were offered for a number of days. Excavations have additionally brought to light evidence of the existence of a *bouleuterion*, the meeting place of the council of the federation. According to an inscription, the *basileus* of Ephesus was the president of this council.[18] It seems that under the dominion of the Lydians and later of the Persians no *Panionia* feast was held. It was probably replaced for a time by the feast of Ephesus.[19] People who came from the rural area were probably shocked at the moral standards of the citizens of Ephesus, and it is likely that those with high moral standards like the Jew, Paul, would have regarded the city as immoral. The Artemis of Ephesus held the whole population of the city in her breasts by two main roads leading to the temple. Like the queen-spider she spun a web which encircled the people of Ephesus. With her magic power she charmed them, surrounding the city with her walls. This "great"[20] temple of Artemis was destroyed by fire on the night of the birth of Alexander the Great (21 July, 356 B.C.) but it was later rebuilt by Deinokrates.

According to Antipator of Sidon, the temple of Artemis in Ephesus was one of the seven wonders of the world in antiquity.[21] The rebuilt temple existed in all its splendour down to the third century A.D.

"Melie Geschichte aufgrund der Quellen und des Grabungsbefundes", in: *Jahrbuch des Deutschen Archäologischen Instituts*, 23. Erg. Heft (Berlin 1967) 78ff. An inscription found in Priene confirms the destruction of Melite (Melie) probably at the beginning of the 7th cent. B.C., see: *RE*, Suppl., XII, col. 252. Cf. G. Kleiner, "Panionion, Geschichte aufgrund der Quellen und Bodenforschung", in: *Jahrbuch des Deutschen Archäologischen Instituts*, 23. Erg. Heft, 8. He shows that Ephesus and Miletus played the main role in the Ionian Federation.

[17] The excavations are described in the "Ergänzungheft XXIII" to the *Jahrbuch des Deutschen Archäologischen Instituts* (Berlin 1967), by G. Kleiner, P. Hommel, W. Müller-Wiener, "Panionion und Melie."

[18] P. Hommel, art. cit. 45-63, esp. 49f. and 62f.

[19] L. Ziehen, art. "Panionia", in: *RE*, XVIII, 603.

[20] O. Jessen, "Ephesia", art. in: *RE*, V, 2754; cf. Acts 19,24ff.; Dio Chrysostom, *The Fortieth Discourse: Delivered in His Native City on Concord with the Apameans* (Loeb Class. Library), vol. IV, 116f. (translated by H. L. Crosby) (1956; reprint, 1962).

[21] C. Schneider, *Kulturgeschichte des Hellenismus*, vol. I, 683-84 (AG 9,58). D. Magie, *Roman Rule*, vol. II, notes to pp. 887-888, states: "The earliest canon of the 'Seven Wonders' seems to have contained, besides the Temple of Artemis, the wall of Babylon, the statue of Zeus at Olympia, the 'Hanging Gardens' at Babylon, the Colossus at Rhodes, the Pyramids of Egypt and the Mausoleum at Halicarnassus."

On the occasion of the feast of Artemis (March, the month of the Goddess), the statue of the Goddess was carried in a procession in which boys and girls in gala dress took part (*exodus* of Artemis). On the sixth of March the feast came to a climax . Sacrifices were offered to the Goddess, dances were performed in her honour [22] and young people were placed under her protection.[23]

With regard to "sacred prostitution," it has not been shown that the priestesses played the role of the sacred prostitute officially. But the practice is supposed to have been current in this cultural milieu.[24] During the feast the Ephesians might have enjoyed "public sex" in the wood of Orthigia which was five hours walk from the city.[25]

To appreciate the spirit of the city of Ephesus, one must bear in mind that alongside the city's wealthy ruling class composed of Roman citizens, favourites of the Roman emperor and successors of the Asian land-owners, there existed a vast "middle class" engaged in handicrafts, fishing, textile production and trade of all kinds. The city's well-known silversmiths appear to have been organized in a kind of guild, and their flourishing silver industry was closely linked to the temple and cult of Artemis. They made statues of the goddess, images of her temple, and the famous amulets inscribed with the magic words—the "Ephesia grammata." [26] In Acts 19,21-29, Luke describes dramatically the activity of these silversmiths and their violent demonstration against the apostle Paul. This demonstration does not appear to have been merely "religious," however. Social reasons also seem to have played a part in it, as the silversmiths were fearful of the effect of Paul's preaching on the profits of their industry which was so intimately connected with the cult of Artemis,[27] and they felt their livelihoods endangered. The crowd came together, shouting without knowing the purpose of the assembly, as if they had been hypnotized *en masse* (cf. Acts 19,32).[28] This incident reveals a city which was a hot-bed of magic, fortune-telling and mantic arts, and it also suggests that the liberation of man from magic or oppressive superstition might involve much more than a setting at nought or a rejection

---

[22] C. Picard, *Ephèse et Claros* (Paris 1922) 326ff. also see, *RE*, V, 2760ff.

[23] C. Schneider, *Kulturgeschichte des Hellenismus*, vol. I, 685, note 2.

[24] C. Picard, op. cit., 233.

[25] G. A. Zimmermann, *Ephesus im 1. christlichen Jahrhundert* (Diss. Leipzig 1874) 78ff.; F. Rienecker, *Brief an die Epheser*, 25-26. We should not exaggerate the "low morality" of the people of Ephesus. It is possible that a positive element of the religion of Artemis existed for the acceptance of the gospel of the Christians and a certain "base" or "consonantia" towards Christianity among the people who believed in the Artemis. Cf. R. Oster, art. cit. (note 7), 38ff.

[26] Cf. *RE*, V, 2771ff.

[27] Cf. Acts 19,25ff.; W. M. Ramsay, *The Church in the Roman Empire before A.D. 170* (London 1892) 130f.

[28] About the historical value of the description of Ephesus in Acts 19 and about Luke's way and art of writing in this chapter, see E. Haenchen, *Die Apostelgeschichte* (Göttingen 1965⁵) 492-514; H. Conzelmann, *Die Apostelgeschichte* (Tübingen 1963) 110-14.

of the goddess. It might, in fact, constitute a challenge, a revolutionary call to change the existing social structure of the city.

Ephesus was the homeland of the magic words ("Ephesia grammata") which were believed to have the extraordinary power of exorcising evil spirits.[29] One who spelled the six words of Ephesia grammata [30] or who wore the amulet engraved with the magic words was said to have super-natural power. From the city of Ephesus the use of the magic words spread far and wide through the Greek cities.[31] Magicians and fortune-tellers enjoyed a flourishing "business" in the Artemision.[32] Until the beginning of the third century A.D. sorceresses, spiritualistic media and exorcists used the magic words to expel demons and to tell the future. Ephesus was the centre of the industry of books on magic that enriched the city. Here the mystery cults flourished. Inscriptions offer a great deal of evidence for the existence of quite a number of mystery religions and organizations in the city. The best known of these groups was the organization of the so-called Kuretes.[33]

This description of the city might lead one to think that the intel-lectual life of Ephesus was not of a very high standard and that its critical sciences were at a low ebb. Such was not the case. The city's famous library of Celsus offers adequate testimony to the tenor of the city's intellectual life. Archeological investigations have turned up the ruins of this library at the southern tower of the Agora (now reconstruct-ed). It occupied one side of the small square on the western side of this tower.[34] The date of the library's institution is still a matter of debate, but it was completed before A.D. 117. An auditorium stood nearby.

Many "philosophical" conceptions of that Hellenistic period can be traced back to Ephesus. Our letter is the witness of "popular philosophy," "Gnostic" influence and "popular" ethics, as taught according to the syncretistic way of instruction in the time of the "Middle Platonic" period.[35]

The city of Ephesus was also a city of "show business." It was

---

[29] Kuhnert, "Ephesia grammata" in: *RE*, V, 2771-2773.

[30] According to Clemens Alex., *Strom.* V, 242, the six words were: "askion, ka-taskion, tetrax, lix, danameneus, sision." And Picard, op. cit., 443, alludes to an ancient link with the Hittite empire.

[31] Kuhnert, *RE*, V, 2772.

[32] Picard, op. cit., 131.

[33] Cf. D. Knibbe, *RE*, Suppl., XII, 284-287, on the "Kretes", col. 286f.; R. Oster, art. cit. (n. 7), 38, says: "... a special college of the priests of Artemis, the Curetes ...."

[34] W. Alzinger, "*Ephesos*" in: *RE*, Suppl. XII, 1630ff.

[35] The term "philosophy" is found only in Col 2,8. The subject matter is not confined to this letter, however. In a very similar way it is found in Eph.; cf. O. Michel, "*philosophia*" in: *TDNT* IX (1973) 172-88. For a summary of the philo-sophical activity of that time with reference especially to Col and to Luke's work, cf. E. Lohse, *Der Brief an die Kolosser und an Philemon*, 144-46, 186-91; J. Dillon, *The Middle Platonists* (London 1977). Cf. A. Momigliano, *Alien Wisdom, The Limits of Hellenisation* (Cambridge 1975), see, esp., chapter 6, 123ff.; F. Zeilinger, *Der Erstge-borene der Schöpfung* (Wien 1974) 118ff.

provided with theaters [36] and gymnasiums [37] for the leisure and education of its citizens. In the month of Artemis, in keeping with a tradition which long pre-dated the christian era, competitions in sport and music were held in honour of the goddess.[38] From inscriptions it may be deduced that originally this was the festival of the *koina*, the federation of cities in Asia Minor, and remained so at least until the time of Augustus.[39] In addition to being a religious-political assembly, it became an occasion for contests in athletics and music.[40] In Pergamon, Smyrna and Ephesus, this festival was held in three successive years. The fourth year it was held in another city.[41] From A.D. 113-116, it was continued in honour of Rome.[42] Competitions in music and drama entertained the the people of Ephesus.[43]

Inscriptions and reliefs from Ephesus show that cruel games between gladiators and beasts satisfied the citizens' hunger for blood. The stadium and circus were used for this purpose.[44] The citizens' intoxication with these brutal contests in Roman times is in sharp contrast to the ancient Greek's love of cultural entertainments.

The immigration of Italian settlers into Asia Minor began in the second century or early in the first century B.C. The "Romans" constituted groups in all the more important cities such as Pergamon, Ephesus and Priene.[45] A rapid increase in their numbers very soon led to considerable friction between them and the native inhabitants. In 88 B.C., the king Mithridates, who had his residence in Ephesus, massacred many thousands of these settlers.[46] Later on the Romans chose Ephesus and not Pergamon as the capital of the province of Asia because of the natural, historical, economic and strategic advantages of this site. Ephesus became the seat of the proconsul.

Here a large group of Roman citizens — the so-called "residential Romans," who were mostly businessmen — engaged in trade. In reality, these men were the harbingers of Roman exploitation. At the beginning of the reign of Augustus they are mentioned as the *"conventus civium Romanorum qui in Asia negotiantur."* [47] The publicani, the Roman tax-collectors, had their offices and banks in the city. These unscrupulous men plundered even the property of the goddess Artemis. The Ephesians,

---

[36] W. Alzinger, *"Ephesos"*, in: *RE*, Suppl., XIII, 1625ff.
[37] Ibid., 1611ff.
[38] D. Knibbe, *RE*, Suppl., XII, 278.
[39] D. Magie, *Rule* ..., op. cit., II, 1294, note 54.
[40] Ibid., 1294, 1298.
[41] Ibid., 1295.
[42] Ibid., 1295, note 57.
[43] D. Knibbe, *RE*, Suppl., XII, 280.
[44] Ibid.
[45] D. Magie, *Rule* ..., vol. I, 162ff.; vol. II, 1051, note 6.
[46] Ibid., 163ff., 216ff.
[47] Ibid., 165; *RE*, Suppl., X, 259f.

however, sent a delegation to Rome and their representative, the famous geographer Artemidoros, obtained from the Roman senate an abrogation of the decisions of the publicani. The fishing rights were given back to the temple of Artemis,[48] and the goddess enjoyed once again her monopoly in this area. The temple organized an enormous loan system which helped finance the Roman campaigns. The Romans, in fact, far from changing the socio-political and economic structure of Ephesus, found themselves rather supporting it.[49] The history of the city of Ephesus shows clearly the enterprising character of its inhabitants. At the same time, it demonstrates the cleverness and realistic political mind of the Ephesians. They managed to hold on to much of the wealth of the city and temple, and they were able to retain their own traditions. The influence of the goddess Artemis endured through the centuries.

Despite Persian kings and Roman tyrants, Ephesus retained its flavour and its steady activity. In spite of the large number of slaves in the city and the uninterrupted influx of foreigners and especially of people from the mountainous inland regions, Ephesus integrated everybody. At the beginning of the Christian era we find here a kind of industrialized society with division of labour, with employers and workers, with guilds and trusts, all having a common interest and intent on the utilization of the city's natural resources and abundant manpower. Little is known about the thousands of slaves which the wealthy citizens of the city and the cult of Artemis possessed (cf. Eph 6,5ff.). Their presence ensured the continuing prosperity of Ephesus.[50]

Economically powerful, this city with its wealth of cultures and variety of relgions was the melting pot of East and West. It was to this city of unity and diversity that the Apostle came bringing the Good News. Despite the many negative features of city life, the Apostle opens his letter with a song which may have been inspired by this environment. He writes:

> Blessed the God and Father of Our Lord Jesus Christ, who has blessed us in Christ with every spiritual blessing in the heavenly places ... (Eph 1,3).

And he might have addressed the citizens:

> Remember, you had no hope, you were without God, with the world about you (cf. 2,12).

---

[48] *RE*, Suppl., XII, 260.
[49] C. Schneider, op. cit., 683.
[50] Cf. F. Reinecker, *Brief an die Epheser*, 9; F. Lyall, "Roman Law in the Writing of Paul — Slaves and the Freedman": *NTS* 17 (1970) 75; C. Picard, *Ephèse et Claros*, 132f.; S. S. Bartchy, *First-Century Slavery and 1 Corinthians 7,21* (SBL Dissertation Series 11; 1973) 63ff.

2-2: The Basic Fact in the Community of the Ephesians: Living Together of "Old" and "New" Christians

The analysis of the situation which the author of the letter to the Ephesians gives in 2,11-13 reveals not only the positive aspect of their paganism: "there was no Christ for you, you were strangers to the community of Israel, outside God's covenants of the promise, who had no hope, you were without God, with the world about you" (Eph 2,11-12).

After having explained the sense of unity which had existed for centuries in the pagan city of Ephesus, in her hinterland and in the whole "Ionian federation," we want now to clarify the basic experience of the Christian community in Ephesus to whom the apostle addressed the letter. The basic experience is the fact that two groups lived together in the one community: one group was addressed as "you" and the other was "we"-group of people who stood together with the apostle.

As a first step of our analysis, we will cite the instances in Eph 1,3 - 3,21.

In Eph 2,11, the "you" group of people is directly addressed for the first time: "... (you) remember that then (once) you were the heathen in flesh ..." and they were described as former heathen. Therefore, and because of the opinions of many authors who identify the "you" group of people simply with "pagan Christians," we must investigate what is meant by the author of the Eph when he used the word "heathen" (*ethnē*). In relation to the notion of "heathen," image of "way" (*hodos*) plays a very important role in the description of the two groups and the description of the new status in which they lived together and formed one community. The image of "way" is also a key image in ancient religions in the Hellenistic world, in the Old Testament and in Judaism, also in the Far East. This is the reason why we try to explain these texts with regard to the image of "way." It will now be possible to undertand the qualities which — according to the letter — characterize a way of life as "being heathen," and this will be presented in the following paragraphs.

2-2-1: *Preliminary Remarks: the Context of 2,11 and its Meaning*

Before explaining verse 2,11, we would like to make a brief comment on Chapter 2. In Eph 1,3 - 3,21 we find a peculiar use of the personal pronoun, that is, as the subject and the object of whole paragraphs. The first and second persons are used alternatively in a dialectical manner.[51] In vv. 11-13 of Chapter 2, which appear to form a unit, the writer addresses himself directly to the addressees (i.e. "you") in the second person

---

[51] Take, for instance, the first person plural: 1,3-12; 1,14 *hēmōn* ("our"); 2,3-10; 3,12; 3,20-21. The second person plural: 1,13; 2,1-2.5b.8-9.11-13.19-22; 3,2.4. 3,18-19. See R. A. Wilson, " 'We' and 'you' in the Epistle to the Ephesians": *StEv* (TU 87; Berlin 1964), II, 676-80, esp. 677ff.; D. Jayne, " 'We' and 'you' in Ephesians 1,3-14"; *Exp* 85 No. 5 (1974), 151-52.

plural with the verb *mnemoneuete* ... ("remember ..."). The object of this "remembering" is given by the adverb *pote* ("once" or "then") in Eph 2,11.13. The adverb *pote* is not only one of the characteristic elements of this section; it also refers back to *pote* in Eph 2,2, which is associated with "you walked" (*peripatēsate* ...) in the same verse.. The verb *peripatein* (to walk) acts as a kind of inclusion word in the section 2,1-10 (see 2,2; 2,10). "Remember" in v. 11 contrasts with *nuni* ("now") in v. 13. This adverb may indicate the present situation of "you." If we take a look at the whole of Chapter 2, we find that the change of "then" and "now" plays an important role also in Eph 2,1-10. In 2,11-13, the time aspect of the language gives way to a spatial aspect. Eph 2,13 is a kind of transition to the following section. It reminds us already of the key-words of the citation from Isaiah in Eph 2,17.[52] Another key-word in Eph 2,11ff. is *ethnos* (heathen) which occurs here for the first time in the letter. In the previous section 2,1-10, the word *ethnos* is not yet verbalized, although v. 11 refers back to the situation of the heathen with the adverb *pote* (then).[53] Eph 2,11 opens with the participle *dio* (therefore) which refers back to vv. 1ff.[54] What has been explained in the previous section is now re-expressed in terms of its relationship to so-called salvation history. "Your manner of walking" as Gentiles (2,1-3) and salvation (2,5b.8) are, in 2,11f., put into the perspective of Christ and Israel (2,12).

The verses 11-13 of Ch. 2 seem to form a prelude to the "hymn of peace" in 2,14ff. At the same time they perform the function of summarizing and deepening for the group addressed as "you" what has been said about both groups in Eph 2,1-10. What was stated about the reality and the manner of "walking" (*peripatein*) is now explained explicitly according to the new situation in Christ.

The second person plural verb *mnemoneuete* (remember) governs two objective clauses in Eph 2,11.12 introduced by *hoti*. Eph 2,11 runs thus:

> Remember, then, that once (*pote*) you, the heathen in (the) flesh, were called the Uncircumcision by those called the Circumcision made by hand in flesh.

Firstly, we will examine the meaning of the term "heathen" (*ethnē*). *What did the phrase "the heathen in flesh" mean to this author?* In many passages in the New Testament, the term *ethnos* or *ethnē* has the

---

[52] Elsewhere in the Pauline letters: Rom 10,8; 13,11; Phil 4,5.
[53] The word *ethnos* occurs in Eph 3,1.6.8, in relation to the Pauline mission (vocation) and revelation, and in Eph 4,17; cf. also Col 1,27.
[54] H. Schlier, *Der Brief an die Epheser* (Düsseldorf 1962³) 119 (henceforth, Schlier, *Komm.*). A. Lindemann, *Die Aufhebung der Zeit* (Gütersloh 1975), 146 (henceforth, Lindemann, *Die Aufhebung*). J. Gnilka, *Der Epheserbrief* (Herder Komm., Band X-2; Freiburg 1971), 134, note 4 (henceforth, Gnilka, *Komm.*).

meaning "nation(s)" or "people(s)" with no particular distinction. In a number of passages, however, the word is used as a technical term corresponding to the Hebrew *goiim* in the Old Testament and denoting "peoples" other than Jews or Christians.[55] A further and more profound use of the term refers to "the heathen" as a viewed from the standpoint of the church or of the true Israelites according to the spirit (*kata pneuma*).[56] K. L. Schmidt rightly classifies this word as a technical term.[57]

For the author of the letter to the Ephesians, however, the term appears to have a wider significance. The word occurs five times in the letter.[58] On three occasions (3,1.6.8) it is used in the Pauline missiological sense which the apostle developed as he preached and carried out his apostolic activities. Here, the word appears to denote not only a "fixed" group but it also suggests a prophetic role for the heathen.[59] Eph 4,17ff. contrasts the manner of life of the heathen (*ta ethnē*)[60] with "your" present way of life.

What did the author of the letter to the Ephesians have in mind when he stated: "... you were the heathen ... (2,11)"? Does he primarily intend to classify the two "traditional" groups, the Jews and the heathen? Or does he want to point out the difference between the Jewish Christians and the Gentile Christians and to demonstrate the superiority of the former over the latter in his community? If we look at the text carefully, we find that the author says more than this. He tells them: "... you were the heathen in flesh" (*ta ethnē en sarki*). The phrase *ta ethnē en sarki* has a parallel in Eph 2,11b *legomenē peritomē en sarki* (so-called Circumcision in flesh). This is followed by another phrase: "You were the heathen in flesh, those called Uncircumcision" (2,11). Here, the author *relativizes* the meaning of "the heathen." At the same time he calls the Jews *those called Circumcision made by hand in flesh* (... *legomenes peritomes en sarki cheiropoietou*). *These Jews called "you" the Uncircumcision.* He understands the status of both groups (the former Jews and the heathen) in relation to their new situation in Christ. A most important point is that the author of Ephesians views the former pre-Christian existence of their groups from his in-Christ experience. Both the former Jews and the former Gentiles were *in flesh*. "You" were in flesh as well as those who called "you" the Uncircumcision. The author of Ephesians describes the former state of both groups in similar fashion without indicating the superiority of one or the other. This is clear

---

[55] K. L. Schmidt, "*ethnos*", in: *TDNT*, II, 369ff.
[56] Schmidt, art. cit., 371.
[57] Schmidt, art. cit., 370.
[58] Besides our verse: 3,1.6.8.; 4,17.
[59] It is strange that in the letter to the Colossians this word occurs only once, in 1,27 (which is parallel to Eph 3,5ff.).
[60] Some texts add *loipa* to *ta ethnē*: see B. M. Metzger, *A Textual Commentary on the New Testament* (1971) 605 (henceforth Metzger, *Text Comm.*).

from the parallel statements about both groups in 2,1-10 and 2,11-12 insofar as they retain their former way of life.

By devaluating the strongly Jewish concepts of *ta ethnē* and of *akro-
bystia*,[61] the author gives his readers to understand that he views both
groups from a third standpoint, that is, an in-Christ standpoint. We can
apply this to Christian today. Only Christians concerned exclusively with
outward observance may be classified as similar to the heathen and the
Jews of our text. The author of Ephesians has his own criterion for
his understanding of "nations." It is neither "theoretical" nor "legal,"
but it is a "sense," a sense which comes from his deep experience "in
Christ."

2-2-2: *The Image of the Way for the Conduct of Life*

The classification of "heathen" or "circumcision" is by no means to
be understood as a static denomination. The author of Eph is thinking
of "being heathen" in dynamic terms, because he wants to initiate for
his readers a process of practical comprehension of the new situation.

If we look closer at the text, we see that the words "being heathen"
and "being in Christ" are internally connected with the word-group of
peripatein (to walk) in the sense of "way of life." We can say that the
image of "way" (*hodos*) synthesizes several word-groups related to such
a manner of life. This image was widespread in antiquity. We find it
also in many other ancient religions. Therefore, it is necessary to mention its background and function before we explain what the "being
heathen" means in our letter. In fact, it represents a fundamental pattern
of thought for the description of the new unity of the two groups in one
community in Christ. And it shows the dynamic criterion of the author
of Eph for distinguishing heathen and believers in Christ.

The word-group "to go", "to walk" etc., in the letter to the Ephesians [62]
is used in the sense of "human conduct," "manner of life." [63] The notions
of human conduct and of human walking converge in the religious use
of the image of the "way," found already in the Old Testament. The verb
peripatein is frequently used in the Septuagint not only in a spatial sense,
but also in a religious or ethical sense to denote a way of life.[64] In the
Hebrew and Greek bible, the word-fields of "way" and "walk" with their
many cognate terms are used in reference to human conduct.

Man's life is symbolized by the image of the "way".[65]

---

[61] Cf. Lindemann, *Die Aufhebung*, 146f.; S. Hanson, *The Unity of the Church in
the New Testament. Colossians and Ephesians* (ASNU 14; Uppsala 1946) 141. Cf.
Rom 2,24ff.

[62] *peripatein*: Eph 2,2; 2,10; 4,1; 4,17; 5,2.8.; 5,15; *anastrephein*: 2,3; *anastrophē*: 4,22.

[63] G. Bertram, "*pateō*", in: *TDNT*, V, 944f.; idem, "*strephō*", in: *TDNT*, VII, 715-
17, esp. 717.

[64] Idem, art. cit., V, 942-43.

[65] Cf. Ps 119,105; Is 53,6. See W. Michaelis, "*hodos*," in: *TDNT*, V, 51, in relation

God's eyes are on all men's ways (Jer 16,17; 32,19) and he has them
in his hands (cf. Dan 5,23), so that one can commit his way to the Lord
and trust in Him (cf. Ps 37,5). "Way" is not only a symbol of human
life, however. It can also signify death. David goes the way of all the
earth (1 Kings 2,2). All mankind goes this way (cf. Jos 23,14) and never
comes back thence (Job 16,22). In many passages of the Septuagint the
term *hodos* signifies "way," "manner of life," "conduct." We find a paral-
lelism of "ways" (*hodoi*) and "works" (*erga*), for example, in Ex 18,20 and
Jer 33,13, and there is a correspondence between *tēn hodon autou* (his
way) and *autos epoiēsen* (what he did) in Job 21,31. In Jer 4,18, *hodoi*
(ways) and *epitēdeumata* (behaviour) are combined and *tropos* (side road)
and *hodos* (way) are related in Deut 5,32f. In a large number of cases, a
man's actual conduct is referred to as his *hodoi* (ways) in a purely factual
manner and, as will often be clear from the context, with no ethical
evaluation.[66]

"Way" assumes a positive or negative meaning with the addition of
a qualifying word or phrase.[67] The criterion for its being positive or
negative is based on whether one follows the will of God. When man
walks according to God's will and lets himself (his conduct) be governed
by God's commandments, then he can be said to be walking along the
way of God. There is a way of sinners (cf. Ps 1,1: *en hodōi hamartōlōn*),
that is, of those who do not listen, who pay no heed, who persist in
disobedience with evil and stubborn hearts (cf. Jer 7,24).[68] A prophetic
appeal is made to the people to return to the law, the commandments,
and the statutes of the Lord. "Give up your evil ways; keep my commandments and the statutes given in the law which I enjoined on your
forefathers and delivered to you through my servants the prophets" (2
Kings 17,13f.; see also Jer 25,5: "if each of you will turn from his wicked
ways and evil courses ..."). Thus the people will return to the Lord who
will have pity on them (cf. Is 55,7).

Man should pray for the Lord's guidance in order to follow his way
and walk in his truth (cf. Is 55,7). The way which God shows his people
is a way which leads to salvation; the way which he commands is a way
of life (cf. Deut 30,15f.): actually called the "way of life" (cf. Ps 16,11;
Prov 5,6). The one who strays from this way will perish. He will not
live long in the land he enters (Deut 30,17f.; cf. Ps 73, esp. v. 2).

In Greek literature there is the image or parable of the two ways

---

to God's requirement. "...the way of the Lord is the manner of life which He
requires of man." Cf. F. Nötscher, *Gotteswege und Menschenwege in der Bibel und
in Qumran* (Bonn 1958) 47ff.

[66] W. Michaelis, art. cit. V, 50-51. Ex 18,20 states: "... teach them the ways in
which they should go, and the works (*erga*) which they must do."

[67] See, for example, Jer 6,16; Prov 8,20; Jer 25,5; Prov 8,13; 1 Kings 15,34.

[68] Cf. W. Michaelis, art. cit., V, 51-52.

which, as we shall see later, constitutes an allegory on the choice of one's manner of life.

The motif of the two ways, which later became so important, is found already in the Old Testament as a figure of speech for two types of conduct which man must choose. To obey or not to obey the Lord is the central theme of the Old Testament. In other words, there are two courses of action open to Israel; either she "enters the covenant" by being obedient to God or by her disobedience she holds aloof. To these two ways of life belong "life," "blessing" and "cursing" (cf. Deut 11,26f.; 30, 15f.).[69] It is obvious that the "way" (*hodos*)-passages are all in some sense antithetical. God's ways are contrasted with those of man's own choice. The scheme of the two ways which is found in Greek literature and which permits a choice of manner of life is not found in the Old Testament. Nevertheless, it does present us with the image of two opposing ways representing two different possibilities of human conduct.[70]

The allegorical use of the image of the way found in the Pseudepigrapha and in Rabbinic literature was taken over from the Old Testament. The verb "walk" is attested in the context of conduct, behaviour, mode of life[71] while "work" and "way" are paralleled, for example, in Jub 22,16; 1 En 61,8f. and Sib III, 233. The term "way" is used metaphorically in a special manner in this literature. In Jub 12,21, the right way is contrasted with walking in the deceitfulness of one's heart (cf. Sib I, 23ff.). Similarly, in Jub 7,26, the paths of destruction are contrasted with those of righteousness. In the admonition of II Bar 85,12 Baruch admonishes his readers that at the end of time there is no more place for repentance and a change of ways. One can no longer alter one's way and enter another. In II Esdras 7,12ff., it is stated that after the transgression of Adam the ways of this world became narrow, sorrowful and painful, full of perils and great toils. The ways of the future world, however, will be broad, protected, and will bring the fruits of immortality.[72] This metaphorical use of the term "way" is, as we shall see later, different from its use by the Greeks (the usage found in Greek literature).

The aspect of the choice of manner of life is found in 1 En 91,18f. where exhortation to follow the way of righteousness is accompanied by a warning against the way of violence.[73] A clear example of this is found in II En 30,15: "I called his name Adam and showed him the ways, the light and the darkness, and said to him, 'This is good and that evil'" (cf.

---

[69] See also Prov 2,12.20; 4,14f.: "good and bad", "just and wicked" are connected to the notion "way." Cf. F. Nötscher, op. cit., 64ff., esp. 68f. (note 65).

[70] Cf. W. Michaelis, art. cit., *TDNT*, V, 53-54.

[71] Ibid., 56. The Pseudepigraphs speak of "ways" less frequently than the Old Testament.

[72] See, R. H. Charles, *The Apocrypha and Pseudepigrapha of the Old Testament*, vol. II (Oxford 1913) ad locum.

[73] W. Michaelis, art. cit., 57.

42,10b). Test Asser 1,3-5 (cf. Jer 21,8; II En 30,15), which may be older than II Enoch, offers another example of the metaphor of the two ways:

> Two ways hath God given to the sons of men, and two inclinations, and two kinds of action and two modes (of action) and two issues. Therefore, all things are by twos, one over against the other. For there are two ways of good and evil and with these are the two inclinations in our hearts discriminating them ....

This is one of the oldest examples of the metaphor of the two ways.[74] Here, however, the motif of the two ways is applied allegorically in order to explain the two inclinations of man, inclinations which later received a psychological explanation. Although the metaphor of the two ways in the context of human conduct found a wide and varied use in the Old Testament, it seems that the rabbis did not make much use of it.[75] Deut 11,26 and 30,19 do not provide instances of the use of the metaphor of the two ways, but the rabbis took them to mean that when God set life and death, blessing and cursing before the people, he propounded two ways.[76]

The use of the metaphor in bBer 28b is more in accordance with that of the Old Testament. When R. Eliezer fell ill, his disciples went to visit him. They said to him: "Master, teach us the paths of life so that we may through them win the life of the future world." In this the reference is not to human conduct but to the twofold judgement. On a similar occasion, Rabban Yohanan ben Zakkai began to weep in front of his disciples who had come to visit him. The cause of his weeping, he explained to them, was that he did not know on which of the two ways God would send him at the last judgement. In this case, the ways are the "ways" of destiny after death.[77] Another example is found in bAb 2,9, where R. Yohanan gave a test to his rabbis in which he asked them to ascertain the nature of the good way unto which a man should cleave and of the evil way which he should avoid. Each rabbi brought his answer, but R. Yohanan preferred that of R. Eleazar, namely, good and bad heart respectively.[78]

---

[74] R. H. Charles, op. cit. 343; W. Michaelis, art. cit., 58 and note 46. For the dating of this literature, see D. S. Russell, *The Method and Message of Jewish Apocalyptic* (SCM; London 1964) 36ff.; G. W. E. Nickelsburg, *Jewish Literature Between The Bible and The Mishnah* (SCM; London 1981).

[75] W. Michaelis, art. cit., 58, note 48.

[76] H. Strack - P. Billerbeck, *Kommentar zum Neuen Testament aus Talmud und Midrasch* (München 1926; reprint 1951) vol. I, 461ff.

[77] *The Babylonian Talmud, seder Zeraʾim*, ed. by I. Epstein (London 1948), *Berakoth*, 28b, page 173. For the life of Rabban Yohanan Ben Zakkai, see J. Neusner, *A life of Rabban Yohanan Ben Zakkai (Ca 1-80 C.E.)* (Leiden 1962) esp. 172ff.

[78] *The Babylonian Talmud*, (Seder Nezikin: *Shebuʾoth - Makkoth - Eduyyoth - Aboth*): *Aboth*, translated into English with Notes, Glossary and Indices by J. Israelstam (London 1935), chap. II, Mishnah 9, page 19f.

It is clear that the motif of the two ways is the product of human psychology. A "good heart" and a "bad heart," as is well known in Jewish anthropology, lead men to two different types of conduct.

This imagery is also found in Greek literature where it has a very long history.

The verb *peripatein* means "to walk around" or "to stay," but its figurative sense, "to conduct the walk of life," is not attested in classical Greek. In the first century B.C., at the time of Philodemus, however, the verb is often used figuratively with the meaning "to live" (De Libertate 23,3).[79]

In the classical Greek world, the image of *hodos* (way) seems to have been used in relation to the "manner of life." Life was compared to a way, but was not called a way. The phrase *hodos biou* (way of life) did not refer to a man's lifetime (life, destiny), but signified a form, a manner of life.[80]

Parmenides of Elea (born c. 515-510 B.C.) developed the image of the "way." A disciple of Xenophanes, he was influenced by Ameinias the Pythagorean, and Zeno was in turn his disciple.[81] He used the notion of the "way" in his religious-philosophical poem whose central theme was the nature of the "way of Seeming" and the relation between "it" and the "way of truth." [82] Parmenides sought to proclaim the "truth" (*alētheia*) which he had learned from the mouth of the goddess.[83]

The way on which Parmenides walks is far from the pathways of men. No mortal can find it.[84] The only true way marks off "what is"

---

[79] H. Seesemann, "*Pateō*," in: *TDNT*, V, 941.
[80] W. Michaelis, "*hodos*," art. cit., *TDNT*, V, 43.
[81] See W. K. G. Guthrie, *A History of Greek Philosophy*, vol. II (Cambridge 1965) 1-3.
[82] Ibid., 4-5.
[83] Ibid., 7-8. The prologue of Parmenides' poem begins as follows: "The mares that carry me as far as my heart ever aspires sped me on, when they had brought and set me on the far-famed road of the god (i.e. the Sun), which bears the man of knowledge over all cities. On that road was I borne, for by it the wise steeds took me, straining at the chariot, and the maidens led the way. And the blazing axle in the axle-boxes made the sockets sing, driven on both sides by the two whirling wheels, as the daughters of the Sun, having left the house of Night, hastened to bring me to the light, throwing back the veils from their heads with their hands ... And the goddess welcomed me graciously, took my right hand in hers, and addressed me with these words: Young man, who comest to my house companioned by immortal charioteers with the steeds that bear thee, I greet thee. No evil lot has sent thee to travel this road — and verily it is far from the footsteps of men — but Right and Justice. It is meet for thee to learn all things, both the unshaken heart of well-rounded truth and also what seems to mortals, in which is no true conviction. Nevertheless these things too shalt thou learn, namely that what seems had assuredly to exist, being indeed everything" (Parmenides, B, I, 1ff.). W. Jaeger, *The Theology of the Early Greek Philosophers* (Oxford 1947) 94, states: "Of all the Greek writers who are known to us, Hesiod is the first to have given the word 'truth' such a pregnant and philosophical sense. He proclaims the 'truth' about Being which is eternal and without beginning, and which is opposed to appearance and to all the deceptive 'opinions of mortals'."
[84] Parmenides, B, I, 29-30.

and it is eternal, neither coming into being nor perishing.[85]   It is like a round ball.[86]

Parmenides laments that mortal men roam about on the path of error and he complains about their wandering minds.[87]   The sole right way leads to the goal of knowledge.[88]   The two-way scheme appears in the later pythagoreanism as a religious symbol.[89]   Parmenides' use of the motif of the two ways may be based on a carry-over of religious symbolism into the intellectual process of philosophy.   It is not known how far back the motif of the two ways goes, but its antiquity is vouched for by Hesiod (c. 700 B.C.) in his "Works and Days" (*Erga kai Hemerai* 287ff.; Theogony 911f.).   Here we find the allegory of the two ways in the form of the narrow way of *aretē* and the broad way of misery.   The narrow way is mentioned briefly.   The way which leads to *aretē* is fully depicted.   It is long and steep, then reaches a height; at first it is rugged and difficult, but on the heights smooth.[90]

In a later development of Hesiod's theme in the Prodicosfable (Xenophon, *Memorabilia* II, I, 21-34; 428/7-354 B.C.) the two ways are interpreted in a different manner.

The two ways which confront young people as soon as they attain the age of discretion are not said to be short or long, easy or difficult, smooth or steep.   Rather, both ways have the same goal, namely, life itself.   They are not, as in Hesiod, roads which lead to *aretē* or *kakia.* The point is rather whether one takes the way of life which consists in virtuous conduct or not.   The character of the *hodoi* is not clear.   The image of the two ways is not an essential part of the original fable of

---

[85] Fr. 8, vv. 1-21. Cf. Guthrie, op. cit., 26ff.

[86] Fr 8,42-9; Guthrie, op. cit., 43ff.

[87] Parmenides, B, 6,6; Guthrie, op. cit., 20ff.; Jaeger, op. cit., 96-97. Fr. 6: "What can be spoken and thought of must be, for it is possible for it to be, but impossible for nothing to be.   This I bid thee consider, for this way of inquiry is the first from which I hold thee back.   But also from this one, on which mortals, knowing nothing, wander two headed; for helplessness in their own breasts guides their erring mind.   They are borne along, both deaf and blind, mazed, hordes with no judgement, who believe that to be and not to be are the same and not the same, and the path of everything is one that turns back upon itself."

[88] Jaeger, op. cit., 98.

[89] Jaeger, op. cit., 99, note 27. R. Joly, prefers the concept of life and does not see the metaphorical "genre" of "way." *Le thème philosophique des genres de vie dans l'antiquité classique* (Bruxelles 1956) 172.   Western philosophy in its initial stages made use of many images.   In the course of time, a certain rationalisation took place.   The old images were applied and "translated."   It is possible that part of their contents was not expressed with more abstract concepts. Cf. Michaelis, art. cit., 44, note 7.

[90] Hesiod, *The Homeric Hymns and Homerica*, translated by H. G. Evelyn-White, (Loeb Classical Library; Cambridge; reprint 1974) 25: "To you, foolish Perses, I will speak good sense.   Badness can be got easily and in shoals: the road to her is smooth, and she lives very near us.   But between us and Goodness the gods have placed the sweat of our brows: long and steep is the path that leads to her, and it is rough at the first; but when a man has reached the top, then is she easy to reach, though before that she was hard."   See also 24.

Prodicos. What is essential to the fable, however, is the appearance of the two women in the vision of Hercules. The women, Arete and Kakia, approach Hercules along two different roads and seek to win him over to their respective sides. Arete is the goal of one way, Kakia, the guide on the other. The image of the way is weakened in this case and the mention of the two ways in the introduction in the women's war of words hardly serves to invest the image with greater weight than it properly has.[91]

The use and application of the so-called "Hercules-at-the-cross-roads" motif in later literature lent the fable wide favour.[92] The idea of the choice between two possibilities is found in Hesiod.[93] This idea was later transferred to the ethical field.[94] Despite the variations in the use of the image or motif of the two ways in Greek literature, the motif itself is older than the fables of Prodicos and Hesiod, going back perhaps to the literature of the ancient Near East.[95]

Finally, it should be stated that the image of the way is well known far beyond the western world. It was an important notion in the Far East where it still is a well-known concept.[96]

2-2-3: *The Way of "Being Heathen"*

We have treated the use of the metaphor of the two ways in the Old Testament and in Greek literature as background material for the teaching on the two ways of life contained in the letter to the Ephesians. The writer of the letter appears to have this background in mind and this enables him to address his message to his mixed audience in terms which are comprehensible both to those of a Hellenistic cultural background and to those whose cultural background is Jewish. The author contrasts the way of the heathen which is characterized by the Pauline term *to ethnos* (the heathen — Eph 4,17ff.; 2,11f. cf. 2,1; also Col 3,7) and the way

---

[91] The Prodicos fable begins thus: "Aye, and Prodicus the wise expresses himself to the life effect concerning Virtue in the essay 'On Heracles' that he recites to throngs of listeners. This, so far as I remember, is how he puts it: "When Heracles was passing from boyhood to youth's estate, wherein the young, now becoming their own masters, show whether they will approach life by the path of virtue or the path of vice he went out into a quiet place, and sat pondering which road to take. And there appeared two women of great stature making towards him ..." (Xenophon, *Memorabilia,* II, I, 21ff.) the translation is by E. C. Marchant; O. J. Todd, Xenophon, IV, *Memorabilia* ... (Loeb Class. Library; London 1968) 95ff.

[92] W. Michaelis, art. cit., 45-46.

[93] In *Theog.* 911f. See Michaelis, art. cit., V, 44, note 7.

[94] Ibid., V, 47, note 7. R. Joly, op. cit., "Genres de vie" traces it down to the Renaissance. See his conclusion, 187-93.

[95] Cf. F. Dornseiff, *Antike und alter Orient* (1952); P. Walcott, *Hesiod and the Near East* (1966); M. L. West, *Early Greek Philosophy and the Orient* (Oxford 1971).

[96] Cf. Laoz [c. the beginning of the 4th cent. B.C.; according to K. Fukunaga, *Loshi (Laoz) Chugo-ku Koten* (Chinese Classic 10; Tokyo 1978) 25f.] begins the exposition of his doctrine with his notion "way", see ch. 1.4.14.21.25.37.38. etc. Also cf. Juan dz (c. 370-300 B.C.), (K. Fukunaga, *Soshi,* Chinese class. 12; Tokyo 1978) 58ff.

of life in Christ. Reality is seen in terms of this contrast throughout the letter.[97]

Let us now examine what the "way of the heathen" involves for the author of the letter. Its characteristic elements are:

1. "Walking in the futility of their minds" - Eph 4,17ff.
2. "Being dead through transgressions and sins" - Eph 2,1-2 [98]
3. "By nature children of wrath"; - Eph 2,3
4. "Having no hope and without God" - Eph 2,12
5. "You who once were far off" - Eph 2,13

1. Walking in the futility of their minds (RSV - "Living" for "walking")

Having treated the constitution of the church (the mystery of communion) and the special gifts which serve to build up the body of Christ, the author continues with an admonishment [99] which is, in reality, an exhortation. He calls on those addressed not to allow their way of life to revert to the way of life of the heathen.[100] The term "heathen" (*ethnē*) is used in a decidedly negative sense here,[101] and the author reminds those to whom he addresses himself ("you") of the manner of life among the heathen.[102] In describing this way of life (*ta ethnē peripatei* ...) now from his perspective, the author is not just recalling a way of life renounced once for all, but he is also presenting an ever-present danger for those who have learned Christ (Eph 4,20 of falling back into a way of life which has been abandoned).[103]

The first characterization of the way of the heathen is that conveyed by the phrase *peripatei en mataiotēs tou noos autōn* [104] — "walking in the futility of their minds".[105] The term *mataiotēs* (futility) appears to be one of the basic human feelings that underlie Pauline anthropology.

The terms *kenos* and *mataiotēs* are very similar. But whereas *kenos* has the basic meaning of being without content, and thus worthless, *mataiotēs*, which also conveys the idea of being worthless, has the basic

---

[97] Ex gr. 2,13; 2,4ff. esp. 2,10. In the hortatory part, 4,1; 5,1f.; 5,8f.; 5,15ff.

[98] *RSV*: "dead through ... trespasses and sins in which you once walked."

[99] Cf. 1 Thess 4,1.6. H. Schlier, *Komm.*, 209; J. Gnilka, *Komm.*, 222, note 1.

[100] Schlier, *Komm.*, 210.

[101] Gnilka, *Komm.*, 223; compare with Eph 3,6.

[102] Gnilka, *Komm.*, 223.

[103] J. Ernst, *Die Briefe an die Philipper an Philemon an die Kolosser und die Epheser* (Regensburg 1974) 360. A. Lindemann, *Die Aufhebung*, 71, notes that the text is based on the Revelation-schema of "then"-"now."

[104] In the Pauline letters, the word *peripatein* occurs 33 times, and it expresses a way of life. It is constructed with particles, *kata* or *en* or with a dative. See H. Seesemann, *"peripatein"*, in: *TDNT*, V, 944-945.

[105] The translation taken from *RSV*. The word-group *"mataiotēs-mataios"* etc. is used in the LXX: Ps 38,6; 143,4.; Qoh 1,2; 2,1 (36 times in Qoh.). It is used also in the Pauline letters: 1 Cor 3,20 (Ps 94,11); 1 Cor 15,17; Tit 3,9; Rom 8,20; Eph 4,17; Rom 1,21. See O. Bauernfeind, *"mataiotēs"*, in: *TDNT*, IV, 523.

meaning of being deceptive, or ineffectual.[106] *Mataiotēs* may also signify vanity.[107] For the author, the notion of *mataiotēs* (*mataios*) carries the connotations of changeability, transcience, illusion, idleness, emptiness, futility, foolishness, purposelessness. The term *nous* in this passage signifies "mind" insofar as the mind prepares the attitude (disposition) for action or for conduct and expresses the inner orientation or moral attitude.[108] Thus the manner in which heathens conduct their lives is characterized by the description of their minds as wavering, unsteady, going astray, wandering about in vain and not seeing their futility.[109] It is further characterized by the participial phrases *eskotōmenoi tē dianoia ontes* (being darkened in the understanding) and *apēllotriōmenoi tēs zōēs tou theou* (alienated from the life of God) of Eph 4,18.[110] With these two phrases, the author of the letter goes to the heart of what being a heathen entails. The first phrase states that the manner of life of the heathen is characterized by his darkened understanding (*dianoia*)."[111] The author traces the defect of disposition (*nous*) back to defects of consciousness, of the faculty of spiritual and moral understanding,[112] of sensitivity, of the power to grasp or to comprehend ourselves and other persons and things. Thus, the heathen far from being enlightened by the *dianoia* (understanding), is in fact adversely affected by it.[113] His condition of being darkened affects not only intellectual and speculative understanding but also affects his whole (human) existence.[114] He is trapped in this condition. It is paradoxical that "understanding" should bring about the condition of "being darkened."

---

106 Bauernfeind, art. cit., 519.

107 Schlier, *Komm.*, 211, note 2. The wisdom of this world, whichever it is, and however outstanding, is folly in the eyes of God (cf. 1 Cor 3,19). Reflections, thoughts and discussions of the wise are futile (cf. 1 Cor 3,20; Tit 3,9). And without the resurrection of Christ, the faith is futile (cf. 1 Cor 15,19).

108 See J. Behm, "*nous*," in: *TDNT*, IV, 958; Schlier, *Komm.*, 211f., translates "das Vermögen (und die Tätigkeit)." Cf. Col 2,18 and Rom 1,28. The counterpart of this disposition is "to be renewed in your minds (Eph 4,23)," see also Rom 12,2.

109 Cf. Jer 2,5 (LXX); Col 2,1ff.; 1 Cor 1,18f.

110 Schlier, *Komm.*, 212; Gnilka, *Komm.*, 223.

111 M. Barth, *Comm.*, 500, translates the phrase "Intellectually they are blacked out," but the phrase seems to mean more. Cf.: Eph 1,18; 2,3; Col 1,21; Heb 8,10; 10,16 (Jer 31,31-34); 1 Pet 1,13; 2 Pet 3,1; 1 Jn 5,20; Mt 22,37; Mk 12,30; Lk 10,27 — (Deut 6,4-5.); Lk 1,51.

112 J. Behm, art. cit., *TDNT* IV, 966.

113 Cf. M. Zerwick, *Graecitas Biblica* (Roma 1960) 38. But it is used together with the passive perfect participle of the verb. We take this as meaning "through" or "by". Cf. Blass-Debrunner-Rehkopf, *Grammatik des Neutestamentlichen Griechisch* (Göttingen 1976) § 191.1. The participle of *einai*, *ontes*, with the passive perfect participle of *skotoō* emphasizes the condition which the perfect participle *eskotômenoi* implies. See Blass-Debrunner-Rehkopf, op. cit., § 352, note 4. Cf. Col 1,21; Lk 23,53.

114 The following authors translate the phrase thus: Schlier, *Komm.*, 209: " verdunkelt in hirem Verstand"; Gnilka, *Komm.*, 221: "in der Denkkraft verfinstert"; J. Ernst, *Komm.*, 360: "verfinstert in der Gesinnung"; M. Barth, *Comm.*, 498: "Intellectually they are blacked out." Cf. Gnilka, *Komm.*, 223; on the variations of the reading, Tischendorf, *NTG7*, 453; Schlier, *Komm.*, 212, note 2.

A similar paradox related to the human condition is found in Rom 1,18ff. St. Paul says: "For (*gar*) the wrath of God is revealed from heaven against all ungodliness and wickedness of men who by their wickedness suppress (*katechontōn*) the truth. For (*dioti*) what can be known about *God is plain to them*, because God has shown it to them ... (v. 21) for (*dioti*) *although they knew God* they did *not* honour *him as God* (*hōs*) or give thanks to him, but they became futile in their thinking and their senseless minds were darkened." [115] The wickedness of man prevails over, withholds, suppresses the truth.[116] This suppression which results from the wickedness of man reveals the truth.[117]

The anger of the Justice of God confronts the deceit of men whose manner of life alienates the truth and does not accept or acknowledge the reality of their creatureliness.[118] Such a distorted disposition of mind is alluded to in Rom 1,21: "for although they knew God they did not honour him *as* God ..." (*dioti gnontes ton theon ouch hōs theon edoxasan* ...).

To know God is not merely to draw a practical consequence from theoretical knowledge. It also implies an acknowledgement and is, therefore, close to the phrase *en epignōsei echein* (to acknowledge) in Rom 1,28.[119] Thus, the distorted disposition of mind in Rom 1,21 consists in the fact that men, although they know God, do not manifest this concrete knowledge honestly.

Man displays his knowledge of God by being aware of his own creatureliness, then accepting and acknowledging it, as well as honouring God and giving thanks to him as the Creator. This manifestation of man's knowledge of God must take the form of "worship." [120] Those who do not manifest this knowledge, *eo ipso facto*, distort the truth, and they become futile in their thinking. Consequently, the heart, the very core of man's being (cf. 1 Cor 14,25) which only God discerns, becomes darkened (cf. 1 Th 2,4; Rom 8,27).

The "futility in thinking" and the "senseless heart" have definite consequences for the manner of life of the individual.[121] This is pointed out by Eph 4,19 (cf. Rom 1,24) which describes the effects of this futility of mind on the lives of the heathen: They become callous and give themselves up to licentiousness, greedy to practise every kind of uncleanness.[122]

---

[115] The translation is taken from *RSV*.
[116] H. Schlier, *Der Römerbrief* (Freiburg 1977), Band VI, 47ff. esp. 50 and note 4.
[117] Schlier, ibid., 50 says: "... Das, was die Menschen in oder mit ihrer *adikia* 'niederhalten', ist hier *hē alētheia* genannt."
[118] Schlier, ibid., 51.
[119] Cf. Schlier, ibid., 55.
[120] Schlier, ibid., 55-56.
[121] Cf. Rom 1,24. See the verb *paradidōmi*: 1 Cor 5,5; 2 Cor 4,11; Tim 1,20; 2 Pet 2,4.
[122] Text D lat syp arm read *apēlpikotes* instead of *apēlgēkotes*. See Gnilka, *Komm,*. 225. K.-A. Bauer, *Leiblichkeit das Ende aller Werke Gottes* (Gütersloh 1971) 140ff.

The second participial phrase *apēllotriōmenoi tēs zōēs tou theou*...[123] describes the heathen as being in a state of estrangement or alienation[124] from the life of God.[125] The verb *apēllotriōmenoi* is used also in Eph 2,12 in reference to the heathen who are said to have been estranged from the citizenship of Israel (*politeia tou Israel*).

· These two participial phrases which qualify the main clause describe the same reality from two different yet complementary points of view. The state of being darkened in their understanding is at the same time the state of their being estranged from the life of God.

In Eph 4,18, the state of the heathen is described in spatial language referring to the interiority of man's conduct.[126] Man's nearness to or distance from the life of God is gauged from the experiential knowledge of God (how one conducts one's life).[127] The cause of this alienation from the life of God is given by two *dia*-clauses: *dia tēn agnoian tēn ousan en autois* (through the ignorance which is in them) and *dia tēn pōrōsin tēs kardias autōn* (through the hardness of their hearts).[128] These not only give the "*causa-agens*" for the condition of the heathen but also the result. In the first clause, the author of the letter is not referring to a subjective ignorance (*agnoia*) for which one can provide an apology,[129] nor is he blaming the heathen for the ignorance displayed in their manner of life from his subjective but enlightened (Eph 1,18) point of view.[130]

In Rom 8,18-24, St. Paul speaks about the subjection of the creatures to futility in hope, the hope of the perfect liberty of the sons of God and of the redemption of their bodies. We must pay attention to the importance of hope, which is one of the key notions in the letter to the Ephesians: cf. 1,18; 2,11f.; 4,4.

[123] Apart from Eph 4,19, the verb *apallotriousthai* is found in only 2 more occasions in the New Testament: Eph 2,12; and Col 1,21. Col 1,21 may be a different version of Eph 4,18; 2,12; 2,1f, which seems to have had a similar tradition. Cf. E. Lohse, *Der Briefe an die Kolosser und an Philemon* (Göttingen 1968) 104ff.

[124] Genitivus separationis: see Blass-Debrunner-Rehkopf, *Grammatik* § 180 and note 2.

[125] In the Pauline letters, the phrase, "of the life of God" (*tēs zōēs tou theou*), does not occur elsewhere in the New Testament. "... *tou theou*": genitivus auctoris or originis: see Gnilka, *Komm.*, 224, note 1.

[126] Cf. Eph 2,11ff.

[127] This life of God includes the "communion" with "Israel" (2,12). Thus the author of Ephesians appears to have experienced in himself a unifying and integrating experience of the Christ of Israel which embraces communion with God, with the apostles and with his community.

[128] Blass-Debrunner-Rehkopf, op. cit., 222. *Dia*-phrases go with the participles, not with the main sentences *peripatei*.... See Schlier, *Komm.*, 213, note 2, The authors discuss to which of the two participles these two *dia*-phrases relate. See Gnilka, *Komm.*, 224, note 2. M. Barth, *Comm.*, 498, has another interpretation and he says: "...Intellectually they are blacked out. Because of their inherent refusal to know (God) and of the petrification of their hearts, they are excluded from the life of God."

[129] Schlier, *Komm.*, 13. Cf. Acts 3,17; 17,23; Heb 5,2; 1 Pet 1,14. In 1 Cor 15,34, Paul uses ironically the similar word *agnoia*: see H. Conzelmann, *Der erste Brief an die Korinther* (Göttingen 1969) 331.

[130] M. Barth, *Comm.*, 500, translates the *agnoia* by "refusal to know". We must be careful here for the so-called heathen in Asia Minor enjoyed a highly developed Greco-Roman culture.

The Greeks took *agnoia* to be an intellectual requirement for moral corruption.[131] In this case, however, it refers rather to ignorance in the biblical sense. *Agnoia*, then, does not merely imply incapability of reasoning nor an inability to grasp reality. It involves the total existence of man: emotions, sensibilities, will, action and life.[132] It comes from his own understanding through his distortion of the truth and endures that understanding does not go hand in hand with an experience of the living God.

The second causal clause, which modifies the first clause,[133] specifies the central feature of being a heathen—the hardness of heart.

The "heart" in the N.T. is the centre of the psychosomatic life of man, the nucleus of his inner human life. It is the seat of feeling, of emotion, passion and desire, but also of the will, intention and understanding. It is the source of reflection and thought. It is the very core of man which no one may violate. When the Jew spoke of the heart he had in mind the whole inner life of man with its willing, feeling and thinking. The heart is truly the core and the unifying factor of human existence. Thus it is supremely the one point in man to which God turns, the place in which religious life is rooted, the source which determines moral conduct.[134]

The noun *pōrōsis* is found twice in the Pauline letters.[135] Apart from Eph 4,18, this peculiar term is related to a disposition of mind of the chosen people, Israel.[136] In Eph 4,18, however, the author applies this term to the condition of the heathen. Has he a particular reason for doing this?

In Greek literature, the noun *pōrōsis* has a rather medical nuance [137]

---

[131] Gnilka, *Komm.*, 224.

[132] Cf. M. Barth, *Comm.*, 500-01, and 119ff. esp. 121. He says on page 501: "... two parallels, Rom 1,19-21 and 1 Thess 4,5, suggest that in the translation of Eph 4,18 the object ("God") must be added to the text." But God cannot be a so-called "object" of human cognition. Even highly intellectual philosophers or theologians may be in danger of this kind of *agnoia*. The author of Ephesians seems to have been concerned not with "objectified" knowledge of God but with the self-distorted mind of man. With regard to 1 Thess 4,5, see B. Rigaux, *Saint Paul. Les épîtres aux Thessaloniciens* (Paris 1956) 509.

[133] Schlier, *Komm.*, 213, note 4, subordinates this phrase to the first *dia*-phrase as its explanation.

[134] See F. Baumgärtel, *"kardia"*, in: *TDNT*, III, 605-07. J. Behm, *"kardia"*, in: *TDNT*, III, 608-13. Behm states in page 610: "... *kardia* in the LXX is often interchangeable with *psychē, dianoia, pneuma, nous* etc... but in contrast to even these synonyms it relates to the unity and totality of the inner life represented and expressed in the variety of intellectual and spiritual functions. As the references of the passages in the New Testament: Rom 10,1; 1,24; 1 Cor 4,5; 7,37; Rom 2,5; 6,17; Eph 6,5; Rom 10,9f.; 2 Cor 4,6; Eph 1,18.

[135] Eph 4,18; Rom 11,25. And the verbal form *pōroō* is found in the following passages: Rom 11,7; 2 Cor 3,14.

[136] Cf. Mk 3,5: Jesus in the synagogue on hardness of heart. Mk 6,52; 8,17: hardened hearts of Jesus' disciples. Also cf. Jn 12,40.

[137] See Liddell-Scott, *pōrōsis, pōroō*. Also: Hippocrates, *Aër* 9; id., *Fract* 47; ib., 23; Galen 1,387.

and does not bear the figurative sense found in the Bible. Originally it referred to a kind of marble,[138] but later on it was used by medical writers to identify a node or a bony formation on the joints or for a callus or ossification which served as a mortar to unite the portions of a fractured bone.[139] The noun does not occur in the Septuagint but the verb *pōroun* is used in Job 17,7 and Prov 10,20 to translate the Hebrew verb *khh*.[140]

However, the O.T. contains a number of expressions which are close to the expression in Ephesians. In Ex 4,21, for example, the Lord says: "... I will harden his heart ...".[141] In Ez 2,3-4, he says to Ezechiel: "... I send you to the people of Israel, to a nation of rebels ... the people are also impudent and stubborn ...".[142] In Is 46,12-13, he speaks to the people in exile: "Hearken to me, you stubborn of heart, you who are far from deliverance: I bring near my deliverance, it is not far off, and my salvation will not tarry; I will put salvation in Zion, for Israel my glory".[143]

In using an expression which is very similar to these expressions, the author of Ephesians is recalling the history and the background of the O.T. in order to provide an explanation for the way of life of the heathen which is diametrically opposed to the way of life in Christ (*hymeis de* ... see Eph 4,20ff.). Through the hardness of their hearts they are estranged from the life of God.[144] This inner condition of their being has definite consequences for the way of life which they lead (cf. Eph 4,19).[145]

To sum up the first characteristic of "being heathen," it is a defect in a disposition for acknowledging the truth. Because of distorted understanding, it is a condition in which the whole person is darkened by his very understanding. The state of being darkened in his understanding

---

138 Theophrastus, *Lap.* 7; Aristotel, *Meteorologica* 410.

139 See J. A. Robinson, *pōrōsis* and *pērōsis*, in: *JThS* 3 (1901-1902) 81.

140 Job 17,7: thus B text reads. A Ss text read *pepēronta*. Prov 10,20: A text reads thus. Instead, B reads *pepurōmenos*. The idea of insensibility could be translated from the organs of feeling to the organs of sight. Cf.: Gen 27,1 (LXX: *ēmblynthēsan*); Deut 34,7 (LXX: *ēmaurōthēsan*); Zech 11,17 (LXX: *etyphlōthēsetai*). See Robinson, art. cit., 81ff.

141 *hzg*: Qal. Pi: Ex 4,21; 7,13.
   kbd: Qal. Hi: Ex 8,11, 9,7.
   gšh: Hi: Ex 7,3.
   ʾmṣ: Pi: Deut 2,30.

142 *hzgy-lb*

143 Cf. Deut 29,18f.; Lam 3,65.

144 In *sklērokardia*, the heart is regarded as the seat of the will: in *pōrōsis tēs kardias*, it is regarded as the seat of the intellect. Robinson, art. cit., 92.

145 Cf. Rom 1,24; 1,26.28. The dualistic understanding in *Test Jud* 18,3; 11,1: the *yeser* is blinded by fornication and the evil *yeser* blinds the mind. Cf. Gnilka, *Komm.*, 225. M. Barth, *Comm.*, 526-29, writes an excursus about the indictment of the gentiles. But indictment does not appear to be the main intention of the author of Ephesians. Rather, he "sees" mankind from the deepened level of his life. From his point of view, there are only two types of human conduct. It does not mean that one is simply Christian and the other is non-Christian (i.e. pagan, heathen). Because external or nominal (ritual) ("cultural") Christians are the same as nominal Jews who were circumcised (cf. Eph 2,11).

is at the same time the state of his being estranged from the life of God. What is worse is that the heart—the core and the unifying factor of human existence—is hardened. He loses the dynamism of life, of reality, and this in turn results from his inner distortion of reality. Consequently this condition goes hand-in-hand with his way of life.

2. "Being dead through transgressions and sins" (Eph 2,1-2)

Eph 2,1-2 does not describe the manner of life of the heathen as explicitly as Eph 4,17ff. Nevertheless, this text is worth mentioning because it recalls how they ("you") conducted their lives in the past (*pote* — v. 2) and is closely related to Eph 2,11ff. through the particle *dio* (therefore) of 2,11 which refers back to 2,1f.

The main concern of Eph 2,1-3 is to provoke an awareness among the two groups ("we" and "you") of having shared the same way of life in the past (... *pote peripatēsate* ... *kai hymeis pantes anestraphēmen pote* ...") and at the same time to bring home to them their basic equality and common starting point (2,3ff.). They are thus provided with the proper disposition for their experience of the action of divine grace (2,4ff.) and for a profound unity between them (2,14ff.).

The identification of these two groups has been a subject of much debate and various suggestions have been put forward.[146] It seems likely that the we-group represents an old group of Christians (the traditional Christians)[147] which includes St. Paul and his fellow Jewish Christians, but which does not exclude the so-called heathen or gentile Christians (cf. Eph 1,14; 2,3ff.; 2,10.14ff.; 3,12). The you-group appears to be composed of new though not necessarily newly-baptized Christians. It is possible to understand a number of texts as referring to newly baptized

---

[146] Take for instance: P. Joüon, "Notes philologiques sur quelques versets de l'Epître aux Ephésiens" (1,12; 2,1-3; 2,15; 3,13.15.; 4,28; 5,18.19.; 6,9.19-20.): *RSR* 26 (1936) 455-56. He understands that the "we" were from Judaism and the "you" were from paganism. Schlier, *Komm.*, 106, 108: "We" i.e. the Jewish Christians. J. A. Allan, *The Epistle to the Ephesians* (London 1959) 71 says: "... the changes from 'you' to 'we' and vice versa in this passage (Eph 2,3) have no clear significance ...." R. A. Wilson, " 'We' and 'you' in the Epistle to the Ephesians", in: *StEv* (TU 87; Berlin 1964) II, 676-80. He concludes on page 679: "... 'We' in the Epistle always refers to all Christians. 'You' always refers to a much smaller group, in some way distinct from other Christians; but the subject of the first half of the Epistle is the act of God by which this particular group has been united with the rest of the Church, while the second half consists of elementary moral instruction to them." D. Jayne, " 'We' and 'you' in Ephesians 1,3-14": *Exp* 85, 5 (1974) 151-52. K. Staab, *Die Thessalonicherbriefe die Gefangenschaftsbriefe* (Regensburg 1969⁵) 132. S. Hanson, *The Unity of the Church in the New Testament Colossians and Ephesians* (Uppsala 1946) 142. See also L. Ramaroson, "Une lecture de Ephésiens 1,15-2,10": *Bib* 58 (1977) 398, note 22. W. Rader, *The Church and Racial Hostility* (Tübingen 1978), studies the history of interpretation of Eph 2,11-22 and gives us a warning against social-cultural prejudices and preconceptions which affect the exegesis of the text.

[147] See H. Conzelmann, *Der Brief an die Epheser* (NTD 8; Göttingen 1976) 95.

[148] E.g. J. Coutts, "The relationship of Ephesians and Colossians": *NTS* 4 (1957-1958) 203-04.

Christians (cf. 1,13; 2,1f.5b.8-9.14ff.) [148] but "new" has not just a chrono-logical sense. It may be understood as implying that the group is still in the process of the total realization of its integration into the we-group (cf. 1,13.17ff.; 2,19ff.; 3,16ff.) whose members have already experienced the fact of salvation and have realized it in themselves (cf. 1,12.19; 2,7). However, the you-group is already a part of the we-group in so far as its members have attained to some realization of the mystery of the will of God in Christ.[149]

The author's profound experience of the action of God which is trans-parent in Eph 2,4-7 lies at the centre of the section 2,1-10. This is clear from the fact that the principal verbs are found in vv. 4-5: "But God while we were dead ... made us alive with Christ ..." (*kai ontas hēmas nekrous tais paraptōmasin synezōopoiēsen tōi Christōi ...*).[150] The implications of this loving gift of God are specified more closely by *syn* (together with) [151] which is prefixed to the three main verbs.[152]

All three verbs are in the aorist and recount a past event.[153] In characteristic Pauline terminology the writer states in Eph 2,5b.8-9 that "you" have been saved (*chariti este sesōsmenoi*). At the same time he admonishes the recipients ("you"), reminding them that their salvation comes gratuitously from God. Their proper disposition, therefore, should be characterized by a lack of boastfulness about their salvation, an attitude which is in line with, and which was inherited from, the Pauline tradition. Having shared a sinful past and now sharing the gift of salvation, there is no place for a boastful attitude (*kauchēsis*) in their inner dispositions.[154] Eph 2,10 which sums up the previous verses (*autou gar esmen poiēma ...*) affirms the fundamental fact of "our" common origin, our "creature-liness". We are created in Christ Jesus (*ktisthentes en Christōi 'Iesou ...*)

---

[149] The personal "you" in Chapter 3 is directly opposed to the "I" of Paul. This antithesis is found in the Pauline tradition. "You" is used in the prayer of the apostle in Eph 3,14ff. which foresees the growth of the Christians into the full perfec-tion of Christ. "You" represents a group which is almost prophetically foreseen in the future completion of the mystery based on the fruit of Paul's mission (Eph 3,1ff.). This group (cf. 3,1-13) includes not only those addressed in the present but looks for-ward and also addresses those who will form part of this group in the future. This means that "you" must be understood in relation to those other "*you*"'s outside the present community (cf. 3,1ff. 13). Cf. Lindemann, *Die Aufhebung*, 106-207. We are not discussing here how this union is reached but are simply stating and reflecting upon the important fact that old and new Christians, "we" and "you", lived together in one community and shared a common existence.

[150] B. M. Metzger, *Text. Comm.*, 602, says: "The reading *en tōi Christōi* (p46 B 33 al) seems to have arisen from either accidental dittography of the previous *en*, or from deliberate assimilation to *en Christōi 'Iēsou* in v. 6." Se also Lindemann, *Die Aufhe-bung*, 118-19 and note 80.

[151] Cf. J. Ernst, *Komm.*, 301.

[152] These three *syn*-verbs, *synezōopoiēsen*, *synēgeiren* and *synekathisen*, and their meaning will be treated in our discussion on the manner in which the unity in the "body" will take place. See page 142ff.

[153] Lindemann, *Die Aufhebung*, 106-07.

[154] Cf. J. Sanchez Bosch, *"Gloriarse" según San Pablo* (AnBib 40; Rome 1970) 164ff.

for good works (*epi ergois agathois*) [155] which God prepared beforehand, that we should walk in them. The verb "walk" has a different meaning here from what it has in Eph 2,2f. where it refers to the conduct of one's life. In this case it denotes the manner in which the way prepared by God is realized. The divine determinism (*proētoimasen ho theos*) makes possible a development in our lives. There are a number of links between Eph 2,10 and 2,14 (cf. *autou — autos; gar — gar; esmen — estin; poiēma — poiēsas; ktisthentes — ktisēi* [v. 15] *en Christōi °Iesou — en*-phrases) and v. 10 may be said to lead up to v. 14 which forms the climax of the section 2,1-22 of the letter.

We will now examine the manner of life of "you" as described in Eph 2,1-2.[156]. Verse 1 runs thus: "And you [157] being dead through your sins" (*kai hymas ontas nekrous tois paraptōmasin kai tais hamartiais hymōn*). It is stated there that "you" were dead [158] and the condition of being dead came about through [159] "your" transgressions and sins. This condition is defined in terms of man's relationship to God, of his communion with God. One who is in sin is dead in respect of this communion.[160] At the same time this communion implies a communion between men.[161]

The Bible presents sin as a power of death and as a state of estrangement from God, the source of life. In the Pauline letters, the notions of sin and "being dead" are closely linked.[162] Rom 6,23, for example, states: "The wage (*opsōnia*) paid by sin is death; but the free gift of God is eternal life in Christ our Lord".[163]

Death, in fact, is not only a punishment for sin, it is also its end and

---

[155] Compare the meaning of the same word *ergōn* in 2,9.

[156] Schlier, *Komm.*, 100, interpreting the conjunctive particle *kai* in 2,1, sees a connection with the previous part of the letter 1,23. Here, however, we feel unable to follow the logic of the author of Ephesians because, in chapter 1,3ff. he sings the "hymn" about his (in the text, "*our*") experience which is self-evident to him, but not so to us. The experience is something like a "crude" fact. We sense a kind of oriental pedagogy given by an enlightened master who sees his way.

[157] Schlier, *Komm.*, 100, says: "... Mit *kai hymas ontas* ... beginnt dieser Abschnitt in einem weitausholenden Anakoluth, in dem der einstige Zustand der Heidenchristen und ihre damalige Lebensführung beschrieben werden .... Aber vielleicht ist das *kai* einfach ein "und" im Sinne einer anknüpfenden und fortführenden Partikel." Gnilka, *Komm.*, 113, note 1. M. Barth, *Comm.*, 211, translates it by "*especially.*" See also L. Ramaroson, art. cit., 393-94.

[158] R. Bultmann, "*nekros*" in: *TDNT*, IV, 893.

[159] The associate dative or instrumental? Blass-Debrunner-Rehkopf, op. cit., § 198. We follow the translation of M. Barth, *Comm.*, 213.

[160] Lindemann, *Die Aufhebung*, 107 and note 5. F. Mussner, "Beiträge aus Qumran zum Verständnis des Epheserbriefes", in: *Ntl. Aufsätze* (Festschrift J. Schmid; Regensburg 1963) 196, compares Eph 2 with 1 QH 11 8b-14.

[161] Cf. 2,14ff.
　　　4,18: "being estranged from the life of God"
　　　2,12: "being estranged from the citizenship of Israel".

[162] Cf. Rom 5,12ff.; 6,16; 7,5; 10,23f.

[163] Cf. Rom 8,14f. 23.; 1 Cor 1,8; 2 Cor 2,15; Rom 7,14-25.

consummation, its fruit and crown.[164] Thus understood death is, of all things, that which can reveal what sin is.[165] The awareness of "being sinful" is a level of enlightenment which one cannot reach merely with the aid of ethico-philosophical self-examination (reflection). God's act of grace and love alone can awaken men from the death of sin (cf. 2,4ff.) and enable him to recognize sin in his past and in the present. The consciousness of sin, therefore, is part of the revelation brought by Christ (cf. 1,7f.).

In 2,1, the author does not conceive of death as physical or spiritual as we moderns do; at least, he does not say whether it is physical or spiritual.[166] The juxtaposition in this verse of the "transgressions" and the "sins" (hamartiai) which are linked by the particle kai [167] has no parallel in the Pauline corpus [168] where transgressions are mentioned in the context of the Pauline theology of sin.[169] We may ask what the reason for this juxtaposition is? Was the term hamartiai deliberately chosen because the author is addressing himself to the "you"-group of people? Or being aware of the heterogeneous groups with their own particular traditions, is he consciously widening the range of meaning of these terms? Or is this simply a characteristic of his style or of his rhetoric? We have not found a convincing reason for the juxtaposition of the two terms here,[170] but, whatever the reason is, it should be kept in mind that the two terms have practically the same meaning [171] and that sin does not denote a personified power. Thus, the author of Ephesians presents sin in a light different from that of St. Paul in the letter to the Romans (cf. esp. 5,12ff.). For Paul the power of fate is closely linked with that of death and the sin of man is the basis of death's rule (basileuein). Sin is the author of evil and it involves not only the individual act, but it is also a state which affects all humanity. The individual is always in this all-embracing state.[172] For the author of Ephesians, however, sin is something different. He does not adopt the meta-history of sin. Instead, he appears to have taken over the Pauline theology of sin and to have adapted it to the situation which

---

[164] Cf. Rom 6,21.

[165] See S. Lyonnet - L. Sabourin, *Sin, Redemption and Sacrifice* (AnBib 48; Rome 1920) 55.

[166] Schlier, *Komm.*, 100f., says: "... und es war ein realen Tod, dessen vorausfallenden Schatten nur der leibliche Tod ist, es war nicht ein Tod, 'im übertragenen Sinn', denn die eigentliche Wirklichkeit ist die durch das Verhältnis zu Gott bestimmte ...." Gnilka, *Komm.*, 113; M. Barth, *Comm.*, 212.

[167] "Sin" is not singular as in Rom 5,21; 6,23; 1 Cor 15,56.

[168] Compare Rom 4,25; 5,15ff.; 11,11f.; 2 Cor 5,19; Gal 6,1; Eph 1,7; 2,5; Col 2,13.

[169] The parallel phrase of 2,5 omits the "sins" hamartiai. Col 1,14 which is parallel to Eph 1,7, uses hamartiai instead of paraptōmata.

[170] P. Benoit, "Rapports littéraires entre les épîtres aux Colossiens et aux Éphesiens", in: *Ntl. Aufsätze*, (Festschrift J. Schmid; Regensburg 1963) 13-14.

[171] Schlier, *Komm.* 101, interprets thus: "... Es ist vielmehr ein predigtmäßiger Doppelausdruck, der die fülle der Sünden betont, die ihr heidnisches Leben durchwaltete."

[172] See W. Grundmann, "hamartanō", in: *TDNT*, I, 309f.

confronts him. Eph 2,2 must be considered with 2,1. Here, sin is presented in a different light from that of Romans.

Sin itself is not the main subject under discussion in vv. 1-2 but the
two modes of *peripatein* (walk i.e. way of life) which are qualified by
the two participial phrases. This is made clear by the temporal contrast
conveyed by "then" (*pote*) (2,2.3.11.13.) and "now" (*nyn*).[173] Verse 2, which
is subordinate to v. 1, further explains the condition of death in mythico-
cosmological terms as a condition which is under the influence of a cosmological power: "[the sins] in which [174] you once walked following (*kata*)
the age (*aiōn*) of this world, following (*kata*) the prince of the power of
the air, the spirit that is now at work in the sons of disobedience." "Your
walking in the sins" is qualified by two *kata*-phrases and thus the author
is referring to a manner of life following the age (*aiōn*) of this world [175]
and a manner following the prince of the power of the air. The noun
aiōn is singular here [176] as also is the term *archē* of the following phrase.[177]
It is stated that their ("your") way of life while they remained in their
sins was influenced or ruled by the totality of power.[178] This power in
so far as it works against God takes the form in human conduct of disobedience (*apeitheia*). It is the spirit which is at work now and which
entraps the insincere, the unfaithful, the disobedient (2,2b). The author
of Ephesians does not say "following this age," but "following the age
of this world".[179] He heaps up mythico-cosmologically pregnant notions
one after another either from Hellenistic or from Jewish traditions.[180]

The term *kosmos* in v. 2 is not conceived chronologically in opposition
to another *kosmos*,[181] nor has it negative connotations.[182] The author of

---

[173] Paradoxically "being in Christ" makes man (here "you") aware of his sinful
past, an awareness which affects not only the "you" group but also the "we"-group.
Eph 2,13 does not state explicitly the condition of "*being* in Christ." The *einai* (to
be) in Christ is already a meaning which man interprets according to his "ontology."
On the analysis of tenses of verbs, see page 108ff. To be aware of our sinful past
is the turn-about for our present condition of being in Christ. This is equally valid
for the both groups.

[174] The *hais* is a feminine plural form of the relative pronoun and so is grammatically linked to "sins" (*harmartiai*).

[175] H. Sasse, "*aiōn*", in: *TDNT* I, 197ff. esp. 207, sees a personified *aiōn* in the
Hellenistic syncretism. The same author, "*kosmos*", in: *TDNT* III, 868ff. esp. 885, 893.

[176] Compare Eph 1,21 (the two traditional contrasting ages: this age and the age
to come. 2,7 (plural); 3,9.11.21.

[177] Compare: Eph 1,21 *pasēs archēs*; Eph 6,12 (plural); Col 1,16 *archai*.

[178] Cf. G. Delling, "*archē*", in: *TDNT*, I, 479ff. esp. 482-483. N.B. "power" or *energeia* is one of the important notions in our letter.

[179] F. Mussner, *Christus, das All und die Kirche*. Studien zur Theologie des
Epheserbriefes (TrThSt 5; Trier 1968²) 26f. Is ..*aiōna tou kosmou toutou* an explanatory genitive?

[180] Does he try to demythologize these views of the world in order to move the
Christians to his inner freedom?

[181] Cf. Eph 1,4; 2,12. Strack-Billerbeck, IV, 799ff. The author appears to have
adapted a traditional eschatological expression here.

[182] See 1 Cor 3,19; 5,10; 7,31. *Ho aiōn houtos*: Rom 12,2; 1 Cor 1,20; 2,6.8.; 3,18;
2 Cor 4,4.

this so-called captivity letter (cf. 3,1; 4,1) notes how men are entrapped by the condition of life.[183] In so far as he walks in sins, man falls under the power of the prince of the air in a superhuman sphere and is unable to free himself from his bonds.[184] The author does not intend to describe these "powers" and we should not, therefore, try to objectify or personify them. The main point of Eph 2,2 is the manner of life which is expressed with the aid of two *kata*-phrases.[185] It is the man who goes astray who is bound and entrapped.[186] In so far as he lives in his sins, he is under the influence of this evil power experienced as transcendent. The author views "your" conduct of life in the past (*pote*) from his inner (transcendent) freedom.

The second characteristic of "being heathen," then, is a conduct of life which is entrapped by the power which is at work amongst the insincere and the disobedient to God. It is a condition bound by the evil power and by his sinful conduct of life, the result of his distorted heart.

3. "By nature children of wrath" (Eph 2,3)

The author of Ephesians then goes on to describe the manner in which "we all" once conducted "our" lives.

In Eph 2,3, he states: "In these also (*kai*)[187] we all once lived in the passions of our flesh, following the will of the flesh and the mind, and we were by nature children of wrath like the others" (*en hois kai hēmeis pantes anestraphēmen pote en tais epithymiais tē sarkos hēmōn, poiountes ta thelēmata tēs sarkos kai tōn dianoiōn, kai ēmetha tekna physei orgēs hōs kai hoi loipoi*).

The first two words, *en hois* (in whom) refer back to the previous phrase, "the sons of disobedience" (*en tois huiois tēs apeitheias*).[188]

The question arises as to whether "we all" (*hēmeis pantes*) denotes[189]

---

[183] Lindemann, *Die Aufhebung*, 51.
[184] Ibid., 56ff. See also W. Foerster, "*exousia*" in: *TDNT*, II, 562ff. esp. 567, idem, "*aēr*" in: *TDNT*, I, 165f.
[185] Cf. Eph 4,22. Also the *kata* in Eph 1,19; 3,7.20.; 4,16.
[186] Compare G. Delling, "*stoicheō*" in: *TDNT*, VII, 666-87. See also Col 2,6-3,4 esp. 2,8.20, and Gal 4,3 (with the relation to the Law.)
[187] *Kai* has the meaning "also" here; see H. Conzelmann, *Der Briefe an die Epheser* (NTD 8; Göttingen 1976) 95.
[188] Schlier, *Komm.*, 106, says: "... Das *en hois* ist nicht auf *ta paraptōmata kai hai hamartiai* zu beziehen. Dann müßte das Relativpronomen ... wie in V.2 femininisch und nicht neutrisch sein. Es gehört zu dem unmittelbar vorangehenden *en tois huiois tēs apeitheias*." Also Gnilka, *Komm.*, 116; Lindemann, *Die Aufhebung*, 111. M. Barth, *Comm.*, 216 states: "... The relative pronoun translated by 'these ways' is masculine or neuter. It refers more likely to the Gentile-born 'rebels' than to the remote 'lapses' of vs. 1 ...." P. Joüon, "Notes philologiques sur quelques versets de l'Epître aux Ephesians", *RSR* 26 (1936) 455f. L. Ramaroson, art. cit. (n. 196), 399 says: "... Bref, nous pensons que la proposition relative *en hois anestraphēmen* de 2,3 est attribut du couple *paraptōmasin* et *hamartiais* de 2,1."
[189] The texts A D read *hymeis*.

all the Jewish Christians, as in Eph 1,11f.,[190] or all Christians who conducted their lives in the past as sons of disobedience. Here we must treat this carefully, as the author of Ephesians does not explicitly "oppose" the Jewish and the non-Jewish Christians.[191] It is an historical fact that believers in Jesus Christ came from both Jewish and non-Jewish backgrounds. What does happen in v. 3 is that the writer by using Jewish-Pauline terms (*sarx, tekna, orgē,* etc) deepens the statement of vv. 1-2 (*pote ... peripatēsate*: ... you once walked).

Verse 3 is framed by *kai hymas* (also you) of v. 1 and *kai hēmas* (also we) of v. 5a. The we-you opposition does not imply opposition or discrimination in the community, but rather the fact that the "you"-group is, as was mentioned above,[192] incorporated in the we-group, the community composed of those old believers who have realized the Gospel in a certain sense in their lives. The author of Ephesians reminds us that "we all once (*pote*) lived (*anestraphēmen*)[193] in the passions (*epithymia*) of our flesh, following (*poiountes*) the will (literally: the wills: *ta thelēmata*)[194] of the flesh and of the mind (literally: "of the minds": *tōn dianoiōn*)."

The word *sarx* (flesh) which occurs twice in this verse has a negative sense here.[195] But the term itself does not denote a demonic "power" in a dualistic understanding of man.[196] Here it is part of the phrase *en tais epithymiais tēs sarkos hēmōn* (in the passions of our flesh). The *epithymia* (passions) are the passions or desires which impel one and which imply an anxious self-seeking.[197] This self-seeking is explained by the following participial phrase: following the will(s) of the flesh and of the mind(s) (*poiountes ta thelēmata tēs sarkos kai tōn dianoiōn*). Here the author is referring to the whole man who conducts his life in the passions of his flesh in so far as[198] he realizes the will of the flesh and the mind. It is

---

[190] Schlier, *Komm.*, 106.

[191] Lindemann, *Die Aufhebung*, 111 and note 29; 112 where he states: "... Nachdem den Lesern die christliche Interpretation vorchristlicher Existenz gegeben wurde, wird noch einmal im Wir-Stil generalisierend gesagt, da alle Menschen einst unter dem aion dieser Welt standen, auch 'wir' christen, mit einer Unterscheidung zwischen Juden- und Heidenchristen hat das nichts zu tun." Cf. also Gnilka, *Komm.*, 116.

[192] Refer to page 36ff. and 104ff.

[193] G. Bertram, "*anastrephō*" in: *TDNT*, VII, 715ff., esp. 717, in the sense of conducting life. Cf. Eph 4,22 (*anastrophē*); cf. Gal 1,13; 2 Cor 1,12.

[194] In opposition to *ta thelēmata* (the wills) notice *to thelēma* (the will) in Eph 1,9; 5,17; 6,6; also 1,1.5.; 1,11.

[195] Compare the same term in Eph 2,11.14.; 5,29.31; 6,5.12.

[196] See Lindemann, *Die Aufhebung*, 112-13. Cf. E. Schweizer, "*sarx*" in: *TDNT*, VII, 137 says: "... One sees how *sarx* can take on an increasingly personal demonic character. What was among the Gentiles the aeon of this world or the prince of the air was *sarx* among the Jews."

[197] Cf. Eph 4,22; Gal 5,16 and compare Eph 6,12. See F. Büchsel, "*epithymia*" in: *TDNT*, III, 171. K.-A. Bauer, *Leiblichkeit das Ende aller Werke Gottes* (Gütersloh 1971) 142 and note 13. With regard to the notion of *sarx* (flesh): A. Sand, *Der Begriff "Fleisch" in den paulinischen Hauptbriefen*. Biblische Untersuchungen. Bd. 2 (Regensburg 1967) 240ff., 210f.

[198] The participle *poiountes* is conjunctive to indicate the manner in which an

noteworthy that the author of the letter included the word *dianoiai* (minds) after the *sarkos* (of flesh). In doing this he appears to have tried to avoid a misunderstanding of the traditional notion of *sarx* which might be taken to imply a dualistic understanding of man — one substance with respect to which the flesh is evil and the mind good. The use of the two terms, flesh and mind (*tēs sarkos kai tōn dianoiōn*) is in question.[199] His intellectual or spiritual faculty is included.

It can be adversely affected by a life lived in (*en*) sins or following (*kata*) a sinful way of life (cf. vv. 1-3). What really matters then is how one conducts one's life.[200] The term *to thelēma* (the will) has a positive meaning in the Pauline letters [201] where it is always used in the singular. In Ephesians, however, it is the plural form of the noun that is used and it has a negative sense.[202] The author of Ephesians may have deliberately chosen this plural form to underline the deliberate contrast to the singular form which is used of the will of God (Eph 6,6; also 1,9 — the mystery of the will of God — cf. 1,5.11). The author of Ephesians stresses the need for believers in Christ Jesus to discern the will of God (5,17).[203]

In the following verse (v. 3c), summing up the condition in which "we all" lived, the author states that "we" were by nature children of wrath like the others (*kai ēmetha tekna physei orgēs hōs kai hoi loipoi*). We cannot deduce from the use of this term [204] the ethical view that human nature is evil nor that we, in our natural condition as descendents of Adam, were through procreation evil children of wrath by virtue of our "*natura humana*".[205]

---

action takes place, what precedes it and what accompanies it; see Blass-Debrunner-Rehkopf, *Grammatik*, § 418,5.

[199] E. Schweizer, "*sarx*" in: *TDNT*, VII, 137, says: "... The division of man into *sarx* and *dianoiai* is surprising"; see also pages 102, 104.

[200] See the previous pages on Eph 4,17f., 30ff. Cf. Lindemann, *Die Aufhebung*, 113-14.

[201] Compare *to thelēma tou theou* (the will of God): Rom 1,10; 2,18; 12,2; 2 Cor 1,2.; 8,5; Gal 1,4; 1 Thess 4,3; 5,18; Tim 1,1; 2,26.

[202] The only other occurrence of the plural form is found in Acts 13,22 (*panta ta thelēmata mou*).

[203] Cf. Col 1,9; 4,12.

[204] Dative of respect: Blass-Debrunner-Rehkopf, op. cit., § 197.2; *physei* is translated "by nature". Cf. Gal 2,15; Acts 4,36; Lk 1,5.

[205] It does not mean that *physei* (in an instrumental sense) we were sons of anger. Bauer-Arndt-Gingrich, *A Greek Lexicon of the New Testament*, 877, interpret thus: "... we were, in our natural condition (as descendants of Adam), children of wrath." M. F. Sadler, *The Epistles of St Paul to the Galatians, Ephesians and Philippians* (London 1892) 167: "... By nature can mean nothing else than 'by birth'. By our natural birth we received from the first Adam a taint of evil ...." H. C. G. Moule, *The Epistle of Paul the Apostle to the Ephesians* (Cambridge 1910) 70: "... By nature: i.e. by our unregenerate state in itself, not only by circumstances ...." E. F. Scott, *The Epistles of Paul to the Colossians, to Philemon and to the Ephesians* (London 1930) 164: "... by nature (i.e. in their natural state ...)". I. Knabenbauer, *Comm. in S. Pauli Epistolas ad Ephesios, Philippenses et Colossenses* (Parisiis 1912) 73: "... *physei* exhibet ... pronitatem naturalem, formitatem, i.e. refertur ad desideria carnis nostrae, quae ex ipsa natura oriantur." P. Pokorny, *Der Epheserbrief und die Gnosis*

According to the Jewish Apologetic, only the one who is gentile by nature is subject to the anger of God (the judgement). The Jews, on the other hand, are saved by the Law from the power of nature.[206] This scheme does not fit Eph 2,3 very well. The author of Ephesians includes all the members of the community to which he belongs, the new and the old believers, in this radical state of "being fallen." His scheme, in fact, is that of conversion to the life of Christ — once sinful, we are now saved by grace.[207] The term *physei*, therefore, is simply opposed to the divine act of grace (cf. vv. 5b.8) which is mentioned in the following verses (vv. 4ff.: *ho de theos...*).[208] The antithesis between the gratuity of divine salvation and the "being entrapped in sins" or "boasting about one's own works" (cf. vv. 5.8f.) is in stark contrast to the gratuity of divine salvation. To the total gratuity of divine love the corresponding inner attitude is that of total surrender or of entrusting oneself completely to God. Men without grace ("we" in the text) or men who refuse to respond to grace[209] are sons of anger.

The word "anger" (*orgē*) alludes to the eschatological judgement.[210] Instead of the more common phrase "the anger of God" (*hē orgē tou theou*),[211] the author has "by nature sons of anger" (*tekna physei orgēs*). This phrase, compared with 5,6 which contains a traditional expression of the eschatological judgement (*erchetai hē orgē tou theou epi tous huious tēs apeitheias*), refers to an actualization (realization) of "the anger" in man's conduct of life.[212] The way of life which is based on a fundamental *hybris* (arrogance, insolence) and which comes from the intimacy of the human heart,[213] led to a form of the divine anger,[214] the negative expression of God's love. Following our own wills of the flesh and of the mind we were unfaithful to God. In the community, we old believers as well as you new believers, were dead without the merciful love of God (cf. Eph 2,4f.).

(Berlin 1965) 113, sees a relation with a gnostic thought: "... Statt der gnostischen individuellen Befreiung von den Mächten, die durch die Erneuerung der eigenen göttlichen Natur geschieht, werden hier die Menschen von Natur (*physei*) für Kinder des Zorns erklärt." On the history of the interpretation of this phrase, see J. Mehlmann, *Natura filii irae. Historia interpretationis Eph 2,3 eiusque cum doctrina de Peccato Originale nexus* (AnBib 6; Rome 1957).

[206] H. Köster, "*physis*" in: *TDNT*, IX, 274f., 267. Cf. Wis 13,1f.; Josephus, *Ant.* 4,193.

[207] Köster, art. cit., 251ff., esp. 274f. He identifies "we" with the Jewish Christians and "you" with the Gentile Christians. Cf. Rom 2,14f.; 11,21.24.

[208] Schlier, *Komm.*, 107. Lindemann, *Die Aufhebung*, 115.

[209] Regarding "sons of anger": see Blass-Debrunner-Funk, op. cit. (English translation), § 162,2. the genitive of possession. Cf. Eph 5,8; 5,1ff.

[210] Cf. G. Stählin, "*orgē*" in: *TDNT*, V, 430f.; for the expression, "sons of anger"; see *Apoc. Mos.* 3: "Cain is a son of anger"; *skeuos orgēs* — Rom 9,21ff.

[211] Cf. Eph 5,6; Col 3,6; Rom 1,18ff.; 1 Thess 1,10. See Gnilka, *Komm.*, 250, and note 1.

[212] The thought of judgement as in 1 Thess 1,10 does not seem to be present here.

[213] Cf. G. Stählin, art. cit., 423.

[214] Cf. H. Kleinknecht, "*orgē*" in: *TDNT*, V, 383ff. Cf. Rom 1,17f.

It seems preferable to take the following phrase "like the others" (*hōs kai hoi loipoi*) as being ambiguous. The non-identification of "the others" appears to correspond more closely to the author's intention of presenting the community as a unity. He is not referring to two opposing groups such as we find in Romans (Jewish Christians and "the others" as the Gentile Christians leaves much to be desired). Another solution which takes "we" to refer to the Christians with "the others" referring to those not yet Christians, can easily leave one open to the charge of being biased by a preconception derived from a background of different denominations of Christian churches. Is it proper to interpret the phrase from the point of view of a "discriminating" mind?[215] Does "the others" denote the gentiles[216] or the rest of mankind — the non-Christians?[217] The best solution to this problem appears to be that "the others" refers to those people whose way of life may be described as universal among the heathen (cf. Eph 4,17ff.; 2,1-3; also 2,12). Too restrictive an identification of "the others" is hazardous as it may lead to a discriminatory attitude among us Christians as to who "the others" may be.[218]

There were Jews who insisted that some of their brethren had become "sons of disobedience." There were also the so-called heathen who clung to their own way of life in sins, refusing the truth. This description is also applicable to us Christians today who do not follow the manner of life in Christ. However, the author's main concern is not primarily that stated in 2,1-3, but rather to lead the members of the community to the reality of the event of Christ, through the merciful love of God, and to an awareness of their common sinfulness (cf. Eph 2,4ff.: But God, who is rich in mercy ...) with a view to deepening the unity of the community. To sum up, the characteristic of "being heathen" is the condition of a man who, while recognizing the will of the flesh, continues to give way to his passions and makes no effort, indeed refuses, to respond to the grace of God.

4. "Having no hope and without God" (Eph 2,12)

It has already been pointed out that Eph 2,12 is composed of two objective clauses governed by *mnemoneuete* (remember — *Dio mnemoneuete hoti*... v. 11). In this verse, the author calls on his readers to

---

[215] Cf. Stählin, art. cit., 438, note 392.

[216] E.g., Schlier, *Komm.*, 107. E. Gaugler, *Der Epheserbrief* (Zürich 1966) 89.

[217] Lindemann, op. cit., 114: ... "*hoi loipoi*" = die übrigen Menschen, d.h. die gegenwärtigen Nicht-christen. J. Ernst, *Komm.*, 304: "... Das Gilt nicht nur für die Judenchristen, von denen hier direkt die Rede ist, sondern auch von den 'Übrigen', d.h. von den Heidenchristen." Gnilka, *Komm.*, 117: "... Wie auch die übrigen findet noch einmal uns alle, die wir jetzt in der Gemeinde sind, mit der Allgemeinheit, den Söhnen des Ungehorsams, zusammen." See also note 3. M. Barth, *Comm.*, 211, translates it by "the rest of mankind."

[218] See the previous pages 20f. on 2,11.

remember "that at that time you were without Christ, estranged from the citizenship of Israel and strangers to the covenants of the promise, having no hope and without God in the world" (*hoti ēte tōi kairōi ekeinōi choris Christou, appēllotriōmenoi tēs politeias tou Israel kai xenoi tōn diathēkōn tēs epaggelias, elpida mē echontes kai atheoi en tōi kosmōi*).

This condition of the you-group in the past (*ēte*) which the author recalls is denoted by *pote* (v. 11), a term which is also found in v. 2. This is put in opposition to the present condition of the group (cf. v. 13: *nyni de . . .*: But now . . .)[219] which is described in v. 13. Through this antithesis, the author focusses on a specific point in "your" way of life and in particular on how the awareness of the condition (cf. 2,1ff.) of being sinful or as being ensnared by sin arose.[220]

Taking a closer look at this condition in the past, we may ask what the phrase "at that time you were without Christ" signifies. The opposite condition is mentioned in the following verse, namely, the condition of life in Christ Jesus. It is noteworthy that the phrase "without Christ" lacks the article before Christ [221] and also lacks the name "Jesus".[222] What is the significance of this? Is Christ in v. 12 the official name of the Messias who was promised to the Jews? If so, the meaning of the phrase is that "you" did not have the Messias of the Jews.[223] The context shows that naturally they did not have any Christ and certainly not Jesus Christ.[224] The author wants to express in a different and more concrete way what has been said in v. 11 in regard to their ("your") manner of life and he has done this by using the phrase "without Christ".[225] In a certain sense we can say that the Jews were "with Christ". In so far as they expected a Messiah according to their own idea they may be said to be with Christ in their own expectation.

---

[219] Lindemann, *Die Aufhebung*, 148, note 21.

[220] This depends on the interpretation of the phrases: *en tōi haimati . . .* (2,13); *en tē sarki autou* (2,14); and *dia tou staurou* (2,16).

[221] Compare Eph 1,3; 4,15; 5,21; 6,6 etc.

[222] Cf. Eph 2,13; 2,5.7.10.

[223] F. Mussner, *Christus das All*, 77: "... Die Heiden waren, ohne Messias, d.h. ohne die jüdische Hoffnung auf den verheissenen Heilbringer ...." In this line of interpretation, the phrase "at that time" (*en tōi kairōi ekeinōi*) may indicate the epoch of Salvation History before and after the Messiah.

[224] E. Gaugler, *Der Epheserbrief* (Zürich 1966) 103, says: "... Damals aber waren sie—außerhalb Israels—auch *choris Christou*. Es bezieht sich aber dennoch nicht auf den präexistenten Christus (gegen von Soden). Der Gedanke ist tatsächlich: die Juden hatten Christus, die Heiden nicht. Ohne den Christus hatten die Heiden noch keinen Anteil an den Vorzügen der israelischen=der Heilsgemeinde." We can ask ourselves if Gaugler presupposes that the Jews had Christ in the sense of the author of the Ephesians, because in Eph 2,11, the Jews who did not follow the conduct of life in Christ were also "heathen." Also cf. E. Haupt, *Die Gefangenschaftsbriefe* (Göttingen 1902) 71, "... Nicht davon ist im Zusammenhang die Rede, daß das Judentum Christum schon hatte, aber die Heiden nicht, sondern daß die Heiden, als sie Christum nicht hatten, auch die religiösen Güter des Judentums nicht hatten, welche ihnen erst als Christen zu teil geworden sind."

[225] Cf. Lindemann, *Die Aufhebung*, 148, states: "... Christos bezeichnet das Heilsereignis als Ganzes."

If one takes the acknowledgement of Christ in one's life and the manner of life in Christ as the criterion of being with or without Christ, then it can be said that the Jews who do not commit themselves to Christ in their actual lives are "without Christ" from the standpoint of the author, whose yardstick is the extent to which one conducts one's life in Christ. This criterion may also be applied to nominal Christians. In any case, whatever the Jews hoped about Christ and whatever the Christians now know about Jesus Christ, the heathen at that time did not in any way benefit from it.

Their way of life at that time was "estranged from the citizenship of Israel" (*apēllotriōmenoi tēs politeias tou Israel*).[226] The expression, "the citizenship of Israel" does not refer to the state of Israel which had not existed for a long time and membership in which the Greek of Asia Minor can hardly have thought worth seeking. Nor can it refer at all to citizenship in the literal sense, since Christian status would not be a true counterpart to this. It is used rather in the figurative sense of the privileged religious position of Israel as the recipient of the promise.[227]

Even in Rom 11,26, Paul does not state that "all Jews will be saved," but that "all Israel will be saved..." Most importantly, the contestation against the Pauline mission and Paul's sorrow for his kinsmen by race (cf. Rom 9,1ff.) are the underlying assumptions of the letter to the Ephesians. Israel is not just the whole of its individual members; it is the bearer of the promise and the recipient of its fulfilment.[228] It has obtained the privilege in so far as it participates in the promise fulfilled by Christ. It may be described as "the people of God".[229]

Citizenship in Israel is a pledge of the heavenly citizenship which is now being prepared and which is identical with the Church.[230] We must not overlook the concrete situation of "you" which is described in traditional Jewish terminology. While Israel does not open herself to Christ and does not accept him yet, she still belongs not to this time (*nyni de...*: "But now": 2,13) but to that time (*tōi kairōi ekeinōi*: "at that time": 2,12). In this situation, irrespective of whether the Jews are "real Israel" or not, "you" were at that time without Christ, estranged from the citizenship of Israel.

The author of the letter goes on to describe "your" situation as strangers to [231] the covenant of the promise.[232] The privileged position

---

226 See page 40ff. on Eph 4,17f. *politeia* is found twice in the NT; in Eph 2,3 and Acts 22,28.

227 H. Strathmann, *"politeia"* in: *TDNT*, VI, 534. Lindemann, *Die Aufhebung*, 148-49, says: "...sondern 'Israel ist einfach der Name für Heil und Gottverbundenheit', so wie das Stichwort *ethnē* pauschal für 'Gottlosigkeit' steht."

228 W. Gutbrod, *"Israel"* in: *TDNT*, III, 386ff. Cf. Schlier, *Komm. Röm.*, 340.

229 W. Gutbrod, art. cit., 387.

230 Gnilka, *Komm.*, 135.

231 *xenos* with genitivus; see Blass-Debrunner-Rehkopf, *Grammatik*, § 182,3.

232 J. Schniewind - G. Friedrich, *"epangelia"* in: *TDNT*, II, 582ff. esp. 583. Note 58

of Israel is enunciated in Rom 9,4f.[233] The messianic gift of salvation is promised to Israel[234] while the promise, the covenant and the guidance of God form the community of Israel as such. For Paul, the notion of "promise" (*epaggelia*)[235] is the principle of the life of Israel (cf. Rom 4,13f.; Gal 3,16ff.). This promise has been accomplished in Christ (cf. Rom 15,8 — note the plural form; and 2 Cor 1,20) and since then has been fulfilled through the spirit (cf. Gal 3,14; 2 Cor 1,22; 5,5).[236]

According to Ephesians, the fruits of this promise[237] were shared in Christ Jesus through the Gospel (cf. 3,6; 2,19ff.). "You" were estranged from this promise and so did not have any hope and were without God.

The term "hope" (v. 12) does not occur in the Synoptics, in John's gospel nor in the Apocalypse of John. It is found eight times in Acts and 36 times in the Pauline letters.[238] The frequency of occurrence of the term in the Pauline letters shows its importance for Paul. The verbal form *elpizein* is not found in the letter to the Ephesians.[239] The phrase "having no hope" (*mē elpida echontes*) denotes "your" situation at that time as viewed from "your" present situation.[240] The same expression[241] is found in 1 Thess 4,13, but there it has a different meaning.[242] The "hope" of Eph 2,12 is not so specific that it cannot allude to hope in the resurrection or future salvation or the parousia.[243] "Your" situation is

states: "... Eph 2,12, as in Gal 3,16 *epangelia* is closely linked to *diathēkē* in meaning." Here, the *diathēkai* in the plural form may allude to the covenant with Abraham (Gen 15,7-21; 17,1-22) and with Moses (Ex 24,1-11) (cf. Rom 9,4; Gal 4,24), but must be thought of from the viewpoint of the accomplishment of the new covenant (cf. Jer 31,31-34; 32,40; Is 53,3; Ez 37,26 and in our letter: Eph 1,13; 3,6 etc.). Cf. Gnilka, *Komm.*, 136. T. J. Deidun, *New Covenant Morality in Paul* (AnBib 89; Rome 1981) 228: "More particularly: it is obvious from our discussion that, in Paul's view, the religion of the New Covenant is not, first and foremost, a doctrine nor, in the literal sense, a cult, but a divine-human '*peripatein*': God's activity in man's ... This integration of religion and morality, which is more or less implicit in all New Testament writers, is particularly characteristic of Paul ..., being based on his peculiar understanding of the rôle of the Spirit, and, more particularly, on his interpretation of Ez. 36,27, in the light of which he sought to explain his faith experience."

[233] The textual problem whether the text reads a plural or singular form may be solved with B. M. Metzger, *Text Comm.*, 519. Cf. Rom 3,2.

[234] Cf. Rom 4,13ff.; 15,8; Gal 3,16; 4,24.

[235] "Paul's inquiry concerns the relationships between *nomos* and *epaggelia*, between human action and divine grace (Rom 4), between the demanding will of God and His will to give (Gal 3)". See J. Schniewind, art. cit., 582. Ephesians, however, does not use Paul's key-term *nomos* here but later in 2,14ff., where he places it at the root of the phenomenon of "enmity."

[236] Schlier, *Komm.*, 120-21.

[237] Here the "promise" is in the singular and this term is not found in Colossians.

[238] Heb: 5 times; 1 Pet: 3 times; 1 Jn: once.

[239] The cognate verb *proelpizein* in 1,12.

[240] Cf. Lindemann, *Die Aufhebung*, 150. On "hope": see R. Bultmann, "*elpis*" in: *TDNT*, II, 517ff.

[241] Compare Acts 24,15; Rom 15,4; 2 Cor 3,12.

[242] Gnilka, *Komm.*, 136, note 3.

[243] B. Rigaux, *Saint Paul. Les épitres aux Thessaloniciens* (Paris 1956) 366, says: "... Toutefois, avec Bultmann, on peut légitimement remarquer que les énoncés de

described in Jewish-Pauline terminology and especially in terms of the hope of Israel.

The indefinite nature of the phrase "having no hope" appears to indicate a condition of man who closes his heart to others, adheres mentally to the age of this world, abandons himself without letting himself trust in the dynamism fo God working towards the wider horizon of his view and life, and continually seeks his own self-based security, which is rooted in those people who do not follow and do not want to follow the way in Christ described in the previous verses vv. 1ff. Fatalistic thought, ideology, philosophy or theology which may become ideologies to bind and to suffocate dynamism of life in Christ, have often resulted from these or similar conditions of man.

From the viewpoint of the author who hopes in Christ, "you" did not have a hope at that time.[244]

It should also be noted that in the three passages in Ephesians (1,18; 2,12; 4,4) in which hope is mentioned, it is not described in terms of the tension between the past and the future, between the "already" and the "not yet." With the help of traditional expressions, the author has presented in a new and creative way the eschatological fact which was understood according to a linear time concept of past-present-future.

In the human experience of daily life man believes and loves and from his or her mutual communion springs forth hope based on joy. For Paul, hope (*elpis*) with faith (*pistis*) and love (*agapē*) form a stereotyped triad which conveys the fundamental experience of primitive christianity, and experience which comes from the preaching of the Gospel. By this triad, Paul expresses a fundamental attitude of Christ Jesus himself and of his followers. The triad occurs for the first time in 1 Thess 1,3.[245] It is also found in 1 Cor 13,13 in the sequence faith-hope-love, where Paul explains the importance of love in comparison with faith and hope, neither of which goes beyond the end of earthly life.

Comparing Paul's wording with similar philosophical statements of that time, it is clear that Paul used *agapē* instead of *eros* (love).[246] Some

---

Paul se groupent autour de trois centres unifiés: l'attente de l'avenir, la confiance et la patience dans l'attente: que l'espérance est dirigée totalement vers des choses qu'on n'a pàs encore vues, cf. Rom 8,24-25: que l'idée de patience est présente, cf. Rom 5,4-5; 15,4; avec celle de confiance, cf. 1 Cor 15,19; 2 Cor 1,10; 3,12; Phil 1,20 ..."

[244] Cf. Eph 1,12.

[245] The triad occurs in the following form: "remembering before our God and Father *your work of faith and labour of love and steadfastness of hope* in our Lord Jesus Christ" (*mnēmoneuontes hymōn tou ergou tēs pisteōs kai tou kopou tēs agapēs kai tēs hypomonēs tēs elpidos tou kyriou hēmōn °Iēsou Christou emprosthen tou theou kai patros hēmōn*). Cf. B. Rigaux, *Saint Paul. Les épîtres aux Thessaloniciens* (Paris 1956), ad loc.

[246] Porphyrus, *ad Marc.* 24: *tessara stoicheia malista kekratunthō peri theou, pistis, alētheia, erōs, elpis.* "And there is no evidence in Greek patristic writings of the distinction which is repeated so often in exegetical works; see Lampe's *Patristic Greek Lexicon,* agape and erōs; on the contrary, they are expressly equated" (Mary Grosvenor).

authors are of the opinion that Paul, in 1 Cor 13,13, was coping with gnostic tendencies but that is not easy to prove.[247]

There three key-words are found in many passages in the Pauline letters.[248] In the parallel passages of Col 1,4f. and Eph 1,15ff. "hope" appears to play an important role. The order of the triad, which is the same as in 1 Thess 1,3, follows the order of experience and reflects the proto-experience of Christ.

In Col 1,5, hope is not put on the same level as faith (*pistis*) and love (*agapē*). Nevertheless, the fundamental pattern of the *Ur-Erfahrung* of faith and love are dynamically linked to the hope (*dia tēn elpida*: through the hope).[249] We see that the expressions which describe "hope" in Eph contain more than one feature. We are not at this stage obliged to determine positively what these expressions mean. We will do that later, when we treat Eph 1,18.[250] But it is already clear what the negative expression wants to say here. All the experiences mentioned above, the hope of 'Israel' and the initial experience of Christian life in a community—surely the development of hope in a full Christian life—are excluded when the apostle states: "you were without hope."

The author then goes on to describe the situation as "(being) without God" (*kai atheoi*). The term *atheoi* is a hapax in the N.T.[251] In Eph 2,12, it clearly signifies a practising atheist. It does not mean that those who practice Hellenistic or Pagan (i.e. non-Jewish or non-Christian) religions cannot have a knowledge of God.

In the present context, *atheos* indicates a manner of life seen from the standpoint of believers in Christ.[252] It is not a superficial denomination of Jewish Christians who insist that they have the true God. It is rather a description of "your" situation in the past from the point of view of one who has experienced God's relationship with his people in Christ Jesus. This is clearer in Eph 2,14ff.

The *atheoi* are people who are bound to something or are bound by themselves or by something which they can conceive or imagine, in

---

[247] H. Conzelmann, *Die erste Brief an die Korinther*, 270ff.

[248] E.g., Gal 5,6; 1 Thess 3,6; 1 Cor 16,13f.; Philem 5; Gal 5,5. 1 Thess 5,8; Rom 5,3ff. In Eph 6,17, *elpis* is not mentioned. See Conzelmann, *An die Korinther*, 270ff. E. Lohse, *Kol.*, 45.

[249] E. Lohse, *Kol.*, 46ff. esp. 48, says: " ... Das Sinnen und Trachten der Glaubenden gilt darum dem, was droben ist (3,1). Der Begriff *elpis* ist damit aus einem zeitlich eschatologischen Verständnis in eine von räumlichem Denken bestimmte Vorstellung übertragen. In der Trias Glaube, Liebe, Hoffnung wird im Kolosserbrief nicht die Liebe als die größte unter ihnen gepriesen, sondern die *elpis*. Sie kann daher geradezu als Inhalt der Frohbotschaft schlechthin bezeichnet werden, durch den Glaube und Liebe ihre Begründung erfahren." Lindemann, sums up the hope, *Die Aufhebung*, 194: " ... die *elpis* ist der *Christos en hymin*, d.h. die Hoffnung richtet sich auf das bereits gegenwärtige Heil." Also compare Rom 15,13.

[250] See Chap. 4, page 154ff.

[251] Gnilka, *Komm.* 136.

[252] Cf. Lindemann, *Die Aufhebung*, 150. Cf. 1 Cor 8.4-6; Ignatius *Trall.* 3,2; 10,1.

such a way that they will not acknowledge God. The first attitude of the
atheoi is this condition of being ensnared. Even God becomes an object
who ensnares man, in so far as man conceives Him without being aware
of his (man's) reality. Practical atheism is worship by the ignorant, the
short-sighted, the self-sufficient, the hedonist or the careless.[253] The "godless" attitude of man comes from his inner self-sufficiency or his self-
glorification, whether he is conscious of it or not. Defiance of God
springs from self-glory.[254] On the level of a community, self-glorification
of a nation or state or of a culture, or sometimes of a religion, can lead
to the manipulation of authentic elements of religion by a political power
and to the secularisation (in a negative sense) of the authentic character
of religion.[255]

In the Hellenistic period, belief in God was very much overshadowed
by the widespread belief in fate, a belief which sometimes has an heroic
and fatalistic character and at other times a magical and astrological one.

It is out of such a belief that the fear of the *stoicheia tou kosmou*
arises, against which Paul addresses his message of the cosmic supremacy
of Christ and of the all-embracing scope of his death (cf. Col 2,8ff.).[256]

The replacement of a belief in God by philosophic (in modern sense)
or gnostic enlightenment can also lead to a subtle form of atheism if
man neglects the concretely somatic realisation of the will of God in his
life. To know one God in the sense of philosophic monotheism can
amount to atheism. Jewish monotheism which denied polytheism and
emptied the world of gods can also be described as atheism.[257] It is ironical
that the Jews who condemned Jesus as the messenger of the devil[258]
made the same charge against the community of Jesus.[259] *Aire tous atheous*
("take away the atheists") was the anti-Christian war-cry of the non-Christian mob.[260] The believers in Christ did not merely reject this charge,
they threw it back at their accusers as in Eph 2,11f.

Once "in the world" (*en tōi kosmōi*) "you" had no God and no hope.
The irony of this statement is clear once we realize that the word
"kosmos," in the Greek order of things, embraced all the gods. The
inhabitants of the Hellenistic cities of Asia Minor had a highly developed
cosmology and philosophy.[261] According to the author, however, some of
these people were "without God."

---

[253] E. Stauffer, "*atheos*", in: *TDN*, III, 120f. Cf. Is 22,13; Jer 54,ff.; Ps 10,4; 14,1ff.
Rom 1,30; 3,10ff.; 1 Cor 15,32.; Josephus, *Bell.* 5,566.
[254] Cf. Eph 1,21; 2,1ff.; 6,10ff.
[255] See above, Stauffer, art. cit., 120f. Cf. Ez 28,2; Dan 11,36; 2 Thess 2,4.
[256] Stauffer, "atheos", 120f.
[257] Josephus, *Ap.* 2,148.
[258] Lk 7,34; Jn 10,20.
[259] Acts 5,39; 9,5; 23,9.
[260] *Mar. Pol.*, 3,2; Just., *Apol.* 1,13,1.
[261] See the previous page on *Kosmos* in Eph 2,2, page 36ff., especially, 40f.

We may sum up the fourth characteristic of "being heathen" which denotes also the former condition of the you-group people. It is described in 2,12 in Jewish-Pauline terminology, especially in terms of the hope of Israel. The "your" condition of "having no hope", however, includes a double level of hope. One level refers to "your" way of life in the past "at that time" when you were apart from Christ and from "us", i.e. the community who believed in Christ "At that time" you were living in sins and were bound by the power of this world, seeking yourself, and being ensnared by your own distorted minds and hearts, then, you were blind to the reality of God in Christ. This manner of life is simply a life without hope.

The second level of hope is a specific one for which man is asked to pray in order that he may himself respond totally to the hope of the calling of God who is now at work in him who has become a member of the community. And this condition of "having no hope" at the same time implies godlessness.

5. "You who once were far off are now brought near" (Eph 2,13)

In this verse, the author comes to the present situation of the "you": you without hope, who were far off, are now brought to God's source of salvation. "But now you are in Christ Jesus, through the blood of Christ, you have been brought near, you were once far off" (*nyni de en Christōi ʾIēsou hymeis hoi pote ontes makran egenēthēte eggys en tōi haimati tou Christou*).

The present situation in opposition to the former one is indicated by the words, *nyni de ...* (but now ...). The content of 2,13 is opposed to the "your" condition of the past (*pote*, then) which is described in 2,11f., and which refers further back to the manner of conduct of life described in 2,1f. And this verse 2,13, at the same time, becomes a link verse to the following section of 2,14ff.

The expression *pote ontes makran* (once being far away) serves to link verse 2,13 to the previous verses, where the situation of "being without Christ" of 2,12 is described. The opposite situation is described "but now you [are] in Christ Jesus" (*nyni de hymeis en Christōi ʾIesou*) in 2,13.[262] The main intention of verse 2,13 is to describe the present situation through spatial-language, instead of time-language like *pote* and *nyn* (then and now) to show the counter-situation to what is stated in 2,11f. The author of the Ephesians describes the situations in the following spatial terms: *makran* (far) and *eggys* (near). These contrasting terms allude to Is 57,19 which in Eph 2,17 might be a kind of quotation. But the reason why the author of Eph switches his diction from

---

[262] S. Hanson, *The Unity of the Church in the New Testament. Colossians and Ephesians*, 146. Lindemann, *Die Aufhebung*, 151.

time language to space language is also internally connected to the spatial wording and the image of 2,14ff.[263]   Verse 2,13, therefore, prepares us for the spatial image of "building" in 2,19ff., where, after the "hymnic" part of 2,14ff., "your" present situation, i.e. incorporation into the citizenship of the saints, is described in terms of the image.[264]

Now here in 2,13 we will examine the meaning of "being far" and "being brought near" (precisely, "having become near" in the Greek text).[265]   In the context of Is 57,19, the word "far" meant the Jews who were in Exile, and the "near" were those who came back home.[266]   According to some rabbinic interpretation, those who are "far off" are sinners who became converted, and those who are "near" denote justified men within Israel.[267]   And the Hebrew verb "to bring near" (*qrb*) is applied to non-Israelites outside the community of Israel, consequently non-Israelites may denote heathen.   But we must be careful not to assume that in every case those who are far are necessarily the heathen.[268]

The rabbinic interpretation of Is 57,19 about the "far" and the "near" concerns also the relation of man to God within Israel and is not intended to refer to the counter-status of Israel and non-Israel.[269]   Therefore, we cannot say simply that the "near" means the Jews, and the "far" the heathen.[270]

Another interpretation, this time without basis in Judaism, is that the "far" and the "near" are supposed to denote not the Jews and the heathen, but the cosmic powers.[271]   In this context of 2,13, the two terms indicate concrete persons: the "you" who once were far.   The author of Ephesians does not state who are near in Eph 2,17, where he adds "you" (*hymin*) to the quotation-like sentence of 2,17, but he, peculiarly enough,

---

[263] Eg.: the two become "one" (*hen*) (2,14); the partition wall *to mesotoichon* (2,14); the body *sōma* (2,16), the access *hē prosaggōgē* (2,18).

[264] In 2,19ff., the author again addresses the "you" directly after 2,11ff.

[265] In the Pauline letters, the term *makran* occurs only in Eph 2,13.17. On the word *eggys*: cf. Phil 4,5; Rom 10,8; 13,11 as well as our passages Eph 2,13 and 2,17.

[266] Cf. C. Westermann, *Isaiah 40-66* (London 1969) 330.

[267] Strack-Billerbeck, I, 167, states: "... Erst 'den Fernen', u. dann 'den Nahen' (Die 'Fernen' d.h. die, die Gott erst fern waren und dann in Buße sich ihm zuwandten; die 'Nahen' d.h. die, die als vollkommene Gerechte Gott immer nahe waren). Dagegen sagte R. Jochanan: Wer ist der 'Ferne'? Derjenige, der sich von Anfang an von der Übertretung ferngehalten hat. Und wer ist der 'Nahe'? ... Der erst der Übertretung nahe war (in Sünden lebte) und nun sich von ihr entfernt hat (in Buße)." Cf. also id. 215f.

[268] Strack-Billerbeck, III, 585ff. Cf. Gnilka, *Komm.*, 137, and some thoughts parallel with Qumran: F. Mussner, "Beiträge aus Qumran zum Verständis des Epheserbriefes," in: *Neutestamentliche Aufsätze* (Festschrift für J. Schmidt) (Regensburg 1963) 197.

[269] See Strack-Billerbeck, III, 586.

[270] Lindemann, *Die Aufhebung*, 154 and note 55.

[271] J. Gnilka, "Christus unserer Friede — Ein Friedens- Erlöserlied in Eph 2,14-17," (Festschrift H. Schlier) (Freiburg 1970) 200. Cf. H. Schlier, *Komm.*, 122, says: "... Christus gibt den 'Ort' an, an dem man Gott nahe ist. Christus selbst der 'Raum' der Nähe Gottes. Aber 'in Christus Jesus' sind die ehemaligen Fernen Gott nahe gekommen: *en tōᵢ haimati tou Christou*."

does not add "us" (*hēmin*) before the word *eggys* (near).[272] He appears to have avoided an attitude of contestation which induces a feeling of superiority over the newcomers, "you." If we would understand the word "near" in the sense of the Jews and the "far" as the heathen in the passages of Eph 2,13.17, the verse of 2,13 could mean: "you" (are) now in Christ Jesus, who once were the heathen, you are brought near, namely you became Jews in the blood of Christ. This is clearly not the intention of the author.[273] With different nuances, many authors interpret the two terms (*makran*, *eggys*) as referring to the Jews and the heathen respectively,[274] but the author of Eph never emphasises the disunity or contestation between Jews and Gentiles, nor between Jewish Christians and the gentile Christians at first reading of this text, at least.[275] In our letter there was a Pauline problem, the counter-position of the Jews and the Gentiles, or of the Jews and the Greeks. Such a problem appears to be the background of the present community of Ephesians. The contestation between the Jews and the gentiles had become the proto type of disunity to clarify what was meant by unity, what enmity implied, and what the gospel brought to humanity. At least, it seems clear that the first interest of the author of Eph is not the disunity of the Jews and the heathen (or the gentiles) nor that of the Jews and gentile Christians because we cannot find explicit statements about a contra-position or disunity between Jewish Christians and gentile Christians in our letter.

---

[272] P. Stuhlmacher, "Er ist unser Friede (Eph 2,14)," *Neues Testament und die Kirche* (Für R. Schnackenburg), (Freiburg 1974) 346 and note 39.

[273] S. Hanson, op. cit., 142f. finds a difficulty in interpreting the term *eggys* and says thus: "... Their state as Gentiles is designated by *makran*, and this has been exchanged for *eggys*. What does this mean? In v. 17 *hoi eggys* denotes the Jews, but in v. 13 the sense is hardly that the Gentiles have become Jews, for that would contradict the fundamental thought of this section; as we shall see, *eggys* must here have a more general meaning of 'near' i.e. near God and the gifts of grace He offers the Church."

[274] Cf. P. Stuhlmacher, art. cit. (n. 272), 348, states: "... v. 13 verkündet die wunderbare, von Gott in Christi Sühnetod ermöglichte und vollzogene Zusage ... Gott (hat) im blutigen Tode Jesu Heil und Vergebung für die Fernen, d.h. die Heiden, (und für die Nahen, d.h. die Juden) gestiftet und eben damit die bisher durch das Gesetz von seiner Heilswirklichkeit Ausgeschlossenen durch Christus in seine Nähe gezogen." G. Schille, *Frühchristliche Hymnen* (Berlin 1965) 25, says: "... Der Verfasser hingegen trennt zwischen fern und nah absichtlich, als meine 'fern' die Heiden und 'nah' die Juden, um die Aufnahme der Heiden in die Bürgerschaft Israels hervortreten zu lassen ..." P. Benoit, "L'unité de l'Eglise selon l'Epître aux Ephésiens": *Stud. Paul. Congressus 1961* (An Bib 17; Rome 1963) I, 62f., states: "... Comment s'est opéré ce merveilleux changement? Par le Christ, ainsi que Paul l'explique aux vv. 14-18 qui séparent les vv. 11-13, où est décrite la séparation, des vv. 19-22 où est décrite la réunion. Par le Christ qui 'supprime dans sa chair', en mourant sur la croix, 'la haine' qui opposait juifs et païens, 'pour créer en sa personne les deux en un seul Homme Nouveau, faire la paix ... .'" J. Coutts, "The Relationship of Ephesians and Colossians": *NTS* 4 (1957-1958) 201-07, 206, says: " ... at Eph 2,13 the author alludes to the latter passage, *hymeis hoi pote* .... The author has interpreted *hoi makran* to mean you Gentiles, and *hoi eggys* to mean the Jews, and the repetition of *eirēnē* as the confirmation that there is to be peace to each of the two. Thus the work of the Second Adam is set in the Messianic context of the messenger of God promised in Isaiah ... ."

If one takes into consideration the word "access" (*prosagōgē*) in 2,18,[276] "to be far" indicates only a "distance" of man from God, and "to be brought near" (2,13) (*egenēthēte eggys*) means a closeness to Him. But this is a rather one-sided interpretation.[277] It is still insufficient to interpret the "nearness" (*eggys*) in the sense of closeness to *God*. The meaning of "to be far" relates to a manner of life as we explained it above (cf. 2,1ff.; 2,11f.; 4,17ff.). Therefore the distance is also a distance between men, and concretely in our text, a distance between the "you" and the "us." "To be brought near" (*egenēthēte eggys*) means that both "we" and "you" draw closer together. In this pregnant sense, "our" nearness is at the same time nearness to God.[278] Having stated the fact that you who were far off were evangelized (2,17), the author of Eph uses the word "father" to whom we all draw near (2,18). The "father" in a certain cultural milieu shows the origin of brotherhood. In the case of our letter, without doubt he is the father of Jesus Christ and of all.[279] To sum up, the last characteristic of "being heathen" is a condition of "being far off": from the citizenship of the saints, from our community in Christ, and from God. The author of Eph resumes the "your" manner of life in the past by the spatial idiom "far" in oposition to "your" present condition in "our" community. You were brought near through the blood of Christ.

As far as we can judge from the letter, these five qualities mentioned above define what the author of Eph means when he speaks about "heathenness". By "being heathen", the author denotes a kind of life and its consequences and presuppositions which should belong definitively to the past of his hearers. The meaning of "being heathen," dynamically understood, contains a warning to us Christians of today as well. Heathenness has always something to do with us Christians. It is a hindrance and an obstacle to the new unity the author wants by his letter to bring to the recipients.

---

[275] H. Merklein, *Christus und die Kirche* (SBS 66; Stuttgart 1973) 25, says: "... Der Verfasser will ja nicht sagen, daß die ehemaligen Heiden nun Juden geworden sind. Die Begriffe sind zwar die jüdischen, aber der Verfasser sieht sie ganz aus seiner (christlich-ekklesiologischen) Sicht. Erst von Christus her werden sie in ihrer ganzen Bedeutung verifizierbar. Außerdem ist zu betonen, daß die Juden nicht qua Juden 'Nahe' waren, genausowenig wie die Heiden qua Heiden 'Fernen' waren. Nahe waren die Juden, insofern sie unter der Gottesvolkidee standen. Deswegen kann der Epheserbrief sagen, daß die Heiden jetzt nahe gekommen sind, weil sie jetzt in Christus zur Kirche gehören ...."

[276] Cf. Eph 3,12; Rom 5,2. N.B. "we have access ..." *echomen ... tēn prosagōgēn ....* *Echomen* is the first person plural of the present indicative of the verb *echein*. See below, page 108ff.

[277] Lindemann, *Die Aufhebung*, 155.

[278] Col 1,20ff., where we can find the contrasting time-language of *pote* and *nyn* (v. 21-22), but not the dialectical way by changing personal pronouns, "you" and "we." Cf. H. Merklein, "Zur Tradition und Komposition von Eph 2,14-18": *BZ* 17 (1, 1973) 79-102, 101f. According to the author, Col 1,21f. is the background of Eph 2,11-18.

[279] Cf. Eph 3,14f.; 1,2, etc.

2-3: Unity of "Old" and "New" Christians

Now we come to explain the basic experience: the fact of unity between old and new Christians in the same community. This fact, in the context of Chapter 2 of Eph, is described mainly in 2,14-18. Therefore, it would seem essential to make an exegesis of these verses. We feel that the whole letter is permeated by the motive of unity. But especially here in 2,14ff. the author of Eph states the fact of reconciliation and the unity of both groups. And we shall deal with this fact of unity in the following Chapter because the author of Eph appears to persuade and lead his readers not only to an understanding of the fact of unity, but also to a fuller and deeper comprehension of it and its actualization in their conduct of life.

Christe is Our Peace

The author of Eph exalts the fact that they were brought close together by the cross, by the blood of Christ. He goes into a description of the consequences for the present community. "For he is our peace" (*Autos gar estin hē eirēnē hēmōn*) (2,14). Various authors discuss whether this part (2,14ff.) beginning with "For he ..." (*Autos gar*)[280] could have been originally an independent hymn; and they try to reconstruct its original form.[281] But we will examine the text as it stands. The author of Ephesians prepares the you-group of people for the consequence which happened to "us" and was brought to "us" by the death of Christ on the cross. The author relates 2,14ff. with the preceding part, 2,1ff. For we can observe that the verse 2,14 develops 2,10, which states the creation in Christ Jesus[282], and 2,13 explicitly relates to this section of 2,14ff. as we explained above. Not only are we God's handicraft (*poiēma*) created in Christ Jesus (*Autou gar esmen poiēma*... 2,10), but now our peace is Christ (*Autos gar estin hē eirēnē hēmōn*... 2,14).[283]

---

[280] G. Schille, *Frühchristliche Hymnen*, 24, takes *gar* as "recitativum." But we follow R. Deichgräber, *Gotteshymnus und Christushymnus in der frühen Christenheit* (StUNT 5; Göttingen 1967) 166, who understands it as a causal linking *gar* (for).

[281] Schlier, *Komm.*, 123 and note 1. Schille (see the above note 280). P. Pokorny, "Epheserbrief und gnostische Mysterien": *ZNW* 53 (1962) 160-94, esp. 182f. J. T. Sanders, "Hymnic Elements in Ephesians 1-3": *ZNW* 56 (1965) 213-32, esp. 217f. J. Gnilka, "Christus und der Friede — Ein Friedens-Erlöserlied in Eph 2,14-17" in: *Die Zeit Jesu* (Festschrift für H. Schlier) (Freiburg i.Br. 1970) 190-207, esp. 193ff. The same author, *Komm.*, 147ff. and "Die Kirchenmodell des Epheserbriefe": *BZ* 15 (1971) 161-84, esp. 170. H. Merklein, "Zur Tradition und Komposition von Eph 2,14-18": *BZ* 17 (1973) 79-102, esp. 80ff. P. Stuhlmacher, " 'Er ist unser Friede' (Eph 2,14)" in: *Neues Testament und Kirche* (Für R. Schnackenburg)) (Freiburg 1974) 337-58, esp. 341ff. Cf. G. Giavini, "La Structure litteraire d'Eph. II, 11-22": *NTS* 16 (1969-1970) 209ff.

[282] Cf. page 58.

[283] We find a similar way of expression which appears to have an emphasis upon "him" or "he" (*auton, autos*):
Eph 1,22: *... kai auton edōken ...*
    4,10: *... ho katabas autos estin ...*

The basic feature of the Greek concept of *eirēnē* (peace) is that the word does not primarily denote a relationship between several people, or an attitude, but a state, i.e., "time of peace" or "state of peace," originally conceived of purely as an interlude in the everlasting state of "war." [284] The notion of "peace" in the OT has a rich content. The term is used often with other important words as with *emeth*, *berith* etc.[285] The meaning of "peace" in our passages (vv. 14.15.17) [286] shows it to be a matter of relation.[287] Let us stress further the point or meaning of relationship.[288] In our passage, Eph 2,14ff., the author appears to have had in mind Is 57,19 (cf. Eph 2,13.17). There the peace is an expectation for the future, but here in Eph 2,14ff., the peace exists now.[289] Here this peace is even "personified." The author of Eph is saying: "...He (Christ) is our peace".[290] The identification of Christ [291] with peace occurs only here in the Pauline letters. The meaning of the sentences, "For He is our peace" (2,14) is described in the term of his activity in the following passages.[292] Paying attention to the word "peace" (*eirēnē*) we find the same term at the end of v. 15 as the object of the participle *poiōn*: *poiōn eirēnēn* (making peace) (cf. 2,17). The author of Eph does not use in v. 15 the aorist participial form, *poiēsas*. Why? Is the present tense of the "*poiōn*" the same as the "*ktisēi*" (created) of the main verb of the *hina* sentence in 2,15? [293] We feel here a double time, namely,

---

4,11: ... *kai autos edōken* ...
5,23: ... *autos sōtēr tou sōmatos.*
Cf. Col 1,17: ... *kai autos estin* ...
1,18: ... *kai autos estin hē kephalē tou sōmatos tēs ekklēsias* ...
On the possible relation of Col 1,15-20 to Eph 2,14ff., see H. Merklein, "Zur Tradition ...", 95f.

[284] See W. Foerster, "*eirēnē*" in: *TDNT*, II, 400ff.

[285] See G. von Rad, "*eirēnē*" in: *TDNT*, II, 402ff.

[286] Elsewhere the term occurs in our letter: 1,2; 4,3; 6,15.23.

[287] W. Foerster, art. cit., 415, takes this in the sense of a state and says: "... We may say that *echthra* (enmity) and *eirēnē* (peace) are here objective states which take many different forms in the human race.

[288] Cf. Lindemann, *Die Aufhebung*, 160, states thus: "... *Eirēnē* meint im Epheserbrief 'Ganzheit', Beseitigung alles Trennenden ...." In many passages of the Old Testament the term denotes relationship rather than a state. The connection between the two words (*berith*: "covenant") and *shalom* (peace) is so strong that *shalom* seems to have become a kind of official term. The thought may be that the relationship of *shalom* is sealed by both parties in a covenant. The *shalom* is also a gift of Jahweh who alone can bestow it. And the *shalom* of the O.T. is one element of the eschatological expectations. See G. von Rad, art. cit., 403ff.; cf. Foerster, art. cit., 406ff. about *eirēnē* in the Septuagint and in the rabbinic writings; cf. Strack-Billerbeck, III, 587.

[289] See the present verb *estin* of 2,14 and the *echomen* of 2,18. See later page 110.

[290] Cf. Is 9,5: ("prince of peace"), and Mich 5,4.

[291] If the *autos* (he) is understood as *theos* (God), it would be difficult in our context of 2,14ff. Cf. Schlier, *Komm.*, 124; Gnilka, *Komm.*, 138; Lindemann, *Die Aufhebung*, 160.

[292] P. Stuhlmacher, "Er ist unser Friede" ..., 348f., explains this "peace" in opposition to a static understanding.

[293] Cf. Schlier, *Komm.*, 135.

the time accomplished in Christ ("*ktisēi en autōi* ...": he might create in him) and the time when "you" stand now.[294] In accordance with the grammar, we do not want to exaggerate the difference of the tenses of the verb and participle.[295] With regard to the meaning of peace in 2,14ff., we can discern a triple relationship: at first, the relationship between Christ Jesus and his God, which is the major and fundamental premise and basis for all consequences. The second is our relationship with our fellow men, based on the relationship between Christ Jesus and his God, and the last, our relationship through Christ to God the Father.[296] The fact that He is our peace was brought about by his deeds, shown by three participles: *poiēsas* (made) in 2,14; *lysas* (broken-down) in 2,14; *katargēsas* (abolished) in 2,15.

The first deed is: "He made both one" (*ho poiēsas ta amphotera hen*) (2,14). The verb *poiein* (to do) and its cognate word sometimes allude to a divine deed of creation. The New Testament takes for granted that God is Creator.[297] In our letter to the Ephesians, the term *poiein* occurs 10 times [298] and the cognate word *poiēma* once, in Eph 2,10.[299] The word *ktizein* (to create) is used often in Colossians and in Ephesians.[300] But the substantive noun *ktisis* (creature), does not occur in Ephesians.[301] Taking into consideration that the author of Eph uses the language of "creation" in Eph 2,10 and in the *hina* sentence of 2,15, "that he might create ... in him one new man ..." we feel a nuance of divine creation of man in these phrases, especially in 2,14 where he states: "... He made both one." We have therefore to identify who were the "both" (*ta amphotera*).[302] Whom or what did He make into one? What is meant by "both" (*ta amphotera*)? These questions become more serious after seeing the difference in gender of the same term in 2,16.18 (*tous amphoterous — hoi amphoteroi*). And in addition to these, we will be puzzled how to interpret "the two" (*tous duo*) in 2,15.

As possible background to our verse 2,14ff., it would be helpful to check some passages of the O.T. The passages of Is 9,5ff.; 52,7; 57,19 might be interpreted by the author of Ephesians through the event of Christ Jesus which was described in Eph 2,13-18; the promise of the message is accomplished, so that "He", Christ Jesus, becomes the peace.[303]

---

294 See page 108ff.
295 Cf. Blass-Debrunner-Rehkopf, *Grammatik*, § 339, 2.
296 Cf. Rom 5,1f.; Lindemann, *Die Aufhebung*, 160.
297 H. Braun, "*poieō*" in: *TDNT*, VI, 462.
298 Compare: Eph 1,16; 2,3; 2,14.15; 3,11.20; 4,16; 6,6.8.9.
299 Elsewhere in the New Testament: Rom 1,20.
300 Eph 2,10.15; 3,9; 4,24; Col 1,16 (bis); 3,10. In the other Pauline letters: Rom 1,25; 1 Cor 11,9; 1 Tim 4,3.
301 But in the Pauline letters: Rom 1,20.25; 8,19.20.21.22.39; 2 Cor 15,17 and Gal 6,15 with the term *kainē* (new); Col 1,15.23, *ktisma*: 1 Tim 4,4.
302 This term occurs only in Ephesians: 2,14.16.18.
303 Cf. P. Stuhlmacher, "Er ist unser Friede", 347ff.

The scattered people will be gathered (cf. Ez 34,7ff.), and one shepherd will be set over the people, the Lord will become their God, God's servant will be a prince among them. God will make with them a covenant of peace (cf. Ez 34,20ff.). God himself makes their ruler draw near and he shall approach God, for no one ventures of himself to approach God the Lord (cf. Jer 30,21). If we consider the word-field and the thoughts of Eph 2, we see that the author of Eph again and again alludes to traditional language, and we think that he contemplated the passages of the O.T. from his living experience of "being in Christ." Together with the Jewish tradition about the eschatological union of Jews and Gentiles and reunion of separated Jewish tribes, Ez 37 might have inspired the motifs of Eph 2. We might compare the phrase "he made both one" (2,14) with Ez 37,17: "He joined the two together for you into one wood, and they will be one in your hand." Especially in the following parts of Ez 37,15-28, occur many verbs, which are also used in the description of the new situation of unity and peace in Eph 2, 14-21. It is quite clear, however, that the images, the ideas, the concepts and words are different from the description of eschatological peace in Ez 37. And Is 57,19 serves as a foil for the wording in Eph 2,17. Despite many "allusions" which shine through the text of Ephesians, we surely cannot say that we have an unmistakable use of Scripture-quotations. We can only say that the author of Eph attempted to express a new reality. Now we come to the examination of the meaning of the *ta ampho-tera* (the both) in 2,14.

One interpretation, in which authors see different nuances takes the line of a "cosmic" explanation: the "both" of 2,16-18 means two groups of people, but the "both" of 2,14 means two cosmic spheres.[304] The other line is that "the both" of 2,14 grammatically[305] denotes concrete groups of men, or the two groups consisting of the Jews and the Gentiles.[306] We feel that the term *"amphoteroi"* itself is ambiguous and appears to have a double sense, because in 2,14 the same term is neuter plural while it is masculine plural in 2,16 and 2,18. The neutral form of 2,14 (*ta ampho-tera*) probably is attracted by the neutral form of *hen* in 2,14, and it is to show the collective sense of the neuter plural form of *amphoteroi*.[307]

---

[304] Cf. Col 1,20. Cf. Schlier, *Zeit der Kirche*, 302. Schlier, *Komm.*, 124. J. Gnilka, "Das Kirchenmodell des Epheserbriefes": *BZ* 15 (1971) 161-84, esp. 170. Gnilka, "Christus unser Friede ...", 196 and his commentary of Eph., 139 and 149. G. Giavini, "La structure", 210, note 1 says: "... deux zones mystiques de l'espace; celle du ciel et celle de la terre ...." Lindemann, *Die Aufhebung*, 160f. P. Pokorny, "Epheserbrief und gnostische Mysterien": *ZNW* 53 (1962) 160-94, esp. 182f., sees a parallel to the gnostic documents.

[305] Cf. Blass-Debrunner-Rehkopf, *Grammatik*, § 138,1, (something like 1 Cor 27) states: "The neuter is sometimes used with reference to persons if it is not the individuals but a general quality that is to be emphasized."

[306] S. Hanson, *Unity*, 143. Cf. H. Merklein, *Christus und die Kirche*, 29ff. P. Stuhlmacher, "Er ist ...", 345. M. Barth, *Comm.*, 263.

[307] F. Mussner, *Das All*, 81.

At the same time, being attracted to the collective sense or quality of
poiēma (handicraft, creatura) of 2,10, the neuter plural form was probably
chosen.   Considering the two nations, which is alluded to by Ez 37,22
(LXX): *duo ethnē... hen ethnos*), who will become one, the author of
Eph probably chose rather the ambiguous expression: *ta amphotera*
(*... ta ethnē*), in order to allude to opposing groups in the tradition
and to a possible form of opposition in the world.   On the other hand,
we cannot negate the fact that the author of Ephesians received the
Pauline tradition: the conflict between the Jewish and the Gentile peoples
through the Pauline Gospel, was based on Paul's experiences of his mission.   The opposition between the Jews and the Gentiles (the Greek),
between the believers in Christ from the Jewish religion and those from
non-Jewish religions, was the Pauline experience in his preaching the
Gospel.[308]   From a deeper perspective of St. Paul, the "discrimination,"
whatever form it may take, is contradictory to "being Christians".   For
instance, Gal 3,28 where Paul says: "... There is neither Jew nor Greek,
there is neither slave nor free, there is neither male nor female; for you
are all one in Christ Jesus (cf. Rom 10,12; Col 3,11)."   Any human self-
distinction from others that normally originates from an inclination to
boast (*kauchēsis*), causing disunity, has nothing to do with the believers
in Christ.   In Eph 2,14ff., the author's main concern does not seem to
be to solve an existing opposition between the Jewish and the Gentile
Christians in his community, not in any way the enmity between the
Jews and the gentiles.   Rather, the proto-opposition of the Jews and
the Gentiles which was reconciled and was brought to unity by Christ,
is now applied to the "present" situation of the Ephesian community.
As Paul states in Gal 3,28; Rom 10,12; Col 3,11, the "both" of Eph 2,14
probably comprehends the "twoness" of things or peoples which causes
opposition, disunity and enmity.   In the text of 2,14-18, the meaning of
"both" (Eph 2,14.16) (and "two": *tous duo* in 2,15) gradually come to
converge to "both of us" in 2,18 (*... echomen .. hoi amphoteroi ...: ...* we
both ... have ...).   Therefore, the author is concerned firstly with the
unity of the "we" group and of the "you" group of people in his actual
present situation.   We repeat, we cannot simply understand that the
"we" means the Jewish Christians and "you" the Gentile Christians.   However, we cannot exclude the possible allusions of the term "both" in 2,14,
to the two cosmic spheres or to the two spheres of peoples.   This term
is too ambiguous to define its meaning clearly.   It may comprehend the
Jewish and gentile spheres of peoples and similar spheres of community
composed of two really different groups.

---

[308] The historical problem is discussed by M. Hengel, *Judaism and Hellenism.
Studies in their Encounter in Palestine during the Early Hellenistic Period*, 2 vols.
(Philadelphia 1974); see also F. Lentzen-Deis, in: *Theologie und Philosophie* 46 (1971)
285-289.   For Eph, see Schlier, *Komm.*, 134.

Having stated that Christ is our peace, who has made both into one, the author of Ephesians continues to explain the fruit of this peace: "and [309] (Christ) has broken down the dividing wall of hostility" (*kai to mesotoichon tou phragmou lysas, tēn echthran*) (2,14b). The main question is how to interpret "the dividing wall" (*to mesotoichon tou phragmou*) (literally: the partition-wall of the fence).[310]

Authors have discussed the possible origin and meaning of the partition wall. According to some authors, it alludes to a wall standing in the precincts of the Jerusalem temple, which separates the Israelites from the heathen.[311] Another allusion is that the dividing wall is the separating curtain between the Holy of holies and the Holy inside the temple. In this case it is the ritual separation between the divine sphere and the human one that is stressed.[312] M. Barth suggests other allusions to the commandment to "build a fence around the law or to the Sinai fence".[313] H. Schlier distinguishes three levels of the probable meaning or origin of "the dividing wall": First, the Torah in the sense of the wall which protects Israelites and at the same time divides them from the other peoples (Gentiles). Secondly, the image which originates from Jewish Apocalyptic literature, meaning the world and the heavenly wall which makes a frontier between the cosmic spheres. Finally, the cosmic wall and the Torah as wall are associated by the author of Ephesians.[314] But the evidence which Schlier presents is late [315] and such a mixed interpretation (Torah and the cosmic wall) lacks confirmation.[316]

The author of Ephesians, seeing the church formed historically by the two groups of peoples, namely by the Jews and the Gentiles (the division itself is Jewish), and looking back to the traditional image of the law and alluding to the cosmic barrier dividing the heavenly sphere and the earthly sphere (the divine and the human), applies the fact of the division of those peoples and of the inaccessibility of humanity to the divine world to the actual community to whom he speaks. The unity and the division of the two peoples (the Jews and the Gentiles) are used here by the author as the theological base for the unity of the community, by using the Jewish-nuanced-law as the dividing wall.[317] The separation

---

[309] With Schlier, *Komm.*, 124, we take this *kai* (and) as the explanation of the first participle *poiēsas*.

[310] The genitive noun *tou phragmou* ("of the fence") is an explanatory genitive; M. Barth, *Comm.*, 263; M. Zerwick, *Graecitas Biblica* (Romae 1960) n. 33; A. Lindemann, *Die Aufhebung*, 160, note 87; H. Merklein, art. cit., 31 (see note 281 above); F. Mussner, *Christus, das All*, 81, note 51; Schlier, *Komm.*, 124.

[311] See M. Barth, *Comm.*, 283f.

[312] Ibid., 284.

[313] Ibid., 284f.

[314] H. Merklein, art. cit., (above, n. 281), 38f.; M. Barth, *Comm.*, 285f.; Schlier, *Komm.*, 142f.

[315] H. Merklein, art. cit., 39f.; M. Barth, *Comm.*, 285f.

[316] H. Merklein, art. cit., 39.

[317] Ibid., 30.

has to do with the law and its statutes and interpretations. This separation caused the enmity between Jews and Gentiles; this fact leads to
enmity against God from humanity as a whole which is represented by
the Jews and by the Gentiles.[318] Therefore, the dividing wall is interpreted as the enmity: "Christ has broken down the dividing wall of the
enmity (tēn echthran) (2,14b).

The term echthra (enmity) must be important to the author of
Ephesians, because it occurs again in 2,16b: "... bringing the hostility
to an end": literally: "... killed the enmity in him (... apokteinas tēn
echthran en autōi ...)".[319] An individual who does not accept the equality
of humankind before God by reason of privileged consciousness or feeling of superiority over other peoples is easily led to a sectarian mentality,
and consequently to enmity whenever the other does not follow his
ideology or his way of thinking or his manner of life.[320] A sect or fac-
tion or dissension or disunity [321] is incompatible with a man who is called
a believer in Christ Jesus (cf. 1 Cor 1,9ff.).[322] It is universally attested
as a human weakness that such a sectarian attitude of mind or self-
righteousness causes "quarrels" (eris), then finally hostility, between one
and another (cf. 1 Cor 1,11).[323] This source of enmity, the dividing wall,
was broken down by Christ.

The third fruit of the peace brought by Christ is abolition of "the
law of the commandments in regulations": "in his flesh he has abolished
the law of the commandments in regulations" (en tēi sarki autou,
ton nomon tōn entolōn en dogmasin) (2,14c-2,15a). The dividing wall
has to do with the law of the commandments. The "law" in 1,15a
is not likely conceived as a general law. The author of Eph states clearly
the (ho) law (nomos) with the singular form and with the article. Not
only to the Jews but also to Paul, the law was holy (hagios: cf. Rom 7,12),
spiritual (pneumatikos: Rom 7,14) and good (kalos: cf. Rom 7,16). And
Christ is the end [324] of the law, so that every one who has faith, may be
justified (Rom 10,4). In these above-mentioned passages the law itself
gains a positive evaluation. We ask ourselves, then, what was meant
by saying that this law was abolished.[325] While he indicates a certain

---

[318] Cf. M. Barth, Comm., 286.

[319] G. Schille, Frühchristliche Hymnen (Berlin 1965) 24-26, says that the enmity
(tēn echthran) is a gloss. The enmity from the standpoint of the author of Eph is to
show the application of the traditional heritage to his addresses.

[320] Cf. Gal 5,20ff. Strack-Billerbeck, III, 590; 3 Macc 3,4.

[321] Paul treats the disunity and sectarian mind in the community in 1 Cor 1,10 -
4,21. See H. Conzelmann, Der erste Brief an die Korinther (Göttingen 1969) 45ff.

[322] Cf. 1 Cor 11,18; 12,25.

[323] Because the "fleshly" man does not conduct life according to the Spirit, but
according to "man" (anthrōpon), he gives rise to sectarianism and quarrels. They walk
in sins. Cf. 1 Cor 3,3ff.; Eph 2,1-3; 4,17ff.; 4,22ff. Cf. also Gal 5,16; Rom 1,29; 13,13;
2 Cor 12,20. Rom 8,7.

[324] Cf. Gal 3,24. See Schlier, Komm. Röm., 311.

[325] See M. Barth, Comm., 287.

freedom from the law (cf. Rom 7,2.6; Gal 4,3ff.; Gal 5,13ff.), we cannot find a passage where Paul states that the law itself is abolished (see: Rom 3,31; Gal 3,17ff.). It is a superficial interpretation of Eph 2,15 to say that the author had in mind the abolition of the law of the commandments. The law does not mean a mere collection of the commandments.[326] The author states "the law of the commandments" (... *tōn entolōn*). The commandment (*entolē*) itself also is holy, just and good (cf. Rom 7,12). As Eph 6,2 shows, the commandment denotes an article of the law (cf. Rom 13,9; 1 Cor 7,19; 14,37). We must notice that the author of Ephesians adds the phrase "in regulations" (*en dogmasin*) after the law of the commandments: ... *tōn nomōn tōn entolōn en dogmasin*. This "in regulations" (*en dogmasin*) may show how the author of Eph understands the Pauline law of the commandments and applies it to his situation where he stands.[327] He penetrates the reason why the law of the commandments resulted in separation and enmity, and the reason why the holy, just and good law stood in the way of the Jews reaching unity and caused enmity from both groups, from the Jews and the non-Jews. This explanation depends upon an interpretation of how one understands the *en dogmasin* (in regulations).[328]

Primarily, the word *dogma* means "decree," "ordinance," "decision," "command" and then "doctrine," "dogma." [329] The law of Eph 2,15 does not likely consist in the commandments *and* (equivalently) the single regulations.[330] The three words, the law, the commandments and the "regulations" should not be understood as equivalent: [331] "the law" (*tōn nomōn*) is the object of *katargēsas* (abolished), the expression 'commandments' (precisely, "of the commandments": the genitive) is designed to modify the law, and the "regulations" are tied with the particle *en* (in), not with *kai* (and) (*en dogmasin*).[332] It is right to say that the law of

---

[326] P. Stuhlmacher, "'Er ist unser Friede' (Eph 2,14). Zur Exegese und Bedeutung von Eph 2,14-18": *Neues Testament und Kirche* (Für Rudolf Schnackenburg) (edited by J. Gnilka) (Freiburg 1974) 337-58, esp. 350.

[327] Cf. M. Barth, *Comm.*, 288f.

[328] The *dogmasin* does not have an article.

[329] Bauer-Arndt-Gingrich, *A Greek-English Lexicon of the New Testament*, ad locum; our phrase is translated "the law of the commandments in (single) ordinances."

[330] P. Stuhlmacher, "Er ist unser Friede", 350, states: "... Daß das Gesetz abgetan ist, das Gesetz, das in V. 14.15, im Anschluß an jüdisch-kosmologische Sprechweise als 'Trennwand des Zaunes' und dann christlich als 'Gesetz mit seinem Geboten und Satzungen' bezeichnet wird, versteht man am besten, wenn man folgendes bedenkt. Für das Judentum was das ihm geoffenbare Gesetz nicht nur eine Gebotsammlung, sondern zugleich Grundlage seiner Lebensordnung und Schutzwehr seiner Lebensweise."

[331] Cf. Lindemann, *Die Aufhebung*, 172 and note 148. He suggests the phrase *en dogmasin* is a comment influenced by Col 2,14, and in note 148, referring to H. Merklein, *BZ* 17 (1973) 100, states: "... aber das Bezeichnende an dieser Stelle ist doch die Verbindung von den Begriffen gleicher Bedeutung."

[332] Schlier, *Komm.*, 118 translates this phrase: "... das Gesetz der Gebote, die Satzungen sind, vernichtete." H. Conzelmann, *Komm.* (*NTD* 8; Göttingen 1976) 98, translates the particle *en* (in) in the sense of "with" ("mit").

the commandments, namely the law, consists of the commandments, but
we cannot say that the law of the commandments consists in regulations.
The text does not say this.[333] In our opinion, rather a "fixed" and
"absolutized" manner of the human reception of the law is questioned.
This is a universal problem when a law takes effect on man and binds
him and alienates him.[334]

If the law of the Jews was not a mere collection of legal articles,
but a principle and protection of their life, it would be something
equivalent to the *stoicheia* or "philosophy" (cf. Gal 4,3) in the Hellenistic
world. And if so, it would be difficult to understand that Christ has
abolished the law of the commandments. We feel the solution will
be found in the meaning of the *en*-construction: *en dogmasin* (in regulations). In the Pauline letters the word *dogma* occurs only in Eph 2,15
and in Col 2,14. So, at first, we have to examine the meaning of the
word in Col 2,14 [335] in order to understand the probable meaning of our
verse 2,15.

In Col 2,6ff., the community who accepted (*parelabete*) the Lord
Jesus is encouraged to conduct its life in him and to remain unshakeable
in its faith. The author of Colossians admonishes the community to
beware lest it should be ensnared by philosophy and by empty deceit
(cf. Col 2,8; Eph 5,6). "In Hellenistic language usage the word philosophy was used to describe all sorts of groups, tendencies and points
of view, and thus had become a rather broad term...".[336] Not according to Christ, but according to the element of the universe (*stoicheia
tou kosmou*) [337] they walked, and were entrapped by the philosophy. As
the result of the "entrapping", philosophy stands against philosophy, tradition against tradition, and claim against claim. The *dogma* was significant
for the controversy over philosophy (cf. Col 2,20). The Colossians use
the term *dogma* in the context of the "dead-situation" by sins and in the
forgiveness of sins (cf. Col 2,13ff.; Eph 2,1ff.). "Where there is forgiveness of sins, there is freedom from the 'powers' and 'principalities,'

---

[333] Gnilka, *Komm.*, 132, translates thus: "... das Gesetz der aus Verordnungen
bestehenden Gebote, ..." see also 141. F. Mussner, *Christus, Das All*, 82f., 83, note 25.

[334] Cf. Schlier, *Komm.*, 125f., esp. 126, says: "... Die große Tat Christi, durch die
er sich als 'unser Friede' erwiesen hat, ist letzlich also die Beseitigung des Gesetzes,
so wie es in seinem vielfältigen Geboten als *dogmata* begegnet." H. Merklein, *Christus und die Kirche* (SBS 66; Stuttgart 1973) 33. Barth, *Comm.*, 253, translates the
phrase: "... He has abolished the law (that is only) the commandments (expressed)
in statutes." See ibid., 264ff. and 287ff.

[335] E. C. Best, *An Historical Study of the Exegesis of Colossians 2,14* (Rome 1956),
examines the Church Fathers' interpretations of this verse.

[336] See E. Lohse, *Colossians and Philemon* (translated by W. R. Poehlmann, and
R. J. Karris) (Philadelphia 1971) 94ff. Here it indicates the "heresy" of Colossae, see
below page 83, note (47).

[337] See Lohse, ibid., 96ff.

[338] Ibid., 106.

there is life and salvation." [339] Colossians 2,14 runs thus: "God wiped out the certificate of indebtedness which was made out against us, which — because of regulations — was against us, and he removed it, he nailed it to the cross".[340] The word "regulations" (*dogmata*) does not mean the stipulations of an edict of grace (decrees of grace), but binding statutes or regulations.[341] In Hellenistic Judaism the commandments of God are called also "regulations" (*dogmata*). Also the teaching of the "philosophers" in those days demanded that followers observe regulations. These regulations ruled over the life of the followers and defined their manner of life.[342] In Col 2,20, the verbal form of dogma *dogmatizein* is used and the verse runs thus: "If, therefore, with Christ you died to the elements of the universe, why do you want to have regulations imposed on (*dogmatizesthe*) you as if you still lived in the world: (v. 21). Do not handle, do not taste, do not touch." Here are described the people on whom regulations were imposed in opposition to the people who believed and followed Christ in whom the entire fullness of deity bodily dwells (cf. Col 2,9). Clearly the "philosophy," which had been introduced into the community, had so strongly influenced many Christians that they were ready to acknowledge the binding power of the "regulations." [343] The author of the Colossians warned them lest they should go back to their manner of life in the past. He pointed out their attachment to the *stoicheia tou kosmou* (the elements of the universe). The rules for eating, ceremonies and liturgies are the shadow of what is to come (cf. Col 2, 16f.), and do not have absolute values. The vision and the worship of the angels, even though they seem highly spiritual, cannot liberate man from becoming puffed up without reason by his earthly mind (cf. Col 2, 18f.). The regulations which contain the prohibitions (...should not... do not..., must not...) and the doctrine of man are practised with the reputation of wisdom and with ascetism of body. They often served to satiate the flesh, however. Highly sophisticated religions or philosophies based on "tradition of man" could not free man from enslavement to the flesh.[344] Such a condition is shown by the dative *tois dogmasin* in Col 2,14. And it appears to indicate a something similar in the case of *en dogmasin* (in regulations) in Eph 2,15. Even the holy, just and good law of the commandments alienates man and prepares a base for contestation and finally causes enmity.[345] It is quite interesting that

---

[339] It is interesting to see the Latin translation of the verse. Cf. *Epistula ad Colossenses, Vetus Latina* (edited by H. J. Frede) (Freiburg 1966-1971), 420ff.

[340] The translation is from E. Lohse, *Col.*, 92.

[341] Lohse, ibid., 109, and in the note 107, Eph 2,15 is translated thus: "... by abolishing the law of commandments and regulations." Cf. G. Kittel, "*dogma*" in: *TDNT*, II, 230ff.

[342] Lohse, *Col.*, 110 and note 114.

[343] Ibid., 123.

[344] Cf. ibid., 123ff. F. Zeilinger, *Der Erstgeborne der Schöpfung* (Wien 1974) 169f.

[345] Cf. M. Barth, *Comm.*, 290f.

the phrase *ton nomon tōn entolōn en dogmasin* may be put another way: *ten philosophian tōn aletheiōn en dogmasin* (the philosophy of the truths in regulations). From where comes contestation? Why does man distinguish himself from other peoples? From where comes the enmity for centuries in human histories, even in the very world of religion itself?

If the dative *dogmasin* of Col 2,14 could denote the "binding regulations," the *en dogmasin* (in regulations) [346] of Eph 2,15 could show the condition of man who could not free himself from the "binding statutes," as man is bound by the law and he himself binds others on behalf of the law. Because of this, even the holy, just and good law of the commandments became the source of alienation and of enmity. So it might become "the" criterion to bind oneself and others.[347] The law as comprehended by a distorted mind cannot give an inner freedom. If the law gives a reason for boasting or a criterion to judge others, it contains an acute malice which is often hidden from men.[348]

Therefore, Christ abolished the law of the commandments in regulations, which causes the "division" and the "enmity" by His self-surrender ("*Hingabe*") of his whole life, especially by his cross.[349] He abolished any form of "doctrine," article, principle, belief and conduct which are absolutized by our human "fixed" way of comprehension, without inner freedom and love which are opened to the "somatic" communion.[350] The unity meant here is neither theoretical nor dogmatic, which remains always "marginal" among men who have different ways of comprehension and

---

[346] If we compare all the *en*-constructions in Eph, we find that the *en*-construction of our verse 2,15a (*en dogmasin*) belongs to the very few cases with a negative sense: *en sarki* in 2,11; *en pleonexia* in 4,19; *en hais* (*en tais hamartiais*) in 2,2; *en tais epithymiais* in 2,3; *en tēᵢ kybeiaᵢ* in 4,14; *en mataiotēti tou noos autōn* in 4,17. The *en*-constructions with a negative sense indicate the counter-conditions which are shown by the many positive ones: *en Christōᵢ en pneumati, en agapeᵢ, etc.* Also see our Chapter 3, page 98ff.

[347] Cf. Rom 13,8ff.; Gal 5,13ff.; 1 Tim 1,3ff.

[348] St. Paul, in opposition to the "binding law" which man cannot observe, speaks very often about the newness of the message he brought with him, and alludes to the new law or the new heart in Jer 31,31ff. and Ez 36,24ff. Compare: 2 Cor 3,3ff.; Gal 4,21ff.; 1 Thess 4,8f.; Rom 2,28f.; 3,27ff.; 8,2ff.; 10,5ff.

[349] The author of Eph already mentioned that by the blood of Christ, "you" were brought near in Eph 2,13 (on this see H. Merklein, *Christus und die Kirche*, 26). Christ destroyed the enmity by his "*Hingabe*" ("self-surrender") of his whole life. The phrase *en tēᵢ sarki autou* should not be understood either as materialistic or dualistic. It shows, on the one hand, the way of His "*Hingabe*" of his whole life as man, (cf. Rom 8,3; Gal 4,4), on the other hand, it shows the climax of his "*Hingabe*" on the cross, because of the phrase "through the cross" in Eph 2,16. By his "*Hingabe*," he abolished the law of the commandments of the yokes which caused the enmity (cf. Gal 2,19). Cf. P. Stuhlmacher, art. cit. (note 281), 352; Schlier, *Komm.*, 125. We can observe that the flesh (*sarx*) and the *sōma* ("body") in Colossians are apparently not so clearly distinguished as the usage in the Ephesians. Ephesians never associate *sōma* with *sarx* as in Colossians: Col 1,22.24; 2,1.5.11.13.18.23; 3,22. Eph 2,3.11.14; 5,29.31; 6,5.12. Cf. H. Merklein, op. cit., 49ff.

[350] This kind of "fixation" very often suffocates an inner dynamism of the Body with the Head and the hope of the divine calling. Cf. our Chapter 3-7, p. 124ff. and Chapter 4 on hope, p. 154ff.

interpretation. Such unity (often in some sense uniformity) cannot attain to the unity which Christ brought to us. The obstacle towards the unity between man and man and between man and God can be overcome by the deeper unity which we will try to expose in the following chapter.

The final sentences of vv. 15b-16 tell creation of the two and the reconciliation of both: "so that he might create in himself one new man in place of the two so making peace, and might reconcile us both to God in one body through the cross, thereby bringing the hostility to an end" (RSV) (*hina tous duo ktisēi en autōi eis hena kainon anthrōpon poiōn eirēnēn, kai apokatallaxē tous amphoterous en heni sōmati tōi theōi dia tou staurou, apokteinas tēn echthran en autōi*). The words "...create the two..." (*...tous duo ktisēi...*) reminds us of the passage of Gen 1, 26ff.,[351] and the unity of husband and wife in Eph 5,22ff. and the profound mystery of Christ with his Church. The two are the fundamental units of the unity, which we mentioned concerning the meaning of the both (*ta amphotera*).[352] The terminology of "new" and "to create" (cf. 2,10; 3,9; 4,24) alludes to the eschatological time of salvation.[353] This creation of the new man really happened in him (*en autōi*).[354] Christ created the two into (*eis*) the one new man. "The one new man" on the one side means that the two are created into the unifying new community, and on the other hand it means Christ himself who made the foundation of the new man.[355] Christ himself is our peace, who made the bridge between the two groups, between the two persons, unifying them into one, so making peace.[356]

The next-to-final sentence is: "and he might reconcile both in one body to God, through the cross, thereby bringing the hostility to an end" (literally: "...killing the enmity in him") (v. 16). The word *apokatallassō* (reconcile) occurs only here and in Col 1,20.22 in the New Testament. Paul normally uses the word *katallassō* (and *katallagē* to mean the reconciliation to God (cf. Rom 5,10; 1 Cor 7,11; 2 Cor 5,18ff.; Rom 11,15). But Ephesians states that *Christ reconciled both* to God.[357] One difficulty of this passage is how to understand the phrase "in one body" (*en heni sōmati*).[358] The catch-word "one" (*hen*) together with the opposing terms "peace — enmity" shows the main concern of the author of Ephesians in this section of 2,14ff.[359]

---

351 Schlier, *Komm.*, 133f. F. Mussner, *Christus, das All*, 86f. H. Merklein, *Christus und die Kirche*, 41.
352 Cf. the previous pages 58f.
353 Cf. Schlier, *Komm.*, 125.
354 With B. M. Metzger, *A Textual Commentary*, 602 and 615f., we read *en autōi* not *en heautōi*.
355 We follow H. Schlier, *Komm.*, 135. Cf. 2 Cor 5,17f.; Gal 3,28; 6,15.
536 Cf. H. Merklein, *Christus*, 42ff. Cf. Mt 5,9; 3 Enoch 26,8; 42,7.
357 Merklein, op. cit., 44f.
358 Compare: Rom 12,4f., 1 Cor 12,12.
359 *hen* (one) in v. 14; *eis hena kainon anthrōpon* in v. 15; *en heni pneumati* in v. 18. Cf. Eph 4,4f.; Col 3,15; 1 Cor 12,13.

The meaning of the phrase "in one body" (*en heni sōmati*) is that both of "us" become one. According to some authors,[360] the *sōma* (body) of this verse alludes to the body of the Crucified, or it has a double meaning of the body, namely, the body of the crucified Jesus and the body of Christ in the sense of the Church. Perhaps this line of exegesis may be reached by harmonizing our verse 2,16 with Col 1,22 where it is stated that "he has now reconciled in his body of flesh by his death..." (*nyni de apokatēllaxen en tōi sōmati tēs sarkos autou dia tou thanatou...*).[361] The body in the sense of community or church belongs to an image-field. On the other hand, the body of the Crucified or the body on the cross is the body which once was subject to suffering and death. There are two different levels of language between the body of the Crucified and the body of Christ, the Church. We cannot "harmonize" both "bodies" epistemologically. One is the image, the other is the "physical" body of the Crucified. What we can comprehend is the fact of faith that we have now been receiving the influence of the result of the crucifixion of Jesus. The continuity between the body of Christ on the cross and the body of Christ, the Church (i.e. the community) is not a matter to be thought out materially nor substantially. There is, however, a continuity between the divine dynamism at work in Jesus Christ himself and the same dynamism within the community in Christ which has been initiated by His total "*Hingabe*" (self-surrender) on the cross. We may claim that the *en heni sōmati* (in one body) means neither ideological nor philosophical nor cultural unity but the "somatic" unity of both of "us" in the community of Ephesians, as if they were one body in relation to the Head, Christ.[362] We repeat that the *sōma* (body) in this verse 2,16 is figurative and should not be understood in a material sense.

Both groups cannot become one-body of the Crucified of Christ Jesus. It means that Christ reconciled both in one body, in one community through the cross (*dia tou staurou*). The possibility of the unity between the "opposed" groups is now open to humanity. It was the fruit of peace brought by the "*Hingabe*" of Jesus on the cross which was the climax of

---

[360] Schlier, *Komm.*, 135. Schweizer, E., "*sōma*" in: *TDNT* VII, 1024-1094, esp. 1077. Similarly, E. Percy, *Der Leib Christi in den paulinischen Homologumena und Antilegomena* (Lund 1942) 44, and the same author, *Die Probleme der Kolosser- und Epheserbriefe* (Lund 1946) 381. The critique to a notion of body by J. A. T. Robinson, see R. H. Gundry, *Sōma in Biblical Theology with Emphasis on Pauline Anthropology* (Cambridge 1976) 239.

R. Jewett, *Paul's Anthropological Terms* (Leiden 1971) 201f.

[361] Lohse, *Col.*, 64., says: "... by addition of 'of flesh' (*tēs sarkos*) the body is characterized as the physical body which is subject to suffering (cf. 2,11). Thereby Christ's body that was given to death is clearly distinguished from the Church which is the body of the exalted Lord ... ."

[362] The following authors, with their different nuances of the interpretation on "the body" in 2,16, take the line of ecclesiological or social-community sense: R. H. Gundry, op. cit., 239; A. Lindemann, *Die Aufhebung*, 175; J. Ernst, *Komm.*, 318; H. Merklein, *Christus und die Kirche*, 45ff.; K. M. Fischer, *Tendenz und Absicht des Epheserbriefes* (Güttingen 1973) 50f.; Gnilka, *Komm.*, 142f.

his dedication to God. The somatic unity between the members of the community (and the community herself) was the result of the dedication of Jesus Christ, especially of his cross. In this way the crucified body became the source of unity and reconciliation and has become a theological "cipher" for the reconciliation (of both) to God and to men. To prove our point we mention the two *en autōi* (in him) in 2,15-16. The *en autōi*, namely the formula "in Christ," gives the proto-structural determination for the creative act of God: God acts in Christ. This formula is the main frame of reference according to the author of Ephesians.[363] Here, in the verse 2,15-16, the subject is Christ himself. Christ works in the community as a generative structure: God works in Christ. The "in him" at the end of 2,16 does not mean in the body of the Crucified. If we look back to the previous passages, the "in Christ Jesus" in 2,13 together with the phrase "in the blood of Christ" (*en tōi haimati tou Christou*) is stated in parallel with the "in one body" (*en heni sōmati*) with the "through the cross" in 2,16.[364] And the "in one body" of the verse 2,16 corresponds to the phrase "in one spirit" (*en heni pneumati*) in 2,18. The somatic unity of both groups becomes now the sine-qua-non condition for the divine unity: in one spirit.[365] "For[366] through Jesus Christ, in one spirit we both now have the access to the Father" (*hoti di'autou echomen tēn prosagōgēn hoi amphoteroi en heni pneumati pros ton patera*). Especially, the "you," the addressees who have heard and received the Gospel of peace of Jesus Christ (cf. 2,17), are united with "us", and all together have access in one spirit which is the gift of God through Jesus Christi (cf. Eph 4,4).

Verse 2,17 treats again of the peace: "And he came and preached peace to you who were far off and peace to those who were near" (*kai elthōn euēggelisato eirēnēn hymin tois makran kai eirēnēn tois eggys*). The meaning of the *elthōn* (coming: participle aorist) alludes to the coming of the earthly Jesus and the coming of the exalted Lord.[367] The moment of coming and preaching the Gospel indicates that the salvation-event was realized in Jesus Christ himself, and that this event of Jesus Christ continually promotes the process of the evangelization of those who were far off and those who were near. Jesus came to accomplish the Gospel

---

[363] See page 91ff. on the formula "in Christ."

[364] In the following paragraph 2,19-21, the two *en*-constructions (*en hōi*: in whom ...) are used to denote the divine act in Christ that integrates the "you" into our community by using the image "building."

[365] With Lindemann, *Die Aufhebung*, 179, note 180, " spirit " is not here meant as the Holy Spirit in the theology of the Trinity which was developed later.

[366] We take the *hoti* as declarative. See M. Zerwick, *Graecitas Bibl.*, § 259f.; R. Mussner, *Christus, das All*, 104; Gnilka, *Komm.*, 146, note 2.

[367] See Lindemann, *Die Aufhebung*, 176 and notes 165-166. According to Schlier, *Komm.*, 137f., the *elthōn* (coming) indicates the event of Redeemer (saviour). His interpretation is strongly influenced by the "ascending and descending"-image of Eph 4, 8ff. And Lindemann, op. cit., 176f. claims that the *elthōn* does not indicate a certain moment of the salvation-event but resumes the work of Christ.

in himself and consequently this fact affects us. As we mentioned above, Eph 2,17 is not simply a quotation of Is 57,19. The author of Eph appears to use the verse of Is 57,19 intentionally for his motif because he adds the personal pronoun "to you" (*hymin*) before *tois makran* (those who were far off). The author has his message to address to those who were far off: Christ himself is coming to them.

The author of Ephesians concludes this section 2,14-18 with the description of our present situation. In 2,18, he no longer speaks of unity of the both or of unity with God but he states the present togetherness of us. The very fact of togetherness in the community is itself the dynamic condition for access not to a god as such, but to God the Father. Before the Christ-event which is mentioned in 2,14ff. we had no possibility of an intimate relation with God, but now we have the decisive breaking point to gain access to the Father: through Christ Jesus. God is now the Father and both of "us" who are reconciled in one body to God are drawing near to Him in one spirit.

CHAPTER 3

"Christ-Agogical" Way of Unity

3-1: General Introduction for Chapter 3

In the previous chapter, we described the basic experience of the Church of Ephesus: the existing unity of "old" and "new" Christians in the community, in Christ. It is true that this unity seems to create a problem for the community, or, at least, it is one of the great preoccupations of the apostle who writes this letter. His ultimate purpose, however, is deeper than the unity of all the members of his community in the same spirit and in common experiences. He wants to accomplish his ministry of apostleship and of a preacher of the Gospel especially by conducting all his addressees to the fulfilment of their Christian faith, love and hope. The realization of the mystery of God's will is more than the unity of a community, of "old" and "new" Christians. He intends to promote the "unity in Christ" of the city of Ephesus, of the surroundings of the city, and of the whole universe. The means he adopts to conduct his addressees deeply into this mystery can be found in the first part of the letter in a special way. The author of Ephesians here shows his purpose clearly, and he uses his rhetorical and literary means according to his motif, or purpose. The great difference of this letter from most of the other letters of the NT is the "hymnic" part at the beginning. It is internally related to the intercessory-prayers in 1,15ff. and at the end of chapter 3 of Eph (3,14ff.), and to the many instances in which the apostle speaks about the interior growth of his hearers in "comprehension" of the mystery of the divine will and of hope, in faith and love. A "perceptive" word-field, or so-called "intellection" words, form one important element of our letter. The apostle wants to introduce and to conduct his hearers into a certain *epignōsis* (comprehension).[1]

---

[1] One of characteristics of our letter is the "perceptive" line of thought. For the author of the Ephesians states that God has made known to us the mystery of His will (see Eph 1,9). This perceptive communication of the Divine will forms one of the main elements of our letter. Beside the two intercessory prayers, the inner comprehension of God's will appears to be related to the Pauline insight and his mission to the Gentiles (see Eph 3,1ff.). And in many passages, we find " perceptive " words:

sophia; phronēsei: 1,8
gnōrisas: 1,9
sophias kai apokalypseos: 1,17
epignōsei: 1,17

And so we now investigate the first part of the letter. We shall avoid giving a full exegesis and a kind of commentary, but seek to deepen the ideas which have been already studied in our second chapter. The purpose of the apostle is to help his hearers and to conduct them practically, not only by admonishing them, but by "walking together" (syn-peripatein), by praying with them, and by singing together with them the song of the new reality, of the new city, of the new community in Christ, which makes possible a fulfilment of the will of God.

We started the analysis of our study with Chapter 2 of Eph, more precisely with 2,11, following our present experiences of a church which consists in two groups of believers: of old Christians and neophytes. There the accessibility for our present experience of being Christian is the inner logic for starting with Chapter 2 of Eph rather than with Chapter 1 of Eph. For the author of Ephesians abruptly (it appears to us) begins his letter with the "hymn" of 1,3ff. and presents us with a "crude" fact of his experience with his traditions.

The "hymn" of Eph 1,3-14 sings out "our fact," which is entirely

---

pephōtismenous tous ophthalmous: 1,18
eis to eidenai ... tis ... tis ... kai ti ...: 1,18-19
dianoiōn: 2,3
apokalypsin egnōristhē: 3,3
anaginōskontes noēsai tēn synesin ...: 3,4
egnōristhē: 3,5
apekalyphthē: 3,5
phōtisai tis ...: 3,9
gnōristhē ... sophia ...: 3,10
katalabesthai: 3,18
gnōnai ... gnōseōs: 3,19
nooumen: 3,20
epignōseōs: 4,13
tou noos ...: 4,17
eskotōmenoi tēs dianoias: 4,18
alētheia: 4,21
tou noos: 4,23
alētheias: 4,24
alētheian: 4,25
ginōskontes: 5,5
skotos ... phōs ... phōtos: 5,8
phōtos: 5,9
dokimazontes ti ...: 5,10
tou skotous: 5,11
elegchomena hypo tou phōtos: 5,13
phaneroumenon phōs: 5,14
epiphausei: 5,14
aphrones ... syniete ti ...: 5,17
eidotes ... ti ...: 6,8
eidotes: 6,9
skotous: 6,12
alētheia: 6,14
gnōrisai to mystērion: 6,19
eidēte: 6,21
gnōrisei: 6,21
hina gnōte ...: 6,22

based upon the fact of the "unique" relation of Jesus Christ with his God.[2] This fact of the unique relation includes a dynamism within "us" and a determining perspective for "us" and for the hearers or addressees.

Chapter 1 of Eph does not present us with a polarity like that of "then" and "now", nor that of "far" and "near" which we studied in the previous chapter when treating of the unity of old and new Christians. Generally, Paul speaks in his main letters of a polarity or a tension which man experiences in his life and existence: death-life (this exists in a different manner in 2,1ff.), sin-grace, slavery-liberation, old-new, flesh-spirit, law-Gospel, etc. However in Chapter 1, the author of Ephesians does not mention these kinds of polarity experienced in the life of Paul and in the life of the pauline communities. Rather, our letter seems in these communities, *to show a tension between the whole and the parts, and an integration of the parts into a unity.* He appears to refer to *a dynamic tension between the community to which "we" belong and the other groups, and the integration of the whole into the community in Christ, and, then, the relation between the church and the world.* Even when we treated the two ways of "leading one's life", [3] we felt that the main concern of the author of Ephesians appears neither to compare the two manners of life (heathen and Christian), nor to explain man as such who lives in the tension between the two poles: the conduct of life in Christ and that of life enslaved by the powers at work in the heavens (cf. Eph 2,2; 6,10ff.). His main concern is not simply to encourage a beginner to learn an elemental doctrine of the faith, but rather to encourage him *to "walk" ahead in Christ.* To this end, his interest is to encourage a group to come into a full awareness of what happened in Christ, and to integrate themselves totally into the communion which God caused to be brought about in Christ. We must be careful that this communion which formed the community does not become a "self-seeking" group or a self-introverted one. The deeper man gets involved in communion, the more dynamically he goes out towards those outside. This phenomenon is addressed at first not to an individual *but to a community itself.* Because the author expresses his conviction of faith for this: namely that God unites all things in Christ (cf. Eph 1,10) and Christ is our Head (cf. 1,23).

Theory and praxis

But here we meet a difficulty. Even though we understand the fact of the faith come about in Christ, we cannot realize ("somatize") it in all corners of our life. The understanding of the fact of being in Christ

---

[2] It will be shown by the expression *en Christō* and the similar *en* -constructions. See page 91ff.

[3] See our Chapter 2. pp. 20ff.

does not invariably promote unity or deepen experience in Christ. Even if we had known the unity of God and man, the unity of our fellow-men, and even if we had fully perceived the closeness to God and to our fellow-men, we know that this closeness was brought to us by Christ Jesus (cf. 2,14ff.). Despite the theological knowledge we have, we could not be moved to reach the closeness and attain the unity mentioned in the previous chapter. There, we studied the meaning of "being heathen," the root of the enmity and disunity. Histories of the world teach us that even Christians could have hatred and disunity and divisions. To be Christian and to indulge in discrimination or hate are really things which do not go together. According to the author of Ephesians divisions and disunities have nothing to do with man in Christ. Even if we understand the event of Christ and fully perceive the meaning of the mystery, such knowledge would remain mere "knowledge" unless we give our assent to the fact and "somatize" it in our life. It is one thing to know, another to do what we know. It is one thing to know what the unity is, another to actualize and somatize it in all corners of our life.

Task

Our task in this chapter is to describe the meaning of *the special kind of unity which unites the members of the Ephesian community among themselves, together with the apostle, with the writer of the letter.* The answer to our question must be found in the letter as a whole, but especially in the first part, at the beginning of the letter where the main theme is exposed. From 1,3-14 we think that the author of Eph shows his main concern, his motif of the unity and the fact of promoting this unity. Our main concern in the examination of 1,3-14 is not to recon-struct the "original" form.[4] It is more important for us to look for the inner unity of 1,3-14 with the rest of the letter, especially up to the end of the first part of our letter, 3,21, because the structure and the sequence of thought, the method of argumentation, the style, the special choice of words, all the elements of the text together teach the fundamental mes-sage: the total realization and execution of the Divine will in Christ.

The unity is reached[5] by the integration of faith and behaviour within

---

[4] C. C. Caragounis, *The Ephesian Mysterion: Meaning and Content* (CB New Test. series 8; Lund 1977) 41-45, quotes the authors. Regarding our proposal for a division of the text, see below 87ff.

[5] S. Hanson, in his monograph (*The Unity of the Church*, 1f.), gives us three notions of unity: "'Unity,' as well as the Greek *henotēs* is, of course, formed from the cardinal *unus*: *heis*: *hen* and the word originally refers to number. The word has this sense when we speak of e.g., the unity of God: There is only one God. ... [And] ... unity between two persons, e.g. between the Deity and the divine king, between God and Christ ... In this case, the meaning of unity closely approaches that of identity. Finally, we have the aspect that is most important to our investigation, viz. unity in multitude, as when we speak of the unity of a people, of the Church or of cosmos."

an individual person and also inside a group. It is reached by the integration of what we believe and what we show in our concrete life according to our belief, by the integration of what we think and what we do. Such a "unity" is aware of its relativity. There exist other "unities" around it, even if it can become a part of other greater unities. This is true for a community and for an individual. The real unity results from unity of faith, volition, reason, emotion and action. Especially when we speak about the unity between God and man, we should not forget that the unity is meant analogically. God is a person, but at the same time, He is not a person as we humans are. The unity between God and man is shown by the way in which the latter has acquired that unity with his fellow-men and unity in himself. But there is an inner aspect which reaches deeper. Experience between two men can show unity between man and the Creator, between man and the Redeemer. It can be "seen" only through "new eyes," however (cf. Eph 1,17). While we believe that Christ brought reconciliation and that he united both the peoples who were far off and who were near, we who are the so-called Christians (cf. Eph 2,11) have not yet reached the full unity of men and the unity of men with God. We have not yet reconciled our fellow-men in the world, even within the Christian churches! In the previous chapter, we tried to explain the origin of "prejudice" and the distorted mind and heart which are an inherent character of our human thinking and doing, so that they prevent unity among men. Any "comprehension" can easily become an ideology or an ideal which binds other men. Even high ethics or philosophy can entrap man so that they prevent him from a conduct of life the genuine reality of which he does not always perceive and they hinder his complete unity with men and God. In opposition to these dangers of thought and of comprehension, we want to explain an aspect of reaching a real unity, which may better explain the full meaning of the letter of Eph. In our opinion, the first part of the letter 1,3-14 is as a whole pregnantly arranged for the following passages, according to the essential theme: *comprehension of unity*. And this unity which combines the community of Eph has a special character. We may call it *the "somatic" unity of the community.*

3-2: Style and Language

As soon as we start to read this letter, we notice clear differences in its style and language from the former Pauline letters. It is true that most of the characteristic elements of the language of Col and Eph can be found in the former Pauline letters.[6] But Col and Eph differ con-

---

[6] This was the problem discussed in the monograph of E. Percy, *Die Probleme der Kolosser- und Epheserbriefe* (Lund 1946), but he did not evaluate the characteristic changes arising from the many instances of peculiarities in Col and Eph. The pecu-

siderably from the other letters. We will mention shortly the main instances. The author of Eph uses astonishingly long sentences. The text
which interests us (1,3-14) is grammatically one sentence.[7] Ephesians shows
a characteristic tendency to use relative clauses. We cannot say that
in Col and in Eph we find more relative clauses or relative pronouns
than in the former Pauline letters. The frequency of the relative clause
itself does not show characteristic differences from the former Pauline
letters. But if we examine their stylistic functions in Col and Eph, we
will notice the difference.[8] Especially, the former Pauline letters make
greater use of a relative clause which is put before its main sentence
to be defined, and a relative clause of "correspondence."[9] Ephesians
never uses such relative sentences as the ones found in Rom 2,1; 2,12.23.
etc.[10] Instead, Col and Eph prefer an "annexing style."[11] Namely, the
relative pronoun links the previous sentence or phrase or word in order
to determine and to clarify or to repeat the same idea in a different
manner. This kind of relative sentence is certainly to be found in the
former Pauline letters, but the frequency of the usage considered in relation to lengths of the letters Col and Eph reveal their characteristic style.[12]
And this style is confirmed by the frequent use of relative pronouns
followed by the conjunction *kai*, which is one of the characteristic features
of "loose construction of phrases." This kind of *kai* is relatively frequent
in Col and in Eph.[13] There are many other proofs for the "agglutinative"
character or mentality of this style.[14]

---

liarities in Col/Eph can be found in the Pauline letters *somewhere*. And he concludes,
therefore, that they are Pauline. But such an accumulation of these peculiarities
repeated in so many instances are no longer Paul's style. If such a formulation or
expression is found very often in (Col and) Eph, this datum does not constitute *a difference of mere "quantity" but of "quality."* See the methodical consideration of
W. Bujard, *Stilanalytische Untersuchungen zum Kolosserbrief als Beitrag zur Methodik
von Sprachvergleichen* (StUNT 11; Göttingen 1973) 14-20.

    [7] The other instances: 2,1-4; 2,4-7;; 2,11-12; 2,14-16; 2,19-22; 3,1-7; 3,8-12; 3,14-19; 4,
11-16. etc. Cf. M. Barth, *Comm.*, 5; A. van Roon, *The Authenticity of Ephesians* (Leiden
1974) 105ff.

    [8] See W. Bujard, op. cit., 66.

    [9] Bujard, op. cit., 66, states: " ... Der Vergleich der jeweiligen Zahlen macht deut-
lich, daß Paulus im Unterschied zum Kol und zum Eph sehr häufig einen Relativsatz
voranstellt ... ."

    [10] Ibid., 68. Bujard puts Eph 6,8 in parentheses because of the textual problem.
See 66.

    [11] Bujard, op. cit., 67: "locker aufügender Stil."

    [12] Ibid., 68.

    [13] Eph 1,11.13 bis; 2,3.22. Col 1,29; 2,11.12; 3,7.15; 4,3. See Bujard, op. cit., 69-70.

    [14] In this limited study, we observe that Colossians and Ephesians like to use
relative clauses: relative pronouns (*nominative*) followed by *estin*:

    hos estin ...; hētis estin.
    Col 1,7.15.18.24; 2,10.17.22; 3,5.14; 4,9.
    Eph 1,23; 3,13; 4,15; 5,5.
    And the preposition *en* with a relative pronoun like *en* with *hō̧i* is more often
        used in Eph:
    Eph 1,7.11.13.bis; 2,21.22; 3,12 (the second instance in 1,13 could possibly represent
        also *en tō̧i euaggeliō̧i*)

Ephesians shows a characteristic tendency to make use of prepositions, especially of the prepositions *en* (in) and *eis* (into),[15] and of participial constructions,[16] also an abundance of phrases where nearly synonymous nouns are connected in a genitive construction.[17] And we find a number of "repetitions" and near-synonymous expressions often combined by the conjunction *kai.*[18] This characteristic is often described as

---

Col 1,14 (parallel to Eph 1,7); 2,11; 2,12 (3 times).
And another difference from Colossians is that Ephesians associates a cognate noun and verb:
1,6: ... *tes charitos autou hēs echaritōsen* ... (... his grace with which he was gracious ...)
1,7-8: ... ... *to ploutos tēs charitos autou* ... *hēs eperisseusen* ... (... the riches of his grace ... which he lavished)
1,20: ... *energeian* ... *hēn enērgēsen* ... (... working ... which he worked ...)
1,21: ... *onomatos onomazomenou* (name that is named)
2,4: ... *agapēn* ... *hēn ēgapēsen* (love ... with which he loved) ...
3,7: ... *dōrean* ... *dotheises* (gift ... given ...) ...
3,19: ... *gnōnai* ... *gnōseōs* (... to know ... knowledge ...) ...
3,19: ... *plērōthēte* ... *plēnōma* ... (... you may be filled ... fullness ...)
4,7: ... *edothē hē charis* ... *tēs dōreas* (the graces was given ... the gift ...) ...
4,8: ... *ēchmalōteusen aichmalōsian* (he captured captivity ...) ...
This kind of usage does not occur in Col. It appears that Eph wants the addressees to deepen and to appreciate meanings of these cognate-words.
Cf. H. J. Cadbury, "The dilemma of Ephesians": *NTS* 5 (1958-1959) 91-102, esp. 98.
[15] We will treat these prepositions later on page 92ff.
[16] Such a participle in the nominative continues sentences: Eph 1,3: *eulogēsas* ...; *proorisas* ... in 1,5; *gnōrisas* ... in 1,9 etc. Bujard, op. cit., 62-63, esp. 63, says: " ... Auch wer alle aus den Paulusbriefen aufgeführten Fälle für genaue Analogien zu den Stellen aus den Kol hält, kommt nicht um die Feststellung herum, daß die Fortführung des Satzes mit Hilfe eines im Nominative stehenden Partizips im Kol (und im Eph) unverhältnismäßig häufiger begegnet."
[17] E.g.: Eph 1,5 *eudokian tou thelēmatos;* 1,11 *boulēn tou thelēmatos;* 1,6.12.14 the praise of his glory; 1,19 *kratous tēs ischuos* 2,14 *to mesotoichon tou phragmou;* 3,7 *dorean tou charitos;* 6,10 *kratei tēs ischuos* etc. Cf. Bujard, op. cit., 156f.
[18] Take for instances:
1,4: *hagious kai amōmous* (holy and blameless)
5,27: *hagia kai amōmos* (holy and blameless)
1,8: *en pasȩ̄ sophia̧ kai phranēsei* (in every wisdom and insight)
1,17: *sophias kai apokalypseōs* (of wisdom and revelation: these are not synonyms but in the same word-field).
2,1: *tois paraptōmasin kai tais hamartiais* (the transgressions and the sins).
2,19: *xenoi kai paroikoi* (strangers and sojourners)
4,14: *klydōnizomenoi kai peripheromenoi* (tossed to and fro and carried about with ...)
5,29: *ektrephei kai thalpei* (cherishes *and nourishes*).
Cf. H. J. Cadbury, art. cit., 99 and also Bujard, op. cit., 147ff. In addition to these mentioned above, we find that pair phrases or clauses are used to explain two aspects of a single fact.
ex. gr.
1,17-18: *pneuma sophias kai apokalypseōs* ... *pephōtismenous tous ophthalmous tēs* ... (spirit of wisdom and of revelation ... enlightened the eyes of ...)
1,20: *egeiras* ... *kai kathisas* ... ([the] raised ... and made ... sit ...)
1,22: ... *hypetaxen* ... *kai auton edōken kephalēn* ... (... put ... under ... and [he] made him head ...)
2,3: *tēs sarkos kai tōn dianoiōn* (of the flesh and of the senses)
2,12: *apēllotriōmenoi tēs politeias tou Israēl kai xenoi tōn diathēkōn tēs epaggelias*

"plerophoric." [19] In addition to these features, we should add the following peculiarities: frequency of *pas* (all) as the plerophoric character.[20] There is no rhetorical dialogue such as we find in Rom 3,1-9; 3,27 - 4,11 etc. And the vocative *adelphoi*, or *adelphe* does not occur. There are no rhetorical questions and syllogisms. The rhetorical logic is normally indicated by a conjunction like *ei*, *gar*, *men*, *de*. But these conjunctions rarely occur or simply do not occur, as van Roon points out.[21] Commentators mention these special features of the language of Eph. Its "abundance" and "redundance" of sentence cannot be explained only as a peculiarity of the author of Eph. These characteristics of style and language have to be seen in relation to the milieu of the author of Eph. Often this question has been discussed together with the problem of its destination.[22] Discussion has been aroused by the fact that the letter does not carry the name of the recipients or the title in the old witnesses.[23] Some authors think that the letter was a kind of encyclical document, which might be sent from some "official" to members of local churches. In place of the addressee's name a blank was left where names of different localities of addressees could be written and filled in when the letter was sent. If it was an encyclical letter, what was its purpose? In order to communicate information? or to communicate official decisions of a "central" church with her local churches? Or in order to give a synopsis of the former Pauline letters?[24] It is difficult to accept this

---

([were] alienated from the citizenship of Israel and strangers to the covenants of the promise)

2,12: *elpida mē echontes kai atheoi* (having no hope and godless)

2,16: *apokatallaxē̜.. apokteinas tēn echthran...* (reconciled ... destroyed the enmity ...)

2,19: *sympolitai tōn hagiōn kai oikeioi tou theou* (co-citizens of the saints and members of household of God)

3,8-9: *tois ethnesin euaggelisasthai ... kai phōtisai pantas tis ...* (to evangelize the gentiles ... and to illumine all that ...)

3,16-17: *... krataiōthēnai ... katoikēsai ...* (... to be strengthened ... to dwell ...)

3,17: *errizōmenoi kai tethemeliōmenoi* (being rooted and grounded)

3,18-19: *... katalabesthai ... gnōnai ...* (... to comprehend ... to know ...)

[19] See Bujard, op cit. (N. 6), 146ff.

[20] van Roon, *The Authenticity*, 102f.

[21] Ibid., 102f. And Bujard, op. cit., 26ff., indicates the following similar statistic: Eph has fewer adversative conjunctions: "*anti toutou*" and "*toutou charin*" occur in Ephesians. But the hypothetical and consequent conjunctions are less frequent in Eph. Final conjunctions are relatively numerous however.

[22] On the problem of the authorship cf.: C. R. Bowen, "The Place of 'Ephesians' among the Letters of Paul": *AngThR* 15 (1933) 279-99; C. L. Mitton, "Unsolved New Testament Problems: Goodspeed's Theory Regarding the Origin of Ephesians": *Exp* 59 (1947-1948) 323-27; idem, "Important Hypotheses Reconsidered, VII: The Authorship of the Epistle to the Ephesians": *Exp* 67 (1955-1956) 195-98; P. N. Harrison, "The Author of Ephesians": *StEv*, vol. II (Berlin 1964) 595-604.

[23] Gnilka, *Komm.*, 1ff., treats the history of the study and the place of the problem. Also cf.: A. van Roon, *The Authenticity*, 72ff. N. A. Dahl, "Adressee und Proömium des Epheserbriefes": *TZ* 7 (1951) 241-264; H. J. Cadbury, "The Dilemma of Ephesians": *NTS* 5 (1958-1959) 91-102; R. Batey, "The Destination of Ephesians": *JBL* 82 (1963) 101.

[24] See M. Barth, *Comm.*, 36ff. and esp. p. 39f.

hypothesis, because we possess no parallel from antiquity where the recipient of a letter remains unidentified.[25] The style and language must be considered especially in relation to its content and to the intention of the author in writing and composing this document known as the letter to the Ephesians. The author of Eph, in spite of a less characteristically Pauline flavour, addressed this letter not surely to "fictional" addresses, but to concrete people.[26] In the previous chapter, we already examined in a more general way who the recipients were (in the text, the "you"-group of the people). They were not simply the Gentile Christians, in opposition to the Jewish Christians; while we understood the "historical" fact that the Jews and the Gentiles together enjoyed unity through the coming of Christ and a consequent evangelisation. We believe that this letter to the Ephesians had its home ground in a specific soil, in a certain cultural and local origin and in its own purpose. The affinity in style and language of the letters to the Colossians and the Ephesians at least indicate a similar background and milieu.[27] We think that this letter was a part of a living process of religious experience both of an individual, the writer, and of his community. The origin of Eph should not be understood simply as a literary process in the modern sense.

An experienced man like Paul does not need to model his writings on those of the past, nor does he need books of his tradition before his eyes to be able to compose a new writing. While such an author prays, reflects, preaches and uses his experience to convey a message and its practical implications for his people especially with his collaborators, he is more aware of "the way" of his preaching and guiding his people to the stage of his experience. He is dependent upon the Pauline tradition, and he learned it, but he is not "enslaved" by literary traditions. He explained and applied it, and he used his freedom in the line of the same faith and conviction and content as Paul tried to live and which he preached. We are conscious of the affinity of such a process with what still happens in religious guidance in our part of the world in the Far-East. The real "guru" or "master," in a religious experience, does not need any literary study. Even though he once learned and now uses traditional doctrine and its expressions, he is free from them. The first step of all such experience is the imitation and following of a master. From there a complex process of living takes its rise. Pseudonymity should be considered in the frame of such a process. It had positive value in antiquity. It was not a forgery in the modern sense, neither a simple imitation nor mere fiction. For whatever purpose it might have

---

[25] Gnilka, *Komm.* 4; A. van Roon, op. cit., 78.

[26] Gnilka, *Komm.*, 6; A. van Roon, op. cit., 79f. With regard to the doctrinal considerations and intentions, see M. Barth, *Comm.*, 31ff.

[27] This could be more true if both letters were written by the same hand, as van Roon thinks, op. cit., 439ff. and 204ff. Cf. A. Vanhoye, "L'épître aux Éphésiens et l'épître aux Hébreux": *Bib* 59 (1978) 198-230.

been used, it can surely also show the inner relation of a master with his disciples. On this point our letter eloquently teaches the unity of the author with Paul and with the disciples. The form of the letter has to be understood as an effective way of communication with the followers of the master and the people around him. The "fixed" way of communication or form is also important to show the special way of the master's teaching.[28]

3-3: Literary Genre

Like Col, Ephesians differs from the rest of the Pauline literature in its style and language, because it has a special message and it expresses a special development of the Pauline doctrine and "gospel." [29] From the observations of many commentators it can be seen that the question of "style" and "language" are not merely "formal" or external ones. They concern its content. As we have said, the letter to the Ephesians is a real "letter." [30] But Schlier was right when he described it as also a *"Mysterienrede,"* a mystagogical introduction into the mystery of God in Christ.[31] We need to take into serious consideration these suggestions. In our own day we find a similar phenomenon. Repetitions, apparent tautologies, a special kind of "baroque" language belong to a reflective and meditative language. In Eph, style and language are witness to a special literary genre, a special " pre-consensus," acceptance and understanding between the author(s) or the speaker(s) and the readers or the hearers of the letter. It is obvious that we cannot demonstrate the special genre or way of communication between the author and the readers of the letter to the Ephesians if we base our judgement only on stylistic elements and on the redundant language. We have to investigate the whole writing as a text. We must study the general sequence of thought, the line which the author proposes to follow in order to lead his hearers from their initial condition to the situation and state of soul and faith

---

[28] See: J. A. Sint, *Pseudonymität im Altertum* (Innsbruck 1960) esp. 157ff.; W. Speyer, *Die literarische Fälschung im heidnischen und christlichen Altertum. Ein Versuch ihrer Deutung* (München 1971). See the critical review: *Bib* 54 (1973) 434-36 (J. Gribomont) and H. Widmann, "Die literarische Fälschung im Altertum", Bemerkungen zu W. Speyers Monographie, art. in: *Antiquariat* (Wien 1973) 169-74. N. Brox, *Falsche Verfasserangaben*. Zur Erklärung der frühchristlichen Pseudepigraphie (SBS 79; Stuttgart 1975).

[29] See Schlier, *Komm.,* 18-19; Gnilka, *Komm.,* 29ff. esp. 31-32. M. Barth, *Comm.,* 6-10, and the history of the research in Percy and Bujard. Good insights also come from a comparison with Qumran texts, see K. G. Kuhn, "Der Epheserbrief im Lichte der Qumrantexte": *NTS* 7 (1960-1961) 334-46; and also cf. B. Rigaux, "Révélation des Mystères et Perfection à Qumran dans le Nouveau Testament": *NTS* 4 (1957-1958) 237-62.

[30] Schlier, *Komm.,* 16-20.

[31] *Komm.,* 21f. See also H. Conzelmann, *Der Brief an die Epheser,* (NTD 8; Göttingen 1967) 87, who states that the letter is a "meditation" on the church.

which he wants to accomplish in them. In the present work, we must limit ourselves to a more general outlook. A detailed analysis of similar writings in the ancient church, especially of the church Fathers, could possibly show that we had more than a single and unique text of this kind.[32]

As a first step, we wish to point to some differences between Eph and Col. The second step will then be an analysis of the complete structure of the letter to the Ephesians in itself. This second step will begin with a precise investigation of some units of the letter to the Eph which specially interest us because of their "style" and "function" and content.

Col is more dependent upon the "classical" Pauline letter. It starts with the usual proemium which presents the sender and the addressee(s) and it expresses a salutation and a wish for a blessing in Col 1,1-2.[33] We find the almost same opening in Eph 1,1-2, even though the problem of the addresses (the Ephesians?) is uncertain because of the textual variants.[14] At the end of both letters, we read a salutation and blessing expanded by personal greetings from companions of the author. The relation of these two endings has been investigated. Some authors think that Ephesians is an imitation of Colossians.[35] Eph 6,23-24 has a distinguishing feature however. The author of Eph uses the third person to address the recipients, while most Pauline letters prefer a direct "you" or "your." Even in the final blessing Ephesians differs from Col. At any rate, both writings are intended to be "letters." The difference — in spite of many internal correlations — becomes evident immediately after the opening. Col 1,3ff. is an expansion of the common thanksgiving or blessing of God which includes the theme of the letter.[36] We are quite accustomed to such a thanksgiving from the Pauline formula of letters.[37]

---

[32] Patristic evidence, regarding the term "*mystagōgē*", is indicated by W. H. Lampe, *A Patristic Greek Lexicon* (Oxford 1961), ad locum. For the wider background, cf. K. Prümm, "*mystères*", in: *Supplément au Dictionnaire de la Bible*, VI (Paris 1960) col. 1-225.

[33] E. Lohse, *Colossians and Philemon* (Philadelphia 1971) 5ff.; H. D. Betz, "The Literary Composition and Function of Paul's Letter to the Galatians": *NTS* 21 (1975) 357-79, esp. 355f. Cf. K. Berger, "Apostelbrief und apostolische Rede zum Formular frühchristlicher Briefe": *ZNW* 65 (1974) 190-231.

[34] See B. M. Metzger, *Text. Comm.*, 601; Gnilka, *Komm.*, 1f.

[35] The Colossians follows the names which we find in Philemon (Col 4,7ff.): see Lohse, *Col.*, 170ff., esp. 175ff. Is Eph 6,21-24 an imitation of Colossians? See Gnilka, *Komm.*, 320f. A. van Roon, op. cit., 4ff. and 94ff., studies the history of the research and mentions authors who claim that Eph is the imitation of Col or, Eph depends on Col (literary dependence).

[36] P. T. O'Brien, *Introductory Thanksgivings in the Letters of Paul* (Leiden 1977) 69ff.

[37] Lohse, *Col.*, 12ff., summarises the evidences for the Hellenistic letters from which Paul borrowed. At the beginning of his letters he mentions thanksgiving to God, the Father of Jesus Christ. Cf. W. G. Dotty, *Letters in Primitive Christianity* (Philadelphia 1973) 31ff.; P. T. O'Brien, *Introductory Thanksgivings in the Letters of Paul* (Leiden 1977) 63ff.; Cf. P. Schubert, *Form and Function of the Pauline Thanksgivings* (Berlin 1939) 4ff. 12ff.; B. Rigaux, *Paulus und seine Briefe* (München 1964) 167ff., esp. 171f.

But it should be pointed out that Paul does not indicate only the subject in his "prayers." In the thanksgiving parts, he describes the experience which he wishes to provoke in his hearers. From this starting-point, he begins his motive for writing and his arguments. Immediately after the opening 1,1-2, there follows a kind of "hymn" (1,3-14). It is most important to note, therefore, that we do not find a "thanksgiving" followed by an "intercession" at the beginning of Ephesians.[38] This is a significant difference from Colossians. Coming to Eph 1,15, we find the introduction-vocabulary and formulation which remind us of a "thanksgiving," which is similar to Col 1,3ff.[39] In Col 1,9ff., there follows the "intercession" which Paul used to add after the "thanksgiving" in his letters.[40] The kind of intercession-prayer follows in 1,17ff. immediately after the mention of faith and love in 1,16 (hope appears later in 1,18).[41]

The relationship of Eph 1,15ff. to Col 1,3-5 seems to be obvious, at least according to the word-field and the formula. Eph 1,15ff. has some ideas in common with Col 1,9ff. For instance, *epignōsis* (comprehension) is one of key-words for both letters (Col 1,9-10; Eph 1,17-18; cf. Eph 1,8b-10; Col 1,6).[42]

The main point for our investigation is the different use of the "hymn." In Col 1,12-20, a kind of "hymnic" text is inserted as argument and motivation for the admonition after the "intercession-prayer" (1,9-11) which leads to an "application" to the actual situation of the hearers of 1,21ff.

---

[38] 2 Cor 1,3ff. and 1 Pet 1,3ff. have similar wordings beginning with *"eulogētos ..."*. On 1 Cor 1,3ff., see O'Brien, op. cit., 233ff. Cf. Schubert, op. cit., 8f.; J. T. Sanders, "The Transition from Opening Epistolary Thanksgiving to Body in the Letters of the Pauline Corpus": *JBL* 81 (1962) 348-62. Cf. J. Coutts, "Ephesians 1,3-14 and 1 Peter 1, 3-12": *NTS* 3 (1956-1957) 115-27.

[39] Schubert, op. cit., 33ff., esp. 34 states: "Strangely enough this thanksgiving, as far as basic structure is concerned, resembles most closely not that of Colossians, though it belongs to the same pattern, but that of Philemon ...." Also see 43ff. On page 44, Schubert says: " ... The thanksgiving of the pseudo-Pauline Ephesians is included here, because it represents the only occurrence of *eucharistō* of the 'thanksgiving type' in the whole NT outside of the genuine Pauline letters and is moreover obviously a conscious imitation of the genuine Pauline thanksgiving, particularly (as is everything in Ephesians) by Colossians. The formal and functional characteristics of the first and proper proemium, of course, served much better the purpose of this pseudo-Pauline document". O'Brien, op. cit., 3. note 5 and 233ff. and 239.

[40] Schubert, op. cit., 21; Lohse, *Col.* 24f.; O'Brien, op. cit., (N. 36), 82f.; Compare 1 Thess 2,13; (Phil 1,9); Eph 1,15ff.; Cf. G. P. Wiles, *Paul's Intercessory Prayers* (Cambridge 1974) 156ff.

[41] The role of the "hope" is remarkable in both letters. Ephesians incorporates the "hope" (*elpis*), one element of the "triad," into the content of the prayer of intercession requested by the readers. See 154ff.

[42] In Col 1,9ff., the author intercedes for "you": that you may be filled with the knowledge of God's will and lead a life worthy of the Lord and toward all good pleasure that you be fruitful in every good work and grow through the knowledge of God. See: Lohse, *Col.*, 24ff.; O'Brien, op. cit. (N. 36), 82ff.; J.-N. Aletti, *Colossiens 1, 15-20. Genre et exégèse du texte Fonction de la thématique sapientielle* (AnBib 91; Rome 1981), esp. 170f. We will treat Eph 1,8b-10 later and there we will find that "knowledge" or "comprehension" is the essential aspect of Ephesians as well.

("then" — "now") (*pote — nyni*).[43]   Col 1,21f. with the admonition of 1,23 is nothing else than a continuation of the original intention of 1,9f.[44]

Eph 1,15-21 cannot be explained as a simple conflation of Colossians or other similar letters, nor a simple expansion of the ideas of Col 1. It is true that the person "apostle" and his function in the church(es) is treated similarly in Col 1,23 and Col 1,24-29 (also Col 2,1-5), and in Eph 3, 1-8. But here again the difference is marked. According to Eph., Paul is not the *diakonos* of the Church (see Col 1,25) while both letters agree in referring to Paul as the *diakonos* of the gospel (see Eph 3,7; Col 1,23). One of the serious differences is that Paul himself in Eph 3,1ff. becomes the object of consideration, the "person" on whom the addressees, "you," make a theological reflection, specifically, on the Pauline insight into the mystery of Christ (3,3ff.). Chapter 2 of Ephesians is formulated in "hymnic" wording (see 2,4ff.; 2,14ff.).[45]

The peculiar thing in Eph is that we find another new intercession-prayer in 3,14-21 which ends up with a doxology.[46] Col 2 deals with the Colossian "heresy." [47] The problem of such a self-redeeming attitude and the practices which come in a certain way close to fulfilment of some Jewish laws are not the object of the letter to the Ephesians. We feel these contents of Col 2 behind the wording of Ephesians, in the back of the author's mind as something like a remote "background" sound of an on-going stage performance. On the contrary, the text of Ephesians resembles a continuous invitation to deepen the "knowledge" of the basic truths, which are expressed at a more practical level in Colossians. The theme of "knowledge" (comprehension) is also prominent in Colossians (see Col 1,6.9.10; 2,1; 3,10), but Ephesians presents it more specifically: the comprehension of the unity (see Eph 1,8b-10).

In Col the "initial" faith-love-hope-experience is the starting point and the common experience of the community to which the apostle alludes, and which he provokes in order to develop awareness of the actual dangers and to help his hearers in overcoming them (see 1,3ff.).[48] But in Ephesians the triad is not the initial experience of the community like the Colossians under the single preacher Epaphras, who initiates the strategy of the writer.[49] Instead, the author of Eph lets the whole community start

---

[43] See Lohse, *Col.*, 32ff., esp. 41ff. The affirmation about the situation of the hearers also occurs in Eph 2,1-3; 2,11f. See pp. 36ff. and 45ff.

[44] Cf. Lohse, *Col.*, 62f.

[45] See the previous Chapter 2-3, 56ff.

[46] See below, pp. 166ff.

[47] Lohse, *Col.*, 92ff.; J. S. Stewart, "A First-century Heresy and its Modern Counterpart" in: *ScotJTh* 23 (1970) 420-36; T. H. Olbright, "Colossians and Gnostic Theology": *RestorQuart* 14 (1971) 65-79; G. R. Beasley-Murray, "The Second Chapter of Colossians": *RevExp* 70 (1973) 469-79.

[48] Cf. Lohse, *Col.*, 15ff. The intercession of 1,9ff. is closely related with the content of 1,3ff. See Lohse, *Col.*, 24.

[49] Cf. Lohse, *Col.*, 22-23.

a song of 1,3ff. The hearers should listen to them, to their great "chorus." The first "act," after the preliminary statement addressing the listeners from the letter of the great Apostle Paul (1,1-2), is the common expression and the shared experience of those present in the community.[50] Only in 1,15ff., at the second act, the author himself enters the scene, and shows himself to be a single person (*kago* ... in 1,15).[51]

In the beginning of the letter, the author at once draws the attention of the hearers away from himself to the thanksgiving and intercession which everybody was accustomed to expect at the beginning of a letter.[52] The author goes back into the group of the "we," of the big "chorus" to which he belongs.[53] Only after the long "hymnic" explanation of the present situation, where "we" and "you" stand, is the authority of the Apostle Paul put into the foreground. In Eph 3,1ff., the Apostle is not only the main actor of the scene but the content of theological reflection. Paul was the prisoner of Christ Jesus[54] and the great witness who carried the "stigmata" of his Lord.

The text of Eph 3,1ff. does not have "personal" flavour. This is

---

[50] Later we will treat this point about the personal pronouns more precisely. See page 104ff.

[51] There is no mention of *egō Paulos* ("I, Paul") as in 3,1, *Toutou charin egō Paulos* ...; Col 1,9 which is a parallel passage to Eph 1,15 starts *dia touto kai hēmeis* ... (Therefore, we ...); Lohse, *Col.*, p. 14, states: "... The thanksgiving does not begin with 'I give thanks,' but with 'we give thanks', as in the letters to the Thessalonians. Although the plural form is used here, there is no difference in meaning between it and the singular form. From time to time in Col 'we' and 'us' appear, but it is still the apostle as an individual who speaks. The thanksgiving and the intercession of the letter continue the plural form, but it is later replaced by the singular as shown in the phrase, 'of which (the gospel) I, Paul, became a minister....'" Blass-Debrunner-Funk, *Grammatik des Neutestamentlichen* § 280, state: "The literary plural (pluralis sociativus), i.e. the use of *hēmeis* instead of *egō* and the 1st person plur. of the verb instead of the 1st sing., is a widespread tendency among Greek authors as well as in vulgar texts and other languages. The writer (or speaker) thereby brings the reader (or hearer) into association with his own action. This plur. is frequently sought in Paul; however, as the salutation in his Epistles shows, he is usually writing in the name of two or more persons and where this is not the case ... no such plurals are found: cf. Col 1,3 ... with Eph 1,15f. ..." Ephesians, however, reaches the climax by the progression from the "chorus" (we-you-styles) to the single man, the *Egō* of the author or the apostle, in 1,15. In the case of Eph, the use of the plural "we" and the singular *egō* have a meaning. The change indicates a dynamism by which the addressees may acknowledge the comprehension of Paul and of the "we"-people (including the author of Eph) (cf. 1,15ff.; 3,1ff.; 3,14ff.). We observe that Prof. M. Carrez, gave a paper about the "we" in II Cor on the occasion of the congress: Studiorum Novi Testamenti Societas (34th General Meeting, 20-24, August, 1979 in Durham), and saw a theological importance in the "we." And now, published: "Le 'Nous' en 2 Corinthiens": *NTS* 26 (1980) 474-86.

[52] Eph 1,15-16.

[53] Cf. what we have said about the "we"-group in the previous chapter and pp. 104ff.

[54] The historical fact that Paul was sometimes imprisoned in jails, constitutes the basis of the statement of Ephesians that Paul was *desmios* (prisoner) in Christ Jesus for you the Gentiles (see Eph 3,1.13; 6,20). The Pauline imprisonment gained a "theological" significance: the imprisonment became a stigma of the witness, of what he preached. He was first of all the prisoner in Christ and was bound by Christ's mystery.

not the warm-hearted Apostle Paul whom we knew from the former letters. Here, he speaks in hieratic solemnity, like the preacher in a big
assembly, at a "theatre" or "odeion," like the hierophant of a liturgy, like
a conductor who guides them deep into the mystery, as if he is saying:
"Not only 'we' but also 'you' listeners are actors of this 'drama.' His
explanation began in Eph 1,15, even if the formulas of thanksgiving and
intercession were used at the beginning. Later, from v. 19 onwards, this
'prayer' or 'hymn' is a 'mystagogical' sermon. Meditation and speech
are intermingled with admonition and exhortation. In a true sense, we
can call the second parts of both letters 'paraenetical,' because in Col 3
and Eph 4 the admonitions form part of a continuous current." [55] It is
true that the letter to the Ephesians remains more "elevated" even here
in the paraenetical part. The paraenetic part of Eph is permeated to a
greater degree by the theme of chapters 1-3. In both letters, the "doctrine" was explained in the first part, and in the paraenetic part more
"applied." And in both letters, the special kind of "doctrine" is used
in the motivations and argumentation, sometimes shorter sometimes
longer, or more explicitly, of the "moral" admonitions. Also the
"Haustafeln" [56] are clearly permeated by the "doctrine." In Eph 5,22ff.
the image of the body leads to one of the finest texts about the mystery
of the unity between man and woman (husband and wife).[57]

   Therefore, we prefer to call the genre of the letter to the Ephesians
"mystagogical." It is a mystagogical letter, not simply a pastoral Pauline
one. We may be allowed to call it precisely a "Christ-agogical" letter,
being distinct from "mystagogical" in the sense of mystery Religions.[58]

---

[55] The case of Ephesians seems to be very clear. It begins in Chapter 4 with
the parenetic wordings: *parakalō oun hymas egō ...* (4,1). See the major commentaries.
Cf.: J. Gnilka, "Paränetische Tradition im Epheserbrief", in: *Mélanges bibliques en
hommage au B. Rigaux* (Gembloux 1970) 397-410; W. G. Dotty, *Letters in Primitive
Christianity* (Philadelphia 1973) 37ff.; C. J. Bjerkelund, *PARAKALO: Form, Funktion
und Sinn der parakalo-Sätze in den paulinischen Briefen* (Oslo 1967) 179ff.
[56] Compare: Col 3,18ff.; 1 Tim 2,8-15; Tit 2,1-10; 1 Pet 2,13-3,7; *Did* 4,9-11; *Barn*
19,5-9; *1 Clem* 21,6-9; *Epist. Polyc* 4,2-6,3.
[57] Cf. J. P. Sampley, " 'And the two shall become one flesh.' " *A Study of Traditions
in Ephesians 5,21-33* (Cambridge 1971).
[58] We should like to define the term "Christ-agogical" which we created. The
Greek word, *agōgē* has the sense of "way of life", "conduct". By adding "Christ",
we mean a manner of life, but a Christian way of life and conduct (cf. 1 Cor 4,17; 2Tim
3,10; *1 Clem* 47,6; 48,1). The word *agōgē* occurs only in 2 Tim 3,10. According to
K. L. Schmidt, the word may mean "manner of life". And it refers to an education,
to those who are guided and educated, namely, children. The reference of *agōgē*
may be decisive in understanding the meaning of *agōgē*, in the sense that it refers
to the result of education rather than to education itself, i.e., to the way in which
the man who is guided conducts himself in life, to his breeding, behaviour, mode
or manner of life (*TDNT*, I, 128-129). It refers to philosophical schools as well (cf.
G. W. H. Lampe, *A Patristic Greek Lexicon* [Oxford 1961] 25). Therefore we use
the word *agōgē* in the sense of "learning how to live one's life in Christ". Eph
4,20f. is, then, quite suggestive of our definition of the notion "Christ-agogical" way.
There the author of Eph states: " you did not so learn Christ" (*hymeis de ouch houtōs
emathete ton Christon*). This is a most unusual use of *manthanō*. To learn a

The investigations of the "hymnic" and "liturgical" character of its language have developed our knowledge of such an attitude. But these "hymnic" and "liturgical" characteristics do not adequately describe the nature of the text in its entirety. The author's function is that of a leader for the "you"-people in the letter (i.e. the recipients) into the mystery. The whole letter uses the "strategies" of christ-agogical piety and religious partnership, in so far as he is a wise man and master in the experience and he has the duty and the joy of leading and helping other religious peoples. He sees himself as one member of his group: not merely the writer of the letter but at the same time a participant. He must exercise his authority but that authority is embodied in a longer and more widespread tradition of the community which chose this leader.

They (the community) chose him on the grounds of communally "proved" indications witnessing that he has penetrated to the core the experience of God's fact in Christ, as a disciple of the apostle.

The Christian church(es) (the leader(s) and community members as well) understand her leaders *as instruments not so much of the church but of Christ who is the "Head" of the community (the body)*. This is a

---

person is more than merely learning about Christ's existence and his teaching and doctrines (see M. Barth, *Comm.*, 529ff.). The same Christ is also the subject matter of learning. And in the next verse Eph 4,21, the author of Eph continues: "assuming that you have heard about him (Christ) and were taught in him (in Christ) ..." (*ei ge auton ēkousate kai en autōi edidachthēte* ...). To listen to Christ (Eph 4,21a) implies more than mere hearing *of him* or hearing *about him*. The readers of Eph surely did not see Jesus personally with their eyes. They listened to Christ in those people "proclaiming Him" (in the case of Ephesians, the apostle and the group of "we"-people in the community). For our definition of the word "Christ-agogical," the verse Eph 4,21b, "you were taught in him (Christ), as truth is in Jesus," is important. It certainly means that the recipients i.e. ("you") were taught by Christ. But still we may ask how Christ taught them, by what means they were taught to lead their life in Christ, for Christ was invisible to their eyes and untouchable to their senses in the present somatic manner of being and life.

We would suggest that they were taught in Christ in so far as the truth of God was actualized and somatized in a man, Jesus. By such an interpretation we envisage an inner analogy of life and of dynamism between Jesus and the recipients of Eph, then between Jesus and us present believers in Christ. It is an analogy between the manner of life of Jesus and our manners of life. The real active subject in our letter is God who acts in Christ. He acted in Christ towards the members of Eph. He spurred them and led them and directed them as He guided Jesus, in truth. Christ is presented at the same time as a message and a teacher, a lesson and a dynamism, of the community to follow him. The medium and the message are not only inseparable but completely identified. The concrete medium of this community, however, is the apostle and those who stood together with the apostle, who listened to Christ and to a certain extent accomplished the ways God willed for their life. Through these predecessors of the faith who comprehended how to lead a life in Christ, the recipients, in a concretely somatic manner, could "learn Christ." They abandoned themselves and entrusted themselves to the guidance of God at work in Christ.

By so doing, they were led to an inner comprehension of God himself who was revealed in Christ Jesus. Therefore, the "Christ-agogical" way is already in itself a "knowledge" and comprehension of God such as Jesus might possess during his life on earth. On the Mystery religions cf., K. Prümm, "Mystères", in: *Supplément au Dictionnaire de la Bible*, VI (Paris 1960) col. 1ff.

serious and important claim, and we must avoid "divinization" of man and "idolatrisation" of human leaders in socio-politico-religious institutions.

In a real sense, we can say that the authentic *Mystagōgos* is not the leader, but the Head Christ within His community. Therefore, the leader should be as much assimilated to the fate and the destiny of Christ and to the image of Christ. He must be the follower of Christ. He is the man who "*walks with*" (*symperipatein*) his hearers and with his master(s), with Christ and his disciples. By partaking of the same dynamism of the body of Christ and of the apostle and the leader, the recipients or the believers are in a process of completion. They will become aware of the consciousness and the comprehension which the leader wants and intends to accomplish in them.

If they follow the dynamism of the body, they will become aware of the inner comprehension which is at the same time the power to "somatize" what they are aware of. All other knowledge comes to naught. This is what we intend to show as the sense of the mystagogical genre, or precisely, the sense of the "Christ-agogical" genre of the letter.

3-4: Structure of Eph 1,3-14

Having explained the general aspect of our interests in the epistle and the special features of its style and language, we have evaluated its characteristic genre as "Christ-agogical." Now we come to study the text 1,3-14 in detail, so as to afford more proof for our proposition mentioned above. At first then, we shall investigate the structure of Eph 1,3-14 in order to bring into prominence the meaning of the text and its sequence of thought. Then, we will be able to clarity one specific aspect of the author of Eph and explain his main concern in Eph 1,3ff. in relation to the rest of the letter. And we shall be able to suggest a probable function for the "hymnic" part in relation to the rest of the letter.

Since E. Lohmeyer,[59] most exegetes agree that the "hymnic" text of Eph 1,3-14 is carefully composed.[60] For our purpose it is not necessary to determine a possible earlier form of a real "hymn," which perhaps was used by the author of Eph. We are interested in the intention of the author himself, and this can be seen by examining the actual form of the text. Up to the present, more than one "disposition" or "division

---

[59] E. Lohmeyer, "Das Proömium des Epheserbriefes," in: *Theol. Blätter* 5 (1926) col. 120ff.

[60] Against the judgement of E. Norden, *Agnostos Theos*, 253, note 1; cf. especially J. T. Sanders, "Hymnic Elements in Ephesians 1-3": *ZNW* 56 (1965) 214-32, esp. 223f. He tries to prove that the passages Eph 1,3-14 are not quotations. This is seen in the similarities of language and style between these passages Eph 1,3-14 and the rest of the section 1,15-3,21. On the structure see also, 87ff., and Gnilka, *Komm.*, 58f.; M. Barth, *Comm.*, 97f.

in strophes" has been proposed for this text. The earlier exegetes were aware especially of the grammatical and literary elements. They held a strict interdependence of "form" and "content".[61] For most authors the main problem consisted in the difficulty in establishing a "general principle" for the division of the "hymn".[62] During many years of serious research, almost all possible approaches of textual analysis have been attempted. With many authors, we are convinced that every method has its own right; not only literary, "stylistical," and all kinds of "external" elements have to be respected, but also the more modern linguistic and semantic considerations as well.[63] Instead of repeating earlier proposals,[64] we propose to explain our own opinion which adopts suggestions from many authors.

The division appears clearly if we look at the grammatical construction of the long sentence of vv. 3-14 together with the preposition which introduce smaller units which go to make up the verses, and if we respect the function of the verbal forms which express "movements" and "actions."

The first unity of the long sentence 1,3-14, which is conceded by most authors [65] grammatically is verse 3:

Blessed be the God and Father of our Lord Jesus Christ who has blessed us in Christ

with every spiritual blessing in the heavenly places.

Eulogētos ho theos kai patēr tou kyriou hēmōn
ᵒIēsou Christou,
ho eulogēsas hēmas

en pasēᵢ eulogią pneumatikēᵢ
en tois epouraniois
en Christōᵢ.

---

[61] E.g. H. von Soden, *Hand-Komm. z. NT.* III, 1, 2, 1893².

[62] See H. Schlier, *Komm.*, 40, where there is a summary of the proposed solutions. Cf. K. M. Fischer, *Tendenz und Absicht des Epheserbriefes* (Göttingen 1973) 110f.; G. Schille, *Frühchristliche Hymnen* (Berlin 1965) 65ff.

[63] For our proposal two authors especially are helpful: the articles of H. Krämer, "Zur sprachlichen Form der Eulogie Eph 1,3-14": *Wort und Dienst* N.F. 9 (1967) 34-46, and R. Schnackenburg, "Die große Eulogie Eph 1,3-14, Analyse unter textlinguistische Aspekt": *BZ* 21 (1977) 67-87. The former article uses classical philological and literary and semantic methods, the latter is characterized by the more recent "linguistic" attitudes of textual criticism.

[64] See esp. H. Schlier, *Komm.*, 39f. and H. Krämer, art. cit., (N. 63), 34-41.

[65] E. Lohmeyer, art. cit. (N. 59), considers vv. 4 and 5 as a single "strophe"; C. Maurer, "Der Hymnus von Epheser 1 als Schlüssel zum ganzen Briefe": *EvTh* 11 (1951-1952) 151-72, esp., 154, follows Lohmeyer's position. J. Schattenmann, *Studien zum neutestamentlichen Prosahymnus* (Göttingen 1965) 1-10, bases his analysis upon a supposed Greek rhythm "of quantities". He considers v. 3a the "title" of the hymn.

This verse 3 is a "formula of benediction," known from the OT and Qumran examples [66] and found in the NT and in Jewish literature.[67] It constitutes the "title" of this text.[68]

Of special interest for the understanding of the whole "hymn" is the double verbal form, *eulogētos* (blessed) and *ho eulogēsas* ([who] has blessed.)[69] Such a "parallel' use of the same root word runs through the whole text.[70]

In order to divide the following verses, we have to respect the many instances of the formula or "quasi-formula-like," *en Christō* ("in Christ") and its equivalents. Semantically it dominates the whole content and message of this text. We observe that these formulas are doubled at the end and at the beginning of v. 7 and vv. 10/11 and vv. 12/13. But such an "accumulation" of formulas in itself is not a principle of division or structure.[71] It has to be confirmed by other elements.

In fact, the *kathōs* (i.e. as) in v. 4 opens a series of phrases which are similarly constructed.[72] At the beginning we find a finite verbal form: *exelexato* (v. 4), *echomen* (v. 7), *eklērōthēmen* (v. 11). The *en Christō* ("in Christ") of v. 3 (at the end) is resumed by the formulas of *en autō*, "*en hō*" ("in him", "in whom"), which are connected with these main verbs. Verses 13 and 14 are differently constructed and will be analysed later.[73]

The next verbal form after the main verbs in vv. 4-12 is the aorist participle: *proorisas* (v. 5), *gnōrisas* (v. 9), *proorithentes* (v. 11). And the

---

[66] See K. G. Kuhn, "Der Epheserbrief im Lichte der Qumrantexte": *NTS* 7 (1960-1961) 334-46; S. Lyonnet, "La benediction de Eph 1,3-14 et son arrière-plan judaique," in: *A la rencontre de Dieu* (Memorial A. Gelin; Le Puy 1961) 341-52.

[67] See R. Deichgräber, *Gotteshymnus und Christushymnus in der frühen Christenheit* (Göttingen 1967) esp. 64ff.

[68] Cf. R. Schnackenburg, art. cit. (N. 63), 78f.

[69] See R. Deichgräber, op. cit., 72f.

[70] See above, p. 76, n. 7.

[71] See J. T. Sanders, art. cit. (N. 60), esp. 223f.; H. Schlier, *Komm.*, 39f. The *en Christō* or the similar expressions can be found repeated one directly after the other: vv. 6/7; 10/11; 12/13. In addition to these prepositions *en* with *Christō* or personal relative pronouns, we find the two *en*-constructions in v. 4 and in v. 8: *en agapē* ("in love") and *en pasē sophia kai phronēsei* ("in every wisdom and insight"). These two *en*-constructions help to indicate division or structure of the text as well. The *en agapē* ("in love") in 1,4 goes together with the following participial sentence *proorisas ...* in v. 5. The reason: its word-field. The words of 1,5-6 show the similar word-field of significations which are in correlation to each other: *proorisas* ("predestined"), *huiothesian* ("sonship"), *eudokian* ("favour"), *thelēmatos* ("of will"), *charitos* ("of grace"), *echaritōsen* ("bestowed", "favoured on"), *ēgapēmenō* ("beloved"). These terms denote "love-relation." In like manner, the *en agapē* in 1,4c and the *en tō ēgapēmenō* in 1,6c form a kind of inclusion and are in correspondence. With Gnilka, *Komm.*, 77; Schlier, *Komm.*, 52f.; Schnackenburg, art. cit. 73. The same thing is true for the case of the verse 1,8b: "in every wisdom and insight." The verse 1,8b starts a new semantic unity, namely, a "noematic" or "perceptive"-word-group or field: *gnōrisas* ("has made known"), *mysterion* ("mystery").

[72] On the conjunction *kathōs*, see Blass-Debrunner-Rehkopf, *Grammatik*, § 453, 2. Cf. 1 Cor 1,6.

[73] See our pages 90 and 105ff.

divine will is expressed by a *kata*-phrase ("according to", see vv. 5.7.9.11)
and a final or consecutive construction with a particle *eis* ("into") follows
(vv. 6.10.12).[74]

We conclude therefore that after the "benediction-formula" at the
beginning of v. 3, we have the following parts: vv. 4-6, 7-10, 11-12, and the
verses 13f., whose structure we have yet to explain. All these "strophes"
are dependent upon the introductory verse, "Blessed [be] the God and
Father..." of 1,3; then, what is explicitly expressed as the content of
reflection on the blessing is indicated by the conjunction *kathōs* ("as,"
"since") in 1,4.[75]

Vv. 13-14 do not follow the scheme of the three strophes of vv. 4-12.
They are characterized by the change of persons "we" (in vv. 4-12) into
"you." This change is underlined by the conjunction *kai* at the beginning
of v. 13 (*en hōi kai hymeis*...: "in whom *you also* ...") and at the beginning of the second half of this strophe (*en hōi kai pisteusantes*...: "in
whom (which) (*you*) *also believing* ...").

The aorist participles in vv. 4-12 have God as their grammatical and
logical subject. Instead, here in vv. 13-14, the subject of the two aorist
participles are the recipients of the letter, "*you*." The order of main
verb — aorist participle of vv. 4-12 is reversed: the participles come
first. And the participles are doubled. It appears that the emphasis is
meant to lie on the addressees "you." A *kata*-phrase referring to God's
will does not exist in this paragraph. But the preposition *eis*-construction
stands at the end and is doubled: *eis apolytrōsin* ("for redemption")...
eis epainon tēs doxēs autou ("for the praise of his glory"). Without doubt,
this is a last part of this "hymnic" text, in which the recipients of the
letter are directly addressed. Despite the grammatical sense and line of
thought of the text, the link is the *en*-formula (in-formula) which resumes
an *en tōi Christōi* or a corresponding expression. The first *en Christōi* stands at the end of the introduction or the title in v. 3. The whole
text explains God's Act in Christ, in the past, present and future.

If we look closer at the text as whole, we see that the second strophe,
vv. 7-10, is longer and in a certain way fuller in its line of thought. It
contains not only the *en hōi* ("in whom")-relative construction, but also
it contains such formulas as: *en autōi* in v. 9; *en tōi Christōi* in v. 10; *en*

---

[74] Cf. G. Schrenk, "*thelēma*": *TDNT*, III, 56f. (1938); H. Krämer, art. cit., 41;
R. Schnackenburg, art. cit., 74f. J. Cambier, "La Benediction d'Eph 1,3-14": *ZNW* 54
(1963) 58-104, is keen on the *eis*-phrase *eis epainon* ... ("into praise ...") and makes it
the criterium-refrain formula for the division of the strophes: vv. 4-6, 7-12, 13-14. See
also, S. Lyonnet, "La Bénédiction de Eph 1,3-14" in: *A la Rencontre de Dieu*,
(Memorial A. Gelin) (Le Puy 1961 341-52, esp. 350; J. Coutts, "Ephesians 1,3-14 and
1 Pet 1,3-12": *NTS* 3 (1956-1957) 113-27, esp. 116f. These authors (Cambier, Lyonnet,
Coutts) appear to us to read into our text the Trinitarian structure. Perhaps the
author of Eph did not think of God as a Trinity such as later developed in dogmatic
theology.

[75] R. Schnackenburg, art. cit., 74, sees that the *kathōs* has the same function of
the preposition *kata* with accusative noun.

Christō$_i$ in v. 10; *en autō$_i$* in v. 10. In addition to these, it contains a similarly formed construction at the end of v. 8: *en pasē$_i$ sophia$_i$ kai phronēsei* ("in every wisdom and insight").

In the first half of v. 7, we have a *kata*-phrase (*kata ploutos tēs charitos autou* i.e. "according to the riches of his grace"), and also in the second half of v. 9, *kata tēn eudokian...* ("according to his favour..."). And especially the *eis*-phrase of v. 10 is enlarged and expanded. The phrase appears to be the central part of the whole text: "to be carried out in the fullness of the times" (*eis oikonomian tou plērōmatos tōn kairōn*). This is followed by an infinitive *anakephalaiōsasthai* and by a double epexegetical explanation of the object of the infinitive. The hymnic style of this text (vv. 7-10) stresses the end of phrases and phrase-units. We have to consider that here is a focusing point of the text. *Ta panta* ("the whole" or "all things") is destined to come under a head (*anakephalaiōsasthai*) "in the Christ." The article of the formula "in *the* Christ" (*en tō$_i$ Christō$_i$*) (v. 10) puts emphasis on it, being compared with the two similar constructions at the end of vv. 9 and 10 (*en autō$_i$*: "in him"). The repetition and epexegetical explanation is the following:

> *Ta epi tois ouranois kai ta epi tēs gēs en autō$_i$* ("the [things] in the heavens and the [things] on the earth in him").

This epexegetical repetition makes clear that the formula *ta panta en tō$_i$ Christō$_i$* ("all things in the Christ") with the aorist infinitive *anakephalaiōsasthai* ("to unite") has importance specifically for the whole text (and also for the whole letter). In the immediate context, it is explained as an act of God already initiated (*...gnōrisas hēmin...* ["...has made known to us..."]). The following context shows that it is a present event that has to go forward towards the future for the meaning of the present life of the "you" to whom the letter is addressed.

If we may sum up shortly the "structure" of this text, we can say that in the form of a Benediction God's Act is hymnically described in 4 steps: vv. 4-6, 7-10, 11-12, and 13-14. The first three are closely linked together, but the last constitutes the "application" which has to be fulfilled and executed by the recipients. A semantic emphasis can be shown with the help of the formula *en Christō$_i$* and of its equivalents. The action in Christ of God who "has provided a head over the whole" stands at a special and central point of the text, and is emphasised by means of its style and language.

3-5: Dimension of the Expression *en Christō$_i$* ("in Christ")

Having set out the structure of Eph 1,3-14, we will choose some remarkable features of this text which we have pointed out. The *en Christō$_i$* ("in Christ") (and its equivalents) is one of them.

Therefore, first, we will examine the possible meaning of the expression *en Christōi*. In this connection the *eis*-phrases are worthy of notice. And we propose to clarify different usage and meanings of the prepositions *en* and *eis* and their constructions, in order to show that the Act of God in Christ, which is described in the distinguished events (see 1,4ff.), has its inner dynamism for the goal or purpose which God has decided to fulfil.

Secondly, we have to explain the function of Eph 1 verses 13-14, especially, the meaning of the change from the "we"-style to the "you"-style. This change must be seen in relation to verbal tenses as well, so that it may indicate the standpoints of the sender(s) and of the recipients of the letter. We feel that the change of the "we"-style to the "you"-style also relates to one of the main motives or intentions of the author of Eph. In our terminology, it may show the "Christ-agogical" dynamism for the integration of the "new" Christians into "our" community. We hope that the analysis of everything mentioned above may indicate the dynamism at work which integrates the "new" Christians into the "old" ones, for the sake of the divine mystery of his will.

According to the analysis of the structure 1,3ff., the second strophe 1,7-10 shows the main and specific insight of the author of Eph. There, the divine mystery of His will is stressed and specified by the verses 1,8b-10: "In every wisdom and insight, God has made known to us the mystery of His will, ... to unite all things in the Christ ...." Therefore we will examine these verses.

At the end of this chapter (our Chapter 3), as the result of the examination of Eph 1,3-14, we shall be obliged to study the significance of the image "Head-Body." By using this image "Head-Body," the author of Eph appears to make a synthesis of what he intends to communicate to his hearers. We will investigate the meaning of the image, so that we may understand the relation of the "Head" to its "Body."

3-5-1: *Clarification of the Meaning of the Expression*

Before we treat the expression "*en Christōi*" itself, we need to clarify a meaning of the preposition *en* in our letter, because the preposition occurs 117 times, and this occurrence is 42,5 percent of all prepositions which the author of Eph uses in his letter.[76] Compared with the similar length of the letter to the Galatians,[77] its frequency in Eph is remarkable. And the percentage of the preposition *en* to all the words in Eph is 4,8%. This is in second place after Colossians (5,5%) in percentage of frequency.[78]

---

[76] See W. Bujard, *Stilanalystische*, op. cit. (in n. 6), 122-25. The preposition *en* is also frequently found in Colossians and 2 Pet and Johanine letters.

[77] See Bujard, ibid., 24.

[78] See Bujard, ibid., 126-27.

Again, if we compare this fact with Galatians, the frequency of *en* in Eph is worthy of notice.[79] From this statistical result, we can simply say that the author of Eph was fond of the *en*-construction (also Colossians).

First, we should like to clarify the meaning of the preposition *en* itself and its possible range of meaning. We will treat here only the preposition *en* with the dative.

The meaning of the preposition in Classical Greek is understood by "in" in English.[80] It has a local meaning: "of place," "position," "state" and "manner." Also it may denote a certain time-span.[81]

In the western semitic languages, the Greek *en* corresponds to Hebrew *b* and similar prepositions.[82] The *b* fundamentally denotes a situation which stays still.[83] But it does not only locate the situation, but also, with certain verbs, denotes a movement within the range of "being stative". The movement which is shown by a verb remains within the "area" which it indicates.[84]

In the Koine Greek, the preposition *en* became increasingly elastic [85] so that we must determine its final meaning by the context or by parallel passages. The preposition *en*, however, *did* not lose the fundamental spatial meaning: "in" or "among." [86] According to N. G. Turner,[87] three factors were at work in the popularity and extension of its use in the New Testament: first, the growing lack of clarity in the dative case; then, the influence of the NT, where *en* had been widely employed to render the much-used *b^e*; but equally important is the influence of Christian ideas, especially in phrases peculiar and vital to the Christian religion like "in Christ." [88]

---

[79] Ibid., 126f.

[80] Liddell & Scott, *Lexicon*, 551.

[81] Ibid., 551f.

[82] J. H. Moulton, *A Grammar of New Testament Greek*, vol. III, *Syntax* by N. Turner (Edinburgh 1963) 261.

[83] Brockelmann, C., *Grundriss der vergleichenden Grammatik der semitischen Sprache*, II Band (Hildesheim 1961) 368. Cf.: W. Gesenius, *Hebrew and English Lexicon of the Old Testament*, translated by E. Robinson (Oxford 1906) 88ff.; J. Levy, *Wörterbuch über die Talmudim und Midrachim*, Band I (Berlin-Wien 1924) 186f.

[84] Cf. Brockelmann, op. cit., 363.

[85] J. H. Moulton, and E. Milligan, *The Vocabulary of the Greek Testament* (London 1930) 209f.

[86] J. H. Moulton, *A Grammar of New Testament*, vol. III, 261. Cf. W. F. Arndt, and F. W. Gingrich, *A Greek-English Lexicon of the New Testament*, ad locum.

[87] Moulton, op. cit., vol. III, 261.

[88] Since the study of G. A. Deissmann, *Die neutestamentliche Formel "in Christo Iēsou"* (Marburg 1892), many authors have discussed the global theme of the expression *en Christō_i en Christō_i ᵒIēsou*, etc. of the Pauline letters. For instance: A. Oepke, *"en"* in: *TDNT*, II (1935) 537-43; W. Schmauch, *In Christus* (Gütersloh 1935) 175 (esp. about Ephesians); F. Büchsel, " 'In Christus' bei Paulus": *ZNW* 42 (1949) 141-158, esp. 148, he interprets the sense of the preposition of Ephesians. R. Bultmann, *Theologie des Neuen Testaments* (Tübingen 1977⁷) 528; W. Grossouw, *In Christ* (Westminster, Maryland 1952); D. Tabachovitz, *Die Septuaginta und des Neue Testament* (Lund 1956) esp. 44ff.; F. Neugebauer, "Das Paulinische 'in Christo' ": *NTS* 4 (1957-1958) 124-38, esp. 136f.; J. A. Allan, " 'In Christ' Formula in Ephesians": *NTS* 5 (1958-1959), 54-62. H.

We must admit that the preposition *en*, especially in the Pauline letters, combined with a person or with the similar personal nouns, indicates a peculiar characteristic. The *en* of some Pauline passages has neither merely instrumental meaning ("by" or "with") nor merely meaning of "within" or "in" in spatial sense. If, for instance, we understand a phrase like "in Christ" in a rigidly local sense, the phrase would be crude and meaningless. On the other hand, it is not a mere metaphor.[89] We must read the *en* of each passage in its context, and bearing in mind that even in the Pauline letters every instance may have its own world of language both of unity of code and of meaning. For this reason, a simple comparison of one *en*-construction with others in other passages of other letters can very often be misleading. We would like to emphasize that the preposition *en* does not lose the fundamental or basic meaning: limitation of locality, "in", "within", "in the sphere of ..." and "in the stretch of ...."[90]

Let us now list all the occurrences of the preposition *en* in Ephesians.

The first group of *en*-constructions are accompanied by a term of "locality": in the heavenly places, in the world, in Ephesus etc.[91]

The next group is the *en* with a personal name or a personal pronoun or persons.[92] We must investigate this usage later on.

L. Parisius, "Über die forensische Deutungsmöglichkeit des paulinische '*en Christō_i*'": *ZNW* 49 (1958) 285-88. J. K. S. Reid, "The Phrase 'in Christ'": *ThTo* 17 (1960-1961) 353-65. A. Schweizer, *Die Mystik des Apostels Paulus* (Tübingen 1930) 122f.

[89] N. Turner, *Grammatical Insights into the New Testament* (Edinburgh 1965) "the mystical *en*", 118ff.

[90] J. H. Moulton, *A Grammar*, op. cit., vol. III, 261f.; A. T. Robertson, *Kurzgefasste Grammatik des Neutestamentlichen Griechisch* (Leipzig 1911) 169, states: "... Immer ist der Bedeutungsumfang des Wortes, bei dem *en* steht, scharf im Auge zu behalten, er bestimmt die Grenze und verleiht so der abgeleiteten Bedeutung Inhalt." We shall limit our study to certain aspects of the usage of the preposition in Ephesians, because we do not know sufficiently about the literary interdependence of the Pauline letters, especially those of the so-called deutero-Pauline letters. Even if Ephesians shows a similarity of terminology and style etc. with Colossians, this fact does not immediately lead to the conclusion that Ephesians depended upon Colossians or vice versa. Diachronical comparison and method must be applied after an examination of the literary unity of one document, as a help to understanding the possible meaning of certain words or sentences.

[91] The verses in the brackets indicate passages paralled in Colossians:

en tois epouraniois: 1,3.20 (2,12); 2,6 (2,12); 3,10 (1,16); 6,12.
en ouranois: 3,15; 6,9.
en deixia_i autou: 1,20 (2,21).
en tō_i kosmō_i: 2,12 (1,21).
en Ephesō_i: 1,1.

[92] *en tō_i Christō_i °Iēsou tō_i kyriō_i hēmōn*: 3,11.
en Christō_i °Iēsou: 1,1; 2,6.7. (2,11-12); 2,10.13; 3,6 (1,23-25); 3,21.
en tō_i Christō_i: 1,10.12.20. (2,21).
en Christō_i: 1,3; 4,32.
en tō_i °Iēsou: 4,21. This peculiar expression is combined with the *alētheia* (truth). In the same passage, the phrase *en autō_i* (namely, *en tō_i Christō_i*) refers back to the *ton Christon* of the previous sentence, 4,20.
en tō_i kyriō_i °Iēsou: 1,15 (1,4).

Thirdly, the preposition *en* is used together with a large number of nouns, which mostly qualify actions.[93] Finally, we find the *en* combined with a notion of time-span.[94]

After this survey of the occurrences of the preposition *en* in our letter, as we mentioned above, the second usage of the preposition *en*, *en* with persons, interests us most, especially, the *en Christō_i* formula. The expression en *Christō_i* appears in Eph 1,3 after the foreword to the letter 1,1-2.[95] Verse 1,3 is the theme-sentence of the "hymnic" part, which gives the reference-frame of the content which the author of Eph describes in the following passages 1,4ff. and of the content which he wants to communicate with his correspondents. If we translate the theme sentence literally in English, it will be thus: "Blessed[96] the God and Father of our Lord Jesus Christ, (who) has blessed us in every spiritual blessing in the heavenly places in Christ." And the last expression "in Christ" is repeated in the whole hymnic part from 1,4 to 1,14 in equal or similar expressions as we showed above.[97] The first *en Christō_i* in 1,3 will be resumed by the *en autō_i* ("in him") in 1,4. As we explained the structure,[98] we observe that double formulas (*en hō_i ... en autō_i, ...*) enclose a new unit of significations. What is expressed in these verses can be divided into several units, which are included in the expression of *en Christō_i* or of similar ones.

---

en *kyriō_i*: 2,21; 4,1.17; 5,8; 6,1.10; 6,21.
en *autō_i*: 1,4 (1,22); 1,9.10; 2,15 (2,14); 2,16; 4,21.
en *hō_i*: 1,7.11.13.13; 2,2.22; 3,12; 4,30.
en *tō_i ēgapēmenō*: 1,6 (1,13).
en *tō_i theō_i*: 3,9 (1,25-26).
en *hēmin*: 3,20 (1,29).
en *hymin*: 5,3.
en *tois ethnesin*: 3,8.
en *tois huiois*: 2,2.
en *autois*: 4,18.
en *hois*: 2,3 (3,7).
en *tois hagiois*: 1,18.

[93] We refer to the list of instances in: K. Aland, *Vollständige Konkordanz zum Griechischen Neuen Testament* Vol., I (Berlin-New York 1977) 400f.

[94] en *tō_i aiōni toutō_i*: 1,21.
en *tō_i mellonti*: 1,21.
en *tois aiōsin*: 2,7.
en *tē_i hēmera_i*: 6,13.
en *panti kairō_i*: 6,18.
en *tō_i kairō_i ekeinō_i*: 2,12.

[95] The expression *en Christō_i* ᵓ*Iēsou* for the first time appears in Eph 1,1. See M. Barth, *Comm.*, 69f.; Gnilka, *Komm.*, 53f.

[96] The Greek participle *eulogētos* denotes the present moment of the laudation in this context. In is not at all a wish that God "*may be blessed.*" It is not *eiē* but *estin.* Because it is a proclamation of the summary of the events in the following passages 1,4ff. is not a request for the blessing of God. Cf. Cambier, art. cit., 62; Deichgräber, op. cit., 72f.

[97] See 87ff.

[98] See pp. 87ff.

At first, the basic and all-inclusive "Event" is the fact that God blessed "us" in Christ (cf. 1,3). This Blessing is explained by the following
events.

In the first unit, from v. 4 to v. 6, the expression "in Christ" is referred to the election before the foundation of the world. The election of
believers in Christ has existed [99] since the creation of the world. In v. 5,
we find the election "directed" toward the future. In other words, the
election has its sense in the future, and its purpose. The aim is the integration of the believers into the sonship of God through Christ Jesus
and so to bring them near to God Himself. The *en Christō*-expression
includes a dynamic aspect of the divine Act in Christ.

The second paragraph (1,7-10) claims that "in him" (namely, "in the
Beloved one" in v. 6b), we have the redemption and the forgiveness of
sins. This is explained with the help of the traditional expressions of
redemption and remission of sins. The *kata*-phrase, "according to the
riches of His grace" indicates the undercurrent of the grace and power
of God, originating in the Glory of God.[100] In this overwhelming grace
of God who gives us forgiveness of sins and liberation from them (this
happened in Christ), God has made known to "us" the mystery of his will.
In 1,8b-10, the author of Eph describes the fact that God has revealed
the inner mystery of his will to us: To gather (to unite) all things in
Christ. Here we have the nucleus of the message of this hymnic part.
Christ, as "Head," is the very inner content of the expression *en Christō*
("in Christ"). We shall explain this point later more in detail. Here we
only remark that the expression *en Christō* is not simply equivalent to
the possible signification of the image "Head-Body." For the moment,
we simply claim that the nucleus event is caused to happen *in the Christ*.[101]

The third unit is vv. 11-12, where the author of Eph applies the revelation to the "we"-group of people, to which he belongs. He states: "In
him, according to the purpose of him who accomplishes all things according to the counsel of his will, we who first hoped in Christ have been
destined and appointed to live for the praise of his glory."

The last unit of meaning from vv. 13-14 states that also the "you"
group of people belong to the inner content of the mystery of His will,

---

[99] A time aspect may be expressed by means of an aim to be reached, but our
author of Ephesians is not inclined to a purely historical or mathematically linear
image of time. Cf. F.-J. Steinmetz, *Protologische Heils Zuversicht. Die Strukturen des
soteriologischen und christologischen Denkens im Kolosser- und Epheserbrief* (FThS 2;
Frankfurt 1969) 76f.

[100] See pages 165f. and 169 note (90).

[101] The expression en *Christō* has a wider range of signification than that of
"Christ". This is clear already from the fact that the author utilizes the expression
in Eph 1,20: *"which (work: energeian) he (God) worked (enērgēsen) in the Christ,*
raising him from the dead, and making him sit at his right hand in the heavenly
places". In 1,20, the traditional expression of resurrection and of enthronization is
expressed as a realization of the Divine Work in the Christ. See Gnilka, *Komm.*, 67.

since the gospel is preached among "you," and "you" have received the spirit. This process of evangelization is also brought to happen in the Christ. The Christ-Event comprehends the "us" and the "you" in unity in the power of the spirit.

Besides the *en Christō*ᵢ-expression in 1,3, we find other *en*-constructions in the same verse: "in every spiritual blessing" and "in the heavenly places" (*en tois epouraniois*). They may help to clarify the meaning of the *en Christō*ᵢ. The "spiritual" (*pneumatikē*ᵢ) must not be understood as "spiritual" in opposition to "material," but as a blessing which works on "us" with the power of the spirit.[102] The term "every" (*pasē*ᵢ) here does not mean the whole in opposition to the part, but the epitome, the sum of all that is called blessing.[103]

The *en tois epouraniois* ("in the heavenly places") is a peculiar usage, which is found only in Ephesians. The phrase "in the heavenly places," however, appears to be important to the author of Eph, because he adds this phrase after the traditional phrase "at the right hand of God" (*en dexia*ᵢ *autou*) in 1,20 and in 2,6, together with the *en-Christō*ᵢ (ʾ*Iēsou*). Both contexts of these passages (1,20; 2,6) speak about the resurrection and the enthronement. The phrase *en tois epouraniois* ("in the heavenly places") must be internally related to the resurrection and to the enthronement of Christ. Except for 1,3, the phrase is always used with a certain power semantic word-field.[104] Perhaps the author of Eph, instead of the traditional term "heavens" (*ouranoi*), chose the word *epourania* ("heavenly places"): grouping the various powers in the heavens, he chose to show us the "position" and the "sphere" of Jesus Christ, who rules over these various powers. At the same time, this is the proclamation of the unique position of Jesus Christ and the announcement of the "break off" of the new power of God for the world and humanity.[105] With Schlier, we under-

---

[102] Cf. Schlier, *Komm.*, 44. The suffix *-ikos* of the adjective *pneumatikos*, according to J. H. Moulton, *A Grammar*, vol. II, 378, denotes an ethical or dynamic relation to the idea involved in the root. Also see A. Urban, J. Mateos, M. Alepuz, *Cuestiones de Grammatica y Lexico* (Madrid 1977) 37, where there is a different interpretation offered by Urban. The term *pneumatikos* occurs three times in our letter: 1,3; 5,19; 6,12; and the word *pneuma* in the following verses: 1,13.17; 2,2.18.22; 3,5.16; 4,23.30. The author of Ephesians, it seems to us, does not substantialize or personify "spirit" as the second Subject who works on "us", that was developed later in the Trinitarian Theology.

[103] M. Barth, *Comm.* 78, note 6; Schlier, *Komm.*, 44.

[104] H. Schlier, *Mächte und Gewalten im Neuen Testament* (Questiones Disputatae 3; Freiburg 1958) 11ff. (The English translation: *Principalities and Powers in the New Testament* [New York, 1961] 11ff.). See also the same author, *Komm.*, 45f.

[105] The traditional term *ouranos(oi)* ("heaven[s]") occurs also in our letter: 1,10; 3,15; 6,9; 4,10. While "heavens" (*ouranoi*) is used in opposition to the "earth" (*gē*) in our letter, *epourania* with the preposition *en* and with a power-terminology or words relating to *energein* ("to work") expresses a kind of "place" of the power of God (metaphorically). Among the passages where one can find the term *ouranos* ("heaven") 4,10 may be significant for an understanding of the expression *en tois epouraniois* (in the heavenly places), in relation to the transcendental rule of Christ and his transcendent position. See Schlier, *Komm.*, 45. and 192f.; M. Barth, *Comm.*,

stand both *en*-constructions (*en Christōi*, and *en tois epouraniois*), in a metaphorically "spatial" sense.[106] The sphere of the expression *en tois epouraniois* ("in the heavenly places") is: a sphere where God, the Father of our Lord Jesus Christ, blesses "us" (1,3); a sphere where Jesus Christ is seated at the right hand of God, and God has put all things under his feet and made him (Christ) transcend all powers (1,20ff.) and a sphere where the Head of the Body is present (1,22f.); a sphere where the "we" are co-risen and co-seated with the "you" thanks to Jesus Christ, and at last, a sphere where the counter-powers were mighty only until the event which happened in Christ (3,10; 6,12). These counter-powers held their spheres in that part of the heavenly places which is called "air." These spheres in the heavenly places are one which affect also the Body i.e. the Community, and exert bad influences on it and are now still at work in the subjects of God who rebel against Him (cf. 2,2).[107]

The spheres are "spaces" insofar as they are open to ruling powers. Man lives under these spheres. However, the blessing of God which happened in Christ has broken through and destroyed these spheres of powers. All these powers are now at the same time under the Christ Jesus, the Head of the Body, which is the Church, insofar as man conducts his life in Christ.[108] To sum up the direction of a possible meaning of the expression *en Christōi*, it shows a "determination" of the Divine Act in relation to "us" and to "you" (i.e. the community). God works in the Christ and has realized his work within us.

3-5-2: *Dynamic Element of the Expression* en Christōi

For the second step of the investigation of the expression *en Christōi*, we will be concerned with certain dynamic elements which are included in the units of the significations constructed by the expression "*en Christōi*." For this purpose, the preposition *eis* ("into")-phrases and final clauses may be important. They appear to indicate a dynamic aspect of the dimensions of the expression *en Christōi*. The dynamism of the Christ-

---

vol. II, 434. J. Cambier, "La Bénédiction", art. cit. (N. 74), 65-66, has a different interpretation, and he states: "... avec l'événement salvifique du Christ, nous sommes transportés dans une autre monde et en un autre temps (cfr. Col 1,12-14) ...." The author of Ephesians, it seems to us, does not oppose this world to another world nor does he make a distinction between this time and the other time (see Eph 1,21; 2,2). It seems to us that those who conduct their life in Christ are already in the heavenly places where God is fully at work. But this implies that Ephesians lacks a future eschatology or the expectation of the parousia, for future salvation. The growth of the body or our human completion in somatic conduct of life presupposes time-spacial development. This development aims always at the future.

[106] Schlier, *Komm.*, 45f. See the other opinion, Urban, op. cit. (N. 102), 40ff.

[107] Cf. Schlier, *Komm.*, 46.

[108] See also Schlier, *Komm.*, 46-48, explained in terms of an existential philosophy. The divine phenomenon which happens in us can be expressed with "time-spatial" words, in so far as "the Body of Christ" is also a kind of "sphere." See below, Chapter 3-7.

fact is often expressed by such a form, as final, imperative, cohortative or exhortative.

In the first unit from the verse 4 to 6, the *en Christō_i* expression is referred to the Act of God who chose "us" before the foundation of the world, so that "we" may be holy and spotless before God (*einai hēmas hagious kai amōmous katenōpion autou*: v. 4),[109] and that, in v. 5, "we" may be destined to be his sons.[110] In vv. 4-5 the author of Eph introduces the twofold moment of the event which happened to "us" in the Christ: the election of the community (i.e. "us") and their destination to become sons (of God), to sonship through Jesus Christ to God the Father (*en agapē_i proorisas hēmas eis huiothesian dia °Iēsou Christou eis auton*...*i*. The latter element tells us the scope of the election, its destination and its sense. The author of Eph switches over from a static description in v. 4 ("*in him*" [*en autō_i*]... "*before the* foundation" [*pro katabolēs*]... "*in front of*" [*katenōpion*]...) to the dynamic description of the election in verse 5-6 ("to sonship" [*eis huiothesian*...]... "to him" [*eis auton*...]... "to praise" [*eis epainon*...]...).[111]

It is clear that the proposition *en* in this context (vv. 4-6) is not understod in the sense of the proposition *dia* ("through"). The phrase *dia °Iēsou Christou* ("through Jesus Christ") of v. 6 must be closely associated with the previous word "sonship" (*huiothesian*). We want to repeat that the reality which is described by means of *en Christō_i*, is the centre of the Divine Event. *En Christō_i* is the mediating point between God and the "us" in our text of Ephesians. It is not enough to say that "Christ" is this centre and mediating point. The expression *en Christō_i* is really this central and mediating function between God and "us" in the text. The expression *en Christō_i* appears to have a wider and deeper range of signification than the meaning of "through Christ" or the like.[112]

---

[109] Cf. A. Oepke, "*eis*" in: *TDNT*, II, 430. R. Deichgräber, *Gotteshymnus*, 73.

[110] Literally, verse 1,5 is translated thus: "predestinating us to (*eis*) *sonship* through Jesus Christ to (*eis*) *him* (God) ...." Perhaps the preposition *eis* is better translated in English by "towards." See M. Barth, *Comm.*, 80.

[111] We understand the *eis auton* ("to him" or "towards him") in the sense of "to God himself." The accusative form of *auton* ("him") occurs in our letter in the following verses: 1,5 (our verse in question); 1,20.22; 4,15.21. Except for verse 1,5, it denotes Christ in the contexts. With J. Cambier, "La Bénédiction", art. cit. (N. 105), 75. Some authors interpret *eis auton* in 1,5 as *eis Christon* ("to Christ"), because of the use of "*auton*" (him) in 4,15. See Schlier, *Komm.*, 54; Gnilka, *Komm.*, 73.

[112] Ephesians takes for granted that the recipients accept Jesus Christ as Mediator. Ephesians goes further however. If we look at *dia*-phrases in our letter, we find that *dia* (through) is twice linked with a person: *dia °Iēsou Christou* in 1,5 and *di° autou* in 2,18. The former passage shows that Jesus Christ is the Mediator of the divine sonship for us, the latter that Christ is the Mediator of the unity between "you" and "us." This unity itself is the access to the Father. This double fact of the unity (between God and men, and between men) was accomplished through (*dia*) the cross: see the other usages of *dia*: 1,7; 2,16. And the church herself is now the mediator of the manifold wisdom of God to the world (see 3,10; *dia tēs ekklēsias*: "through the church"). Compare the rest of the *dia*-phrases: 1,1; 2,8; 3,6.17; 4,6.16; 6,18.

The Divine Act which is described in Eph 1,3-14 happened *"in Christ,"* not only *"through Christ."* [113]   The line of thought, God-Christ-community, may lead to a wrong interpretation and miss the dynamically pregnant meaning of the expression *en Christō$_i$*.[114]   The author's order is: *God-in Christ-community*.   Having clarified the difference of the propositions *en* and *dia* in our letter, we now pass on to study the proposition *eis* itself, because it appears to us tha the sense of the prepositions *en* and *eis* is clearly distinguished in our letter to the Ephesians.

The preposition *eis* with the accusative indicates a motion "into a thing" or "its immediate vicinity" [115]   But since 150 B.C., the proposition was used instead of the preposition *en* ("in") in local sense.[115]   The Pauline and Johannine epistles and Revelation, however, do not appear to confuse local sense of *en* and *eis*.[117]

In the Pauline letters, the sense of the two propositions seems at times to be intentionally distinguished.   As M. Zerwick points out, the Vulgate translation often leads to an alteration in their meaning.[118]

---

[113] Many authors have different methods and theological viewpoints which result in different interpretation of this expression *en Christō$_i$* with regard to the preposition *en*.   See J. Coutts, "Ephesians 1,3-14 and 1 Pet 1,3-12": *NTS* 3 (1956) 1957) 113-127, esp. 117.   Cambier, art. cit., 66.   Deichgräber, op. cit. (N. 67), 73.   A. Urban, op. cit. (N. 102), 38.   F. Montagnini, "Christological Features in Eph 1,3-14" in: *Paul de Tarse apôtre du notre temps. La communauté monastique de S. Paul en mémoire de Pape Paul VI* (Rome 1979) 529-39.

[114] We have to admit a limitation in our comprehension of the "dimension" of *en Christō$_i$*.   Therefore, even the author of the Ephesians, in the name of authority of the apostle, prays for the recipients so that they may comprehend the inner mystery of the divine will which has been realized in the Christ.

[115] W. F. Arndt, and F. W. Gingrich, *A Greek-Lexicon of the New Testament and Other Early Christian Literature* (Chicago 1957) ad locum.   Cf. C. Brockelmann, op. cit., 377.

[116] J. H. Moulton, *A Grammar*, vol. III, 254.

[117] Ibid., Moulton, 255; M. Zerwick, *Graecitas Biblica* (Rome 1965⁶) 99 (70) ff.   In § 97, he states: "Quasi correlativa permutationi inter *apo* et *ek* est confusio quae haberi potest inter *pros* et *eis*, quatenus *eis* non iam necessario ponit 'terminum ad quem' motus in ipsa re, sed interdum in eius propinquitate (= ad)."

[118] M. Zerwick, op. cit., § 107 (77)ff. esp. § 110 (80).   It is peculiar enough, however, that the Vulgata translates this *eis* by *"in" with the accusative*.   We would suggest interpreting its preposition with the clause as the motion of interiority.   See Moulton, *A Grammar*, vol. II, 330.304.   He explains about the *esō* which is *eisō* in the classical Greek.   It meant "inside."   The author of Ephesians appears to have chosen intentionally the two similar meanings of the terminologies: *eis* and *esō* ("into" and "inside").   It is interesting that at the time of Paul there was a conviction of a general agreement about the existence of God or gods.   A kind of interiority, *innate* character of "god" might have been common in the Hellenistic world in the days of Paul.   So, Dio Chrisostom (*The Twelfth*, or Olympic Discourse, XII, 27) (Loeb Classical Library, translated by J. W. Cohoon; reprint, 1977), says: "... Now concerning the nature of the gods in general, and especially that of the ruler of the universe, first and foremost an idea regarding him and a conception of him common to the whole human race, to the Greeks and to the barbarians alike, a conception that is inevitable and innate (*anagkaia kai emphytos*) arising in the course of nature without the aid of human teacher and free from the deceit of any expounding priest, has made its way, and it rendered manifest God's kinship with man and furnished many evidences of the truth, which did not suffer the earliest and most ancient men to doze and grow indifferent

The propositions *eis* and *es* are derived from *ens*. The form *ens* appears to have come into general use in combination with a verb of motion, in opposition to the adverb *exō* ("outside") in ancient times. In Ionian and Attic dialects, the preposition *eis* is prevalent. The meaning is the same as the preposition *en* with the accusative.[119] The inherited use of *en* with the accusative is retained in the Northwest Greek dialects. Elsewhere this was replaced by an extended form *ens*, whence, *eis, es*.[120]

At any rate in our letter, the use and the meaning of the prepositions *en* with the dative and *eis* with the accusative are distinguished. From this fundamentallly local meaning of the preposition *eis* derives the significance of purpose or goal to be reached and also the indication of time in the future.[121] The motion of "in-to" (*eis*) presupposes a starting point and an end-point within a limited sphere.

Having considered these general lines of meaning, we will take a look at the usage of the preposition *eis* in Ephesians. We find 38 occurrences of *eis* exclusively with the accusative.

At first, the three occurrences in 1,5-6 appear to be important for the understanding of the rest of the *eis*-constructions and their development. The verses 1,4c-6 run thus: "in love (God) destined us to sonship through Jesus Christ to Him, according to the favour of His will, to praise of glory of His grace, which he bestowed on us in the Beloved One." What happened in Christ to us, now has a purpose and aim. We were destined to become children of God, and in so doing, we were brought near to God Himself.[122] Objective and intention presuppose movement or dynamism to attain its end. And in 1,8b-10, the author of Ephesians states that God has made known to "us" the mystery of His will in all wisdom and insight according to His favour which He set forth (*proetheto*) in him (Christ) *as His plan and goal* (... **eis** *oikonomian tou plērōmatos tōn kairōn*). The divine communicative act of His inner knowledge also came about in Christ and has its scope and plan. This plan God has executed

---

to them; ..." See ibid., XII, 39-40, and Jac 1,21. The main question in Eph 3,16 is not an "ontological" view about man, but an awareness and its somatic realization of what the author of the Ephesians wants to communicate to his hearers. We will treat this point later (See 200ff., esp. 223ff.).

[119] A. T. Robertson, *Kurzgefasste Grammatik des Neutestamentlichen Griechisch* (Leipzig 1911) 169-70. esp. 170.

[120] C. D. Buck, *Introduction to the Study of the Greek Dialects* (Boston 1910) 135; cf. also 78. About the complicated language situation of the hellenistic world: See A. Thum, *Handbuch der Griechischen Dialekte* (Heidelberg 1909); especially, about the Ionian-Attic dialects, 304ff.; idem, *Die Griechische Sprache im Zeitalter des Hellenismus* (Strassburg 1901) 162ff., about the variations of the Koine Greek; E. Schweizer, *Die Weltsprachen des Altertums*, 27ff.; idem, *Grammatik der Pergamenischen Inschriften* (Berlin 1898) 45; C. Rossberg, *De Praepositionum Graecarum in chartis Aegyptiis Ptolemaeorum Aetatis usu* (Jena 1908) 26ff.; J. Rouffiac, *Recherches sur les caractères du grec dans le Nouveau Testament d'après les inscriptions de Prien* (Paris 1911) 27ff.

[121] Moulton, op. cit., vol. III, 265-267.

[122] Cf. Eph 2,18.

with a view to the scope and completion which he has decided.[123] And
in Christ, "we" were made His heritage (eklērōthēmen ...) and in him
"we" hoped before "you," to praise God's glory (cf. 1,11-12). We hoped
before you, not as a privilege, but because of God's will. The "we" have
the same destination as the "you" (cf. 1,14). The Christ-events are uni-
quely for the praise of the glory of God.[124] The three phrases of "to
the praise of the glory ..." indicate the final purpose of God for the events
in Christ. God initiates his deed of grace to his own praise. Men have
to praise the grace, the glory of God.[125]

   Later, when the author of Eph treats the unity of both in 2,14ff., the
eis-phrase occurs together with the en Christōi (en autōi: "in him") in
the verse 2,15. We have seen already that the unity and the reconciliation also came about in Christ. There, the unity is the creative work of
God in Christ; to that end we are created. Both peoples, precisely, both
"we" and "you," are created in Christ into the one new man, namely,
into the one new community.[126]

   In the next occurrence of eis it accompanies verbs of motion or
growth. The "movement" which the en-Christōi contains is shown by
the help of such a verb of growing or motion. In 2,21-22, the author of
Eph mentions a complementary image, the building, as a help to understanding the meaning of the image "Head-Body" (cf. 1,10; 1,20ff.), and
so to explain the "co-status" of the addressees, the "you"-group of
people.[127] The author says: "In Christ Jesus the whole construction is
joined together (and) grows to a holy temple in the Lord, in whom you
also are co-built (synoikodomeisthe) to (the) dwelling place of God in
spirit." The "growing into ..." (auxei eis ...) a holy temple and "you are
being built together (synoikodomeisthe eis ...) for a dwelling place of God"
are initiated by God in Christ Jesus. The divine act in Christ here also

---

[123] See pages 112f.

[124] About the peculiar phrase, eis epainon ... ("to praise ...") in 1,6.12.14, some commentators think that it is a refrain formula for the structure of 1,3-14 as we explained
(page 90, note 74). These three phrases of "to the praise of glory ..." with their
slight variations seem to have the function of a "refrain formula."

[125] Cf. Gnilka, Komm. 73f.; M. Zerwick, Der Brief an die Epheser (Düsseldorf 1961)
33f., understands this phrase in relation to the creation of God. As a Jesuit, he appears
to have had in his mind the "Principle and Foundation" of the Spiritual Exercises of
St. Ignatius of Loyola. And he explains the phrase to prevent men from interpreting
it in a sense of "egocentric" self-glory of God. But God seeks his own glory, only
God can do it. His self-seeking glory, at the same time, becomes our glory, because
He is God. We should not think of God in a univocal sense.

[126] See the previous pages 67ff. And in Eph 5,31, we find the unity of man and
woman: The "two shall be into one flesh" (... esontai hoi duo eis sarka mian).

[127] Cf. C. C. Caragounis, The Ephesian Mysterion (Lund 1977) 139ff. We do not
reject the historical inclusion of the Gentiles into the Jewish Christian church that
Caragounis mentions, but we should call attention to the standpoint of the author
of Ephesians who does not speak of the Jewish people of past history, but of the
present recipients. In 2,19-22, the sentences are in "you"-style and the main verbs
are present forms: este ... este ...: 2,19; auxei in 2,21; synoikodomeisthe in 2,22. See
below pages 108ff.

is actualized and is being actualized towards the goal. The expression *en Christōᵢ* includes the dynamic moment of growth and development.[128]

The other cases of the *eis*-phrases are different from those mentioned above. They indicate a kind of "effect" or "attitude" toward somebody. Take for instance, in 1,8, we find the sentence "the grace which overflowed *to us*" (... *hēs eperisseusen* **eis hêmas**). And similarly, in 1,19, the overwhelming power of God *to us* (*to hyperballon megethos tēs dynameōs autou* **eis hêmas**); these two cases mean rather that the grace or the power has effect on us. And to Paul personally was gifted the stewardship of God's grace *for* "you" (... *tēn oikonomian tēs charitos tou theou tēs dotheisēs moi eis hymas*: 3,2). Here, it is somewhat similar to the cases of 1,8 and 1,19. The Pauline gift is to have the effect of the divine stewardship of grace on you the gentiles.[129]

At least, the *"eis"* preposition with infinitive clauses shows a final or a consecutive sense. In our letter, there are two cases: "in order that we may be ..." (*eis to einai hēmas* ...) in 1,12 and "in order that you may know ..." (*eis to eidenai hymas* ...) in 1,18. No matter how these clauses may be understood, in a final or consecutive sense, they lend to the main verbs a sense of purpose or scope, or of direction, or alternatively a sense of consequence ("so that") of the main verbs.[130]

We may conclude that the global aspect of these *eis*-phrases for the most part shows a scope or goal to be reached and denotes an incomplete situation or action to its completion. Completion is placed ahead, sometime in a certain future or timespan.[131] The expression *en Christōᵢ* is pregnant with these dynamic elements. "Christ" is not the key-word, but the expression *en Christōᵢ* is the key-phrase in the letter to the Ephesians, which forms the link of the Act of God with the community of Ephesians. The God of our letter, therefore, is situated outside human phenomena, but provides a bridge between Himself and the community as seen in the expression *en Christōᵢ*. In so far as the phenomenon in Christ comes about within us, it is a divine one. The community of Ephesians is characterized through the dimensions of the expression *en Christōᵢ* and its dynamism. The community itself which is united and

---

[128] The *eis* with a verb of becoming or of fulfilling shows also surely a directive "movement": "... to be strengthened ... into the inner man" in 3,16 and "... in order that you may be filled into all the plenitude of God" in 3,19. On these verses, see pages 17f. After mentioning the "going up" and "down" of Christ in order to fulfill the whole (*ta panta*) (see 4,7ff.), the author of the Ephesians states the role of the ministries for the edification of the Body (see 4,11-16). There, also we find several *eis*-phrases with the verb "we attain" (*katantēsōmen*). See pages 140f. below where we treat the Body in relation to the Head. About *mechri* with the verb *katantēsōmen* ("we attain"), see Blass-Debrunner-Rehkopf, *Grammatik*, §455, 3, note 6; § 383.

[129] In 1,15 and 4,32, attitudes of love are mentioned: "your love for the all saints"; "be kind to one another ...."

[130] Blass-Debrunner-Rehkopf, *Grammatik* § 402, 2; cf. § 406.

[131] Compare for example 1,14; 3,21; 4,30.

formed in Christ is a real expression of the dynamism in human history. The reason is, as the author of Eph states, that God united the whole in Christ (cf. 1,10).

3-5-3: *Integration of Groups: the Dynamism between the Writer(s) and the Readers. The Meaning of the Change of the "We"-Style and "You"-Style*

The expression *en Christō$_i$* has another element of dynamism which appears through the interchange of "we" and "you"-styles in 1,3-14. Here we will study the reason why the author changes the style. It is remarkable in 1,11-14.

In Eph 1,11 and 1,13, we find an important sign of the composition. It is the change from the "we"-style to the "you"-style. In the verse 1,11, after the "He"-style (God is the subject, in 1,3-10), the "we"-style starts. And if we look at the receivers of the Divine Act ("God blessed us ...", "destined us ...," "has made known to us ..."), we can observe that the subject, God, acts toward the "us" from the passages 1,3 to 1,10 (except the verse 1,7 where the author states: "in him we have ..." (*en hō$_i$ echomen ...*). What is the author's reason for this change? From what motive did he change them?

When we treated the unity of the "old" and "new" Christians in the previous chapter, we simply suggested that the "we" were not merely the Jewish Christians and the "you" were not merely the Gentile Christians.[132] As we showed above, the criterion for "being heathen" comes from the way of life.

Here, at the beginning of the letter in the "hymnic" part (1,3-14), we notice that the author of Eph expresses by rhetorical means his inner vision of the important motive, namely, the new unification of men. He expresses it also by the change of subjects and the change of receivers of the Divine Act in Christ. This will be another sign of the thesis of the author of Eph: to unite the whole in Christ. By its nature, this is an act of dynamic development in which the letter itself plays a part. Because of this, we would like to show the dynamism of the letter, observing how in the sequence of the text through the change of the personal pronouns the Divine Act of unification is expressed. The Divine Act towards "us" is diffused towards "you" as well. This dynamism is expressed by the change of the "he"-style, the "we"-style and the "you"-style, if we include nominatives, accusatives, datives, and the whole phrasing. We do not mean to imply that the author of Eph was conscious of this change of styles, in the sense that he was reflecting on it.

---

[132] See the previous pages 36f. 41f.

In Eph 1,3-14, we observe the following sequence: In 1,3-6, God acts towards "us" (*hēmas*). The subject is the third person singular, namely, God the Father of our Lord Jesus Christ (see 1,3a). In 1,7-8a to the end of the relative clause "... overflowed to us" (*eperisseusen eis hēmas*), the explicit subject of the passage is "we": "in him we have redemption ..." (*en hōᵢ echomen tēn apolytrōsin ...*). However, the subject who gives forgiveness of sins is, without doubt, God himself. And in the relative clause of 1,8a ("... the grace which overflowed to us"),[133] the giver of the grace is God, too.

In 1,8b-10, the subject is explicitly again God: "He has made known to us the mystery of his will." And we notice that the recipients of this Divine Act (*gnōrisas*: "has made known") are "us" (*hēmin*). In 1,11-12, the subjects again are changed to "we", the same subjects as in verse 7. But if we look at the main verb *eklērōthēmen* ("we were made God's heritage"), closely, it is a passive aorist. Therefore, the "we" is only the apparent subject, the real Actor is God. In 1,13, the subject is suddenly again changed from the "we" of the previous sentence (1,11-12) into the "you." The main verb *esphragisthēte* ("you were sealed with ...") is, however, the passive form of aorist; the implicit subject of the act "to seal" is God: God acts upon "you" too. In the final verse of the hymnic part of 1,14, the subject of the sentence is the relative pronoun *hos*.[134] And we find a genitive form of the personal pronoun, "our" (*hēmōn*): "which is the guarantee of *our* inheritance ... (*hos estin arrabōn tēs klēronomias hēmōn ...*)." Again the "we"-style of the sentence comes up immediately after the "you"-style of the sentence of 1,13. We understand this *hēmōn* ("our") in a synthetic sense, which includes the "we"-group of the people and the "you"-group of the people of the community.

At this point we may remark a certain movement of the text with reference to the change in personal pronouns and in the subjects and recipients of the Divine Act. The author of Eph starts with the "we"-group of the people (1,3-12). The Divine Act affects "us" in the text, then he changes to the "you"-group of the people (1,13), and finally reverts to the "synthetic" "we"-style (1,14).

After the hymnic part, he moves forward to the prayer of intercession for the "you" (1,15-23), as if he prays to fill a distance or different level of awareness and its realization between the "we"-group and the "you"-group of the people. In the prayer of intercession, the style is to address "you" by *Egō* ("I"). Until now, the movement of the text is in the following order: the "we"-circle, the "you"-circle, the synthetic "we"-circle, and at last the intercessory prayer for "you."

---

[133] The relative *hēs* is attracted from *hēn*. See B. M. Metzger, *A Textual Commentary on the Greek New Testament*, 601.

[134] Metzger, *Text. Comm.*, 601. The subject is the spirit, if the pronoun is *ho*, or by the attraction to the gender of the following *arrabōn*, *ho* became *hos*.

After the intercessory prayer, the author of Eph uses peculiar "floating" participial sentences (2,1-2). There, the "you" plays a main role. And in the following sentences, the main actors are changed from "you" into "we" (2,3-7). Then, abruptly, "you" again appears on the stage from the back screen (2,5b.8-9). Verse 2,5b shows a kind of sentence which is put into a bracket. This does not mean, however, that the short sentence of 2,5b is meaningless or a simple addition. On the contrary, perhaps according to the intention of the author, it may touch on his main concern: the unity or the total integration of the "you"-group of people into the "we"-group of people. Specifically, concerned with the awareness which "we" have and its somatic comprehension which "we" realize and actualize, the author wants "you" to be endowed with the gift of awareness and its "somatic" comprehension of the unity and its realization (somatization).

In 2,10, the "we"-style reappears. We interpret this "we" in a synthetic sense: "For we are his handicraft ..." (*autou gar esmen poiēma, ...*). In synthesizes both groups of the previous passages (2,1-9). Therefore, we find a movement of the text similar to that we mentioned above: you-group (2,1-2), we-group (2,3-7), you-group (2,5b.8-9), synthetic we-groups (2,10).

Coming to the verses 2,11-13, the author of Eph again addresses the "you"-group of people, reminding them of their condition of life in the past viewed from the standpoint of "being in Christ Jesus" (cf. 2,13). The condition is referred back to the situation described in 2,1-2. There, together with verse 2,3, the author of Eph refers to enslavement by sin common to the "you"-group and the "we"-group of people alike. Both shared the state of sinfulness in their former manner of life.

After the verse 2,10, the similar zig-zag-dialectic of the change between the "we"-styles and the "you"-styles continues in the following passages.

In 2,14-16, the subject is clearly *autos* ("he"). But we look at the people who are affected by this "*autos*" ("he"), *He* affected "us": "He is our peace, who made both into one ..." (see 2,14). Here, "we" (or "our") presuppose the two groups, namely, the "you" and "we", at the actual standpoint of the speaker.

And in 2,17 in the quotation-like-passage, we read the "you" (*hymin*: "to you": the dative): "... peace to you (who) are far off and peace to (those who) are near ..." (2,17).

In the following passage, the author resumes both groups, the "us" and the "you," saying: "For through him *we* both have access towards the Father in one spirit (2,18)."

And again he changes a sentence to the you-style in the following passages of 2,19-22, in order to explain the co-status of "you"-group of the people with "us."

Then the author begins the new unit of 3,1-13. He is the "representative" of "us", "...*egō Paulos* ("I Paul"), the prisoner of Christ Jesus for the sake of you the Gentiles..." (*Toutou charin egō Paulos ho desmios tou Christou °Iēsou hyper hymōn tōn ethnōn...*) (3,1). Without the main verb of the subject of *egō Paulos*, it is simply stated as a kind of title or theme of this unit.[135] At the end of this unit in 3,13, the verb of *egō*, *aitoumai* ("I beseech") appears. And the phrase "for the sake of you" (*hyper hymōn*) is the inclusion phrase of this unit (see 3,1 and 3,13).

In the verse of 3,2-12, "you" are the subjects who perceive the insight of Paul into the mystery of Christ (cf. 3,3f.), that is, the Gentiles are the "co-heirs," the "co-body," and the "co-partakers" of the promise in Christ Jesus through the gospel (cf. 3,6 and 3,8ff.).[136]

The complementary image, the building, which explains "your" present status in 2,19-22, is here bound to the Pauline mission and Paul's insight. The passages 3,1-13 underline the co-status of the "you" group of people who have put themselves into the context of the Pauline horizon of the Salvation-history. The author of Eph explains the co-status of the Gentiles (together with our community) in his wider horizon according to the key-person, Paul, and his insight and his comprehension in Christ Jesus (cf. 3,2ff.).

Then, the author concludes the first part of the letter (chapters 1 to 3) with the second prayer of intercession for the "you" (3,14ff.). Clearly, there also, it is *egō* (*Paulos*) who prays for you. And finally, the author ends the first part of the whole letter with a doxological passage (3,20-21): "Now to him who by the power at work within us (*en hēmin*) is able to do far more abundantly than that we ask or think, to him [be] glory in the Church and in Christ Jesus to all generations for ever and ever. Amen." This is a doxology of the Divine Power which is at work within "us." In this way, the author of Eph concludes the first part of the letter.

In 4,1ff., the exhortative part starts with the wording, *parakalō oun hymas egō*... ("I therefore, a prisoner in Lord, beg you to lead a life worthy of the calling to which you have been called,...").

Having looked through the changes of "we"- and "you"-styles in the letter, we shall make a short conclusion.

We suggest that the change of the apparent subjects from "we" in 1,11-12 into "you"-style of 1,13 is one of the important characteristics in Ephesians. This motif and the meaning of the change is developed in the

---

135 Cf. Gnilka, *Komm.*, 162.
136 We suggested interpreting this "you" in 3,1ff. in a wider horizon. See above pages 21f.
The actual addressees, "you," in the community and also the other "you" are included, in so far as "you" will meet and encounter the other "you" outside of the community. Here, it shows a dynamic horizon towards the world outside of the community of Ephesians.

following passages. In the hymnic part 1,3-14, the author already supplies hints as to this main objective in this epistle to the Ephesians: unity and integration. He develops it and explains it later.

The verses 1,3-14 show that the fact which takes place within "us" (1,3-12) is followed by the fact within "you" (1,13), and verse 1,14 synthesizes and includes both groups. "We" and "you" together come to be united under the One Head, the Christ. The thesis of the author of Eph is confirmed by rhetorical means, by the change of "we"- and "you"- styles. The change is not only rhetorical, but theological. And it is the *Christ-agogical* sequence of the text.

3-5-4: *Time of the Praise, Time of the Unity: the Present*

In addition to the analysis of the change of "we"-"you"-styles, changes of verbal tenses also confirm our proposal.

In 1,3, the subject, God, determines the first part of the sentences from 1,3b to v. 6. As we mentioned above when we treated of the structure, the content of God's Blessing is shown by the verses following the conjunction *kathōs* in 1,4. The word *kathōs* ("since," or "as") begins an explanation of the verse 1,3, especially of what God blessed and the reason why "we" praise God now.

In this hymnic part 1,3-14 (it is one sentence) the main verb is *eulogētos* ("blessed") in 1,3a. We have interpreted this "*eulogētos*" in the sense of a present act, namely, now in the community, we sing the praise and praise the blessing of God, because He has blessed "us" with every spiritual blessing in the heavenly places in Christ. The aorist participle *eulogēsas* ("blessing") in 1,3b indicates an Act of God in the past. But it relates to the present condition of this community of Ephesians, precisely, the present condition of "us." The Blessing is not merely behind "us" but also actually present to the community. The Divine Blessing has consequences for the present situation. God's Act in Christ originates from the past event, according to our human comprehension of the reality (time spatial and changing), but at the same time has on us a present effect and determines our future.

The heavens touch the earth, the "air" and "the heavenly places" are doubled, and transcendence and reality of this earth overlap. The praise is directed towards the Divine Event in Christ (see 1,4ff.) which took place and is taking place. We interpret these aorist tenses in the sense of the past and in the sense of the past "effecting" the present.[137] As we simply

---

[137] Observing changes of verbal tenses of the hymnic part, we find two verbs in present tense: the *echomen* in 1,7 and *estin* in 1,14. They are in subordinate sentences, however. And one present participle *energountos* is in 1,11. And the rest of the verbs are in the aorist tense except the case of *proēlpikotas* in 1,12. Strictly speaking, the perfect participle *proēlpikotas* is used in the infinitive clause: *eis to einai hēmas ... tous proēlpikotas* .... The author of Ephesians uses this perfect participle deliberately to stress "our" role of being privileged (we hoped before you), for "your" sake.

look through the tenses of the following passages, we find that present and aorist verbal tenses form the basic tone of the main verbs.

In 1,15-23, we see that the main verb *pauomai* ("I stop") is present tense. Here, the apostle prays *now* just as the speaker(s) sings out the hymn of 1,3-14.[138]

In 2,1-10, the main verbs, after the participial sentences and the relative *en* clauses (2,1-3),[139] are *synezōopoiēsen synēgeiren* and *synekathi-*

Speaking of the fact of "our" status of being called, the author invites and integrates the "you" to "our" fact of salvation. Therefore, he changes the style from "we" to "you" in 1,13, stating their initial status of salvation: hearing the word of the truth, the gospel of their salvation, and believing it, they were sealed with the spirit of the promise. See also the following list of verbal tenses (the observation of the tenses in the hymnic part of 1,3-14):

We abbreviate thus: f = future; p = present; a = aorist; i= imperfect; perft = perfect.
1,3:   *eulogēsas* : a participle
1,4:   *exelexato* : a
     einai : p infinitive
1,5:   *proorisas* : a participle
1,6:   *echaritōsen* : a
1,7:   *echomen* : p
1,8:   *eperisseusen* : a
1,9:   *gnōrisas* : a participle
     proetheto : a
1,10:   *anakephalaiōsasthai* : a infinitive
1,11:   *eklērōthēmen* : a
     prooristhentes : a participle
     energountos : p participle
1,12:   *einai* : p infinitive
     proēlpikotas: perft participle
1,13:   *akousantes* : a participle
     pisteusantes : a participle
     esphragisthē : a
1,14:   *estin* : p

[138] In the intercessory prayer of 1,15-23:
1,15:   *akousas* : a participle
1,16:   *pauomai* : p
     eucharistōn : p participle
     poioumenos : p participle
1,17:   *dōēᵢ* : subjunctive
1,18:   *pephōtismenous* : perft participle
     eidenai : perft infinitive
     estin : p
1,19:   *pisteuontas* : p participle
1,20:   *egeiras* : a participle
     kathisas : a participle
1,21:   *onomazomenou* : p participle
     mellonti : p participle
1,22:   *hypetaxen* : a
     edōken : a
1,23:   *estin* : p
     plēroumenou : p participle
[139] 2,1:   *ontas* : p participle
2,2:   *periepatēsate* : a
     energountos : p participle

sen ("co-vivified," "co-raised," "co-made . . . sit"). These are aorists. The verb *este sesōsmenoi* ("you had been saved") in 2,8 and also in 2,5b are perfect tenses to express their solid fact of salvation. In this part (2,1-10) there is only one present verb, *esmen* ("we are") in 2,10.

The short unit of 2,11-13 starts with the imperative *mnēmoneuete* ("remember . . .") to remind "you" of their past life in opposition to their present condition in Christ (see 2,13: *nyni de hymeis en Christōi °Iēsou* i.e. "But now you [are] in Christ Jesus").[140]

In 2,14-18, we find two present verbs: the *estin* (is) in 2,14 and the *echomen* ("we have") in 2,18. The rest of the verbs are mostly aorist participles.[141]

In 2,19-22, all the verbs are present tense to state the co-status of the addressees "you."

3,1-13, begins without the main verb (see 3,1) and at the end of this

---

2,3:   *anestraphēmen* : a
      poiountes : p participle
      ēmetha : imperfect
2,4:   *ōn* : p participle
      ēgapēsen : a
2,5:   *ontas* : p participle
      synezōopoiēsen : a
      este sesōsmenoi : perfect
2,6:   *synēgeiren* : a
      synekathisen : a
2,7:   *endeixētai* : a (subj.)
      eperchomenois : p participle
2,8:   *este sesōsmenoi* : perft
2,9:   *kauchēsētai* : a (subj.)
2,10: *esmen* : p
      ktisthentes : a participle
      proētoimasen : a
      peripatēsōmen : a (subj.)
140 2,11: *mnēmoneuete* : p (imperative)
      legomenoi : p participle
       legomenēs : p participle
2,12: *ēte* : imperfect
      apēllotriōmenoi : perft participle
      echontes : p participle
2,13: *ontes* : p participle
      egenēthēte : a
141 2,14: *estin* : p
      poiēsas : a participle
      lysas : a participle
2,15: *katargēsas* : a participle
      ktisēi : a (subj.)
      poiōn : p participle
2,16: *apokatallaxēi* : a (subj.)
      apokteinas : a participle
2,17: *elthōn* : a participle
      euēggelisato : a
2,18: *echomen* : p

unit in 3,13, we find a finite verb *aitoumai* ("I beseech"), which is present tense.[142]

Then, 3,14-19 is found the second intercessory prayer where one finds the main verb *kamptō* ("I kneel down") in the present tense (3,14).[143]

At the end of the first part of the letter, we find a kind of doxological unit in 3,20-21. There is no main finite verb, a construction similar to the hymnic beginning in 1,3 (*eulogētos*: "Blessed").

In 3,21, the author closes the first part with the words: "to him [be] the glory in the church and in Christ Jesus to all generations for ever and ever. Amen" (*autōi hē doxa en tēi ekklesią kai en Christōi °Iēsou eis pasas tas geneas tou aiōnos tōn aiōnōn. Amēn*).

Having observed these tenses in relation to the changes of the "we"-"you"-styles we mentioned above, we note that the synthetical "we" is

---

142 3,2:   *ēkousate* : a
            dotheisēs : a participle
     3,3:   *egnōristhē* : a
            proegrapsa : a
     3,4:   *dynasthe* : p
            anaginōskontes : p participle
            noēsai : a infinitive
     3,5:   *egnōristhē* : a
            apekalyphthē : a
     3,6:   *einai* : p infinitive
     3,7:   *egenēthēn* : a
            dotheisēs : a participle
     3,8:   *edothē* : a
            euaggelisasthai : a infinitive
     3,9:   *phōtisai* : a infinitive
            apokekrymmenou : perfect participle
            ktisanti : a participle
     3,10: *gnoristhē* : a (subj.)
     3,11: *epoiēsen* : a
     3,12: *echomen* : p
     3,13: *aitoumai* : p
            egkakein : p infinitive
            estin : p
143 3,14: *kamptō* : p
     3,15: *onomazetai* : p
     3,15: *onomazetai* : p
     3,16: *dōi* : a (subj.)
            krataiōthēnai : a infinitive
     3,17: *katoikēsai* : a infinitive
            errizōmenoi : perfect participle
            tethemeliōmenoi : perfect participle
     3,18: *exischysēte* : a (subj.)
            katalabesthai : a infinitive
     3,19: *gnōnai* : a infinitive
            huperballousan : p participle
            plērōthēte : a (subj.)
     3,20: *dynamenō* : p participle
            poiēsai : a infinitive
            aitoumetha : p
            noumen : p
            energoumenēn : p participle

always expressed by means of present tenses, namely, *estin* in 1,14 (it is in the subordinate sentence anyway: *hos estin...*); *esmen* in 2,10: "...We are His (God's) handicraft" (*autou gar esmen poiēma...*); *estin* in 2,14: "For He is our peace..." (*Autos gar estin hē eirēnē hēmōn...*); *echomen* in 2,18: "for through him (Christ) we both have the access..." (*hoti di' autou echomen tēn prosagōgēn hoi amphoteroi...*).

Therefore, these present tenses show the actual condition in which the sender(s) of the letter and the receivers stood.

3-6: Comprehension of the *"Mysterion"*

3-6-1: *God's Act of Giving Us "Knowledge"*

The second unit of the significations in 1,3-14 is vv. 7-10, where the author of Eph states that in Christ "we" have redemption through his blood and the forgiveness of sins, and he goes on to mention God's act of giving "us" knowledge. The comprehension of unity is caused by God. It is God who gives "knowledge." We have already pointed out that the aspect of "revelation" is one of the key-words of this letter.[144] The aorist participle of the verb *gnōrisas* of 1,9 resumes and points to all the texts about "revelation" or "comprehension" in this letter. This comprehension is explained by the author with the following sentence: "in all wisdom and insight God has made known to us the mystery of His will according to His favour which He set forth in him" (*en pasē̜ sophią kai phronēsei gnōrisas hēmin to mysterion tou thelēmatos autou, kata tēn eudokian autou hēn proetheto en autō̜*) (1,8b-9).[145]

We shall begin with an inquiry into the meaning of the verb *gnōrizein*. It has a transitive sense and occurs again in the following verses: 3,3.5.; 6,19. The meaning is "to make known," "to reveal," "to inform," "to communicate".[146] So God accomplishes the "perceptively" communicating Act to "us" in all wisdom and insight. We understand the preposition *en*-construction (*en pasē̜ sophia̜ kai phronēsei*) of 1,8b in a sense of determination of quality. Whatever God does, is done with wisdom and insight. But what has God made known to us? The author of Eph states "the mystery of His will" (*to mysterion tou thelēmatos autou*). The content of the divine "revelation" is termed the mystery of His will.[147] The term *mysterion* was quite widespread in antiquity.[148] The understanding of

---

144 See page 71 and note (1). Cf. A. Lindemann, *Die Aufhebung*, 93.
145 The translation "favour" for the Greek word *eudokia* is from Bauer-Arndt-Gingrich, *A Greek Lexicon of the New Testament*, s.v.
146 Ibid., 162; Schlier, *Komm.*, 93; R. Bultmann, *"gnōrizō"* in: *TDNT*, I, 718.
147 In our letter, the term *mysterion* occurs in the following verses: 1,9; 3,3.4.9; 5,32; 6,19.
148 G. Bornkamm, *"mysterion"*, in: *TDNT*, IV, 802-17; C. C. Caragounis, *The Ephesian Mysterion* (Lund 1977) 3ff. We do not mean the term itself was of common occurrence. Its cultural praxis and similar terms were widespread.

"mystery" as eschatological secret (or mysteries) of the last day which appears in Jewish Apocalyptic literature has an influence on the New Testament terminology.[149]

Expressions like "the secret of creation," "the mystery of history" and especially, "the mystery of times," appear in the later Jewish Apocalyptic literatures.[150] And in the Qumran-texts, we find wording similar to our text of Eph 1,8b-9.[151] What does the phrase "the mystery of His will" in Eph 1,9 mean? Is it a right attitude for us humans to question what the mystery of His will means? Rather, in the text, the author says that God himself has made known the mystery of His will. It is the divine Act in every respect. Still more, the object of the divine revelation or comprehension is the mystery of *His will.* We humans cannot scrutinize "His will." The "knowledge" is his grace. Our right attitude is to pray for it with the community who sings this "hymn" and with the apostle who prays for the addressees (cf. 1,15ff.; 3,14ff.).

In order to understand at least the line of thought of Eph 1,8b-9, it would be helpful to look through the other Pauline passages which mention the term *mysterion,* especially 1 Cor 2,6ff. and Col 1,26f.; 2,2f.; 4,3.[152]

---

[149] Cf. Dan (LXX) 2,18f., 27ff. See Schlier, *Komm.,* 60. and note 3.

[150] See ibid., 60.

[151] Ibid., note 3; Gnilka, *Komm.,* 77. And compare the following verses in the Qumran texts: 1 QS 4,18; 1,7.14.19; 9,17.23; 10,2f. Cf.: E. Vogt, "Mysteria in textibus Qumran": *Bib* 37 (1956) 247-57. E. Lohse, *Colossians and Philemon* (Philadelphia 1971) 74. and note 44. H. W. Kuhn, *Enderwartung und Gegenwärtiges Heil* (St. zur Umwelt des Nt 4; Göttingen 1966) 162, 169f. While some of these texts cite the word mysteries (*mysteria*) in plural form, Ephesians presents one mystery (*to mysterion*). See Schlier, *Komm.,* 62.

[152] According to 1 Cor 2,6ff., what is meant by the word *mysterion* is Christ the Crucified and Glorified Lord. He is the hidden wisdom of God which none of the rulers of this age (*aiōnos toutou*) understood. Cf.: Schlier, *Komm.,* 61; D. Lührmann, *Das Offenbarungsverständnis bei Paulus und in Paulinischen Gemeinde* (Neukirchen-Vluyn 1965), 113ff.; Penna, R., *Il "Mysterion" Paolino* (Brescia 1978), esp. 23ff. And Col 1,26 speaks of the "mystery" as hidden from the ages and the generations, but now (*nyn de*) disclosed to his saints. See Lohse, *Col.,* 74; Gnilka, *Komm.,* 77. and our study of "we"-"you"; the "we" were the first recipients of the Divine "knowledge." And one of "our" main tasks is to transmit this "knowledge" to "you." God wanted to make known to his saints the wealth of the glory of this mystery among the saints (*... ti to ploutos tēs doxēs tou mysteriou en tois ethnesin ....",* Col 1,27). Also compare Col 2,3: "all the treasures of wisdom and insight are hidden in Christ". The content of the mystery there is stated as "Christ among you" (*Christos en hymin*) (Col 1,27). "Since the content of the mystery is nothing other than 'Christ among you,' it is no longer a matter of various mysteries concerning God's eschatological plan as in Jewish apocalyptic. Rather, the revelation of one mystery is proclaimed" (Lohse, *Col.,* 76). The Lord is present in the Gospel, which is accepted in the community, and therefore He is living in the community. It is the good of the Gentiles as well. In Col 2,2, the apostle strives to encourage the communities. "The solidarity of the whole community is founded, maintained and strengthened by love, the bond of perfection. In this unity, the community should attain to all the riches ... of the mystery, Christ" (Lohse, *Col.,* 81). "The object of this insight is expressed in the genitive which is attached to the parallel term 'understanding' (*epignōsis*). It is the mystery of God, which He has made known to His saints among the nations (*en tois ethnesin*) (cf. Col 1,26f.; and Lohse, *Col.,* 81-82)." This understanding of the divine mystery belongs

The link of the "perceptive" element of the mystery and its hidden-
ness is important for the understanding for the relation of Ephesians
with its receivers. In 1,9, the case is dative, "to us" (*hēmin*). The following phrase *kata tēn eudokian autou hēn proetheto en autōi* ("according to His favour which He set forth in him"), which is already
met with in similar wording in 1,5 and later in 1,11, underlines the
sovereignty of the Divine Act.[153] "To make known the mystery of His
will to us" is totally a divine grace and belongs to his sovereign freedom.
And this gift of "knowledge" is set forth in Christ, and is given, as if it
were restricted by God's loving favour for Christ (see 1,5-6 and the similar
en-constructions, "in love" (v. 4b) and "in the Beloved One" as "in Christ").

The word *eudokia* cannot be separated from the *boulē* ("counsel")
(1,11) which in the *proorizein* ("to destine") of 1,5 *protithesthai* ("to set
forth") in 1,9 and *prothesis* ("setting forth," "design") in 1,11, is expressed
as a pretemporal scope. It is more than the determinative will and
counsel as such. It is the content of this counsel as the free-good-pleasure
which, grounded in God alone and influenced by nothing else, is His
gracious determination to save.[154]

It is the determined Act of His love, which did happen already in
Christ the Beloved one (cf. 1,5) and which is now happening to "us." It
is not only the determinism of "time," but also the determinism of love.
We cannot make other men love us by force. Love belongs totally to
one's free will and is an inscrutable "secret" of man. Man cannot know
his reason for loving him or her. Because it is love. Human love is so,
and the divine love is much more than human love.[155] The "pre-temporal"
act of God, which is expressed according to our linear image of time
(resulting from our manner of being, of change and movement), is comprehended and realized in our human manner, that is, in a historical
manner.[156] No other possibility is left for us to be aware of the divine

with the recognition of the divine will (Col 1,9), for whoever has recognized Christ as
the content of the mystery owes him obedience as his Lord" (Lohse, *Col.*, 81, note 111).
This mystery of Christ has to do with the Pauline preaching and with his experiences
of the evangelization (cf. Col 4,2f.; Lohse, *Col.*, 164-65). Compare also Eph 6,19 and
3,1ff. In relation to the mystery, we must pay attention to the fact that the mystery
is hidden from ages and generations but is now manifested to God's saints (see Col 1,
26). According to 1 Cor 2,6ff., God manifested the mystery *to* "us." We should not
underestimate the real sense of "us," any more than in our case of Ephesians 1,9
("God has made known to 'us'"). See Lührmann, D., op. cit., 117.

153 A. Lindemann, *Die Aufhebung*, 92.

154 G. Schrenk, "*eudokeō*" in: *TDNT*, II, 738-51, esp. 746-747.

155 We have examined the verbal tenses of the passages 1,3ff. Here in 1,9, the
author states the divine Act to "us" by the aorist participle (*gnōrisas*) and aorist
middle (*proetheto*). We have interpreted these aorists in the sense of fact that happened in past but at the same time has influence or effect on "us" in the present
situation. See pages 108ff.

156 Lindemann, op. cit., 91f., stresses the presence of the revelation of the divine
will and Eph 1,5, and states: "... Im Epheserbrief ist unsere *huiothesia* dagegen 'vor
aller Zeit' vorwegbestimmt und also zeitlos-'ewige' Realität."

Act and to realize it in our time-spatial-existence.[157] Now "we" have been given the mystery of His will by God Himself. His inner knowledge has been made known. What is it? How do we comprehend it? For what reason was made known the mystery of His will? Before we examine these questions, we must study the following phrase "for (*eis*) the administration of the fullness of times" (*eis oikonomian tou plērōmatos tōn kairōn*: 1,10a).

3-6-2: *Time-dimension of the Unity*

The "perceptively" communicative divine Act, that is, to make known to "us" the mystery of His will, which is celebrated in this hymn by the worshipper(s), is the fulfillment of all epochs.[158] The phrase *eis oikonomian tou plērōmatos tōn kairōn* explains the divine decision which God in Christ had comprehended before all time.[159] God had comprehended Christ for the oikonomia of the fullness of all epochs.[160]

Oikonomia is understood here as "accomplishment," "administration," "execution" in an active sense (verbally: "to lead through," "to carry out," "to accomplish" etc.). The eternal decree of God is therefore to accomplish the "times" fully in the Christ. The plural of "time": *kairoi* means epochs of history, conceived as historical units, almost as living beings. The fulfillment of these "times" is not only a single moment in history. It is this too, but in this moment the author of Eph seeks to describe the effect of the Christ-event which is for him most important, the unifying aspect of this event. Therefore, he does not use *chronos* as Paul does in Gal 4,4. The *kairoi* are "fulfilled" in so far as they are brought into the dimension of God's plenitude, which becomes present and effective in Christ. But this is not yet explained here. The author only states the fact. In communicating to us the knowledge of his (God's) will about

---

[157] Schlier, *Komm.*, 63, says: "...*Protithesthai* meint eine vorzeitliche *prothesis.*" But we *cannot think* timeless being, because we are already living (changing) timely and spacial. Whatever and no matter how we imagine or think or conceive "eternity" or "timeless", it only shows our limitation of manner of life or thought, and only denotes that God is not like our being. We cannot determine or limit God in time and space, as we are limited spacially and temporally. We must see that the "time" and "space" of our manner of being are not negative, however. It is our manner of being which has positive importance for the letter to the Ephesians. See 124ff. ... (body-head).

[158] The "fullness of the times" (*plērōma tōn kairōn*) is not to denote a climax of time like Gal 4,4. There the term *chronos* is used, instead of as in Eph 1,9 *kairos*. Cf. Schlier, *Komm.*, 64, who understands the phrase *plērōma tōn kairōn* as "die göttliche Fülle als Dimension." Cf. also Gnilka, *Komm.*, 79. And compare the similar wording in the Qumran: 1 QS 8,15; 1 QS 9,13-14; 8,4; 9,18.

[159] The notion of time has been discussed by philosophers since antiquity. It always deals with change and movement. We cannot discuss time separately from our mode of being and existence. See G. Delling, *"kairos"* in: *TDNT*, III, 455-62, esp. 461, and *"chronos"* in: *TDNT*, IX, 581-93. Time-space is the double aspect of our reality that shows our dependence. Cf. Gnilka, *Komm.*, 79.

[160] Ibid.

the new reality "in Christ," God accomplishes the fulfillment of the "times." From hence all periods and epochs of time and space, the whole history of mankind, derive their decisive orientation and final determination. We know this only from the revelation of God's will, which became concrete in Jesus Christ.[161] But one must be cautious here not to read into *oikonomia* too much emphasis on *Heilsplan* or some patristic plan of salvation.[162] If we overstress *Heilsplan*, we may limit the time-dimension of the unity (the unifying Act in Christ) "within" the Church or the community to which we belong. We must avoid any "introverted" exegesis of this phrase: the divine administration or its execution is not only for the fullness of the epochs of salvation-history, but also for the fullness of epochs for the cosmic dimension and the world-history of humanity. The *oikonomia* is in the sense of "*Durchführung*" ("execution") in history according to the "plan" of creation, according to the decree of the Creator God.[163]

The phrase *plērōma tōn kairōn* ("the fullness of times") has as its background the idea of consecutive periods of history which are to be crowned and completed by an era surpassing all previous periods. "The belief was expressed that the end-time would fully restore the primeval conditions of paradise. Except by the use of the verb 'to create' for God's first and final action, however, Ephesians shows no interest in developing a recapitulation theory. But history is understood as something different from a haphazard conglomeration of events, from a meaningful cyclical or an ultimately meaningless recurrence of better and worse events. According to this epistle, history makes sense because it moves, or rather, it has already moved, to an apex. That moment is now!"[164] God has executed the fullness of times for his purpose, for his sense, for his principle; in a word, for the unity of the whole in Christ (cf. 1,10bc).[165]

---

[161] J. Reumann, "*Oikonomia*-Terms in Paul in Comparison with Lucan Heilsgeschichte": *NTS* 13 (1966-1967) 147-67, esp. 150, 157 and 162-64. Cf. Gnilka, *Komm.*, 79, note 4; K. M. Fischer, *Tendenz und Absicht des Epheserbriefes* (Göttingen 1973) 117; M. Barth, *Comm.*, 86-88. Schlier, *Komm.*, 64, describes the content of the whole phrase, explaining it in four steps: 1. God made known to us the mystery of His will, he gave us the knowledge of Christ. 2. Thus he accomplishes his eternal decree. 3. In this decree he fixed himself towards Christ, the Christ who was to bring all the times of history into the dimension of God and in this way he "administers" them. 4. The realization of this eternal decision of God takes place now when God is giving us His wisdom, giving us the knowledge of this mystery. Cf. also pages 129ff. where we treat *to plērōma* again.

[162] J. Reumann, art. cit. 164, note 2.

[163] Cf. Eph 1,4; 2,10.14-15. Schlier, *Komm.*, 63ff. As the perspective of horizon of the Pauline insight, see Eph 3,2.9: "... to enlighten all men as to the *oikonomia* of the mystery hidden from generations (*tōn aiōnōn*) in the God (who) creates all (*ta panta*)."

[164] M. Barth, *Comm.*, 128.

[165] The comprehension of unity is the key aspect of the letter: compare the following verses: 1,22f.; 2,1ff.; 2,5-6; 2,14ff.; 3,6; 4,3ff.

Each epoch in human history has been administered and executed for this purpose by the Creator God from his eternity. And he made it known by choosing "us" before the formation of the cosmos (cf. 1,4).

Each epoch, the whole time-dimension, has been administrated by God in view of His goal. Now we who live amidst secularized histories in the 20th century also have the key and the sense of times insofar as we, so-called Christians, conduct our lives in Christ.

3-6-3: *Christ-dimension of the World*

After having explained the permeation of the divine administration for the fulfilment of each epoch, we come to treat the main thesis of the author of Eph:

To unite the whole in the Christ,
the (whole) in the heavens,
and the (whole) on the earth in him.

anakephalaiōsasthai ta panta en tōi Christōi
ta epi tois ouranois
kai ta epi tēs gēs en autōi. (Eph 1,10c).

This is the sense and meaning of each epoch and the content of the divine mystery of His will.[166] God has appointed "times" for this purpose: to unite the whole in the Christ.

Having studied the "hymnic" part (1,3-14) above, we found that the text itself showed this movement towards unity, in regard to the prepositions (*en* and *eis*) and to the relation and the tension [167] between the addresser(s) and the addressees, now in this verse 1,10bc the author of the Ephesians expresses the main synthesis of his theology concerning God's event in Christ by using the image "Head-body."

The verb *anakephalaiomai* occurs only in the following verses in the New Testament: Rom 13,9; Eph 1,10. The verb itself may be derived from *kephalaiōn* (summing up) not from *kephalē* (head).[168] It is rich in allusion and in significance, and is rare in secular Greek and unknown outside literary sources. In accordance with its meaning it signifies "to bring something to a *kephalaiōn*," "to sum up," "to give a comprehensive sum," also "to divide into the main portions". It is hardly distinguishable from *kephaloioun*.[169] The meaning of the verb *anakephalaiōsasthai* in 1,10

---

166 Schlier, *Komm.*, 62, states: " ... Wahrscheinlich ist *kata tēn eudokian autou* bis *tōn kairōn* zu *gnōrisas hēmin* zu ziehen und *anakephalaiōsasthai* als das zu verstehen, was der Wille Gottes will und das sein Geheimnis ist ... Das Ziel aber diese Geheimnisses Willens it: *anakephalaiōsasthai* ...." Cf.: S. Hanson, *The Unity* ..., op. cit., 121; M. Barth, *Comm.*, 89; A. Lindemann, *Die Aufheburg*, 94. Cf. also Eph 3,3-6; 5,32 and Steinmetz, *Heils*, 106f.

167 Cf. H. Weinrich, *Besprochene und erzählte Welt* (Stuttgart 1977³) 33.

168 H. Schlier, *"Anakephalaiomai"* in: *TDNT*, III, 681-82; Gnilka, *Komm.*, 80.

169 H. Schlier, art. cit. Cf. also Liddell & Scott, *Greek-English Lexicon*, ad locum.

must be decided in its context. It relates, without doubt, to the "Head" (*kephalē*) in Eph 1,22; 4,15; 5,23 (cf. Col 1,18; 2,10.19). The audience who listened to the "hymnic" part (1,3-14) at first might not imagine the "Head," but at least they came to hear the following part 1,15ff., especially, 1,22 saying "God gave him (Christ) Head over all for the Church...," they could feel that the author of Eph wanted to express some new insight.[170] The verb *anakephalaiōsasthai* gives rise to a number of significations and images.

The view that the whole cosmos can be compared to the human organ of the body and the view that macrocosmos and microcosmos correspond to each other in their relationships, are attested very early in ancient times.[171] The presentation of the world (*kosmos*) as the Giant-body is to be traced back to ancient cosmological myth or cosmogony. We find similar presentations in different cultural spheres, in the Babylonian cosmogony as in Enuma Eliš,[172] in Egypt,[173] in the Persian "Urmensch" Gayomard,[174] in India,[175] and in China.[176]

In classical Greek literature, Plato conceives of the cosmos as a living being with a soul and pervaded by reason (*Tim* 31b; 32a,c; 39e; passim). "The cosmos as a body is directed by the divine soul which it follows as it is led (*Tim* 47c-48b)."

In the syncretism of late antiquity Iranian concepts were connected with these Greek concepts. As the Pahlave literature illustrates, the supreme God became pregnant and brought forth the entire creation: "And when it had been created, he bore it in his body... he increased and everything became better, and then one by one he created them (everything) out of his own body. First he created the sky out of his

---

[170] Or if they (the Ephesians) were accustomed to the Pauline word *kephalē* in 1 Cor 11 and 1 Cor 12.

[171] E. Lohse, *Col.*, 53.

[172] See K. M. Fischer, op. cit. (N. 161) 69ff.; *ANET*, Akkadian Myths, 67, Tablet IV, (120)-140; 67-8; Tablet, V (Princeton 1969[3]).

[173] *ANET*, 5 (48-55). The theology of Memphis. See also Fischer, op. cit., 70, note 90.

[174] Fischer, op. cit., 69-70.

[175] Ibid., 70.

[176] The *"YiKing"* (The Book of Changes), which is the book of divination, of wisdom, philosophy of the macrocosmos and the microcosmos. It tries to discover the principle (way) of the cosmic divine world which permeates the ethico-political-human world. This document existed in the time of Confucius (551-479 B.C. in the Christian calendar) as a classical document. There, also human organs of body are applied to the macrocosm:

heaven	—	*neck*
earth	—	*belly*
thunder	—	*foot*
wind	—	*crotch*
water	—	*ear*
fire	—	*eye*
mountain	—	*hand*
swamp	—	*mouth*

See W. Honda, *Eki* (Chinese Classic 1; Tokyo 1978) 5ff.

head ... He created the earth from his feet, ... He created water out of his ears ... He created plants out of his hair ... He created fire out of his mind." The cosmos is viewed as the body of the deity and the elements of the universe are viewed as the various parts of that body.

In an Orphic fragment, Zeus is named as the deity who is the "head" (*kephalē*) of the cosmos and is the one who with his power pervades the universe, which rests in the body of the great deity (*Fragment* 168). Other texts similarly describe the heaven as the head of the Pantocrator, the air as his body and the earth as his feet, or again the heavenly world as the head of the All-Deity, the sea as his belly and the earth as his feet.

The Stoic view of nature takes this idea of the body of the All-Deity and conceives of the whole cosmos as being filled by the deity. Men, however, are members of this world-encompassing body which binds all things together. These conceptions also found entrance into Hellenistic Judaism so that Philo of Alexandria speaks of the world of the heavens as a uniform body over which the Logos is set as the head (*Som.* 1,128). The Logos encompasses all things, he fills and defines them to their extremities (*Quest. in Ex.* 2,68). Just as the body of man needs the direction and guidance given by the head (*Spec. Leg.* 3,184), so also the "body" (*sōma*) of the cosmos needs the eternal Logos of the eternal God, which is the head of the universe (*Quest. in Ex.* 2,117) and directs the whole body. As the body is ruled by its head, so the cosmos is subject to the guidance of the divine Logos and thereby is directly under God's care.[177] We can presume that these images of microcosmic application to the macrocosmic organ of the god or the similar divine being were well spread and known in the vulgar forms among the peoples to whom the author of the Ephesians spoke.

"As regards the history of the term *kephalē* in its theological significance, the first important point in secular usage is that it denotes what is first, supreme, or extreme ... But this leads us already to the second aspect, i. e., not merely what is first, or supreme, at the beginning or the end, but also what is 'prominent,' 'outstanding,' or 'determinative.' Thus man's head is not just one member among others ... It is also the first and chief member which determines all the others".[178] Thirdly, *kephalē*, is used in secular speech for the "whole man" the "person." In the *kephalē* we meet the man ... Finally, the *kephalē* is the "man himself" ... It will be seen that in secular usage *kephalē* is not employed for the head of a society. This is first found in the sphere of the Greek Old Testament.[179]

---

177 E. Lohse, *Col.*, 53-54.

178 Philo is reproducing popular ideas when in *Opificio Mundi* 118 he enumerates the seven outward parts of the body, and then says in 118: *"to hegemonikotaton en zōo kephalē."* The point of departure *kephalē* can easily take on the sense of *archē*. See H. Schlier, *"kephalē"* in: *TDNT*, III, 673-81, esp. 673f.

179 H. Schlier, *"kephalē"* in: *TDNT*, III, 673-81, esp. 673-74, and refer to pages 140f. concerning the medical function and meaning of *"kephalē"*.

The LXX adopts the Greek usage. Here, too, in almost exclusive rendering of the Hebrew *r°š*, it denotes the "head" of man or beast. We also find the related sense of "point," "limit," "top," etc. In various expressions a man is often described in terms of his *kephalē*, e.g. *kata kephalēn*. Worth noting is Is 43,4. It is the only verse in which *kephalē* stands for *nfš* "soul"); *kephalē* has here the sense of life. The implied element of what is superior or determinative is expressed in the LXX along with the sense of "man" or "person." *Kephalē* is used for the head or ruler of a society.[180] This use does not contain the further thought that those ruled by the *kephalē* have the relation of a *sōma* ("body") to it. This is particularly clear in Is 1,4ff. (cf. 7,20), where comparison of the people with a human body is implicit in the background. Man's head is mentioned in Test Zeb 9 with reference to the divinely willed unity of Israel.[181]

After having glanced at these meanings of *kephalē* ("head") as its background, let us observe the occurrences of the term in the Pauline letters. We find the word in the following passages: Rom 12,20; 1 Cor 11,3.4.5.7.10.; 12,21; Eph 1,22; 4,15; 5,23; Col 1,18; 2,10.19.

Among these verses of the former Pauline letters, only in 1 Cor 11,3, do we find the statement that the head of every man is the Christ. We will not make an exegesis of 1 Cor 11,3, but we are interested in the procedure or pattern of thought. 1 Cor 11,3 runs thus: "But I want you to understand that

the head of every man (*pantos andros*)	is Christ,
the head of a woman	is man
and the head of Christ	is God."

thelō de hymas eidenai hoti
pantos andros hē kephalē ho Christos estin,
kephalē de gynaikos ho anēr,
kephalē de Christou ho theos.[182]

---

[180] "At Deut 28,1 the antithesis *kephalē/oura* is an obvious starting-point for this sense. To be sure, there is no express reference to Israel as the *kephalē* over others .... But v. 13 in comparison with v. 43f., shows that headship over someone is at issue ...." See Schlier, ibid.

[181] It says: "Do not divide into two heads; for everything which the Lord has made has only one head. He has given two shoulders, hands and feet, but all the members obey one head". Schlier, in the art. cit., 675f., but this comparison does not go beyond the Septuagint.

[182] Cf. H. Conzelmann, *Der erste Brief an die Korinther* (Göttingen 1969) 215-16. Hellenistic Judaism developed, in accordance with Greek philosophy (Platonism and Stoa), "typus/antitypus"-way of thinking (cf. v. 7). God is the archetype of the cosmos and of humanity. Conzelmann states: "Dieser Gedanke wird von Paulus nun in den Dienst der Christologie gestellt. Die Verwandschaft mit der alexandrinischen Schultradition (Sapientia, Philo) ist deutlich. Eine Besonderheit der Schule, aus der Paulus kommt, scheint eikon-Begriffs, den Paulus auch kennt (v. 7), das Wort *Kephalē* gebraucht wird." "...Der Satz, Gott sei das Haupt Christi, enthält die Gedanken:
  a) Subordination Christi,
  b) Präexistenz Christi,

The similar pattern, God — the Head of Christ, Christ — the head of every man, men — the head of women, is found in Eph 5,23 in a different context: "For the husband (man) is the head of the wife (woman) as Christ is the head of the Church, his body, and is himself its saviour."

If the audience of Ephesians were accustomed to the Pauline image in 1 Cor 11,3, and if they were familiar with the Goddess or God who was the head or ruler of their city, they could possibly understand the rich allusion of the image "head" and they could feel the new insight of the author of Eph. Take for instance, in the case of the city Ephesus, the Goddess Artemis (Diana) was the symbol of the unity of the city and the symbol of the ruling role of the Goddess over the citizens. We may, perhaps, be allowed to suppose in the following manner: She is a woman. Christ is a man. According to the Pauline scheme, "man is the head of woman." The combination of the image "head" with the role and function of Artemis-Woman-Goddess really includes a strong insistence on the conviction of their faith about the role of Christ. They understood what the author wanted to communicate to them by using the image "Head-Body." And there were many allusions to a very rich and wider understanding. Now Christ is the head of Artemis who represented her community and her unity. More than this, Christ is the head of the Church, of the city, and of the whole cosmos. Therefore, our Christian unity at first is not *pro patria*, but *pro cosmo, pro Deo*, who acts in Christ.

Another passage where we find the term *kephalē* in the main Pauline letters is 1 Cor 12,21. There "head" is mentioned as one part of the whole body, and it does not have a theological meaning as the single term "head." It is mentioned in the allegorial image of the human organ (body) to explain the unity in plurality in the Corinthian church. What we must pay attention to there is Paul's explanation of unity in terms of the plurality of the church. The theme "unity" is also a very important aspect of our letter to Eph. In 1 Corinthian, however, Paul does not say that Christ is the head of the Church. He states that Christ Jesus is the Lord (*kyrios*).[183]

In addition to being familiar with the image *kephalē* (cf. the verb *anakephalaiōsasthai* of 1,10 and later passages such as Eph 1,22f.), the readers may well have been familiar with an image taken from building. The *kephalē-goniaios* ("cornerstone") together with the similar one *akrogōnias* ("cornerstone" or "capstone") of 2,20 shows the tradition of interpretation on Ps 118,22 in the primitive Christian tradition.[184]

Der Sinn dieses Gedankens ist 8,6 dargelegt." (See page 216). S. Bedale, "The Meaning of *kephalē* in the Pauline Epistles": *JThS* 5 (1954) 211ff.

[183] Compare 1 Cor 8,6: "*all' hēmin heis theos ho patēr, ex hou ta panta kai hēmeis eis auton, kai heis kyrios 'Iēsous Christos, di' hou ta panta kai hēmeis di' autou*" with Eph 4,5.

[184] Cf. Act 4,11; 1 Pet 2,7; Mt 21,42; Mk 12,10; Lk 20,17. Cf. Gnilka, *Komm.*, 156ff.

To conclude consideration of the image "head": the author of Eph presumes that the hearers or the readers had a cultural consensus about the application of the microcosmic organ of human body to the macrocosmic deity as their groundsoil where the author wanted to sow his new comprehension and its expression of the fact of Christ in his community (God's event in Christ). His greatness might be the combination of the image, "Head-body", which is rich in allusions, with the Greek rhetorically nuanced word *anakephalaiōn* ("to sum up").[185] The readers should *view* the two different spheres of allusions and significations, *neither analytically nor separately, but simultaneously at one glance*.[186] Then, they could feel the synthetical standpoint of the writer and the core of his experience, even though they could not comprehend it fully.

In this verse 1,10, the author still does not use the image "head-body," which will clearly appear in 1,22. But the verb *anakephalaiōsasthai* is enough to allude to the cosmic and Christo-Ecclesiological dimension of the signification of Christ for the addressees. After having stated the possible allusions of the image, we must now determine the meaning of the verb *anakephalaiōsasthai* of Eph 1,10. The verb has been translated and interpreted so richly that we cannot define its meaning by any one term in a modern language, as H. Schlier, mentioned in his note.[187]

As known from later passages of our letter, the verb means "to give the head" which is put over the whole, under which the whole is united and is set up.[188] In this sense, we translate the verb "to unite" in an abbreviated form. It is intended to have the sense of the integration of the whole into the One. This "oneness" will be developed and explained in the following passages (1,20ff.), by using the image "head-body"-relation (the body in relation to the head). From chaos to harmony or order, from divisions to unity, from parts to the whole constitute the fundamental drive and movement of this letter.[189]

---

[185] Cf. A. Lindemann, *Die Aufhebung*, 96, note 50.

[186] Cf. H. Weinrich, *Sprache im Texten* (Stuttgart 1976) 283.

[187] Schlier, *Komm.*, 64, note 3.

[188] Schlier, *Komm.*, 65. M. Barth, *Comm.*, 89ff. and on page 91 he says: "... If Col 1,20 is the key to Eph 1,10 then the combination of the two meanings of the Greek verb *anakephalaioō*, which has already been discussed, i.e., 'to unite' and 'to restore,' is the best solution. The meaning of the ambiguous Greek verb is to be derived exclusively from the context of Eph 1,10, and is 'to make (Christ) the head ...'" Lindemann, *Die Aufhebung*, 96, states: "... *anakephalaiōsasthai* bedeutet einfach 'zusammenfasse, summieren.'" Cf. J. Ernst, *Komm.*, 277.

[189] See the previous pages 104ff. and 108ff., etc. In addition to this we mentioned the verb *anakephalaiōsasthai*, the whole or the cosmos itself has its order and its unity. The question is mankind which inhabits the cosmos. Because of their sins (cf. Eph 1,7; 2,1ff. etc.), humans lost the unity and the order (harmony) which God determined before creation. But the unity which existed before creation of the universe is now at hand for "us the community," especially, for "us" this community of the Eph. The prefix *ana-* alludes to a human world which once was divided and now is restored and re-united by the decisive event of Christ. Cf. Lindemann, *Die Aufhebung*, 97; M. Barth, *Comm.*, 90f.

Let us continue with an explanation of the next words *ta panta* ... ("the whole ..."). The world-view of the author of Ephesians is surely different from ours which places us in the space-technological time. And the author did not simply receive his cosmic view from the Old Testament. The Old Testament view divides the cosmos into the three parts: heaven, earth, underworld (*hades*).[190] A trace of this view is in our verses 1,10 and 4,9. Nevertheless, the author's view is near to the Greek one as well. The world view of the ancient Greek was transformed and moderated by the view of the Old Testament. The *ta panta* ("the whole") of the ancient Greek is divided into three spaces: the world of gods, the Empyreum which vaults over the living space of humanity, and the earth, which man thought of as a disk. *Hades* is deemed to be under the earth, the locality of demons and the dead. Gods and men live near to each other. The earth is open to the heavens.

The notion of the *ta panta* in Eph 1,10 includes heavenly and earthly beings, all beings, angels, demons, mankind.[191] It means the wholeness of the creatures on the earth and in the heavens.[192] We should not limit the meaning of the *ta panta* ("the whole") of 1,10 to the powers and the heavenly beings and the church. The author of Eph surely has a wider view of the divine Act in Christ. It is the cosmic unifying event. This attaches to all creatures.[193]

Those who interpret this passage as an event *"within"-churches* of Christians should open their eyes to the positive values of so-called non-Christian-peoples in the world.[194] The Act in Christ is not limited to the conventional Christian churches. It is a late historical fact that our Christian churches are divided. A "divided" church is itself in contradiction to the nature of the Church and an "impossible possibility." [195] We Christians should recognize how much harm these divisions do and how they poison evangelization.

If we look at the recent history of the world, especially the relations of the so-called Christian countries with non-Christian ones, and the attitude of the church to the so-called mission countries, we will be ashamed of ourselves. The hindrance to persons entering the church comes from us, from our "communal" cultural arrogance. Divisions can be the sign

---

[190] Gnilka, *Komm.*, 63f. L. I. J. Stadelmann, *The Hebrew Conception of the World*, (AnBib 39; Rome 1970), see esp. 177ff.

[191] F. Mussner, *Christus Das All und die kirche* (Trier 1955) 66. Gnilka, *Komm.*, 64f.

[192] Ibid., 65.

[193] Ibid., 81.

[194] Caragounis, op. cit., 144, states: "... *Ta panta* shall be reconstituted afresh in Christ and the relation is envisaged as one in which Christ is Lord or Head, i.e. they are subjected to Him. From this thematic presentation the author proceeds to treat the *anakephalaiōsis* in more detail by concentrating on the two chief representatives of 'things in heaven' and 'things on earth,' i.e. the powers and the Church." See M. Barth, *Comm.*, 91, and Schlier, *Komm.*, 65.

[195] Cf. Fischer, op. cit. (N. 172), 78.

of existing sins. The author of Eph, however, does not see divisions negatively. He declared the unity of the two groups who had hated each other (see 1,3ff.; 2,14ff.). The fact of the unity of both groups is the victory of God in Christ and the starting point of peace for the world. It is not sins that distinguish non-Christians from Christians. Both are equal, as groups and as individuals, before God. The difference is that those who conduct their lives in Christ, being aware of the equality of their sinfulness, motivate themselves to move toward unity.

The central point of the unity of the whole is not the cosmos as such or the world as such, which is considered objectively and separately from the human world and societies.[196] It is the human world which God at first aims to unite. But the unity as a result of the Divine dynamism at work in the community of Ephesians (especially, in 1,10), is not limited to a certain community of believers in Christ. It is the cosmic dynamism of God for unification. Therefore, God has made known to us the mystery of His will to unite the whole in the heavens and the whole on the earth in Christ.

3-7: Christ is Our Head

3-7-1: *Ecclesiological Dimension of God's Act in Christ for Unification (God's Act to Provide Head for the Church)*

The author of Eph explicitly uses the image of "Head-Body" in 1,22f: "and he (God) has put all things under his feet and has made him the head over all things for the church, which is his body, the fullness which fills the whole in every way" (*kai panta hypetaxen hypo tous podas autou, kai auton edōken kephalēn hyper panta tēi ekklesiai, hētis estin to sōma autou, to plērōma tou ta panta en pasin plēroumenou*).

In these verses, the act of God in Christ to unite all creatures (cf. 1,10), the dynamism of the unification, is said to have been realized (somatized) within a human relationship in the community of the Ephesians.

The term "body" (*sōma*) is meant to denote a group of people who realize in themselves the dynamism at work in the "cosmic" dimension, and those who intensify their relation to each other according to that dynamism. At this stage of our study, we may explain a possible meaning of the image "Head-Body" which resumes and synthesizes the Divine Act in Christ. We focus particularly on an aspect of the relation and the dynamism between "the Head and its Body." The relation and its dynamism are internally connected with our inner dynamism of comprehending the mystery of the Divine will which unites the whole (cf. 1,8b-10; 1,17ff. esp. v. 18; 3,16ff.).[197]

---

[196] Cf. F. Zeilinger, *Der Erstgeborne der Schöpfung* (Wien 1974), 198f., note 52.
[197] Cf. pp. 112ff., 136. We will treat there the two texts (1,17ff. and 3,16ff.).

We cannot understand fully the significance of the image which the author of Eph wanted to transmit to us, because our way of thinking is always analytical and dualistic.[198] If we try to comprehend it, it escapes us as water leaks through our hands when we try to scoop it up. Only partially do we glimpse a result of the Divine dynamism which once formed the community and worked in the community.

While "God" is actually the grammatical and real subject of the statements in 1,3-14 and the "Giver" of a spirit of wisdom and revelation for comprehension (1,17ff.), and while the receivers of the Gift of God or of the Divine Act are the "we" and the "you"-peoples,[199] in verse 1,23 the church is suddenly the subject. And for the first time in vv. 1,22-23, the noun "church" (ekklēsia) replaces the pronoun "we" (or "us").[200] And this church is stated to be the body of Christ (hētis estin to sōma autou: "which is his body," v. 23a).

The usage and meaning of sōma ("body") in the former Pauline letters is pregnantly rich in its signification and many authors have studied it. By the sōma ("body") in Ephesians,[201] even if it alludes to the application of human organs to the cosmos or cosmic deity, the author of Eph tried to explain the concrete and historical community of Ephesians within the framework of the wholeness of the church.[202] The church in our letter, even though she widens her horizon towards the cosmic dimension or the "universal"[203] church, is an historical entity and a concrete

---

1. "Organic" unity with "saints": somatic consciousness of the unity with the saints (including Paul and his disciples and collaborators). 2. The comprehension of "dynamis" or "energeia."

[198] It was their experience and was a practical knowledge for the unity. A Greek dualistic attitude toward the reality or way of thinking does not fit into the religious experience of the community of Ephesians, even though it is universally attested as a human way of cognition. See the following counter-positioned or dualistic way of cognition: "eidolon—sōma", soul—body, immortal soul—mortal body, atom of soul—body, nous—body, forma—materia ... etc. Cf. E. Schweizer, "sōma" in: TDNT, VII, 1025-44. When we talk about unity, unity must permeate our way of thinking as well. The division between thought and somatic deed or conduct still has a long way to go to reach to a total unity in man and in a community. In this "division" of the mind of man and his act, there is always a danger of a "gnostic" tendency. We are inclined to interpret the image (Head-Body) neither in a "mystic" way which draws a picture in the heavens, nor literally, nor in a materialized conception of the image. Cf. R. Gundry, Sōma in Biblical Theology (Cambridge 1976) 223f.

[199] See the analysis of pronouns ... pages 104ff.

[200] Cf. M. Barth, Comm., 153.

[201] The term sōma occurs in the following verses: 1,23; 2,16; 4,4.12.16; 5,23.28.30. Also cf. Col 1,18.22.24; 2,11.17.19.23; 3,15.

[202] Cf. K. L. Schmidt, "kaleō", in: TDNT, III, 487-536. esp. 509-13. He denies the figurative sense of the image (see page 509) and understands that Christ himself is the Church and his body, and he is the head and the whole body which includes the head (see page 510). Ekklēsia has a wider field of allusions in Greek and Hebrew. In Eph., the word-field of kaleō (klēsis, ekkalesis) which corresponds to the divine vocation (calling the community of the Eph) of the dynamism. See kaleō, klēsis: Eph 4,1.4; Col 3,15; Eph 1,18. Cf. Schlier, Komm., 90; Lohse, Col., 55.

[203] A sense of "universal" should be understood as totality of believers in Christ. It is not a speculative ideal.

community.[204] The church is explained in a metaphor by using the image
sōma ("body"). We will take the image figuratively, by which the author
of Eph sought to transmit to hearers the awareness and realization
(somatisation) of the actual experience of his community. Still accessible
to us today is an awareness of the mystery and an approach to its
realization in our whole conduct of life, in our whole somatic life as man
in our totality because we believe that the same dynamism which once
was at work within the community of Ephesians is also now at work
within us according to our faith in Christ. The "body" (*sōma*) of our
letter is an image for a principle of unification, neither for division of
body (understood as "materia") and "soul" ("forma"), nor for a disunifying
principle for thinking or reflecting *ego* and objectified-*ego*. Because the
image of the body for the church denotes a concreteness in a way of
being, namely, a time-special-way of being. Apart from our human history, the church (body) of Ephesians could not exist. We should not
allow the body to be interpreted by any form of dualism or idealism.
We repeat that the body is an image of unification and it is not a counter-
object of *nous* or "spirit."

The expression *to sōma tou Christou* ("the Body of Christ") in the
former Pauline letters occurs in Rom 7,4; 1 Cor 10,16; 11,24; (11,27); 11,29.
In our letter to Eph, this expression occurs in 4,12, and "his body" (*to
sōma autou*: presumably, "the body of Christ") is mentioned in 1,23a and
in 5,30.[205] Fischer gives three main classifications of the expression "the
body of Christ": the body of the Crucified, the body of Christ in the context of the Lord's supper, and the body of Christ in the sense of the
Church.[206] Ephesians, however, never mentions the body of the Crucified
nor the body of Christ in the context of the Lord's supper. The body
of Christ or "his body" (*to sōma autou*) in Ephesians turns round the
image "Head-Body."

To begin with, we must say that in Ephesians the term "the body
of Christ" is related to the solidarity and unity of members of the community (i.e. social dimension).

1 Cor 10,17; 12,12-27 (cf. 1 Cor 1,13) and Rom 12,4f. indicate a similar
meaning and teach a unity in diversity and a complementary function [207]
of pluralistic members of one body (i.e. a community). Traditional Stoic
or Egyptian thought used *sōma* to indicate a group of people with gods,
a city, a social and political society which are in parallel applied to the
cosmos.[208]

---

[204] R. H. Gundry, Sōma *in Biblical Theology with Emphasis on Pauline Anthropology*
(Cambridge 1976) 223.

[205] B. M. Metzger, *A Textual Commentary*, 609. With him we will take the shorter
reading "... *tou sōmatos autou*".

[206] K. M. Fischer, *Tendenz und Absicht*, 48ff.

[207] Cf. Rom 12,4 and Maurer, C., *"praxis"* in: *TDNT*, VI, 642-44, esp. 643f.

[208] E. Schweizer, *"sōma"* in: *TDNT*, VII, 1034ff. Gnilka, *Komm.*, 99-100. M. Barth,
Comm. 194.

A similar line of thought and usage for the social human dimension and unity is seen explicitly also in Eph 4,25 and in 5,30: "... let every one speak the truth with his neighbour for we are members one of another" (4,25), "... because we are members of his body (Christ's body)" (5,30).

The metaphor of 1 Cor 12 mentions "head" (*kephalē*), but it is as one part of the whole body. And Rom 12,4f. does not speak about "head," but states that all we members in Christ are one body. "For as in one body we have many members, and all the members do not have the same function, so we, though many, are one body in Christ, and individually members one of another." There is no passage in the former Pauline letters which makes use of the image "head-body"-relation, like that of Eph 1,22f. "God has made (*edōken*) him (Christ) the head over all things for the church, which is his body ..."

The image which is applied to the church is a characteristic feature of Ephesians (also Colossians: Col 1,18; 2,19).[209] So, the application of the image to the church (i.e. the community/communities) cannot be explained only by the possible and pregnant usages of the former Pauline letters.[210]

In order to understand the Divine Act in Christ (i.e. the divine dynamism in Christ) in relation to the community (i.e. that is expressed by the image "head-body"), the linking relative clause of 1,20 is one of importance: "*which* (energeia: "*energy*") (God) *worked* (enērgēsen) *in the Christ* raising him from the dead and making (him) sit at His right hand in the heavenly places" (*hēn enērgēsen en tōi Christōi egeiras auton ek nekrōn, kai kathisas en dexiai autou en tois epouraniois*).

Especially, the characteristic repetition of cognate words, the *tēn energeian* (the energy) of 1,19 and the verb *enērgēsen* ("worked") in 1,20,[211] make a bridge between the energy at work in the Christ and the one at work within "us." Both words really show the same divine dynamism and power at work for "us" believers (1,19b).[212] In verses 20-22, as we noticed above,[213] we find two pairs of verbs: the first consisting of two aorist participles, *egeiras* ("rising") and *kathisas* ("making sit") in 1,20 and the second containing two aorist finite verbs, *hypetaxen* ("has put ... [under]") and *edōken* ("[he] gave") in ,22. These pairs of the verbs describe what God worked in Chist.[214]

In the first pair in 1,20, the author of Eph confesses faith in the

---

[209] C. Colpe, "Zur Leib-Christi-Vorstellung im Epheserbrief," in: *BZNW* 26 (Festschrift für J. Jeremias; Berlin 1964²), 172-87, esp. 174. He gives the bibliography about the *sōma* of Christ since 1930 up till 1960 and a short summary of the interpretation of various authors. Cf. Lohse, *Col.*, 55.

[210] Cf. Schlier, *Komm.*, 90.

[211] See page 77 and n. 18.

[212] Compare 1,11; 3,7; 3,20.

[213] See page 77, n. 18.

[214] M. Barth, *Comm.*, 153.

resurrection of Jesus Christ from the dead (*egeiras auton ek nekrōn*) and faith in the enthronement of Jesus Christ at the right hand of God (*kathisas en dexia̧ autou ...*) in 1,20b, and he comprises them in one "dynamis" or energy of God which he caused to happen in Christ (1,20a).

The power-word-group (*dynamis, energeia, ischus*, etc.), of which it is difficult to draw a picture in our minds, resumes and synthesizes the traditional manner of expressing the divinely unique event which was believed to have happened in Jesus Christ.[215] Verse 1,20 is followed by statements which show the absolute transcendence of the Divine Act over any powers (1,21a) and over all time (1,21b). The God Act is demonstrated as a unique power over all. The power itself is described in similar words (*megethos, dynamis, energeia, kratos, ischus*) in 1,19 as one of the content of the gift of awareness. And verse 1,21, using the phrase *en tois epouraniois* ("in the heavenly places"), which denotes not only spatial but also ruling power-milieu or sphere,"[216] states the absolute transcendence of Christ Jesus over all powers, above every name which is named, in every time-spatial dimension (not only this *aiōn* but also the *aiōn* to come).

In 1,21, the author of Eph resumes the previous two acts of God (the two aorists to denote the resurrection and the enthronement) and adds a sense of their transcendence; then, in verse 22, he presents another pair of divine acts, namely, the subjection of all powers and the gift of the "Head" over all powers for the church. Verse 1,22 which looks like a quotation of Ps 8,6 (verse 20 has as parallel a similar allusion to Ps 110,1), stresses again the divine act of the transcendence of Jesus Christ and the subjection of the powers under his feet.[217]

Christ is the Head who transcends all powers and rulers and even the time-space dimension, and such a Head is given for the Church. This rulership of Christ is contained in the image "head." The Act of God towards the Church is characterized by the simple verb *edōken* ("[he] gave").[218]

So, Christ's rulership over the cosmic power is given to the Church. We should not underestimate the meaning of *edōken* ("gave") of 1,22b which is stated in parallel with the verb *hypetaxen* ("subdued", "put under") of 1,22a. Christ is never said to be ruler over the Church, but to have been given to the Church. Christ, the head of the body, is really the gift of God. The author of Eph never states that God appointed

---

[215] Ibid.

[216] See pages 97ff.

[217] It is a traditional interpretation of the Christ-event by using Ps 110,1 and Ps 8,6. Cf. 1 Cor 15,25.27. Gnilka, *Komm.*, 94f. D. M. Hay, *Glory at the Right Hand: Psalm 110 in Early Christianity* (Nashville-New York 1973), esp. 63f.

[218] M. Barth, *Comm.*, 157-58, translates the verb *edōken* by "appointed," presuming the sense of the Hebrew word, "to give." But Gnilka, *Komm.*, 97, states: "... Das Geben ist nicht hebräisch empfunden. Dann wäre seine Einsetzung gemeint. Es ist griechisch konzipiert ...."

Christ to be the head or *the ruler over the Church, but Christ* the Head who is the ruler over all powers is given for the Church.[219]

The Head is not meant to imply a ruler for the Church, but the Church is *his body*, and even *his own body*. The Church belongs to Him while she is subject to Him, and Christ loves her and dedicates himself to her (cf. Eph 5,24-25). This Act of God giving the Head for the Church is the source of dynamism for the unification and the integration.[220]

The next phrase of 1,23 *hētis estin to sōma autou to plērōma tou ta panta en pasin plēroumenou* ("which is his [its] body, the fullness of him [or "of it"] who [or "which"] fills himself [or "itself"] [or "is filled"] the whole in all [or "completely"]"), causes discussion of the Church according to the author of Eph, and it is vital for the present denominational christian churches.[221]

Primarily, the difficulties in interpreting the phrase come from the ambivalences of the words: *to plērōma, tou plēroumenou, ta panta, en pasin*. What does the *plērōma* mean? Is it a description of Christ, or of the body (i.e. the Church)? Does the *to plērōma* have active or passive sense? "Filled" or "filling"? Does the participle *plēroumenou* have passive or active sense? Who fills whom? Who will be filled by whom? How can we understand the *ta panta en pasin*? Is the *ta panta* the object of the participle? or merely adverbial sense? Then, the *en pasin* ("in all") means what? Does it denote church-members or cosmic powers?

As a first step, we want to take the phrase *to plērōma tou ... plēroumenou* in apposition to the previous words *to sōma autou* ("his [the] body"), namely, the Head's body. Grammatically, the words in apposition, *to sōma autou — to plērōma tou ...* sound quite similar. And they have the same gender (neutral) and same structure as substantives with genitive constructions. Some authors take the phrase *to plērōma ...* in apposition to the 12th word earlier *auton* ("him") namely Christ, then implicitly the *tēn kephalēn* ("the head") in 1,22. But it seems to us that this interpretation is rather unnatural and awkward, if we consider the style of Ephesians.

The author of Eph likes an agglutinative form of sentence or line of thought. We find other sentences of similar appositional style in our

---

[219] Gnilka, ibid.

[220] The positive use of the verb *didonai* ("to give") in Ephesians is to denote primarily an Act of God: God gives comprehension and enlightenment (1,17), the Pauline gift for the integration of the Gentiles to the community and his insight (3,2. 7.8; 6,19), and God gives the somatic comprehension of the unity with His power (cf. 3,16ff.), and as the realisation of the divine Act in Christ, Christ gives the somatic roles in the community for each of the members to build the whole body (4,7.8.11).

[221] We quote only: F. R. M. Hitchcock, "The Pleroma as the Medium of the Self-realisation of Christ": *Exp* 48 (1922) 135-50; idem, "The Pleroma of Christ": *ChQ* 125 (1937-1938) 1-18; J. Gewiess, "Die Begriffe *plēroun* und *plērōma* im Kolosser- und Epheserbriefe": *Vom Wort des Lebens* (Festschrift für M. Meinertz; Münster/Westf. 1950) 128-41; C. F. D. Moule, "'Fulness' and 'Fill' in the New Testament": *SJTh* 4 (1951) 79ff.; J. A. T. Robinson, *The Body* (1952) 67-69; F. Mussner, *Christus Das All* (Trier

letter.[222] Those who interpret the *to plērōma* in apposition to *auton* ("him"), make the relative clause *hētis estin to sōma autou* ("which is his body") separate from the following phrase *to plērōma tou ta panta...*, and tend to put the relative clause *hētis estin to sōma autou*, into brackets.[223] By doing so, they underrate it. But the very phrase *hētis estin to sōma autou* ("which is his body") is an aspect of essential importance to the author.[224] Up to this point (from 1,1 to 1,23), there is no description of Christ Himself or the Head itself. The author's (of Eph) main concern is not the description of *kephalē* or "Christ," but the Act of God in Christ, as we have explained when we treated the *en-Christōi*-formula.[225] He explains the Act by using the image "Head-Body"-relation to describe the fact of the community and the character of the community which was formed as a result of the Act of God in Christ.

The church and the community are the main aspect, and the *anake-*

1955) 46ff.; S. F. B. Bedale, "The Theology of the Church," in: *Studies in Ephesians* (1956) 64-75; A. Feuillet, "L'Eglise plēromē du Christ d'après Eph 1,23": *NRTh* 78 (1956) 449-472; 593-610; S. Virgulin, "L'Origine del Concetto di pleroma in Ef 1,23," in: *AnBib* 17-18, vol. (1961) 39-43; R. Fowler, "Ephesians 1,23": *Exp* 76 (1965) 294; A. R. McGlashan, "Ephesians 1,23": *Exp* 76 (1965), 132-33; A. Feuillet, *Le Christ sagesse de Dieu* (Paris 1966) 277-92; R. Yates, "A Re-Evamination of Ephesians 1,23": *Exp* 83 (1972) 146-51; J. Ernst, *Pleroma und Pleroma Christi. Geschichte und Deutung eines Begriffs der paulinischen Antilegomena*, (BU 5; Regensburg 1970) 105ff.; A. Lindemann, *Die Aufhebung*, 213f.; I. de la Potterie, "Le Christ, Plerome de l'Eglise" (Ep 1,22-23): *Bib* 58 (1977) 500-24. See above 75ff.

[222] E.g.
1,13: "... TON LOGON TĒS ALĒTHEIAS, TO EUAGGELION ..."
("... the word of the truth, the gospel ...")
1,14: "... *ho* (or "*hos*") *estin* ARRABŌN *tēs klēronomias* ..."
("... which (or "who") is t h e g u a r a n t e o f t h e ...")
1,17: "... HO THEOS ..., HO PATĒR TĒS ..."
("... t h e G o d ..., t h e f a t h e r o f ...")
1,17-18: "... *dōēi hymin* PNEUMA ... *pephōtismenous tous* OPHTHALMOUS ..."
("... may give you s p i r i t ... the e n l i g h t e n e d e y e s")
2,2: "... KATA TON AIŌNA TOU KOSMOU TOUTOU, KATA TON ARCHONTA TĒS EXOUSIAS TOU TOU AEROS, *tou pneumatos tou nun* ..."
("... a c c o r d i n g t o t h e a e o n o f t h i s w o r l d, a c c o r d i n g t o t h e p r i n c i p a l i t y o f ...")
2,14-15: "... TĒN ECHTHRAN ... TON NOMON ..."
("... the enmity ..... the law ...")
5,23: "... *kai* HO CHRISTOS KEPHALĒ TĒS EKKLĒSIAS, AUTOS SŌTĒR TOU SŌMATOS"
("... a n d t h e C h r i s t h e a d o f t h e C h u r c h, he (is) s a v i o u r o f t h e b o d y")
6,17: "... *tēn machairan* TOU PNEUMATOS, *ho estin* RĒMA THEOU"
("... the sword o f t h e s p i r i t, which is w o r d o f G o d")
Cf. also W. Bujard, *Stilanalytische*, op. cit., 150f.
[223] A. R. McGlashan, "Ephesians 1,23": *Exp* 76 (1965), art. cit., 132; I. de la Potterie, art. cit., 513ff.; Cf. C. F. D. Moule, art. cit., *SJTh* 4 (1951) 81; V. C. Colpe, " Zur Leib-Christi-Vorstellung im Epheserbrief", in: *BZNW* 26 (1960) 177, note 7; R. Fowler, "Ephesians 1,23", art. cit., [n. 221] 294; G. Delling, "*plērēs*", "*plērōma*", etc. in: *TDNT*, VI, 283-311, esp. 304; R. A. Yates, art. cit. [n. 221], 147f. esp. 151; Gnilka, *Komm.*, 98, and see the excursus 3 in pages 99ff.; Lindemann, *Die Aufhebung*, 214; Cf. Schlier, *Komm.* 96ff.; F. Mussner, *Das All*, 46ff., esp. 59f.; J. Ernst, *Phērōma*, 107f.
[224] See above, pages 117ff.
[225] See above, pages 91ff.

phalaiōsis (cf. 1,10) is his primarily theological thesis that helps the new Christians to comprehend the mystery of the Divine will and to be ready to serve to build up the body of Christ (cf. 4,10ff.), which is essentially a *"missioning"* community (cf. 3,1ff.).[226]

J. Ernst, in his monograph,[227] classifies the interpretation of Eph 1,23 in three groups in spite of variations and differences even within the groups.

The first group understands *to plērōma* in an active sense as "completion" (*Ergänzung*). And under this aspect, the participle (*plēroumenou*: genitive masculine or neuter) is taken in a passive sense, namely, "being filled" (i.e. *erfüllt sein*), or in middle voice (i.e. "fills himself" or "itself") (i.e. *erfüllt sich*).[228] Then the description of the Church is: the Church is the completion of him who is filled or fills himself. In this case, the participle *tou plēroumenou* means that Christ is filled (by God or the divinity etc...), and the agent of the participle is not Christ, but God. One of the weak points of this line of interpretation is the danger that Christ could be understood as if he were incomplete and awaited "completion" by the church. In fact, this can be interpreted theologically in good agreement with the exegesis of the church Fathers. Some authors quote Col 1,24 in support of this interpretation, where it is said that the "tribulations" of Christ are "fulfilled" by the sufferings of the apostle for the church who is His Body.[229] In this line of interpretation the expression *ta panta en pasin* is normally understood in an adverbial sense: "perfectly" or "completely." According to this line of interpretation, therefore, the Church is his body (Christ's body), the completion of him who is filled (by God, or by grace, or by wisdom)[230] completely, or who fills himself completely.

The second group takes *to plērōma* in a passive sense and the participle in the middle voice in a transitive sense. Then, *to plērōma* means the

---

[226] Eph 3,1ff. Cf. W.-H. Ollrog, *Paulus und seine Mitarbeiter* (Neukirchen-Vluyn 1979) 119ff.; R. P. Meyer, *Kirche und Mission im Epheserbrief* (Stud. Bibl. Stuttgart 86; Stuttgart 1977) 62, says: "...weil Christus mittels der Kirche seine Relation zum All konkretiziert."

[227] J. Ernst, *Plērōma* ..., op. cit. [n. 221], 105ff.

[228] F. R. M. Hitchcock, "The Pleroma as the Medium," art. cit. [n. 221], 146f.; J. Ernst, op. cit., 111, note 3. The passive sense is supported by the church Fathers and by the use of the word in the New Testament.

[229] J. Ernst, op. cit., 108f. discusses the theological proposals of the Fathers. H. J. Holtzmann again introduces Col 1,24 into considerations about Eph 1,23; cf. Ernst, op. cit., 109f. According to Col 2,9 the plenitude of the divinity is dwelling "bodily" in Christ. The meaning becomes clear when we think of the polemical direction of this phrase. It means that the Powers and Might of the world do not possess the plenitude. For the readers of Col it is important that they become "Filled-Ones" in Christ, who is the head over all powers and authorities (Col 2,10). See also our discussions of the verse pages 133f.

[229] Feuillet, *Sagesse*, op. cit., 267f., 318.

[230] J. Ernst, op. cit., 112 and notes 1-2. Cf. Schlier, *Komm.*, 99; F. Mussner, op. cit. [n. 221], 67.

"plenitude" (*Fülle*) with the implication of being filled by Christ or by God. The Church is, therefore, the plenitude of him who fills the whole. According to this understanding the Church is not the completion of Christ (*die Ergänzung des Christus*), but Christ Himself fills the Church with the divine grace and gift.[231] In this case, most exegetes understand the participle as middle voice with active sense. Then, *ta panta* denotes the wholeness of the world or all things (i.e. as the object of the participle) and the *en pasin* is meant to be instrumental in a modal sense (i.e. "with all" or "in every way"). On this point there are many variations,[232] for instance the phrase *en pasin,* understood by some authors [233] in the sense of all the members of the church, and the *ta panta* denoting the church. Consequently the sentence would bear some such meaning as: Christ fills the church in all its members with all graces and wisdom.

This interpretation, however, misses the "cosmic" horizon and wider dimension of the Christ-event, and is in danger of missing the fundamental feature of the community of Ephesians, the out-growing dynamism, the missionary dynamism of the church, of the body of Christ.[234] Today there is also the danger of an interpreter understanding such a phrase in a too narrow sense. Especially if he is thinking only of his own group or his "church".[235]

The same restriction takes place if *ta panta* are interpreted only in the sense of the "Powers and Might" which are interpreted in vv. 21-22 as a meaning of *panta,* and the *en pasin* does not refer to personal objects but is a description of the all-embracing rule of Christ.[236] This line of interpretation also tends *to limit* the Event of God in Christ *within* the mythically described spheres of powers, so that they miss the cosmic and world-wide Event of God in Christ, which we found in so many other verses of Eph up to now. The church or the Pauline communities should exist and did exist for the sake of service for others, not for herself nor for their own sakes.[237]

Here, we should like to point out that verse 1,23 is better explained in the context of the whole passage. It would seem to describe the func-

---

[231] See Ernst, op. cit. 112, note 4. Cf. A. Lindemann, *Die Aufhebung,* 214f.

[232] Ernst, op. cit., 112.

[233] A. Wikenhauser, *Die Kirche als der mystische Leib Christi nach dem Apostel Paulus* (Münster 1940[2]) 190; I. de la Potterie, art. cit. [n. 221], 522, note 62; Gnilka, *Komm.,* 99, note 1.

[234] "Mission" should not be understood in the sense of the extension of the numbers of baptism by socio-politico-economical force or by cultural violence. Cf. Gnilka, *Komm.,* 109.

[235] Chapter 2 treated of some elements hindering unity between men; one of which is self-closed, distorted mental attitudes in appreciating reality. See pp. 30ff.

[236] F. Mussner, *Christus, das All,* 67. Cf.: J. Ernst, *plērōma,* 113; A. Lindemann, *Die Aufhebung,* 216, says: "... *en pasin* meint konkret daß Christus das All in allen Bereichen füllt."

[237] Eph 3,1ff. and the train of thought of the texts we explained above, pages 104ff. cf. 152ff.

tion and role of the body of Christ, i.e. the Church (i.e. implicitly the community of Ephesians, the "old" Christians i.e. we), together with the new Christians (i.e. "you") for other peoples who have other values and systems of appreciation and culture, for the whole world and even, in today's language of space-science, for the cosmos.[238]

The third proposal, according to Ernst, is to take both *to plērōma* and the participle in an active sense. In this case, one undercurrent of thought is the organic growth of the "body" (cf. 4,16 and its context especially). According to this understanding, the Church is something which is filled by Christ and growing towards the Head Christ. The fact is stressed that the Church originates essentially from Christ the Head and is promoted by Him to build up the body of Christ and to grow by absorbing other peoples into its communion and unity.

The phrase *ta panta en pasin* has a cosmic meaning and is open to the outer-world beyond the community. This understanding approximates the sense of verse 1,10: God has united the Whole in Christ, on the earth and in the heavens. The role of the body of Christ in this human history is to transmit and to promote the key to the unity, the Head, Christ, in whom every value and difference, even different religions, come to meet in the unity without destroying their own diversities. This "unified" dimension (i.e. the community-dimension) should be expanded into the whole world. This is the unifying Event come about in Christ.[239]

Having stated the problems and a couple of examples of the interpretation of verse 1,23, we want to elaborate our opinion somewhat further.

The relative clause *hētis estin to sōma autou, to plērōma tou ... plēroumenou* is, according to our understanding, a description of the Church, using the image "Head-Body," precisely here, as the organic-body-thought.

The *to plērōma* has an active sense in the sense of the stage of being about to go out to transmit its fulness from Christ by God.[240] It is taken for granted that the community of Eph (those addressed) believed its fullness to originate from the Head, Christ, and therefore, the Church is filled by the Head (by his wisdom, life, power, dynamism, etc.).

If we consider the visual and empirical level, the subject is the community. And if we look at the level of consciousness of belief, the subject is surely God at work in Christ. In this sense, "the fullness" (*to plērōma*) resumes the previous words *to sōma autou* ("his body").

The fullness is always the fullness of God at work in Christ. In this sense, we can say that the fullness is that of Christ. The genitive of the participle (*tou plēroumenou*) appears to show that the subject of the

---

[238] Authors who understand a "cosmic" link of the Church and her function in relation to the world. See J. Gnilka, *Komm.*, 98f. 104ff., and M. Barth, *Comm.*, 206f.

[239] Cf.: J. Ernst, *plērōma*, 114; Gnilka, *Komm.*, 99.

[240] A. Lindemann, *Die Aufhebung*, 214, states: "... In der Tat ist *plērōma* in Manifestations- oder Relationsbegriff."

participle is the body itself.[241]   Therefore, sentence 1,23 means: the
Church is his body, namely, the fullness which itself fills the whole in
every way.   Against this interpretation a couple of objections are raised.
There is no instance in the New Testament of the participle of *plēroō*
in the middle voice,[242] nor in our letter to Eph.[243]   But, while limiting
ourself only to Eph and Col, we may ask if it is clear to conclude that
there is no instance of the middle voice at least regarding the sense.
In the case of Eph 3,19 (... *hina plērōthēte eis pan to plērōma tou theou*
[so that you may be filled]), the meaning can be that "you" may be
filled.   But still we can ask, by whom or by which?   It is apparent that
the subject of the action of "filling" is not clear.   We may translate the
sentence as follows: "so that you may be immersed in all the fullness
of God."   The sense of the sentence means more than the English translation: so that you may be *filled with* all the fullness of God.[244]   We cannot understand the verb *plērōthēte* simply in a passive sense.

Another instance is Eph 5,18: ... *alla plērousthe en pneumati* ("... but
[you] be filled with spirit ").   But it is possible also to translate this
"but [you] fill yourself with (in) spirit."   The subject of "filling" is not
merely the spirit but also "you yourself".[245]   The same is true for Col 1,9:
... *hina plērōthēte tēn epignōsin tou thelēmatos autou en pasēi sophiai
kai synesei pneumatikēi* ("... that you may be filled [with] the knowledge
of his will in all spiritual wisdom and understanding" and "that you may
fill yourself...").[246]   The one who does actually "to fill" is God Himself:
God fills "you" with the knowledge of his will.   And we can say also that
"you" will fill yourself with the knowledge of His will, because the author
wants to prepare the Colossians to participate in this action.   For this
latter case, the real agent (God) is included in the apparent agent "you"
(the apparent does not mean unreal).

The next instance, 2,10, is also ambiguous.   The verse says: *kai este
en autōi peplērōmenoi, hos estin hē kephalē pasēs archēs kai exousias*
("and you have come to fullness [of life] in him, who is the head of all
rule and authority" [RSV]).   But literally "and you have been filled in
him, who is the head of all rule and authority."   Despite the passive

---

[241] The genitive of the participle (*tou plēroumenou*) may be explicative or subjective.   Compare, A. Lindemann, *Die Aufhebung*, 215: "... Christus wird in v. 23 der
das All in allem Erfüllende gennant."   Cf. M. Barth, *Comm.*, 205, 209.

[242] See the study of de la Potterie, art. cit. [n. 221], 502f.

[243] The verb occurs in the following verses: Eph 1,23; 3,19; 4,10; 5,18; Col 1,9.25;
2,10; 4,17.

[244] Thus *The Revised Standard Version* (1973), but *The New English Bible* (Oxford
1970²), translates: "so may you attain to fullness of being, the fullness of God himself."   And *The New American Bible* (New York 1970), similarly: "so that you may
attain to the fulness of God himself."   See below, page 178f.

[245] This sentence is contrasted to *mē methuskesthe oinōi* ("Do not get drunk with
wine").

[246] Cf. Blass-Debrunner-Rehkopf, *Grammatik*, § 159. 1.

form of the verb *este peplērōmenoi* ("you have been filled"), the agent of "to fill" is not simply Christ. Because it is stated clearly that *in him* you have been filled.[247]

Therefore, even with the help of these passages which appear to approximate to the sense of this verb in Eph 1,23, we are in no position to determine whether *plēroumenos* is active or passive.

Another difficulty for us comes from the interpretation of the phrase *ta panta en pasin*. For our part, we are not convinced that *in this context* the phrase has an adverbial sense, something like *pantapasi(-n)* ("completely" or " perfectly" or a similar meaning).[248] It appears to me to mean that in order to accept a word as authentic, it must be paralleled elsewhere in the same work. In our letter, *ta panta* appears to be the objects of verbs.[249] And if we check the plerophoric feature of the usage *pas* ("all"),[250] the author of Eph must be conscious of the meaning or of the content of the *panta* with the article *ta* ("the").[251]

If we look closely at verses 1,11 and 3,9: ... *kata prothesin tou ta panta energountos* ... (1,11); ... *en tōi theōi ta panta ktisanti* (3,9), we notice that they are constructions stylistically quite similar to that of Eph 1,23b: ... *to plērōma tou ta panta en pasin plēroumenou* (subject-object-verb). In addition, the *ta panta* in 1,10 and 1,11 clearly mean "the whole" or "all things." [252]

Therefore, we are disinclined to interpret the *ta panta* in 1,23 in an adverbial sense. It is the object of the participle *tou plēroumenou*, no matter how the participle may be meant.[253] Rather, *en pasin* should be taken in an adverbial sense.[254]

We may conclude that the verse 1,23 tells us the role and function of the body of Christ (i.e. the Church) for the world. The incomprehensibly profound unity between the one filling and those who are filled is expressed by the Body of Christ. Growing in the world and filling the world, the body is absorbing other peoples into it; by doing so, it is expand-

---

[247] Cf. *plērōma*: in Eph 1,10.23; 3,19; 4,13; Col 1,19; 2,9; G. Delling, *"plērēs"*, *"plērōma"*, etc. art. cit. [n. 221], 303f.; Lohse, *Col.* 56f.; M. Barth, *Comm.*, 200ff.

[248] R. Yates, art. cit. [n. 221], 151, *pantapasin* in classical sense.

[249] The expression *ta panta* occur in the following verses: 1,10; 1,23; 3,9; 4,15; 5,13.

[250] See pages 75ff.

[251] Instead, *panta* without article *ta* is used in relation to or in the context of the power-word-field: 1,22(bis); 3,20. And compare the *pantas* in 3,6; ... *pantōn* in 4,6 and *panta* in 6,21. Cf. also *hapanta* ("whole") in 6,13.

[252] Similarly, the *ta panta* in 3,9; 4,10.15 denotes or refers to the wholeness of the world, all creatures. See M. Barth, *Comm.*, 342; the textual variants of the *pantas*: see B. M. Metzger, *Text. Comm.*, 603.

[253] Cf. F. R. Hitchcock, "The Pleroma as the Medium," art. cit. [n. 221], 147. The *en pasin* occurs in our letter in the following verses: 4,6; 6,16 (cf. *en panti* in 5,24). These appear to have adverbial force: "in every way," "in all respect," "completely." 4,6 is a kind of formula which indicates the Divine transcendence and immanence and pan-dynamic dimension of God, but the *en pasin* possibly is meant in an adverbial sense.

[254] Compare 1 Tim 3,11; 2 Tim 2,7; 4,5; Tit 2,9; 2,10b; Heb 13,4; Heb 13,8; 1 Pet 4,11.

ing the unity dynamically.[255] It is the core of the dynamism to make a dialogue with different peoples and races, cultures, and even religions, without destroying their identities and differences (cf. 3,10). It "syntonizes" the divine dynamism at work in Christ in the present world, especially in synthesizing the human groups towards the divine execution of the will for the unity of the whole in Christ.[256]

One of the main concerns of the letter is to somatize this awareness of the dynamism at work in Christ and to make it visual and credible for the world and for the cosmos. From another point of view, we may say that the letter is a *Christ-agogical* one to educate and to prepare a full collaborator or a leader of the Pauline mission. Some members of the community/communities are chosen to be drawn into the inner comprehension of the mystery of the divine will on the level of the apostle and his collaborators.

The somatic comprehension of the unity is not merely a theological knowledge or reflection on something, but a living experience of the unity. It transcends analytical comprehension which poses always "objects" and knowing subjects, or some similar epistemological human limitation.

3-7-2: *Relation and Dynamism of the Head to its Body*

"I beseech you therefore, I, a prisoner in the Lord to walk worthy of the vocation to which you have been called (Eph 4,1), with all lowliness and meekness, with patience be forbearing with one another in love (v. 2), eager to maintain the unity of the spirit in the bond of peace (v. 3).

"One body and one spirit, just as you were called in one hope of your calling (v. 4). One Lord, one faith, one baptism (v. 5), one God and Father of all, who (is) above all, and through all, and in all (v. 6).

"To each of us the grace was given according to the measure of the gift of Christ (v. 7). Therefore it is said: 'When he ascended to the height he led a host of captives, he gave gifts to men' (RSV) (cf. Ps 68,18) (v. 8). In saying 'he ascended' what does it mean but that he had also descended into the lower parts of the earth? (v. 9). He who descended is he who also ascended far above all the heavens, that he might fill all things (v. 10). It is he who gave these ones to be apostles, (that some should be apostles), some prophets, some evangelists, some pastors, some teachers (v. 11), for the equipment of the saints (to equip the saints for work of service), for the work of ministry, for building up the body of Christ (v. 12), until we all attain to the unity of faith and of the knowledge of the Son of God, to mature manhood (unto a perfect man), unto the measure of the stature of the fullness of Christ (v. 13), so that we may

---

[255] Cf.: Schlier, *Komm.*, 99; P. Benoit, "Leib, Haupt und Pleroma in den Gefangenschaftsbriefen," in: *Exegese und Theologie* (Düsseldorf 1965) 246-79; J. Ernst, *Plērōma*, 115f.; idem, *Komm.*, 291ff.; Gnilka, *Komm.*, 109; M. Barth, *Comm.*, 200ff.

[256] See our explanation about 1,8b-10 on pages 112ff.

no longer be children, tossed to and fro and carried about with every wind of doctrine, by the cunning of men, by their craftiness in deceitful wiles (v. 14); rather, living the truth in love we let grow the whole into him who is the Head, Christ (v. 15), from whom the whole body, being joined and knit together through every joint of supply (which serves for supply), according to the energy in the measure of every part, makes growth of the body, unto the building up of itself in love" (v. 16).

The function of verse 4,16 is to recapitulate, from the aspect of inner principle, the whole process which is described in this section 4,1-16 which we translated above, especially 4,11-16 which forms one sentence.

With 4,1 starts an exhortatory part of the letter.[257] The author starts with a maxim. The addressees (i.e. the "you" of the community) are to conduct their lives (i.e. to walk) worthy of the vocation to which they have been called (v. 1). He applies this maxim to virtues of conduct for the community life (lowliness, meekness, patience, forbearing each other in love) (v. 2). Then he leads to the admonition which is the scope of these virtues. The author beseeches his readers to be eager to maintain the unity of the spirit in the bond of peace (v. 3). These appeals, therefore, aim at the unity of the community. In the following verses 4-6, we find seven "oneness"-formulas: one body, one spirit... In the form of confession, as in Jewish religion,[258] the author adds reason and theological basis for his admonition. It is clear that this admonition with its theological reasons form a literary unity. Therefore, the first part of this text is Eph 4,1-6.[259]

In the second part, 4,7 onward, he includes himself, using We-style. Now he speaks about different ministries in one church.[260] But they are all seen as the gift of Christ.[261] Immediately verse 7 underlines this aspect: to each of us was given the grace according to the gift of Christ. Then, using Ps 68,8, he presents the role of Christ in a midrashic manner.[262] Descending and ascending, "he gave gifts to men" (v. 8). "It is he who gave these to be apostles, others to be prophets, some to be evangelists, some to be pastors, others to be teachers" (v. 11).

---

[257] W. G. Doty, *Letters in primitive Christianity* (Philadelphia 1973) 37ff.; C. J. Bjerkelund, *Parakalō: Form, Function und Sinn der Parakalo-Sätze in den paulinischen Briefen* (Oslo 1967) T. Y. Mullins, Disclosure: "A Literary Form in the New Testament": *NT* 4 (1964) 44-50; D. C. Bradley, "The Topos as a Form in the Pauline Paraenesis": *JBL* 72 (1953) 283-46; Cf. Schlier, *Komm.*, 207; H. Conzelmann, *Komm.*, 110; M. Barth, *Comm.*, 426.

[258] See M. Barth, *Comm.*, 462f., and Gnilka, *Komm.*, 201ff. Cf. Fischer, *Tendenz*, op. cit., 137f.

[259] Schlier, *Komm.*, 178; Gnilka, *Komm.*, 195; M. Barth, *Comm.*, 452; J. Ernst, *Komm.*, 342-44.

[260] See H. Merklein, *Das Kirchliche Amt nach dem Epheserbrief* (München 1973) 57ff.

[261] See our pages 128f. and Merklein, *Das Kirchliche Amt*, 59ff.

[262] Schlier, *Komm.*, 190ff.; M. McNamara, *The New Testament and the Palestinian Targum to the Pentateuch* (Rome 1966) 78; H. Merklein, *Das Kirchliche Amt*, 65f.; Fischer, *Tedenz*, 139; M. Barth, *Comm.*, 472ff.

In verse 13, he insists upon the "unity of faith",[263] by doing so he refers to the first part as well.

All this acting in love, all these ministries in the Church aim at the building up of the community, the body of Christ. Also the inner knowledge of the son of God depends upon the measure of the "stature" of the "fullness of Christ" (v. 13).[264]

The signification of these texts is therefore to encourage the addressees that they may enter upon the process of the growing mystery of the unity. They should "somatize" the dynamism already at work. Outlines, structure (*Ur*-structure) and order are already given by the "dimension" of the body of Christ. The verses 15-16 put this reality into the image of the body and explain the aspect which is important in this context: the act of Christ in the relation of Head-Body. Using the image, the author resumes in verse 16 what he had said before.

After verse 14 (where the author encourages the hearers so that they may no longer be misled by deceitful human doctrines) he writes: "Rather, living the truth in love, we let the whole grow into him" (*alētheuontes de en agapē auxēsōmen eis auton ta panta, hos estin hē kephalē Christos —* v. 15).[265]

The *ta panta* together with the verb *auxēsōmen* ("we grow": aor. subj.) makes it difficult to interpret verse 4,15. Because the verb has grammatically two possible meanings: transitive and intransitive.

Some authors understand it in an intransitive sense. Then, the *ta panta* is not the object of the verb and consequently it must have adverbial force.[266]

The others take the verb as transitive, namely, "to make grow" or "to let grow".[267] In this case, *ta panta* is the object of the verb *auxēsōmen*.[268]

The verb occurs elsewhere in Eph 2,21, where it clearly has intransitive sense: "in him the whole building grows ... into a holy temple ...."

The verse parallel to Eph 4,16, Col 2,19 presents further difficulty: "not holding fast to the Head, from whom the whole body nourished and knit together through its joints and ligaments, *grows the growth* of God." (RSV translates: "... *grows with a growth* that is from God" — *kai ou kratōn tēn kephalēn, ex hou pan to sōma dia tōn haphōn kai syn-*

---

[263] With M. Barth, *Comm.*, 488f., we understand the unity of faith and of the knowledge of the son of God ("... *tēn henotēta tēs pisteōs kai tēs epignōseos tou huiou tou theou*": in 4,13) in the sense that the unity of the faith and of the knowledge which the son of God holds or has.

[264] G. Delling, "*plērēs, pleroō*", etc., in: *TDNT*, VI, 283-311, esp. 302.

[265] Cf. I. de la Potterie, *La Vérité dans Saint Jean*, Tome II (Rome 1977) 488.

[266] Gnilka, *Komm.*, 217, note 5; H. Merklein, *Das Kirchliche Amt*, 111f.; M. Barth, *Comm.*, 444f.

[267] *Komm.* Schlier, 205f.; J. Ernst, *Komm.*, 358.

[268] Refer to page 135 of text.

desmōn epichorēgoumenon kai symbibazomenon auxei tēn auxēsin tou theou).[269]

In the case of Col 2,19 the verb clearly allows of an intransitive sense, but Eph 4,16 is ambiguous. Because the *ta panta* denotes, as we mentioned above,[270] the whole, all things or all creatures.[271] Especially, if we refer back to the same words in 4,10 which is just the previous sentence to 4,11ff., there the *ta panta* refers to the Whole which Christ fills.[272] We claim that it is the accusative of the object of the verb.[273] We feel that it is *not merely* the accusative of respect or relation. We may say it shows inner and outer "somatic" relation to the whole and its "working on" the body itself from itself to the whole. The body of Christ has the function of making the whole and all peoples grow into the Head Christ.

It is precisely the somatic dynamism of body. The growth of individuals of the community should be seen in the context of the whole, especially in relation and dialogue with other peoples in the world. We must not lose the dynamic relation between the head and its body, and between the body and the whole.[274] The role of the community is not for her sake but for others "outside" her community, so that they may become conscious of the message of the unity and the dynamism at work in Christ and may realize them and "somatize" them.

The dynamic relation of the community to the whole is another essential message of the letter to the Ephesians. It brings the message of reconciliation and itself becomes the bridge for those who fight against each other (cf. 2,14ff.) and restores the harmony with Nature and the cosmos. By living the truth in love, the "we" grow into him the head, and "we" have an important function as a member of the body of Christ, in order to become the bridge of the reconciliation and unity for different races, cultures, religions, groups — and even for the cosmos. In this sense, we let the whole grow to Him as well. So, "we," insofar as we live the truth in love, are the centre of the "axis" of the whole wheel where the divine unification is even now at work.[275]

---

[269] Lohse, *Col.*, 122, note 63, interprets the verb in the intransitive sense. The case of Col 2,19 is clear because the verb has the accusative of content (cognate accusative), *tēn auxēsin* ("the growth"). See Blass-Debrunner-Rehkopf, *Grammatik*, § 153,1.

[270] See pages 123 and 135.

[271] Compare Eph 1,10.23; 3,9; 4,10; 5,13. On this point, Schlier rightly states that the *ta panta* of Ephesians does not have an adverbial sense. See *Komm.*, 206.

[272] M. Barth, *Comm.*, 434, includes all things, heaven, earth, principalities and powers, also the church, the body of Christ. I. de la Potterie, "Le Christ, Plérome de l'Eglise" (Eph 1,22-23): *Bib* 58 (1977) 522, note 62, has other interpretations.

[273] Some claim that the *ta panta* should be interpreted as the accusative of respect or relation. See Blass-Debrunner-Rehkopf, *Grammatik* § 160. M. Zerwick, *Analysis Philologica Novi Testamenti Graeci* (Romae 1955) 432, takes the *ta panta* as accusative relationis: "sub omni respectu". By doing so, however, one may weaken the real relation (somatic) with the whole and other peoples.

[274] Especially, here between the whole body, and between the whole body and the whole, in 4,16.

[275] The central circle of the axis must be "vacuum", where people come to meet

We grow into him who is the head

We find this movement towards the head in the paragraph 4,11-16.[276] The concern of this paragraph is specifically that of the community (i.e. the body). Christ appointed the apostles, the prophets, and some others ministers, to build up the body of Christ. The gift of Christ, by which we understand not simply static "institutionalized" offices, but a dynamic gift with its proper purpose and energy which is at work in the formation of the community, and which aims at the edification of the Body of Christ.

This fundamental structuring-dynamism impels the members of the community to attain to the unity of the faith and the knowledge of the son of God. They all attain to the matured manhood ("the perfect man"), unto the measure of the stature of the fullness of Christ. As a result of this,[277] they are not tossed hither and thither by human deceitfulness, they grow into the head. And without doubt, this growth comes from a practical knowledge of love and its conduct in Christ in daily life (see 4,15; 3,16-19).

Growth comes from the Head ("from whom" [*ex hou*...]) (v. 4,16a).

When we explained the meaning of the head,[278] we did not mention another possible meaning of the *kephalē* ("head"). It is a physical meaning of head or brain.

The image, the "body" of Eph, especially its relation to its head, may have been influenced by the knowledge and skill of contemporary doctors and philosophers. Eph may have presupposed a common understanding of anatomy of those days, because we find a couple of possibly anatomical or medical terms in 4,16 and its context. While semitic thought more or less locates the seat of life in the heart, hellenistic is inclined to lend

---

and to dialogue and to be reconciled and finally to be united. The Church's function must be like this "vacuum," just as Christ emptied himself and died for both groups who hated each other.

[276] See the *eis*-phrases in this paragraph:

EIS ERGON *diakonias*: "for the work of service" (4,12).

EIS OIKODOMĒN *tous sōmatos tou Christou*: "for the building up the body of Christ": (4,12).

... *katantēsōmen* ... EIS TĒN HENOTĒTA *tēs pisteōs* ...: "... attain ... to the unity of the faith ..." (4,13).

EIS ANDRA *teleion*: "to mature manhood" (4,13)

EIS METRON *hēlikias tou plērōmatos tou Christou*: "to the measure of the stature of the fullness of Christ" (4,13).

EIS AUTON: "to him" (4,15) (= to the Head Christ).

These *eis*-phrases (eis with the accustive) show the inner dynamism at work in the community towards the goal. See above our analysis of *eis*-preposition and its phrases, pages 98ff.

[277] The *hina* of 4,14 is to be understood in a consecutive or final sense. See; Schlier, *Komm.*, 203; Merklein, *Das Kirchliche Amt*, 100.

[278] See pages 116ff.

importance to the head: the head is the seat of the *nous* and of *hēgemonikon*.[279]

Among the Greek doctors, Hippocrates and Galen ascribed priority and superiority to the brain or head.[280] According to Hippocrates, the brain was the strongest "power" in man. Organs of senses, and motions of the whole body carry out their work according to the discernment and knowledge of the brain. It commands and the members obey. It is the source of thought and of awareness and the ruler and judge of the whole body.[281]

Galen of Pergamum [282] studied nerves which branched out from the brain and spread to the whole body, to rule and to control all organs and muscles of the body.[283] The brain or head is compared to an "acropolis" of the body.[284] And when Galen explained growth of body and nutrition for it, he introduced a metaphysical principle, "Nature" (*physis*), as the principle of unity of organism (bodies). "The effects (*erga*) of Nature, then when the animal is still being formed in the womb, are all the different parts (*moria*) of its body; and after it has been born, an effect in which all parts share is the progress of each to its full size (*eis to teleion hekastō* ...), and thereafter its maintenance of itself as long as possible".[285]

" 'Growth' (*auxēsis*) is an increase and expansion in length, breadth, and thickness of the solid parts of the animal ... Nutrition is an addition to these, without expansion ...".[286]

"... And further, to be distended in all directions belongs only to bodies whose growth is directed by Nature; for those which are distended by us undergo this distension in one direction but grow less in the others; it is impossible to find a body which will remain entire and not be torn through whilst we stretch it in the three dimensions. Thus Nature alone

---

279 P. Benoit, *Exégèse et Théologie* (Paris 1961) vol. II, 133. J. B. Lightfoot, *Saint Paul's Epistles to the Colossians and to Philemon* (London 1879) 200-01.

280 F. W. Bayer, "Anatomie" in: *Reallexikon für Antike und Christentum*, vol. I (Stuttgart 1950) 430-37. On page 433 he states: "... In das Gehirn verlegte Alkmaion v. Kroton den Sitz der Seele. Dieser Meinung folgten die Hippokratiker und Plato." And the brain is the seat of the spiritual power (see Galen 3,669; 19,315). In opposition to this view, namely, the head-centred function of body, Empedocles, the Sicilian school, locates the central organ in the heart (see Bayer, 434).

281 M. Barth, *Comm.*, 187.

282 He was from Pergamum in Asia Minor (about A.D. 129-199) well educated in his home-city and studied medicine in Alexandria, then, when he was about 25 years old, he started a career as a gladiator-doctor in Pergamum. See: *Der Kleine Pauly, Lexikon der Antike* (Stuttgart 1967) vol. 2, 674f.

283 See *Sieben Bücher Anatomie des Galen*, ins Deutsche übertragen und kommentiert von M. Simon, vol. II (Leipzig 1906) XLIII, LIII, and 169.

284 M. Barth, *Comm.*, 189.

285 Galen, *On the Natural Faculties*, with an English translation by Arthur John Brock (Loeb Classical Library; London; reprint, 1963), I.V., p. 17. And see the introduction, p. XXIX.

286 Ibid., I.V., p. 19.

has the power to expand a body in all directions so that it remains un-ruptured and preserves completely its previous form." [287]   "... Nature is a constructive artist so that the substance of things is always tending towards unity and so towards alteration because its own parts act upon and are acted upon by one another".[288]

Lightfoot believes that the Greek medical parallels to Col 2,19 and Eph 4,16 are sufficiently strong to explain what the author of Eph had in mind. According to him, the head is "the inspiring, ruling, guiding, combining, sustaining power, the main spring of the body's activity, the centre of its unity, the seat of its life".[289]

Despite the possible meaning of "head" in relation to its body, we cannot explain our text 4,16 by the medical anatomy of Galen. We simply claim that Eph 4,16 and its context could presuppose a popular under-standing of anatomy of those days.

As we explained, the unifying Act was ascribed to the head in Eph 1, 10 and 1,23, now the author of Eph says: "from the head (*ex hou*) the whole body, being joined and knit together ... makes growth of its body..." (4,16).

The verb "to fit together" (*synarmologeō*) and "to knit together" (*sym-bibazō*) denote the head's function and action for its body. "All bodily functions of coordination and stabilization take place in the process of growing toward and from the head".[290] The act of the head for the unification is seen among the members of the community. Apart from the unity of the members the body does not grow. The author states that *the whole body* (*pan to sōma*) is joined and knit together.

Now we inquire what is the range of meaning of the *pan* ("whole"). At first, it sums up, without doubt, all the members of the community (4,13: "...we all attain..."). But it is not limited to the present com-munity of Eph to whom the author of Eph spoke. So, we should study a possible or potential widening of the meaning *pan* ("whole").

3-7-3: *Extending Unity: Expanding and Converging Body*

With whom will "we" be joined together? In other words, we ask what is the sense of *syn-* in combination? An extension of the meaning of *syn* [291] "together with" is one of importance in the letter to the Ephesians. Looking through our letter, we find two occurrences of the preposition

---

[287] Ibid., I.VII, p. 29. Cf. Eph 3,18.
[288] Ibid., I.XIX, p. 73. Cf. I.IX, p. 33; I.XIV, p. 75-76; III.XV, p. 327.
[289] J. B. Lightfoot, *Saint Paul's Epistles to the Colossians and to Philemon* (London 1879) 157. Cf.: B. F. Westcott, *Saint Paul's Epistles to the Ephesians* (London 1906) 64f.; M. Barth, *Comm.*, 190.
[290] M. Barth, *Comm.*, 190f.
[291] W. Grundmann, "*syn*", "*meta*", etc. in: *TDNT*, VII, 766-97, esp. 767, 770.

syn: 3,18 and 4,31. Both passages fit the Koine usage of that time as described by Grundmann.[292] Verse 3,18 appears to indicate an essential element of the awareness and comprehension for which the apostle prays for his community: "You may have power to comprehend *with all the saints* (*syn pasin tois hagiois*) what is the breadth and length and height and depth".[293] What we want to say now about this difficult passage (3,18), is that the comprehension consists in the communal character, "together with all the saints".[294]

In relation to the preposition *syn* in Ephesians, if we check the preposition in Colossians, we find a certain difference between Col and Eph. The expression like *syn Christōi* ("with Christ") or *syn autōi* ("with him": with Christ), is not found in Ephesians, but in Colossians: Col 2,13.20.; 3, 3.4.[295] These passages of Col are concerned with the signification of the death-resurrection.

Eph 2,5-6, however, reveals a thought parallel to Col 2,12-13. But in spite of their parallel elements, the expression of Col 2,12, "to be buried with Christ in baptism"[296] is not expressed in Eph 2,5-6.[297] In Eph 2,5, the dative *tō Christōi* ("to" or "for Christ") replaces *syn Christōi* ("with Christ"). It has variations in reading,[298] but the expression *syn Christōi* ("with Christ") is not found even in the various readings of Eph 2,5.

Eph 2,5-6 runs thus: "even when we were dead through our trespasses, (God) made us alive *together with Christ* ... raised us up *together with him* and made us sit *together with him* in the heavenly places *in Christ Jesus*" (RSV translation, except the additions of "together") *kai ontas hēmas nekrous tois paraptōmasin synezōopoiēsen tōi Christōi — ... kai synēgeiren kai synekathisen en tois epouraniois en Christōi ᵒIēsou.*

The Greek original text is not as clear as the English translation above for the italicized words.[299] The author of Eph does not state explicitly in the text what is translated here in the English. We may ask what the author means by "together with Christ",[300] or "together with us".[301]

For the line of thought of 2,1ff. which we have examined,[302] "together with us" is easily understood. And the formula *en-Christōi* at the end

---

[292] Grundmann, art. cit. in: *TDNT*, VII, 770.

[293] Who are the saints in our letter? They are not only Christians? Compare: Eph 1,15.18; 2,19; 3,8 (cf. 3,5); 3,18; 4,12; 6,18; but also see 1,4; 2,21; 5,3.27.

[294] Cf. below, pp. 165 and 174ff.

[295] Cf. Grundmann, art. cit., 781ff. Also see W. Bujard, *Stilanalytische*, 122.

[296] Grundmann, art. cit., 782.785.792f. E. Lohse, *Colossians*, 103ff.

[297] The Ephesians mentions baptism in 4,5 in a different context: "one Lord, one faith, one baptism."

[298] Bruce M. Metzger, *A Textual Comm.*, 602.

[299] The Greek text does not state these three "together with": together with Christ, ... together with him ... together with him ...

[300] See Grundmann, art. cit., 792-93.

[301] Lindemann, A., *Die Aufhebung* ..., 118-19.

[302] See pages 36ff. and the analysis of "we" style and "you"-style in pages 104ff.

of 2,6 suggests interpreting *syn* ("with") in the sense of "together with us." Because the author never puts Christ at one pole and us at the other. The direction of his thought with regard to the divine Act is: God... in Christ... us; we... in Christ... you; we and you... in Christ... the whole.

At any rate, in 2,5-6, the meaning of *syn*-verbs is rather to indicate the togetherness of both groups ("us" and "you"), based on the traditional "proto"-pattern of unity and enmity, all members of the community. Those who are newly incorporated into the community are also made alive, raised and made to sit together with "us" in the heavenly places for the sake of Christ.[303]

This sense of togetherness with members of the community will be clarified when we explain the two *syn*-verbs of our verse 4,16: *synarmologeō* and *symbibazō*. The first verb occurs twice, only in Ephesians 4,16 and 2,21 (in both cases, passive participles). It means "to join together," "to pile together," "to fit together." The second *symbibazō* occurs only here and in Col 2,2 and 2,19.[304] It means "to bring together" "to unite",[305] "to knit together." [306]

The body is held together by the head. The verb *synarmologeō* strongly evokes the parallel passage Eph 2,21. There, the image used is certainly different from that of Eph 4,16. The former is "building," the latter is "body." And we observe that the image of body in 4,16 is overlapped by the image of building.

In Eph 2,19ff., the author of Eph adapts to his community [307] an image from building in order to explain the mystery of the community, specifically the "your" newly incorporated "status" in his community: "So then you are no longer strangers and sojourners, but you are fellow citizens ("co-citizens": *synpolitai*) with the saints ("of the saints": ... *tōn hagiōn*) and members of the household of God, built upon the foundation of the apostles and prophets, Christ Jesus himself being the cornerstone" (RSV: 2,19-20).[308] Then, the following verse 2,21 contains a wording parallel with 4,16:

---

[303] Dative of respect or of cause, see Blass-Debrunner-Rehkopf, *Grammatik*, § 197, § 196.

[304] Lohse, *Col.*, 80f.

[305] Lohse, ibid., states that this verb could be understood in the sense of "to demonstrate" or "to instruct" as well.

[306] G. Delling, "*symbibazo*" in: *TDNT*, VII, 763-66.

[307] Regarding the image "building" and community or church: F. Mussner, *Das All ...* (Trier 1955) 113ff.; J. Pfammatter, *Die Kirche als Bau. Eine exegetischtheologische Studie zur Ekklesiologie der Paulusbriefe* (Analecta Gregoriana 110; Rome 1960) 73ff.; B. Gärtner, *The Temple and the Community in Qumran and the New Testament* (Cambridge 1965) esp. 60-66; H. Muszynski, *Fundament, Bild und Metapher in den Handschriften aus Qumran* (AnBib 61; Rome 1975); Schlier, *Komm.*, 143f.; Gnilka, *Komm.*, 154ff.; M. Barth, *Comm.*, 314ff.

[308] J. Jeremias, "*gonia*," "*akrogoniaios*," "*kephalē gonias*," in: *TDNT*, I, 791-93, esp. 792, says: "... Eph 2,20 like 1 Pet 2,1, describes the community as a spiritual tem-

"in whom [in Christ] the whole structure is joined together and grows into a holy temple in (the) Lord" (*en hōi pasa oikodomē synarmologoumenē auxei eis naon hagion en kyriōi*) (2,21).

"From whom [from the Head Christ] the whole body, being joined and knit together ... makes growth of the body unto the building up of itself in love" (4,16).

It is clear that the two verses share a couple of common thoughts: the wholeness of the structure or building and of the body (*pasa oikodomē — pan to sōma*: "the whole building" — "the whole body") and the togetherness to be shown by the *syn*-verbs; the growth of the building and of the body (*auxei — auxēsin*), the similar purpose and direction of their growth, namely, "unto the holy temple" and "into the building up of the body" (*eis naon hagion — eis oikodomēn heautou*).

Besides the differences of the images and their contexts, we remark one other difference. The growth of the building in 2,21 [309] is defined by the expression "in Christ" (*en hōi ...*). On the other hand, the growth of the body in 4,16 comes from the head Christ (*ex hou ...*).

The former image is to show that the whole structure incorporating "you" grows into a holy temple, together with "us," based on the apostles and prophets, Christ himself being the cornerstone (or the final stone), and "you" also are built together with "us" into the dwelling place of God (cf. 2,22). It shows the expanding building, by the act of the incorporation of "you" into our community.

4,16 shows that the growth originates from the head and underlines the dynamic relation of the head with its body and the inter-relationship of the members of the community. What we wish to underline by this comparison, is that the "togetherness" and "joining"-dynamism is one of the essential aspects of the letter.[310] The different groups come to meet together, to be reconciled even if they fight or hate each other, and to be united together.

For the proper growth of a body every point of contact is crucial. The *haphē* means "touch," "sense of touch," "contact of surfaces," "point of contact." Here in 4,16, it means "point of contact of the body." [311]

---

ple. The Apostles and prophets are the foundation, and Christ is the corner-stone who binds the whole building together and completes it (Eph 2,20f.). Underlying the image is the lofty declaration of Jesus that He is the final stone in the heavenly sanctuary ...."

[309] Verse 2,22 states: "in whom (in Christ) you also are built together [with "us"] into a dwelling place of God in spirit."

[310] In our letter we find other *syn*-words which denote this integrating or incorporating dynamism: *syndesmos* ("bond"): 4,3 (cf. Col 3,14); *sygklēronomos* ("co-heir"): 3,6 (cf. Rom 8,17); *symmetochos* ("co-partaker"): 3,6; *syssōmos* ("co-somatic"): 3,6. These last three words in 3,6, being related to the Pauline insight that "you" the Gentiles are incorporated into our new community, indicate one of the fundamental acknowledgements of the developing plan of the divine will for the world. This pauline comprehension is somatic.

[311] Liddell & Scott, *haphē*, 288.

And the genitive of the word *epichorēgia* denotes "supply," "provision," "provision of a husband for a wife." [312]

Galen, in describing the structure of the human frame, specifies the elements of union as twofold: the body owes its unity partly to articulation, partly to attachment.[313] The relation and contact of contiguous surfaces and the connection of different parts together effect structural unity.[314] The "contacting" part of each body is the most vital and important point where the Head Christ is really creatively at work.[315] This is the reason why the author of Eph states that the whole body is joined together and knit together through every point of contact which serves for nourishment.[316]

The Head provides for the body nourishment, life and direction,[317] which the body needs precisely at the point of contact with other parts of the body.

The whole body is joined and knit together through every contact between differing peoples, at first within their community, and with whole communities of Christ (the whole Church), and then, within the cosmic dimension where God is at work in Christ to unite the whole (within the potential communities of Christ). Each individual of the community is required to become a perfect man and adult by the gift of Christ.[318] By doing so, the whole body grows unto the building up of itself in love.[319]

Every direction of the growth and expansion of the body has its origin in and is originated by the head Christ, causing the mutual love of the community and the love towards the others who still do not know the love of Christ which transcends any knowledge of the world (cf. 3,19).

The Head's energy does not remain external. Having built up the body, it conveys vitality to it. The body is to make its own growth. In this body, human autonomy becomes perfect, and at the same time, it becomes the divine autonomy within "us" as well.

The contact of the community with foreign or heterogeneous peoples might have caused them (the community) to reflect on unity in diversity.

---

[312] ibid., *epichorēgia* and *epichorēgeō*, 673.

[313] See J. B. Lightfoot, *Saint Paul's Epistles to the Colossians and to Philemon* (London 1897) 198f.

[314] Ibid.

[315] *Katº-energeian* ("according to working"). *Energeia* and the similar "power"-languages are designed to indicate the divine work and activity in Christ. What the author of Eph explains in the letter is not only his doctrine of the unity but also his and his community's experience. He felt and experienced the dynamism at work and actualized it and somatized it in his and some of the members of his community's conduct of life. See "power"-languages: Eph 1,11 (*energountos*); 1,19 (*dynamis, energeia, ...*); 1,20 (*energēsen*); 3,16 (*dynamei, krataiothenai, ...*); 3,20 (*dynamenō, dynamin, energoumenēn*); 3,7 (*energeian, dynameōs*) (cf. Phil 2,13; 3,10).

[316] M. Barth, *Comm.*, 447f.

[317] Ibid.

[318] Cf. Eph 4,7.13.

[319] Cf. Eph 3,17f. See below, page 173.

We have studied the special feature of the unity which forms the community of Eph and combines its members. As we examined the first part of our letter (1,3-14), keeping in mind its relation to the rest of the letter, we found that the aspect of the unity among the members of the community together with the apostle, with his disciples and with his collaborators (i.e. the addresser[s] or the sender[s]) was fundamental. The unity there was not static but dynamic. We saw that the text itself held traces of the dynamism and the movement of unification and integration of the new Christians into the "old-but new" community of Christ.

The peculiarity of the language and of its style, and the special thought of the text also show the special literary genre. We have proposed the genre "Christ-agogical" diction in the form of a letter. There existed a previous "consensus" between the writers and the recipients, in order that the latter might be introduced by the apostle and his disciples (i.e. we-people) into a deeper comprehension of the divine mystery of God's will. Especially, we have stressed the aspect of the unity and of the integration which resulted from the divine execution of the mystery of His will (cf. Eph 1,8b-10). This is the meaning of the change of we- and you-styles. The process of deepening the unity is not individual but communal, in view of the cosmic dimension and scope. According to this purpose and intention, the letter was composed. Distinct from the other Pauline letters, Ephesians opens with a hymnic start, its theme, suggesting to us Christ-agogical piety.

All the events are summed up by the blessing of God in Christ (Eph 1,3). The text of 1,3-14 explains God's Act in Christ, in the past, present and future. And God's Act which is "determined" by the expression "in Christ" includes its scope and aim to be reached and to be executed especially with relation to the "you"-group of people (i.e. the recipients i.e. the new Christians). The finality and the scope both presuppose a dynamism to be reached.

As the explanation of our proposal, we have studied the *en Christō*-formula, which is one of the key-expressions to link the Divine Act or dynamism at work with the community of Eph. It is the "determination" of the Divine dynamism at work in the community, because of Christ, in relation to "us" and to "you," and in relation to the whole. God works within "us" and has realized His will partially within the community of Eph, but this is still on the way towards completion in relation to the "you." Here, the title of this thesis, "Somatic comprehension of the Unity" stands. It fills a certain gap between the awareness of the apostle (including "we") and the "you"-people and fills in for "you" the distance between its realization and somatization which at least the apostle and his disciples had already on a certain level attained.

The letter reveals such a "Christ-agogical" dynamism: to introduce "you" into the deeper and fuller awareness of the mystery of the divine will, specifically of his will for such unification and integration, and lead them into its somatization which "we" in part have actualized.

The profound meaning of the expression *en Christō* is a determination of the divine Act for the community which includes its dynamic development: the total integration of the whole, on the level of an individual and community, to the Body of Christ, towards God himself. This fundamental drive and dynamism are expressed explicitly in 1,8b-10, as the main theme of the author of Eph: God has made known to us the mystery of His will, to unite the whole in Christ and to permeate the unifying dynamism into all creatures and into the whole time-space-dimension.

This whole complexity of the divine Act and His dynamism are explained by using the image "Head - Body." Specifically, the intensified and somatized dynamism of God takes the form of community, the Church, the Body of Christ. The body of Christ shows the incomprehensibly profound unity in Christ with God and between men who are Christ's body (i.e. the intimacy and unity of Christ with his body is presupposed). We may say that the expression "in Christ" indicates the somatic intimacy with Christ and his body (with his peoples).

The body of Christ itself is not a group which exists for itself and is not at all an introverted community (i.e. a community for its own sake), but it contains the dynamism to go out to the whole world to serve others in the sense of making dialogue and making itself a bridge between peoples who hate each other, and of reconciling them. It consists of absorbing differences of humanity in any form, into itself, into unity in diversity. The body of Christ, the somatized unity and dynamism, integrating all kinds of differences to One-community of Christ for the Father, grows and expands (cf. Eph 1,23; 4,16). In this way, we believers in Christ all together approach God the Father in one spirit (cf. Eph 2,18).

Because of these tremendous experiences of the community, the speaker stands in front of the audience and with a clear loud voice, with a joyful face, starts to sing out the Blessing of God (1,3ff.). The audience listens to him and watches his face and feels the vibration of his body.

The hymnic tune of thankful joy is the first thing to be shared with the hearers. They are now invited to join in singing the hymn. The speaker says: Listen to the hymn of our community, listen to the heart of the apostle who was caught by Jesus Christ and underwent hardships and suffering, and now was bound in the mystery of God in Christ and chained in a prison for your sake ..., however, listen to his joy and the joy of his collaborators. This is your hymn too! Let the joy of this community permeate your whole body (cf. Eph 5,19f.) even to your deeper emotion.[320]

---

[320] Cf. R. Schnackenburg, "Die große Eulogie Eph 1,3-14 ...," in: *BZ* 21 (1977) 67-87, esp. 83ff.

The first thing of love in Christ is to share the joy. The whole body of the community co-echoes this vibration of joy of the body of Christ, hic et nunc.

Praise God who has blessed us and chose us before the formation of the foundation of the world in Christ, the Beloved One. The audience, listening to the voice of the speaker, feel within themselves, the co-sounding and co-syntonizing of the joy through the body of the speaker, and the "audience" becomes a "congregation". They share the aspiration and breathing of the whole Body of Christ.

We should not underestimate the somatic fellow-feeling of the hymnic beginning of our letter. It is important that the first message of the letter to Eph is to share the vibration of the body of the apostle and of his disciples including the old Christians (i.e. "us") through the hymn.

The origin of joy is not from us humans, but from God Himself. We may say that God cannot help blessing this community in Christ, and "God cannot help loving Christ and his fellow-men." So, God makes the joy springing forth within us. And the blessing of God overflows now from us and to you, and then, to the whole world like water gushing from a spring becomes at last the Ocean.

CHAPTER 4

Prayer, the Indispensable "Modus" of Transmitting the Mystery of Christ

When we considered the verses 1,3-14, particularly 1,8b-10, we noticed the specific importance of the verses 8b-10, in relation to the dynamism of the community of Ephesians (i.e. the dynamism of the Body with the Head), and in relation to a comprehension of the mystery which the apostle prayed for "you" in Eph 1,15ff. and 3,14ff.[1]

In these intercessory prayers, the apostle prays to God that he may give a certain gift of awareness and of the somatization of its awareness for the recipients. The fact that the apostle prayed for these gifts on the behalf of the recipients (i.e. "you") reveals the existence of a certain incompleteness which they yet had to overcome, and that in turn indicates a certain level of awareness and realization of the mystery of the divine will among the "you"- and "we"-group of people (Paul is included among the "we" group of people), lends a movement towards the integration of "you") into the community in Christ. We may say that they had yet some way to go towards the goal. In this sense, there is yet a measurable distance between the two groups of the community of Ephesians in regard to the comprehension and its realization in their lives.

The mystery of God's will which had been made known to "us" (i.e. the "we" group of people) (1,9) has not yet fully been executed by the addressees (i.e. "you").

In order to integrate the recipients fully into the community in Christ, by means of their deepening knowledge of Christ, and by means of their improvement in the awareness and its actualization of the mystery in their conduct of life, the apostle had to pray to God for them (i.e. "you") in Eph 1,15ff. and 3,14ff.

The divine mystery of His will to unite the whole in Christ (cf. 1,8b-10), was the Act of God in the true sense of the word.

At first, it affects(ed) "us," and now affects "you." This inner dynamism of the Act goes hand in hand with the comprehension for which the apostle prayed to God on behalf of those to whom he is writing.

After the verses 1,3-14, we observe that the two intercessory prayers form a frame to the first part of the letter (chapters 1-3). This fact is

---

[1] See the previous pages 112ff.

not purely formal nor a literary device, but the prayers are really meant as prayers: the apostle actually prays.

In other words, the apostle transmits the inner comprehension and the experience of the mystery of the divine will to the hearers, by praying to God for them. We should not forget that the comprehension and its realization are totally a gift of God, which a human analytical mind cannot understand.

What the apostle asked of God for the hearers in these intercessory prayers is a matter of God's grace and will in the true sense of the words.

The apostle, however, wanted to share the gift of God together with the hearers (i.e. "you"). Therefore, he interceded to God for them.

The wish of Paul to share the gift is in intimate relation to the dynamism and the intention of God's will, to make known the mystery of His will to man. The fact that God wants to communicate and to share His inner knowledge of His plan in order to unite "the whole," also to incorporate the hearers, is expressed three times. The first is in the hymnic part (especially in 1,8b-10), and the other two are expressed in the intercessory prayers of the apostle (1,15ff. and 3,14ff.).[2]

The apostle together with the "we" group of the people in the community played the role of the persons who transmit the mystery of the divine will.

On this last point, we have to mention the role of Paul himself in the letter, before we explain the two intercessory prayers.

---

[2] Even the sequences and the grammatical relations in these sentences show a similar structure.

The relation is always:

God (subject)—verb of conferring—thing to give (object of the verb—indirect object(s) (to whom to give)—various clauses to define (*en*-clause, *kata*-clause, etc.).

Eph 1,8b-9a:

"in all wisdom and insight (*en*-clause)—(God) (subject: the verb shows that the subject is God)—had made known (verb: to confer knowledge)—to us (indirect objects)—the mystery of His will (object of the verb).

We may parse this sentence like this:

in all wisdom and insight, God has made known to us the mystery of His will.

Let us now look at the verses 1,17-18a and 3,16-17:

1,17-18a: "(so that) (*hina*)

God of our Lord Jesus Christ, the Father of the glory (subject of the sentence and the actor)—may give (verb)—to you (indirect object)—spirit ... eyes (direct objects)."

3,16-17:

"(so that) (*hina*)

(God the Father) (subject)—may give (verb)—to you (indirect object)—*kata* phrase etc.—to be strengthened (the infinitive verb as the object of the main verb "may give"—*dia* clause— *eis*-clause— to dwell the Christ ("that Christ dwell") (the second direct object)—*dia* clause—*en-phrase*."

4-1: The Role of Paul, the Master of the Mystery of Christ, in Our Experience of the Mystery

"I, Paul, for this reason the prisoner of Christ (Jesus) on behalf of you the gentiles" (3,1) (*toutou charin egō Paulos ho desmios tou Christou [*Iēsou*] hyper hymōn tōn ethnōn*).

In the following pages, we will concern ourselves briefly with the role of Paul himself in the letter. After having explained the function of the "we" group of people in relation to the recipients (i.e. "you") (our Chapter 3), something should be said about how the author of Eph treats Paul in his theology. In 3,1ff., Paul is presented as a key person in making known to them the mystery of Christ and in sharing with them his comprehension of the mystery of the divine will.

Paul himself there becomes a person on whom the hearers made a theological reflection. He appears to have been charged with the function of revealing what was the mystery of the divine will and of the inner living link to incorporate the recipients (i.e. "you") into the community in Christ.

For these reasons, Paul becomes a theme of 3,1-13. Again, after this part, "I" (*egō*) in 3,14 prayed solemnly to God for his readers: that God the Father may give them the gift of the inner life of Christ (which is parallel to the first intercessory prayer in 1,15ff.).

Chapter 3,1 starts with *toutou charin* ("for this reason") to introduce "Paul" (... *egō Paulus* ...).

The meaning of *toutou charin* (for this reason)[3] is to refer back to all the matters treated in earlier chapters; it refers back to the inclusion and incorporation of the recipients (i.e. "you") into the "co-status" of the saints and of the members of the household of God, built upon the foundation of the apostles and prophets, Christ Jesus himself being the cornerstone of the whole structure (cf. 2,19-22).[4]

After the "for this reason," the position of "I Paul" (*egō Paulos*) indicates an emphasis on the person of Paul himself.[5] This verse 3,1 does not have a verb or predicate.[6] We take 3,1 as the theme of the following verses 3,2ff., that means, the author of Eph wants to introduce to the recipients Paul, the prisoner of Christ (Jesus), as the apostle for

---

[3] Blass-Debrunner-Rehkopf, *Grammatik*, § 216,1. We find the same conjunction in Eph 3,14 and Tit 1,5.

[4] Compare Gnilka, *Komm.*, 162; M. Barth, *Comm.*, 326f.; H. Merklein, *Das Kirchliche Amt nach dem Epheserbrief* (München 1973) 161. Also see our pages 144f.

[5] Blass-Debrunner-Rehkopf, *Grammatik*, § 277,1; Gnilka, *Komm.*, 162; H. Merklein, *Amt.*, 161 note 10 and 171, studies the text in comparison to Colossians.

[6] It is an anacolouthon. It seems that introducing a verb "to be" or "to become" is a tendency of certain languages. But this way of starting a text is found in the Bible: Prov 1,1; Eccles 1,1; Mk 1,1. And Ephesians starts a new train of thought abruptly (or so it appears to us moderns) with a pendent or "floating" sentence: see 1,3 which has no *eiē* nor *estin*; the verses 2,1-3 do have a main verb. M. Barth, *Comm.*, 327, discusses this kind of beginning of the verse 3,1.

"you" the gentile.[7] The imprisonment of Paul supplies a theological frame for the first unit (3,2-7)[8] to remind the readers (i.e. "you") of Paul's suffering both for the sake of the gospel and as the follower of Jesus (cf. Phil 1,12ff.).[9]

The fact that Paul was chained probably became the token of his state as bound to the mystery of the divine will and of Christ.[10] And this "chained" status of Paul was on behalf of "you" the gentiles (*hyper hymōn tōn ethnōn*: 3,1). The person Paul himself is internally related to the inclusion of "you" the gentile.

The words *hyper hymōn* ("on your behalf") together with the words *ho desmios* ("the prisoner") show the person of Paul as the main interest of Eph in this part 3,1ff.[11]

Here, the author of Ephesians, however, does not think merely of the recipients (i.e. "you") in the community, but by speaking to "you," he recalls the role of Paul as their predecessor in the faith, as the representative of the "we" group of people in the letter. He widened their view of the mystery of the will of God and of their roles in it for the world. They have internally a relation to the other "you" yet outside their community.[12] Paul himself is given to them as a key person on whom they are to reflect. For Paul was specially gifted by God for the role of transmitting the mystery of Christ to "you" the readers (cf. 3,2-7) and was appointed by God as the key person for the evangelization of the gentiles and as the key person in illuminating the plan of the mystery hidden for ages in God who created the whole (all things) (cf. 3,8-12).

The verse 3,2 explains what Paul represented for the community of Ephesians[13] by using the rhetorical *ei ge* ("as ...," "suppose ...") in order to imply a more definite assumption for the readers.[14]

Ephesians states: assuming that you have surely heard[15] of the plan of God's grace which was given to Paul (*moi*). The execution has shown

---

[7] Gnilka, *Komm.*, 162.

[8] The word *desmios* ("prisoner") in 3,1 forms an inclusion to the similar sense of word *diakonos* ("servant") in 3,7 of the gospel.

[9] Paul called himself *desmios tou Christou ᵓIēsou* ("a prisoner of Christ Jesus") in Philem 1.9 in allusion to his theological reflections on his own imprisonment. Cf. Philem 13, on this verse, cf. Orllog, *Paulus und seine Mitarbeiter*, 101f.

[10] Cf. Eph 4,1; Rom 11,13; 1 Cor 4,15; 2 Cor 11,23; Gal 1,12; Gal 4,12ff., 19f.; Col 1,23f.; 4,18; 1 Tim 1,11; 2,7. Also see Merklein, *Amt*, 172.

[11] The *hyper hymōn* ("on the behalf of you") is a function to include this section 3,1-13. See the same words *hyper hymōn* in 3,13 where the apostle asked the readers not to lose heart over what he was suffering for them, which was their glory.

[12] Gnilka, *Komm.*, 162f., says that the author of Eph did not have a concrete addressee here in mind.

[13] On the words *ei ge*, see Blass-Debrunner, § 454, 2; Gnilka, *Komm.*, 163; H. Merklein, *Amt*, 162.

[14] Gnilka, *Komm.*, 163; M. Barth, *Comm.*, 328.

[15] On the verb *akouein* ("to hear") cf. M. Barth, *Comm.*, 328. Also cf. Eph 1,13.

the manner in which God conceived His plan and incorporated Paul into this plan.[16]   This gift of Paul was not for himself but for "you".[17]

The author of Eph, then, explains the content of the gift of Paul in 3,3ff.[18]

As Paul wrote briefly,[19] he was made to know the mystery by revelation.[20] Paul was given the intimate communication with God[21] and became the key person of the divine plan to preach the gospel for "you" (cf. 3,2-3,7) and to announce the plan of God for all creatures (cf. 3,9f.).

Therefore, his inner comprehension and perception of the mystery became the thing through which the readers might comprehend: "When you read this you can perceive my insight into the mystery of Christ" (3,4).[22] Through his activity as the minister and the apostle for the gentiles, through his suffering and hope, his imprisonment and salvation, his life and death, God revealed what was His will (cf. Eph 5,17).

The essential Pauline insight consisted in the fact that the gentiles have been incorporated into the community in Christ, and they have shared the promise in Christ Jesus through evangelization (cf. 3,5f.).

His mission was to enlighten all nations as to the plan of the mystery hidden from the ages in God who created all things. So that the multiform wisdom of God may be known to the powers in the heavenly places through the church (cf. 3,9-10).

4-2: Hope, Divine Gift of the Somatic Dynamism

The intercessory prayer in Eph 1,15 begins with the conjunction *dia touto*, "for this reason." By this conjunction, the train of thought is

---

[16] See the previous pages 112ff. as well.

[17] Compared with the "Ur-Erfahrung" which happened to "us" (cf. Eph 1,9; 1,8; 1,11-12; 2,7 etc.), the *eis hymas* ("for the sake of you") in 3,2 has an emphatic tone in relation to the vocation and role of Paul. As we have explained about the "you"-style in 1,13 (pages 104ff.), God's strategy to execute His plan must now be acknowledged and realized by the recipients (i.e. "you"). Compare the parallel verse of Eph 3,2 with Col 1,25ff.

[18] The *hoti* ("namely that ...") in the sense of explaining the gift: see Merklein, *Amt.*, 162; Gnilka, *Komm.*, 163, note 5, gives some textual variations.

[19] The sentence *kathōs proegrapsa en oligō* ("as I wrote briefly") did not refer to the other Pauline letters which we have at hand. He (or the author of Eph) refers to the statements mentioned above in the letter to the Ephesians or in other "unknown" letters. On this interpretation, see Gnilka, *Komm.*, 164; M. Barth, *Comm.*, 329; Merklein, *Amt.* 163.

[20] Compare the following verses: Eph 1,9; 1,17. And also cf. Rom 16,25f.; Gal 1, 12; 2,2. About the background and possible meaning of the words *apokalypsis, apokalyptein* ("revelation," "to reveal"): see A. Oepke, "*apokalypsis*," "*apokalyptō*" in: *TDNT*, III, 563-592, esp. 582ff.; O. Lührmann, *Das Offenbarungsverständnis bei Paulus und in Paulinischen Gemeinde* (Göttingen 1971) 75 and 171ff., treats of the meaning of "revelation" in our letter.

[21] M. Barth, *Comm.*, 330.

[22] The clause *synesis mou en tōi mysteriōi* ("my insight into the mystery") alludes to several passages of Qumran documents: 1 QH, 2,13; 12,13; on this see Gnilka, *Komm.*, 165, who refers to the study of K. G. Kuhn, art. cit.: *NTS* 7 (1960-1961) 336.

carried forward.[23] At the same time, it connects vv. 1,15ff. closely with the preceding text. To what exactly does it refer? There are two main possibilities.[24]

If we fix our attention on the personal pronouns which denote the recipients in the context: "to you" (*hymin*) in 1,2; "you" (*hymeis*) in 1,13; "your faith" (*kath' hymas*) in 1,15; "for you" (*hyper hymōn*) in 1,16; "to you" (*hymin*) in 1,17, then the words "for this reason" (*dia touto*) point to referring the verses 1,15ff. back to the passage of 1,13, namely, to the fact that you have heard the word of the truth, the gospel of your salvation, and have believed and were sealed with the holy spirit of the promise.

On the other hand, if we take notice of the effect of the intercessory prayer, which has already brought to a certain level of fruition the "we" group of people (within "us") and which the author of Ephesians now asks for the sake of the recipients in 1,15ff., then the meaning and function of "for this reason" is to refer back to the fact which happened to "us" (i.e. the old Christians), which was explained and described in 1,3-12.

The main verb of the verses 1,15f. is "I do not cease" (*pauomai*), 1,16,[25] followed by the participle *eucharistōn* ... ("thanking ...") (cf. Philem 5; Col 1,4; 1,9).

This sentence states that the sender of the letter has known of the practices of the faith and the love of the addressees.[26] The reaction of the sender to the news about them was the thanksgiving for them. So, the verses run thus: "For this reason, also I because I too having heard of your faith in the Lord Jesus and of your love toward all the saints,

---

[23] You find similar wording in: 1 Thess 2,13; Col 1,9. See Schubert, *Form and Function*, 21; Lohse, *Col*, 24f.; O'Brien, *Introductory thanksgiving* 82f. And with regard to the connection of thanksgiving and intercessory prayer, see Lohse, *Col*, 12ff. Apart from the letter to the Ephesians, the opening of 2 Cor and of 1 Pet are followed by a eulogy, which begins with the wordings "Blessed be God ..." (*eulogētos ho theos*) (2 Cor 1,3; 1 Pet 1,3). The eulogy of Ephesians (1,3-14) is followed by thanksgiving of the normal Pauline letter form (Eph 1,15ff.). On this, cf. Schubert, op. cit., 8, 31, 44. and O'Brien, op. cit., p. 3, note 5 and pp. 233ff. and 239. And refer to the previous pages on the style of the letter to the Ephesians, 75ff. 80ff.

[24] Schlier, *Komm.*, 75 states: "... So liegt der Grund des Dankes, zu dem sich der Apostel nun wendet, in einem Doppelten: einmal in dem, was 1,13f. bzw. überhaupt in 1,3-14 zu sagen war, in dem Segen Gottes bzw. dem Anteil auch der Christen aus den Heiden daran; dann aber auch in dem, was der Partizipialsatz v. 15 selbst enthält, in dem Glauben und der Liebe der Gemeinde, von denen Paulus gehört hatte ..." Also compare Gnilka, *Komm.*, 88; J. Ernst, *Komm.*, 284.

[25] In other Pauline letters, words which have a similar meaning occur: *pantote* ("always") in Philem 4; 1 Thess 1,2; 2 Cor 1,3; Phil 1,4 and *ou pauometha* ("we do not cease") in Col 1,9. About "incessant prayer", cf. G. P. Wiles, *Paul's Intercessory Prayers* (Cambridge 1974) 158ff., and 181ff. We do not think that this thanksgiving and intercessory prayer is merely a literary device. Contemporary Jewish and Christian practices of prayer three times a day and Christ's instructions about "incessant prayer" (cf. Lk 18,1ff.) suggest also that the apostle really prayed often and did not only mean that Christians should live as if they stood always in prayer before God.

[26] Compare Philem 5; Col 1,4.9.

do not cease to give thanks for you, remembering you in my prayer."
After these verses, in 1,17 the content of his prayer follows:

> that the God of our Lord Jesus Christ, the Father of the glory,
> may give you a spirit of wisdom and of revelation in the knowledge
> of him, (v. 18) (having) the eyes of your heart enlightened, so that
> you may know what is the hope of his calling, what are the riches
> of his glorious inheritance in the saints, (v. 19) and what is the
> immeasurable greatness of his power in us who have believed,
> according to the working (*energeian*) of his great might.

As the text shows, the subject of the verb "may give" (*dōēi*) is the
God of our Lord Jesus Christ, the Father of the glory.[27]

In regard to the mood of the verb "may give" (*dōēi*), there are two
possibilities: it may be optative (*dōēi*)[28], or subjunctive (*dōēi*).[29] We take it
in the sense of the optative considering the context which we will explain.

The gifts for which the apostle asked for the sake of the recipients
are "a spirit of wisdom and of revelation in his comprehension" and
"enlightened eyes of your heart." We understand the "enlightened eyes
of your heart" in apposition to "spirit of wisdom and of revelation."[30]
We do not think that the spirit in 1,17 conceived as a gift of God can be
adequately described as a "quality" of man or of a "thing." It cannot be
grasped and experienced merely by the common faculties of man in time
and space. Whether or not a man has this "spirit," is discerned only
through a process of a life in faith, through a conduct of life, through a
manner of life which goes through the course of an historical development.

In the line of this understanding we interpret the two accusatives in
correspondence with each other. They express the same "fact" and
experience from another point of view.[31]

These two accusatives are followed by the "*en*-construction" "in his
comprehension" (*en epignōsei autou*) and by the infinitive-clause "so that
you may know ..." (*eis to eidenai hymas ...*), respectively. We feel that
they follow the two accusatives because of the rhythm of breath needed
to dictate or to read them to others, and especially because of their
meaning in the context. The expression "in his comprehension" in 1,17,
according to this understanding, modifies the preceding expression "spirit
of wisdom and of revelation."[32]

---

[27] The God in our letter is the God of glory: compare Eph 1,6.12.14.
[28] With M. Zerwick, *Analysis Philologica Novi Testamenti Graeci* (Rome 1966³), ad
locum; Gnilka, *Komm.*, 89, note 4.
[29] M. Barth, *Comm.*, 148 takes it as subjunctive along with "telic" *hina*; Caragounis,
The Ephesian mysterion, 65, takes it as subjunctive with a weakened *hina*.
[30] Caragounis, op. cit., 65, mentions the several positions of authors.
[31] Compare Caragounis, ibid., 65f.
[32] With Schlier, *Komm.*, 79; J. Ernst, *Komm.*, 285f. Gnilka, *Komm.*, 90, relates
the phrase en *epignōsei autou* to verse 1,18.

Authors disagree about the meaning of the words *en epignōsei autou,* especially about the sense of the genitive *autou.* Some take the *autou* as genitive objectivus, so that they translate the expression thus: "so that you may get to know Him (God)." [33]

But we take it as genitive subjectivus or auctoris. The meaning, then, will be: "in (the) comprehension which God holds." In a similar way, we have explained also all the other instances, where it would theoretically be possible to think of God as an object of human cognition. We do not think that the letter to the Ephesians ever conceives of God as an object of the comprehension of man.[34] The same term *epignōsis* ("comprehension") occurs in Eph 4,13 in a similar context. There, the genitive phrase "into the unity of faith and of comprehension of the son of God" (*eis tēn henotēta tēs pisteōs kai tēs epignōseos tou huiou tou theou*) also is to be understood in the sense of a genitivus auctoris or possessivus: "until we all attain to the unity of the faith and of the comprehension of the son of God." This comprehension is the one which the Son of God held and possessed.[35]

Grammatically, it would be possible here to refer the *autou* in *en epignōsei autou* also to Jesus Christ, because we have the expression *ho theos tou kyriou hēmōn ᵒIēsou Christou* at the beginning of the phrase in 1,17. Further reasons could be drawn from the context, because the "hymn," 1,3-14, contained very many *en-Christōi*-formulas, and the following context, 1,20ff., speaks about the power of God who raised Christ from the dead and made him sit at his right hand in the heavens, so that he also became the head of his body, the church. For this case, there also would be possible interpretations of the phrase *en epignōsei autou* ("in his comprehension"): "in the knowledge which Christ has and holds" (genitive auctoris), or "in the knowledge about Jesus Christ, namely knowing him" (genitivus objectivus). However, taking into consideration the use of *autou* in the immediate context: "his calling" in 1,18, "his power" (*dynameōs autou*) in 1,19, "his might" (*ischuos autou*) in 1,19, we conclude that *autou* also here denotes not Jesus Christ, but God.

In the preceding hymn, it was God's eternal wisdom and insight, since the foundation of the world, which intended and created and executed the revelation of the mystery of the will of God in Christ. God's own insight and comprehension is the reason and the base and the power and the way which can make it possible that any knowledge of the mystery of his will is revealed.[36] This is expressed clearly also by the *en*-construction in 1,8b *en pasēi sophiai kai phronēsei* ("in every wisdom and insight").

---

[33] Thus, Caragounis, op. cit., 65f. M. Barth, *Comm.,* 148f., understands the *en*-construction thus: "so that you may know him."
[34] See page 71 note (1).
[35] See page 138 note (263).
[36] Compare: Eph 1,9; 3,3f.; 3,9-10; 3,20; 5,17; 6,19. Cf. Chapter 3-6-1, 112ff.

Therefore, we interpret the passage 1,17 like thus: God may give to the readers (i.e. "you") (the) spirit of wisdom and of revelation in (the) comprehension which God holds and possesses. It is precisely the intention of this letter to introduce the readers into this comprehension.

The gift of the spirit of wisdom and of revelation is totally divine and affects the whole man. The core of the human being must be enlightened by God.

The enlightenment shows a totally new view of life, guiding man to a conduct of life in Christ that is exactly opposed to the existence of man whose mind is darkened and who is separated from the life of God, by hardening his heart (cf. Eph 4,18).[37] And the process of penetration by the enlightenment may permeate a whole person, a whole body (cf. Eph 5,13f.).

This fact of permeation can be seen only through his conduct of life. The apostle prays that God may enlighten the eyes of the heart of the recipients [38] and that they may come to know [39] what is the hope of God's calling.

In our exegesis of Eph 2,12, we defined hope as an original experience of Christian life, which is lacking in the "past" of the "heathen in the flesh." [40]

Here, in Eph 1,18, hope comes from the awareness which itself springs forth from the gift of a spirit of wisdom and of revelation, which God holds. The apostle does not mention here the expectation of the Parousia, nor the resurrection of the dead, nor the fulfilment of the Kingdom of God. Therefore one is not justified in understanding hope here in a general way.[41] Surely, hope in our letter is in some way the content of the good news, of the *euaggelion*, but the author never does express in plain words what exactly is the content of hope.[42] To confine the significance of Eph 1,18 *hē elpis tēs klēseōs autou* to the hope in God's call appears at least to be ambiguous.[43]

Perhaps the hope rests on the very fact that the call is God's call and thus it is not something which stems from our simple wish for better things.[44] If so then this must be carried further and arguments must be presented from the text to sustain it.

---

[37] See previous pages 30ff. Chapter 2.

[38] Visual description of divinity is wide spread in antiquity: cf. W. Michaelis, "*horaō*" etc.: *TDNT*, V, 315-58; H. Conzelmann, "*phōs*", "*phōtizō*", etc. *TDNT*, IX, 310-58, esp., 347-49; Schlier, *Komm.*, 79f.

[39] The infinitive clause *eis to ...* is used to denote purpose or result. The meaning of the clause in 1,18 is: "in order to know ..." or "so that (you) may know ..." See Blass-Debrunner-Rehkopf, *Grammatik*, § 402, 2.

[40] See our Chapter 2 pages 45ff.

[41] J. A. Allain, *The Epistle to the Ephesians* (London 1959) 65-66.

[42] Lindemann, *Die Aufhebung*, 194f., states that hope in our letter does not have a future aspect.

[43] R. S. Candisch, *Paul's Epistle to the Ephesians* (Edinburgh 1875) 35.

[44] J. A. Robinson, *St. Paul's Epistle to the Ephesians* (London 1909) 54.

The *tis* ("what") has a nuance of *"qualitas"* rather than of *"quidditas"* ("whatness") and it demands an answer to the question of what kind of hope you have or what exactly you hope for. It is hardly sufficient to understand hope here simply as a hope for something in the future in heaven.[45]

The question arises as to whether the author of Ephesians prays that God may grant the saints discernment among the various hopes that are possible.[46] It is doubtful that this is the case. The letter does not speak of different hopes. Surely the *tis* clauses in Eph 1,18-19 transcend all epistemological limitations of the questioning mind of man, looking for an adequate concept of "whatness."

The context shows that pure human reasoning cannot fully comprehend it. As we have already pointed out, it should not be forgotten that the author incorporates these *tis* clauses into the apostle's prayer of intercession. The full "understanding" of this hope forms part of the process of growth in enlightenment and in the comprehension of the new eschatological situation of the christian.[47] Hope in this case is not a subjective tendency of man but it belongs to what might be called the *res sperata*.[48] It does not have primarily a future aspect because the call (*hē klēsis*) to which the hope is related here belongs to the present reality.[49]

---

[45] J.-M. Vosté, *Commentarius in Epistolam ad Ephesios* (Rome-Paris 1932) 130, states: "... spes maxima in futuram beatitudinem. ..."

[46] M. Barth, *Comm.*, 151, says: "... In 1,18 Paul prays that God grant the saints discernment among the various hopes that are possible. They are to become aware which hope is decisive to them. Not any hope or number of hopes, but just 'one hope' is held and confessed by the Christians (4,4). Eph 1,18 and 4,4, specify the one prospect as 'the hope of your calling' or 'the hope to which you have been called.'"

[47] J. H. Houlden, *Paul's Letters from Prison* (Penguin Books 1970) 275.

[48] J. Belser, *Der Epheserbrief des Apostels Paulus* (Freiburg 1908) 38, says: "... welch eine große und herrliche Hoffnung uns infolge unserer Berufung...." Schlier, *Komm.*, 82, states: "... elpis ist hier das Hoffnungsgut, die res sperata, so wie etwa auch Gal 5, 5; Kol 1,5.27.... Das sachliche Verhältnis der Hoffnung zum Ruf wird sich dahin bestimmen, daß sich im Rufe Gottes die Hoffunung als Hoffnungsgut erschließt. In Rufe Gottes werden wir in die uns rufende Hoffnung gestellt, um in ihr zu stehen." Cf. H. A. W. Meyer, *Handbuch über den Brief an die Epheser*, (Göttingen 1965) 62. E. Gaugler, *Der Brief des Paulus an die Epheser* (Wuppertal 1961) 65, states: "... elpis (Hoffnung) kann an sich 'das Hoffen' und 'das erhoffte,' das Hoffnungs (Erwartungs-)gut beziehen." Gnilka, *Komm.* 91: "... Der Ruf, der die geschichtliche Verwirklichung der vorzeitigen Auswahl ist, bewirkt Hoffnung. Genauer läßt sich die Hoffnung als im Himmel bereitliegende res sperata bestimmen." J. Ernst, *Komm.*, 288, says: "... An die Stelle des 'Hoffens' ist das 'Hoffnungsgut' getreten, das in den Himmeln bereitliegt (vg. Kol 1,5; 1 Pet 1,3f.)...." Conzelmann, H., *an die Epheser* (*NTD* 8; Göttingen 1976) 94, states: "... 'Hoffnung' bezieht hier nicht die Haltung des Erwartens, sondern das erhoffte Gut."

[49] Lindemann, *Die Aufhebung*, 194f., states: "... In Eph 1,18 und in 4,4 ist—in gleicher Weise wie im Kolosserbrief—die elpis selbst die res sperata die keinen Zukunftaspekt hat, weil die *klēsis*, auf die sich die Hoffnung beziehen könnte, gegenwärtige Realität ist. Nach 1,18 ist Hoffnung "der schon errungene Sieg des erhöhten Christus über die kosmischen Mächte und die Verwirklichung der Kirche als seines Leibes unter ihm als dem Haupte; sie ist eine 'Sphären-Wirklichkeit, die bereits ver-

The expression "the hope of the call" (*hē elpis tēs klēseōs*) is found only in Ephesians in the N.T. (1,18; 4,4). The call embraces the whole complex of the eschatological hope.[50]

For the author of Ephesians, the hope must be expressed by the way of life which ought to correspond to the divine calling (4,1.4.). This divine vocation calls us into the unity of the one hope (4,4).[51] In 4,4, the author's main concern is not the hope, but the call.[52] We can conclude therefore that the role of hope in the letter is related to the new mode of expressing the "eschatological reality."

The examination of the phrase *elpida mē echontes* ("having no hope") in Eph 2,12, revealed the double level of this hope. One level refers to "your" way of life "at that time" (past), when "you" were estranged from "us" believers in Christ. The second is a specific hope for which one is asked to pray in order that "you" within "our" community may respond totally to the hope of the calling, and thus act in a way which is consonant with the inner comprehension of what the hope is.

Thus the verb *proelpizein* in Eph 1,12 becomes a key to the understanding of the author's eschatology and the hope in question. The context there is the dialectic between "us" and "you."[53]

If we compare verses 1,11-12 with verses 1,18-19, we observe that the verses 1,11-12 have an internal relation to the content of the "comprehension" prayed for in 1,18f. The verb "*klērousthai*" in 1,11 is difficult to translate. We adopt the meaning of "to be allotted" (namely, an inheritance).[54] The sentence "we have been allotted" (namely, "we have been made His heritage") in 1,11 corresponds to the second *tis* ("what")-sentence of 1,18b: "what is the riches of the glory of His inheritance in the saints" (*tis ho ploutos tēs doxēs tēs klēronomias autou en tois hagiois*).

And the clause "according to (the) purpose of him who dynamizes the whole, according to the counsel of His Will" (*kata prothesin tou ta panta energountos kata tēn boulēn tou thelēmatos autou*) in 1,11 corresponds to the third "what" clause in 1,19: "and what is the immeasurable greatness of his power in us who have believed according to the working of his great might" (*kai ti to hyperballon megethos tēs dynameōs autou eis hēmas tous pisteuontas kata tēn energeian tou kratous tēs ischuos autou*).

And the infinitive clause of 1,12 *eis to einai hēmas eis epainon doxēs autou tous proēlpikotas en tō̤ Christō̤* ("that we had hoped before [you]

---

wirklich ist und in kein Schema einer zeitlich gerichteten Eschatologie sich mehr einfügt.' "

[50] F.-J. Steinmetz, *Protologische Heilszuversicht* (Frankfurt 1969) 137.

[51] The sentence *hen sōma kai hen pneuma ...* does not have an imperative sense. Schlier, *Komm.*, 186; Gnilka, *Komm.*, 200.

[52] Lindemann, *Die Aufhebung*, 195.

[53] See pp. 104ff.

[54] M. Zerwick, M. Grosvenor, *Grammatical Analysis* (Rome 1979) II, 579; cf. Gnilka, *Komm.*, 82f., see also 82, note 7.

for the praise of His glory in Christ") could, then, be understood as corresponding to the first "what"-sentence of 1,18a: "what is the hope of
the His calling" (*tis estin hē elpis tēs klēseōs autou*).

To understand the meaning of "hope" in our letter, we may interpret
the verse 1,11-12 in the following way: In Christ we were made God's
heritage and were His inheritance which consisted in the saints, in the
community of Christ. "We" had hoped before "you" hoped, and "we"
had surrendered ourselves to the power of God who was at work in all
creatures according to the counsel of His will. Now "we," the old Christians, pray to God for "you" a gift: that "you" may "synchronize" your
aspiration with our hope to which God is calling now. For this purpose,
"we" were chosen by God before "you" and hoped before "you."

Coming back to verse 1,18, we find that hope is not defined according to a time-concept, according to the traditional scheme of "already" and
"not yet." We can perhaps say that the "already" and "not yet"-concep-
tion of being in motion is based on a geometrical image of moving or of
changing reality. Such an image of time is "spatially" extended back-
wards (i.e. the past) and forwards (i.e. the future). This "spatial way"
of consciousness of motion is expressed in a linear image: past — present — future, in points which follow each other on a line.[55] A group of
languages has adopted this linear time-image to express the relation of
reality to its surroundings in "time." But the author of Ephesians, even
in using these concepts of the description of time,[56] does not describe
the eschatological reality with any concrete word about the "future"
parousia, the resurrection or the day to come, as we have already said.[57]

This attitude appeals to one whose language does not contain the
time-tenses of the European languages. In Japanese, e.g., reality is expressed in its wholeness, seeing the past together with the future in relation
to the present which is experienced. The Japanese language expresses
the past only in so far as it adds certainty to the notion. The intention
of the speaker or writer is to express conviction about memory of the
past. In a similar way, the Japanese language does use certain auxiliary
verbs — which in modern grammars for the use of foreigners are described
as expressing the Western future tense. But these auxiliary verbs describe

---

[55] See: T. Boman, *Das hebräische Denken im Vergleich mit dem griechischen*
(Göttingen 1952, ⁴1965) 109ff.; O. Cullmann, *Christ and Time* (London 1962, 1967) 48ff.
definition of "time," 139ff. (description of "future"); idem, *Heil als Geschichte.
Heilsgeschichtliche Existenz im Neuen Testament* (Göttingen 1965) esp. "Gegenwart
und Zukunft. Die heilsgeschichtliche Spannung zwischen 'schon' und 'noch nicht' als
Schlüssel zum Verständnis der neutestamentlichen Heilsgeschichte" (147ff.). Cf. also
G. Greshake, *Auferstehung der Toten. Ein Beitrag zur gegenwärtigen theologischen
Diskussion über die Zukunft der Geschichte* (Essen 1969) 228-231, 326ff. cf. "Verstehens-
Aporien bei Barth, Bultmann und Moltmann", 334ff.

[56] He mentions also a traditional expression like "this age" and "the age to come"
in 1,21.

[57] The redemption or liberation (*apolytrōsis*) in 1,7.14 is expected in the future.
Also cf. Lindemann, *Die Aufhebung*, 96f.

not so much real "future" in the sense of a linear time-image as much as
subjective uncertainty about developments of actual events, or guesses
and suppositions of the speaker.[58]

· We may ask ourselves whether the linear time image does really
express the somatic wholeness of reality. Past time affects present time,
and the present event affects the future. That is even more true if we
believe in "eschatological" reality. The writings of the Bible try to express
in different ways the importance of the divine eschatological event. Our
letter to the Ephesians does so with special emphasis upon the divine
power breaking into our present reality.

Thus, the author of Eph is eager to see the present fact of the community which has been effected by the eschatological event of Christ.[59]

This tendency also appears in his notion of hope. He sees a present
aspect of hope. In order to show this, he uses the word hope together
with "calling."

"To hope in" God is generally *to surrender oneself confidently* to
God. It is not merely a subjective feeling of hopefulness. Here we must
remember what kind of god is spoken of in Ephesians to whom man surrenders himself.

The god of Ephesians is a god who is at work in Christ integrating
and uniting the whole in Christ, and intensively and dynamically unifying
peoples into one community of Christ. He is a god who is genuinely at
work, forming the community of Ephesians and making the unity between
them deepen and grow into the reconciliation and unity of the world.

The unity and integration of people is one of the fundamental aspects
of the mystery of God's will in our letter. To that goal, God is at work
and calling men.

This dynamic calling is to form the community and is now really
at work in the community of Eph. The author of Eph comprehends hope
within this dynamism of the community.

In the Pauline letters, the group of terms "calling" (*klēsis, kalein,
eklektos, eklegein, ekklēsia* ...) has a deeply theological meaning.[60] The

---

[58] S. Ono, *Nihongo nobunpo o kangaeru* ("To Consider Japanese Grammar") (Tokyo
1978) 138ff. The ancient Japanese conceived eternity by using a symbol *banjyaku*
(a huge rock) and "time" (*toki*) is understood in the sense of "melting" (thing) or
"getting loose" (N. B.: these two English words are shown in one Japanese word
toku.) On this see S. Ono, *Nihongo o sakanoboru* ("To Trace Back the Japanese
Language") (Tokyo 1974) 182ff. Greek future tenses should not invariably be
translated by a Japanese future tense, which is normally a form of "uncertain guess
or supposition" of the speaker, e.g.: 1 Cor 15,49 *phoresomen* (we shall bear). Cf.
K. Usami, "How are the dead raised?" *Bib* 57 (1976), 468-93, esp. 488.

[59] We have interpreted aorist verbs in the context of Eph 1,3ff., as referring to
some fact that happened in the past but still affects the present community of
Ephesians. See pages 108ff.

[60] See: K. L. Schmidt, "*kaleō*", "*klēsis*", "*eklegō*", etc. in: *TDNT*, III, 487-536;
Schlier, *Komm.*, 82f. K. L. Schmidt, "*ekklēsia*" in: *TDNT*, 501-36. In our letter the
ekklēsia ("church") is the Body of Christ. Because of the dynamic relation of the

author of Eph, having taken account of these theological meanings, appears to have developed a conception of hope which is more in relation to the present. This is the reason why he combines hope with "calling." God's calling creates the community. That does not mean a static profession, status or vocation.[61]   Rather, it relates to the actual conduct of life. Therefore, verse 4,1 encourages the readers to walk worthy of the calling to which they are called: "I, therefore, a prisoner in the Lord (en kyriōi), beg you to conduct your life worthy of the calling to which you are called" (4,1).

The calling must be somatized by their practical manner of life. And the "quality" of the conduct of their life is described in 4,2ff. It is a "walk" in accordance with eagerness and sensitivity in keeping and deepening the unity of the spirit which remains in the bond of peace (cf. Col 3,15). The deeper sense of unity is based upon the calling in one hope to which God is calling them (cf. 4,4).[62]   The calling therefore opens the door to hope.

The first aspect of comprehension asked for in the intercessory prayer in 1,17ff. consists in the awareness of the present impulse of hope. The readers are called to the deeper unity, as we explained above.[63]   They are called into one body and one spirit. They are called to the community of Christ, who is really aware of what the hope of their calling is. The community is the expression of hope and the beginning of complete communion and unity, between man and God, between man and man.

To sum up, the characteristic feature of hope in Ephesians is to see hope in the term of the dynamic present calling of God in the community. It is internally related to the dynamism of integration and deeper unification which is now in process in the community.

The community of Ephesians surrenders herself to God, to the power of God confidently and joyfully.[64]   *It is the power of God who executes His plan to unite the whole in Christ.*

In the second sentence in 1,18b, the comprehension is described as the riches of God's glorious inheritance. The power of His splendour

---

church to the head Christ, the inner divine power is at work to call the "old" Christians and the "new" Christians to form one community of Christ. The term *ekklēsia* ("church") has a rich content both in the Old Testament and in the Greek world. See Schmidt, art. cit., 501ff. We suppose that the audiences of Ephesians understood what the term "ekklēsia" meant in their cultural context, in a hellenistic city like Ephesus. The citizens were accustomed to assemble together and those who were called and assembled by the herald of that city were called *eklektoi*. It is also found on a bilingual inscription from Ephesus (A. D. 103/104) in which the Greek word *ekklēsia* is simply transcribed (see Schmidt, ibid.). Cf. Eph 2,12.19, where we feel the urban sense of the letter.

[61] Cf. Gal 3,28; 1 Cor 1,26ff.; 7,20ff.; 12,13.

[62] About the meaning of *kathōs* in 4,4, we take it in the sense of a base for the unity. See Schlier, *Komm.*, 186; Gnilka, *Komm.*, 201, note 4.

[63] See above, Chapter 3, pages 127ff. especially.

[64] This community of Ephesians sang out the hymn of their community.

gives us the strength and the possibility to reach to His inheritance. The apostle prays that we may come to know this power of God.

The term "inheritance" (*klēronomia*) belongs to a group of words which are based on Jesus-Christ's filial relationship to God in the New Testament.[65] In our letter, it recalls the motif of the election of the community (cf. Eph 1,3ff.; 1,11).[66] This filial relationship of the community to God is understood in our letter not statically but dynamically.[67] Through Jesus Christ, it is not merely a status once for all, but is a status of growth and of a process to God.

The riches of the glorious inheritance of God seem to consist in the community of the saints (cf. Act 20,32).[68] The meaning of "the saints" (*tois hagiois*) here in the verse 1,18 does not denote angels in the heavens,[69] but the concrete people of the Christian communities: the believers in Christ. This communion includes saints in heaven, but that is not explicitly stated. According to our opinion, the saints are really a community of Christians. The following instances support our opinion. In Eph 1,1, the apostle addresses the letter to the saints (being) in Ephesus and to the faithful people in Christ Jesus (Eph 1,1) (*Paulos apostolos Christou ᵒIēsou dia thelēmatos theou* tois hagiois *tois ousin en Ephesōi kai pistois en Christōi ᵒIēsou*).

In 1,4, it is stated that God chose "us" so that "we" might be *holy* and blameless (... *exelexato hēmas ... einai hēmas hagious kai amōmos...*). One of the purposes of the election is that we become holy. This ideal of the sanctification of man is re-expressed in a different context elsewhere in the letter. In verse 5,3, the apostle encourages the readers to behave worthily of their holiness. It is the Christians who might become holy, not angels.

The verse 6,18 is a similar case: the apostle asks the readers to make supplication for all the saints (... *kai deēsei peri* pantōn tōn hagiōn). Among these saints, the apostle Paul is numbered. He was the least of all the saints (3,8): "To me, though I am the very least of all the saints..." (*emoi tōi elachistoterōi pantōn hagiōn...*). To him and to holy apostles of Christ and prophets in spirit, the mystery of Christ has now been revealed (3,5) (... *hōs nyn apekalyphthē* tois hagiois apostolois *autou kai prophētais en pneumati*).

And the following texts decisively denote that the saints (*hoi hagioi*) in our letter are communities of Christians.

---

[65] See W. Foerster, "*klēronomos, klēronomia*", etc. in: *TDNT*, III, 776-85, esp. 783.
[66] J. Ernst, *Komm.*, 288f.
[67] See our Chapter 3, especially page 101.
[68] Cf. our pages 160f.
[69] Gnilka, *Komm.*, 91, takes this sense; M. Barth, *Comm.*, 151, states: "... the saints, with whom the readers of Ephesians have their share, may be either the angels or Israel." N. A. Dahl, "Cosmic Dimensions and Religious Knowledge" in: *Jesus und Paulus* (Festschrift für W. Kümmel) (1975), 57-75, esp. 73, refers to the angels.

The "fellow citizens of the saints" (*sympolitai tōn hagiōn*) in 2,19, even though the words allude to inhabitants in the heavens or angels as we stated,[70] mean at first sight a concrete people, the community of Christians. To those communities, the recipients (i.e. "you") are now incorporated. By this incorporation, they grow into a holy temple in the Lord (2,21).[71] The passage 4,12 strengthens our opinion. In the verse it is stated, "... to equip *the saints* for the work of the ministry for building up the body of Christ (*pros ton katartismon* tōn hagiōn *eis ergon diakonais, eis oikodomēn tou sōmatos tou Christou*). These saints are not angels but men. The body of Christ is a real human community. The immeasurable mystery of Christ had been made known to man. And he was to comprehend it *with all the saints*, namely with all the communities of believers in Christ: "that you may have power to comprehend with all the saints, ..." (*hina exischysēte katalabesthai* syn pasin tois hagiois...) (3,18).[72] To conclude, in all these texts the term *hagioi* ("saints") denotes Christians. By interpreting the saints in the sense of spiritual beings who *are not thought* of as being "somatic," we should lose the reality and the actual experience of the human community of Ephesians, although we do not exclude the existence of spiritual beings.

Therefore, the meaning of "saints" in 1,18 is believers in Christ, the concrete community of Christians.

The communal and sharing character of the divine inheritance itself is, in its deepest sense, the glory of God. The apostle prays to the Father of the glory (Eph 1,17) for the sake of the recipients "you" so that they may be aware of and may comprehend what are the riches of the glory of God's inheritance in the saints.

The third comprehension is of the power of God: "and what is the immeasurable greatness of His power to us who have believed according to the working of His great might" (Eph 1,19) (*kai ti to hyperballon megethos tēs dynameōs autou eis hēmas tous pisteuontas kata tēn energeian tou kratous tēs ischuos autou*).

The author of Eph, piling up the word group of "power" (*dynamis, energeia, kratos, ischuos*) in plerophoric manner,[73] stresses the fact that the surpassing great might of God which is at work in "us," the authors who have believed (cf. 1,11-12; 3,20). The key word "power" alludes to the power of the resurrection of Christ (Eph 1,20; cf. 1 Cor 6,14; Phil 3,10) [74] and at the same time it alludes to the power at work in the community

---

[70] See our Chapter 3 pages 142ff., about the meaning of the particle *syn* ("with").

[71] See also 144f.

[72] Cf. pages 142 and the following pages 166ff. Chapter 4 about the second intercessory prayer 3,14ff.

[73] See pages 75ff., on the style. Schlier, *Komm.*, 85, distinguishes different meaning of these words; also cf. J. Ernst, *Komm.*, 289.

[74] Cf. J. A. Fitzmyer, "To know Him and the Power of His resurrection (Phil 3,10)" in: *Mél. B. Rigaux* (Gembloux 1970) 411-25, esp. 420f.

which is explained by using the image "Head-Body"-relation.[75]   The same power is surely at work in the recipients (i.e. "you"), but here in 1,19, he prays to God that they may receive the gift of the spirit and of the enlightened heart in order to come to comprehend the power at work for us believers.[76]   The apostle prays not merely to comprehend the Credo of the tradition which we lived in, but to acknowledge the comprehension of the power which is here and now at work within us.

And these three comprehensions, of the hope, of the inheritance and of the divine power, are in accordance with the working (*energeia*) of God's great might (*kata tēn energeian tou kratous tēs ischuos autou*).[77]

The particle *kata* ("in accordance with" or "according to") in our letter is used mainly together with the word-group of the divine will or decision (cf. Eph 1,5.7.9.11; 3,11) and with the power word group (cf. Eph 1,19; 3,7.20; 4,16; 6,10: with the preposition *en*; its counter powers: 2,2 . . . also cf. 4,22).[78]

This power of God is at work in all creatures (cf. Eph 1,11; 4,22) and now in a specific divine decision, it is concentrated to form the community of Christ and to permeate the power for unification and integration of the whole in Christ by the integrating "power" of the community of Ephesians,[79] and it is the power of evangelization given to Paul (cf. Eph 3,7f.).   In accordance with this power, the apostle prays to God that his readers may be inwardly aware of the surpassing power of God which is really at work within us in our community (cf. Eph 3,16).[80]

4-3: Comprehension of Four Dimensions

For this reason I bow my knees before the Father (3,14), from
whom every fatherhood in heaven and on earth is named (v. 15),
that according to the riches of his glory
he may grant you
to be strengthened through his spirit with
might in the inner man (v. 16)

---

[75] See the previous Chapter 3 on the Head and Body relation, especially pages 112ff. and 124ff.

[76] Gnilka, *Komm.*, 92f., and on page 92 note 2, he states: "... Für den Wechsel zum Wir ist zu beachten, daß die in die Fürbitte impliziert Mahnung, die sich an die Gemeinde richtet, mit Beginn des christologischen Credo-Satzes aufhört.   So hat der Wir-Satz überleitende Funktion."

[77] We take this *kata* phrase in 1,19b which modifies all the *tis*-sentences (1,18b-19a), and which, at the same time, relates to the following verses 1,20ff., to the power of God which was at work in Christ, to raise him and to make him sit at the right hand of God in the heavens over all powers, and to subdue these powers under his feet and to give him (Christ) over all powers to the Church.

[78] Cf. Col 1,11.25.29.

[79] Cf. pages 104ff., and 117ff.

[80] For the rest of the verse 1,20ff. see pages 127.

> (and) that Christ may dwell in your hearts
> through faith (v. 17a);
>
> being rooted and grounded in love (v. 17b),
> that you may be strong enough to comprehend with all the saints
> what is the breadth and length and height and depth (v. 18),
> (and) to know the love of Christ (which)
> surpasses knowledge (v. 19a),
> that you may attain to the fullness of God (v. 19b).

The passage of 3,14 begins with the words *toutou charin* (i.e. "for this reason" or "on behalf of").[81] The words *toutou charin* ("for this reason") of Eph 3,14 have the function of referring, not only directly to the passage 3,13 and to the whole of chapter 3, but also to the entire content of the letter which is explained from the beginning.[82]

The passages of 3,14-21 are a conclusion of the first part of the letter. The verse 3,14 begins thus: "For this reason, I bow my knees before the Father" (*Toutou charin kamptō ta gonata mou pros ton patera*). The sentence shows the attitude of the apostle towards God the Father. He (Paul) kneels down before God and prays with deepest reverence to God.[83]

Seeing his posture of "kneeling down" to pray, we notice that his attitude of the intercessory prayer, compared with that of the passages 1,15ff., gives those present a solemn impression and braces their spirits.[84]

---

[81] Cf. the same expression: Eph 3,1 and Tit 1,5; and the meaning, see Blass-Debrunner-Rehkopf, *Grammatik*, § 216, 2.

[82] T. K. Abbott, *The Epistles to the Ephesians and to the Colossians* (Edinburgh 1909) 93, states: "... Resumes ver. 1, 'On this account', referring to the train of thought in the latter part of ch. ii. Although the construction was broken off in ver. 2, the thought has continued to turn on the same ideas." J. A. Robinson, *St. Paul's Epistle to the Ephesians* (London 1914[4]) 173f., says: "... *Toutou charin*: The repetition of this phrase marks the close connexion of vv. 1 and 14 and shows that what has intervened is a digression." Schlier, *Komm.*, 167: "... Mit demselben *touto charin*, mit dem der Apostel 3,1 seine Bitte einsetzte, leitet er nun, wo er sich anschickt, sie auszusprechen, den Satz ein. Das *touto charin* wird sich daher auch noch einmal auf das vor Kap. 3 Dargelegte beziehen und nicht etwa auf 3,13 oder 3,2-12." Gnilka, *Komm.*, 180, note 6: "... Man wird darum sagen können, daß *toutou charin* den ganzen Abschnitt 1,16 — 3,13 zusammenfaßt."

[83] Schlier, Komm., 167; art. "*kamptō*", in: *TDNT*, III, 599-600. Compare the similar posture in praying: Rom 14,11; Phil 2,10 and cf. M. Barth, *Comm.*, 377f.

[84] If we compare the wording of Eph 1,15ff. with that of 3,14ff., we find many parallels which indicate the same attitude of the author:

dia touto ("for this reason") (1,15)   :   *touto charin* ("for this reason") (3,14)

mneian poioumenos epi tōn proseuchōn mou ("remembering you in my prayers") (1,16)   :   *kamptō ta gonata mou* ("I bow my knees") (3,14)

ho patēr ... ("the Father ...") (1,17)   :   ... *pros ton patera* ("before the Father ...") (3,14)

pneuma ("spirit") (1,17)   :   ... *dia tou pneumatos autou* ("through his spirit") (3,16)

Showing how much he reveres God the Father, the apostle specifies in the first sentence what kind of fatherhood he ascribes to God.

The relative clause of 3,15 has the function of explaining the "father":[85] "from whom (Father) every fatherhood in heaven and on earth is named" (*ex hou pasa patria en ouranois kai epi gēs onomazetai*). The Greek words *patēr - patria* are not merely for euphony or a play on words.

Indicating the style and the way of thinking of the author of Ephesians,[86] in 3,15, he is thinking of God as the Father of all and the source of the whole.[87] Without doubt, God is revealed to the community of Ephesians and experienced by them as the Father of Jesus Christ (cf. Eph 1,2-3) and as the Father of power and glory (cf. Eph 1,17). He is Creator of all (cf. Eph 3,9) and is creating the community in Christ to follow his way which God prepared (cf. Eph 2,10). He is God the Father who unites the whole in Christ (cf. Eph 1,9-10; 4,6).

This same God, in verse 3,15, is the source of every community and of every family, whichever form of group or nation or city or clan or family we find in the world, in heaven or on earth.[88]

From the Father of Jesus Christ, the gaze of the author is directed to every *patria* which finds its unifying power in this Father. God's fatherhood is reflected in the whole world, in His creatures as their source of "being in a community." [89]

This fatherhood as the source of the whole, is now made known to

---

ho patēr tēs doxēs ("the Father of the glory") (1,17)	:	*kata to ploutos tēs doxēs autou* ("in accordance with the riches of his glory") (3,16)
dynamis ("power") (1,19)	:	*dynamei* ("power" with) (3,16)
pisteuontes ("believing") (1,19) *agapēn* ("love") (1,15)	:	*dia pisteōs* ("through faith") (3,17) *en agapēi* ("in love") (3,17)
kardia ("heart") (1,17)	:	... *kardia hymōn* ("... your heart") (3,17)
ischuos ("might") (1,19)	:	*exischusēte* ("are strong enough") (3,18)
eis to eidenai ... ("so that ... know") (1,18)	:	*katalabesthai* ... *gnōnai* ... ("to comprehend ... to know ...") (3,18-19)
tis ... tis ... kai ti ... ("what ... what ... and what ...")	:	*ti ...* ("what ...") (3,18)
to hyperballon ... ("the immeasurable ...") (1,19)	:	... *tēn hyperballousan* ... ("... the surpassing ...") (3,19)

[85] Cf. B. M. Metzger, *Text. Comm.*, 604, states: "After *patera*, ... a variety of Western and Byzantine witnesses add the words *tou kuriou hēmōn ᵓIēsou*...."

[86] Cf. above pages 75f.

[87] God is referred to as father in patriarchal societies, in contrast to matriarchal societies in other cultural spheres. See G. Schrenk, and G. Quell, *"patēr"* etc. in: *TDNT*, V, 945ff.

[88] J. Ernst, *Komm.*, 336, and G. Schrenk, *"patria"*, in: *TDNT*, V, 1015-19. The verb *onomazetai* ("... is named") does not mean "is named after the Father." On this see M. Barth, *Comm.*, 367f. and 379ff. esp. 382ff.

[89] Compare Schrenk, art. cit., 1018.

the community of Christ. The community of Ephesians has an intimate relation to God. They are "sons" through Christ to God (cf. Eph 1,5).

In verses 3,16-17a, the author of Eph states the content of the intercessory prayer: "that according to the riches of his glory he (God) may grant you to be strengthened with might in the inner man, (and) that Christ may dwell in your hearts through faith" (*hina dō hymin kata to ploutos tēs doxēs autou dynamei krataiōthēnai dia tou pneumatos autou eis ton esō anthrōpon, katoikēsai ton Christon dia tēs pisteōs en tais kardiais hymōn*).

The apostle intercedes for the recipients (i.e. "you"). He has an insight into reality in the radiance of the divine glory. So, he is praying in conformity with the radiance and with the power of the glory of God the Father.[90]

The whole content of the apostle's prayer shows an inner relation to the power of glory of God. He intercedes for two gifts in the form of verbs in the aorist infinitive: "to be strengthened ... with might in the inner man" and "that Christ dwell in your hearts through faith" (*katoikēsai ton Christon ...*).[91] These two infinitive clauses appear to be formed in a parallel manner, in regard to their grammatical constructions. Because the two infinitive verbs are followed by *dia* ("through")-phrases: the first one is "through his spirit" and the second is "through faith." And the first instance has the *eis*-phrase, "in [lit. 'into'] the inner man" and the second one contains *en*-phrase, "in your hearts." [92]

The first gift the apostle intercedes for is an interiorization of the divine power and of its working in us within the community. This interiorization is not at all statically understood, but dynamically.

---

[90] Cf. Schlier, *Komm.*, 168. In our letter, we find a number of *kata* phrases ("according to ...", "in conformity with ..."). Most cases "define" the Act of God in Christ to us. See above, pages 165f. The particle *kata* with accusative means a norm of similarity or homogeneity. It means "according to ..." "in accordance with ... ", "in conformity with ...", "corresponding to...." Liddell & Scott, *A Greek-English Lexicon*, 883; F. Zorell, *Lexicon Graecum Novi Testamenti* (Paris 1961³) col. 662-63, in (6), states: "'de norma,' 'de conformitate vel similitudine': 'secundum,' 'congruenter,' seu 'consentanee ad.'" The *kata*-phrase ("according to the riches of His glory") in Eph 3,16 resumes the significations of *kata*-phrases in the previous passages of Ephesians, which relate to the Divine power and to the Divine decision and will or benevolent grace of His will. This intercessory prayer in 3,16ff., is not merely a favourable or benevolent will or wish of the apostle, but a petition corresponding to the power at work within "us" (see Eph 3,20).

[91] M. Zerwick, *Graecitas Biblica* (Romae 1966⁵), § 252, says: "Aoristus effectivus. Sicut apud verba quae statum significant attentio figitur in actionis initio, ita apud verba quae conatum significant, attentio potest dirigi in *finem* actionis et in effectum secutum...." "Confer Eph 3,16.17, ubi aoristi *krataiōthēnai* et *katoikēsai* de maturitate et perfectione intelligendi videtur esse." Why does the author of Eph ask these gifts in the form of infinitive verbs, rather in form of substantive nouns? We may think that the aorist infinitives indicate, at first, the continuing Act of God in the community, no matter whether some members of the community are aware of it or not, and secondly, denote an unlimited duration of the Act towards a goal. It could be felt that the author of Eph had an experience of the inner life of Christ.

[92] See also 98ff., esp. 100 and note (118).

What does it mean when the author of Eph states that "you" may
be strengthened with power in the inner man? What does he seek to
express when he says "the inner man"?

We want to explain our interpretation of Eph 3,16f. against the background of the concept of "interiority" and of "inner man" in some forms
of Western spirituality.

Quoting the French *Dictionnaire de Spiritualité*, E. Malatesta [93] ob-
serves about "interior man": "... What is said of the various meanings
of interior man ... can be applied to interiority in general."

A first, common sense meaning indicates the thoughts, sentiments
and desires which, although experienced by us, are invisible to the eyes
of others; they are "within" us. Second, the language of interiority,
especially in most of the French spiritual writers of the seventeenth
century, refers to the realm of prayer, recollection, awareness of God's
presence, in sum, to all those attitudes that express a serious purpose
in the pursuit of Christian perfection. Third, a more metaphysical sense
is found in the history of Christian tradition by those who reflect on the
ontological structure of religious experience.

At the conclusion of his article, the author (A. Lalande) seeks a point
of contact between traditional Christian spirituality regarding the interior
man and modern philosophy. He (the French author) suggests that in a
very general way a triple level of interiority can be found in the categories
of contemporary thought. First, within the realm of psychology, that is
interior which "exists in so far as known consciously or which is relative
to consciousness" (...), that is, whatever affects our psychological consciousness ... A second level of interiority is that of the exercise of
freedom in reflecting, deliberating, and judging in relation to the true,
the good and the beautiful. But since our being and the root of our freedom are not identical with our reflection, there is a third level of interiority, that of the "depth of the soul," the level of our existence which is
beyond ordinary consciousness. Although most spiritual writers by "interiority" refer first of all to the second level, "for them, to speak of the
interior man is, definitively, to point toward the most intimate level, the
deepest center, the depth of the soul, where man is called to fix his dwelling place in order to unite himself there to God present and to live his
whole life of action and contemplation in subjection to the Holy Spirit."

According to Western spirituality, perhaps the term "interiority" or
its active form "interiorization" can describe such a phenomenon as is
meant in Eph 3,16ff. But, admitting the fact that man perceives things
spacially, we feel that the term "interiority" presupposes already the
human "spatial" way of comprehension and cognition. According to Far
Eastern spirituality and religious sensitivity, we should prefer to use

---

[93] *Interiority and Covenant* (AnBib 69; Rome 1978) 10f., 13-14.

another expression, in order to focus from the beginning on the level of the interiority (i.e. the innermost level of heart).[94] Instead of "interiority," we should prefer an expression like "somatic interiorization" in the sense of somatic integration of the inmost depth of heart and of the divine dynamic, in order to avoid both a possible dualistic and an individualistic understanding of man.

We think that this mode of comprehension does not fit the case of "inner man" of Eph 3,16, because the verse does not treat an "individual" event but an "inner" event of the community of Ephesians and the mystery of Christ in the community.

Generally speaking, by "somatic interiorization" we mean that man integrates his whole person and his whole somatic way of being and living into the inmost depth of his heart in which God is really at work and where man unites himself to God present and meets and encounters other persons in the deepest level of their being. This process of the somatic interiorization must affect "intellection," "ways of thinking," "emotion and affection," and even "inner unconscious level of man." [95]

Religious peoples of the world are always confronted with the danger of disunity between reason and faith, between thoughts and somatic "Gestalt" as the expression of the inmost depth of heart. We Christians, in spite of our belief in the "salvation history" and in the decisive event of the Saviour Jesus of Nazareth, are no exception, because we often do not show credibility through our deeds and attitudes towards other religious peoples. The credibility comes from a unity between the somatic expression and the inmost depth of heart in which God calls and is at work, and in which man himself becomes himself, and in which man sees the reality as it stands, and in which man is aware of the profound unity of all creatures, and in which man meets with other persons in their depth and unites himself to God present.

"The inner man" in Eph 3,16 should not be understood dualistically and ontologically.[96] Because in the Pauline anthropology "inner man" and "outer man" denote the same man. Whether he is outer or inner man depends upon his attitude to God.[97]

The author of Ephesians is not referring to two opposed parts of man, but rather speaking of an ethical dualism. He speaks of two ways

---

[94] The expression "the depth of soul" already indicates a "dividing principle" of mind at work between "soul" and "body."

[95] We approach the reality at first through our somatic ordering and disposition of ourselves. Then all "higher" faculties of man follow the ordered and disposed body to God. Cf. what we said about "the Body" in chapter 3 and about Eph 1,15ff., above, pages 154ff.

[96] H. Schlier, *Christus und die Kirche im Epheserbrief* (Tübingen 1930) 35, gives the evidences of dualistic and ontological interpretations of "inner man." Also cf. the sources of other religions and philosophies: J. Jervell, *Imago Dei* (Göttingen 1960) 58ff., 247f.; Eltester, *Eikon*, 43ff. We follow more or less J. Ernst, *Pleroma*, 126f.

[97] Ibid., 127.

and two manners of the conduct of life: the conduct of life in Christ
and that of life without Christ or in opposition to God.[98]

The anthropological term *ho esō anthrōpos* in Rom 7,22 is in paral-
lelism to "I" *(egō*: vss. 17.18.20.) or the mind (*nous*: vss. 23-25) and shows
the believer in so far as he is in accord with God's will.[99]

The same expression "inner man" (*esō anthrōpos*) in 2 Cor 4,16 means
man as a creature of God who is renewed every moment, and the "outer
man" (*exō anthrōpos*) shows a man who is transient and is subjected to
suffering and to death.[100]

However, the inner man of Eph 3,16 neither teaches us an inner
phenomenon of an individual person (i.e. my consciousness and uncon-
sciousness) primarily like Rom 7,22, nor is described in opposition to an
outer man.

The author of Ephesians describes, in Eph 3,16ff., a depth of the
dimension of the community, which is analogous to the depth of the
heart of man.

A contrasting description of man is that in Eph 4,22f.   There the
verses present us with opposing manners of life in the image of the old
and the new man.[101]   Those verses describe two ways of life.[102]

According to our proposal, the inner man in Eph 3,16 denotes:

1. the purpose and goal of God who chose the community and makes
it come near to God Himself, making it His son through His beloved
Jesus Christ (Eph 1,5).[103]

2. a man who is created to follow the way which God had prepared
beforehand, the way in Christ (Eph 2,10; 4,22f.).

3. the inner experience of a life in accordance with the dynamic of
God in the community which leads to reconciliation and to unity (Eph 2,
15; 2,21f.).

4. a man who is not yet complete and is in the process of being per-
fected toward the fulness of God (cf. Eph 3,19).

5. the growing awareness of following the "ideal" Christ, which leads
to the unity of the faith and of the comprehension of the "son of God"
(Eph 4,16).[104]

The author states that it leads to total and whole interiorization of
faith, and of the comprehension which the Son of God completed in him-

---

[98] Cf. our Chapter 2 where we have discussed the two ways, pages 23ff.

[99] Cf. J. Behm, "*exō*" in: *TDNT*, II, 698-99; "*esō*" in: *TDNT*, II, 575-76, and also
compare H. Schlier, *Der Römerbrief* (Freiburg 1977) 233.

[100] Gnilka, *Komm.*, 183; J. Ernst, *Pleroma*, 127.   And compare the following passages of the Pauline letters: Rom 6,6; Eph 2,9f.; 4,24; Col 3,10.

[101] Cf. our explanation of Eph 4,17ff., about "walking in the futility of their minds,"
on pages 30ff.

[102] See page 23f. where we analysed *peripatein* ("to walk") and *anastrephein* ("to
lead one's life").

[103] Cf. page 101.

[104] See 100 note (118) and 136ff.

self for the sake of us. This inmost depth of the Son of God cannot be reached by any form of "narcissistic" acts. The "inner man" in Eph 3,16 has to be understood in relation to the inner dynamic of the community which originates in Christ's intimate relation to God.

The "inner man" is a theological "index" (cipher). It "constructs" and "gives form" to the community's faith and comprehension. At the same time, it grows and follows the concrete unification which the faith in the Son of God effects in the community. According to Eph 3,16, this process of "somatic interiorization" is done by the power and spirit of God.[105] From another point of view, Christ dwells firmly [106] in the heart through faith.[107] Verse 3,17 stresses the solid fact that Christ dwells in the heart of the readers: *katoikēsai ton Christon . . . .*

The expression of 3,17, "Christ dwells," has its root in the faith in the Divine presence expressed, e.g., with *Shekinah* in the Old Testament. And Paul also teaches that the believers are temples of the spirit or of God, that Christ dwells in a believer.[108] As we mentioned above,[109] in Ephesians the community of believers is explained by using the image of building and temple of God (see 2,19ff.).

In verse 3,17, the author of Eph states that Christ dwells in the hearts of those he is writing to.

In which heart? Christ dwells in the core of somatic interiorization, in the enlightened heart (1,18), in the heart liberated from the enslaved condition of man, in the heart open to other persons and to God (cf. 4,18),[110] and in the heart which sings a hymn to God (5,19) and in the heart of sincerity and of truth (6,5).

Between the first and the second *hina*-sentence (3,16-17a and 3,18), the author of Eph inserts two participles related to "in love" (*en agapē*): "being rooted and grounded in love" (*en agapē errizōmenoi kai tethemeliō-menoi*).[111] These two participles are directly related to the preceding infinitive verbs ("to be strengthened" and "to dwell") in 3,16-17a, if we consider the image and sense of the words, "being rooted" and "being grounded." Because the "being rooted" (*errizōmenoi — rizein — riza*: "to root" — "root") suggests an image that the deeper it is rooted in soil, the stronger and firmer it becomes; [112] the "being grounded" (*tethemeliō-*

---

[105] Cf. J. Ernst, *Pleroma*, 128.

[106] With Gnilka, *Komm.*, 184, states: "... Aufmerksamkeit verdient das Moment der Dauer, das mit *katoikēsai* bezeichnet ist ..."; also M. Barth, *Comm.*, 370.

[107] Compare: Eph 2,5b.8; 1,15; 1,19; 3,12.

[108] Cf. O. Michel, "*oikos*" etc., in: *TDNT*, V, 119-159. Compare: Rom 8,9; 1 Cor 3, 16; 6,17ff.; Col 1,19; 2,9.

[109] Pages 144f.

[110] Cf. pages 45ff.

[111] The participles (in the nominative) are still dependent on verse 16. They have indicative force. See Blass-Debrunner-Rehkopf, *Grammatik*, § 468.

[112] The image of a tree which sinks its root into the soil is not explicitly stated, but we feel the image of the verb *errizōmenoi* ("being rooted") presupposes an image of tree or plant, as we find in 1 Cor 3,9ff.

menoi — themeliein — themelios: "being grounded, founded, based": "to ground," "to base," "to found," "foundation") shows, on the other hand, an image that the more something is based on a solid foundation, the more firm it becomes. The former alludes to the growth of a tree which stretches its roots into the soil, the latter alludes to an image of building and of a temple (cf. Eph 2,19ff.; Col 1,23; 1 Cor 3,9ff. and its context).

These two images correspond to those images used in the two infinitive clauses. The first, "to be strengthened... in the inner man" in 3,16 indicates a movement similar to the rooting in love in 3,17b. The somatic interiorization must be reached by praticing love and should be done by rooting our actions in the soil of love. The recipients are encouraged by the apostle to be rooted firmly in love.

The infinitive clause "that Christ may dwell... in your hearts" (*katoikēsai ton Christo... en tais kardiais hymōn*) alludes to the image of the firmness and solidity of a building. The process of constructing a building is not to deepen or penetrate further into something, but to build up and pile stones on a solid and immovable foundation. In this way, the author of Ephesians, reminding his readers of the practice of love, makes a synthesis of what the two aorist infinitives mean,[113] and he bridges the following passages 3,18f.

The second and the third *hina* sentences (v. 18-19 and v. 19b) are subordinated to the previous *hina* clause of 3,16-17a,[114] and they show the deepest level of comprehension (verses 18-19a) and the final goal of the apostle in this letter to the Ephesians.

The structure of verse 3,18 is clear enough to be observed: the main verb of 3,18, *exischysēte* ("you may be able," "you may be strong") subordinates the two infinitive clauses as does the verb "may give" (*dōi*) in verse 3,16f.: "to comprehend with all the saints ..." (*katalabesthai syn pasin tois hagiois*) and "to know the surpassing love ..." (*gnōnai te tēn hyperballousan ... agapēn ...*).

The particle "*te*" in 3,19a after the infinitive *gnōnai* ("to know") effects a close link with the previous infinitive clause *katalabesthai* ... ("to comprehend ...") in 3,18.[115]

The contents of the comprehension are quite specific. The former is to comprehend together with all the saints what is the [116] breadth and

---

[113] Cf. Schlier, *Komm.*, 168.

[114] H. Schlier, *Komm.*, 168; Gnilka, *Komm.*, 185; Caragounis, *The Ephesian Mysterion*, 75.

[115] See Blass-Debrunner-Rehkopf, *Grammatik*, § 443. Both infinitives are of a "noematic" word-group: *katalabesthai*: to grasp, to find, to understand, to comprehend; *gnōnai*: to know. Cf. Phil 3,10.12f. Gnilka, *Komm.*, 186 and note 1 about *katalabesthai*: "Das einemal ist das durch *katalabesthai* selbst sichergestellt, das als Erfassen, Begreifen, das Betroffensein von dem Erkannten ohne weiteres miteinschliesst...."

[116] All that follows is to be understood under one article *to*.

length and height and depth, the latter to know the love of Christ [117] which surpasses knowledge.[118]

What does it mean when the author of Eph writes: "to comprehend with all the saints what is the breadth and length and height and depth"?

Why does the author of Ephesians not specify the four dimensions: "breadth, length, height, and depth"? Since the Church Fathers' time, it has been asked "which, whose, or of what" dimensions?

Did the author of Eph have a specific intention when he mentioned the four dimensions? If so, what was it? Or, sceptically we ask if it is right to inquire whose dimensions were meant.

Commentators have tried to solve this, one of the most difficult texts in the New Testament. Some think of a heavenly good of salvation, which is understood by the author of Eph spatially.[119] On this line, it meant God's inheritance among the saints (cf. Eph 1,18), the realm of salvation, or the heavenly city Jerusalem (cf. Rev 21,16f.).[120] Others think of a quality which has something to do with God or a divinity, or the divinity of Christ.[121] Some interpret it as the whole economy of salvation or the all-encompassing mystery of Christ.[122]

Some translations of the New Testament take the four dimensions in the sense of "the four dimensions of Christ's Love" which follows directly in Eph 3,19: "to know the Love of Christ which surpasses knowledge" (3,19a).[123] But the text as it stands does not allow us to assume this, even though the two phrases follow each other directly.

Irenaeus alluded to the four arms of the cross. He combined the four dimensions with the symbolism of the cross. The crucified Christ is the Logos, the word of God almighty in the whole world, and encompasses both its length and breadth and height and depth.[124]

Do the four dimensions represent Wisdom? [125] J. Dupont researched the meaning of the four dimensions in verse 3,18 against the background of Stoic philosophy. He thinks that the meaning of the four dimensions has to do with the wholeness of being, *to hen kai pan*.[126] The

---

[117] Cf. Eph 5,2.25.

[118] ... *tēn hyperballousan tēs gnōseōs agapēn* ...: the genitive ... *tēs gnōseōs* is a genitive of comparison. See: Blass-Debrunner-Rehkopf, *Grammatik*, § 185; Gnilka, *Komm.*, 189, note 5; J. Dupont, *Gnosis. La Connaissance religieuse dans les Épîtres de Saint Paul* (Bruges-Paris 1949) 493ff.

[119] See J. Ernst, *Pleroma*, 131.

[120] See N. A. Dahl, "Cosmic Dimensions and Religious Knowledge," in: *Jesus und Paulus* (Festschrift für W. Kümmel; 1975) 57-75, esp. 57f.

[121] See Ernst, op. cit., 131, note 2 where he specifies authors who hold this opinion.

[122] See Ernst, op. cit., 131; Dahl, art. cit., 57.

[123] *The New English Bible* (Oxford-Cambridge 1970²) 247; *The New American Bible* (New York 1970) 230; *Shinyaku Seisho, Kyōdōyaku* (Ecumenical Translation of the New Testament; Japan Bible Society 1978) ad locum.

[124] See M. Barth, *Comm.*, 396; Dahl, art. cit., 68.

[125] A. Feuillet, "L'Eglise plerome du Christ": *NRT* 78 (1956) II, 593-610; *Le Christ Sagesse de Dieu*, op. cit., 312ff.

[126] Cf. Ernst, *Pleroma*, 132; J. Dupont, *Gnosis*, op. cit., 476ff.

two horizontal dimensions with height and depth, then, encompass the entire world. Comprehension of the cosmic dimensions may stand for knowledge of the whole world and all that is in it.[127] And the author of Eph might describe elsewhere what he presented by *plērōma* and *sōma*, in another manner.[128] H. Schlier [129] sees the cross of Christ in the formula: breadth, length .... According to him, after having studied the possible background of the formula, he interprets it as Christ who is as world-encompassing Anthropos upon the world-encompassing cross.[130]

According to others, verse Eph 3,18 presupposes the tradition of the inaccessibility of the human mind to the divine wisdom or to God which is found in the Bible.[131]

If the four dimensions mean *the cosmic* dimensions, we wonder if it serves to know the immeasurable cosmos. In what way does it relate to the inner mystery of the community in Christ?

The author of Eph was not interested in the inaccessibility of God or of Wisdom; on the contrary, he tried to lead his readers to an inner comprehension of the mystery of God's will, as we have explained above.[132] He teaches us the "modus", and the "way" of attaining the inner comprehension of God which is now to be expressed in Christ and through Christ to us. As Dahl states,[133] " neither the cross-symbolism of Irenaeus nor the anti-gnostic attitude of later gnostics are likely to have been within the horizon of the author of Eph." We must respect the background of Stoic philosophy or Jewish wisdom literatures.

The author of Eph is not interested in natural theology and does not appear to have taught his readers the immeasurable dimensions of the cosmos.[134]

As we have explained above in the previous chapters, the author of Eph teaches us a certain inner comprehension of the mystery of God in Christ, which has been gradually maturing in the community of Ephesians. He is interested in the mystery of community. His main concern is to lead the recipients into a deeper, interior understanding of the mystery of the divine will in order to unite them.

Therefore, according to our proposal, the four dimensions of the formula *allude* (in its full sense) to the inner comprehension of the Body. The author of Ephesians does not give us the specification of the formula (i.e. the four dimensions). We may think that he thought it better to

---

[127] See Dahl, art. cit., 59.
[128] Cf. Ernst, *Pleroma*, 132.
[129] *Komm.*, 174.
[130] Id. 134.
[131] See Dahl, art. cit., 60ff. 70.
[132] Refer to our Chapter 4 and the pages we discussed the first intercessory prayer, 154ff.
[133] Art. cit., 69.
[134] Cf. Dahl, art. cit., 73.

omit the specific dimension. Even we feel that we should not specify the four dimensions. Because the comprehension of four dimensions concerns a comprehension of the community itself. The comprehending subject is the community itself: self-comprehension of the Body.

The readers (i.e. you) are the Body as well as the "we"-people behind the apostle. The inner self-comprehension is totally different from a normal comprehension of being as if it stood outside the man who comprehends. This comprehension of the four dimensions is internally related to our self-awareness and to its self-realization (somatization) of the mystery of God in Christ in the community and in all the communities which belong to Christ.

It relates to the inner comprehension and realization of the divine mystery which is actualized in this community in so far as the believers live in the Body of Christ and conduct life as members of the Body. The comprehension grows in relation to their integration into the Body.

The object of comprehension is not any ordinary tridimensional body. By mentioning the four dimensions, the author of Eph makes us aware of the fact that "you," the comprehending subjects, are placed so to speak at the centre of the "globe" of the Body, whose dimensions "you" may comprehend.

By "your" inwardly enlightened eyes of the heart, you see "forward," both sides of your body, "upwards" and your profoundity "downwards." We will come to explain this at greater length later.

The author surely means that the image of four dimensions could be well understood by the readers and can be understood by many Christians, but not by every Christian. Because the comprehension which the author of Eph teaches in 3,14ff., depends in the first place upon: divine gift and grace (see Eph 1,15ff.; 3,14ff.); [135] one's conduct of life, how a believer in Christ lives as we explained especially in our Chapter 2; the degree of integration among the recipients into the inmost "dynamic call of God at work" in the community, how deeply they integrate and unite themselves with the community of Christ, the Body of Christ.[136]

We shall now try to explain what is meant by Eph 3,18. The image of the four dimensions is dynamic. Let us say that we see a globe extending itself. According to the way in which have we interpreted the whole context, "the Body" is extending. By finding other unities among men or communities in the world and by integrating them into the community of Christ, the Body expands. It deepens these communities by integrating them and bringing them into inner contact with the sphere where God and men are united through Christ. Men become brothers, become members, so to speak, of one family. Here we should apply all

---

[135] See pages 154ff., 166ff.
[136] See our explanation, 124ff.

the examples the author is giving in the "parenetic" part of the letter.[137] This community of believers cannot be understood simply and univocally as the institutionalized local churches. The conduct of Christian life has to do essentially with the integration into the Body.

The "you," for whom the apostle intercedes, are seen standing at the vital "centre" of the Body. They see it absorbing other groups, new groups of men in the city of Ephesus and in the whole world, elevating them to unity with Christ, the Head who is in heaven. The Body grows and extends in the four dimensions as if it were extending into the whole cosmos and reaching to the infinite fulness of God (cf. Eph 3,19b). According to the image, those addressed in the epistle are looking towards this self-expansion. The image is applicable to every individual member of the community. But this member's self-integration, his inmost dynamic call of God must be deepened in accordance with the dynamic of the community of Christ, the Body of Christ. This process is not only an individual one, but communal. This deepening is tending always to others. The comprehension of the four dimensions is the self-comprehension of the community, in relation to all communities of Christ, to every possible community of Christ, through the ages and history of mankind.

Therefore, the author of Eph states that "you" may become strong enough to comprehend *together with all the saints* [138] what is the breadth and length and height and depth (Eph 3,18). It is a communal comprehension in its deepest sense.[139]

This may be the reason why the author does not specify which kind of dimensions are meant. The image is not completely clear. In fact, the four dimensions are "your" and "our" dimensions including the possible and potential stretch of the community of Christ (i.e. the Body). Individual thought and enlightenment and comprehension should serve to enrich the community's inner comprehension. By that point the whole body is enriched.

The communal aspect is also emphasized by the following words of 3,19a: "to know the love of Christ which surpasses (all) knowledge" (*gnōnai te tēn hyperballousan tēs gnōseōs agapēn tou Christou*).

The communal comprehension with all the saints presuposes unity among them. And this unity is the expression of the love of Christ. The community of Christ itself is the "realized and somatized" comprehension of the Love of Christ. The "somatized" form of the love of Christ is expressed by the image of the Body, by its dynamic intimacy and communion (cf. Eph 5,22ff. also). If you are aware of this fact, you cannot resist realizing the inner dynamism of God in your bodies and in your whole life and conduct. And "you" will attain to the fulness of God.

---

137 Cf. Epilogue, 181ff.
138 See our pages 164f.
139 Cf. Gnilka, *Komm.*, 186.

Therefore, the author of Eph states in 3,19b: "that you may attain to all the fullness of God" (*hina plērōthēte eis pan to plērōma tou theou*).[140]

The exact meaning of this last verse of the prayer (before the doxology in 3,20-21) is much discussed among the exegetes.[141] We cannot decide beyond doubt which opinion is right, but we can try to understand the verse in accordance with the explanation we have already offered.

The fulness with which the recipients of the letter will be enriched is surely God's fulness. On the other hand, this fulness must be related to the comprehension and experience the readers are having "in the Body." The act of "filling" takes place in this Body.

Can the wealth of grace and peace and love and mutual understanding which encompasses the readers be "human" in origin? The author has to characterize it as "divine." It comes from God, it is a gift of God, it is tending towards God. The believers are experiencing in faith the gift, which is in fact God Himself. In this context of prayer we have expressions which do not occur in "normal" life.

This experience is mystic in character. If one may compare this kind of experience with similar ones of later Christian mystics, one might employ their expressions. But it would go beyond the scope of exact exegesis to define more 'precisely' the nature of this "fulness of God." We can only say that "in the Body" Christians reach fulfilment of unity with God.

Thus, the first part of the letter comes to end with a doxology: [142]

> Now to him who by the power at work within us is able to do far more abundantly than all that we ask or think, to him be glory in the church and in Christ Jesus to all generations for ever and ever. Amen (3,20-21) (*Tōi de dynamenōi hyper panta poiēsai hyperekperissou hōn aitoumetha ē nooumen kata tēn dynamin tēn energoumenēn en hēmin* (v. 20), *autōi hē doxa en tēi ekklēsią kai en Christōi ᾽Iēsou eis pasas tas geneas tou aiōnos tōn aiōnōn. Amēn*).

From the beginning till the end of Chapter 3, the letter has a prayerful tone. Our studies have already shown that, in our opinion, the "letter" is "Christ-agogical" literature, in our sense, a "mystagogical" document. The author of Eph, after beginning in the form of a letter (1,1-2), expands his message to praise God in Christ (1,3-14).

---

140 The translation in English follows the New English Bible and the New American Bible. The literal translation from the Greek text may be: "that you may be filled into all the fullness of God" (3,19b). Some translate the verse thus: "that you may be filled *with* all the fullness of God." We, however, do not agree with this translation. The preposition *eis* is understood in the sense of "with." But to interpret *eis* in this way is to ignore the dynamic sense of the text. And see the textual variants: Metzger, *A Text. Comm.*, 604.

141 J. Ernst, *Pleroma*, gives an elenchus of the opinions, on pp. 120ff.

142 See: Schlier, *Komm.*, 176f.; Gnilka, *Komm.*, 191ff.; Ernst, *Komm.*, 341f.; Caragounis, *The Ephesian Mysterion*, 76f.

Interceding for his readers in 1,15ff., he leads them into the deeper comprehension of the mystery of Christ which by degrees is approaching realization in the community.

He tries to integrate them into the profound unity of Christ with God (2,1ff.). For this integration of the newcomers the apostle Paul plays the role of transmitting the mystery of Christ (3,1ff.).

For the immeasurable and profound mystery of unity, the mystery of the community in Christ, the apostle, in 3,14ff., again intercedes for his readers that they may attain to an inner knowledge and comprehension of the mystery of the community in Christ. The doxology in 3,20f., relates to all the previous part of the letter.[143]

Now the author of Eph exclaims in a final doxology seeing the profundity of the Divine plan and of God's will for the world, especially for "us," the community, "glory to God in the church and in Christ Jesus." To him, to his power, glory! He is now at work within us. His powerful deed is just beyond our ken.

Even in this verse, the author of Eph shows his main theology which we tried to explain above. The "grace-full" power of God and divine dynamism in the community is his reason for the doxology.[144] And he repeats that the comprehension of the power of God which is at work in us in the community surpasses our human knowing and knowledge (cf. Eph 3,19a).

Remarkably, the author of Eph sums up his insight and vision, saying: glory to the powerful God, *in the church* and *in Christ Jesus* for ever more. Amen (cf. 3,21).

---

143 Gnilka, *Komm.*, 191.
144 Refer to our pages 91ff. and 124ff.

CHAPTER 5

Epilogue

Now that we are approaching the end of our study, we shall briefly recapitulate what we have explained above, and we shall indicate the message of Ephesians for us, today's Christians. Here we shall not repeat the conclusion which we made at the end of our chapters.[1]

5-1: Unity

The Unity in Diversity

The community of Ephesians consisted of two groups [2] and was formed by the "we"-group of people and the "you"-group of people. In full consciousness of their different backgrounds, cultures and religions, they made every effort to live together in harmonious accord. Their community lived together, not because they shared *primarily* a common ideological unity or uniform thought, but an experience, a conduct of life in Christ. Both groups had the same point of departure to form a community and to live together in harmony as one community. They shared equally a manner of life of "being heathen" in the past.

The criterium of discerning and identifying who is a heathen and who is a believer in Christ, is practical and dynamic. The dynamic and practical nature is shown by a motif of "way" (*hodos*) in the letter. We have studied the motif of "way" in the sense of conduct of life (i.e. *peripatein*, "to walk" and same word group).[3] As a result of our study, we showed that the criterium of "being heathen" came from the manner in which man conducted his life. And "being Christian" is not simply a matter of baptism or similar ritual praxis. If we do not conduct our life in Christ, we Christians also could just as well be heathen. This acknowledgement is important for forming a community of peoples who have

---

[1] As was the practice of rhetoricians of old (Cicero, Fortunatus, C. I. Victor, Marianus, Sulpicius Victor, and others). See H. Lausberg, *Handbuch der Literarischen Rhetorik* (München 1973²) 236ff.; the epilogue should not be a simple repetition of what was said before. It should rather be an application of the total content of the previous work. According to those authors, the epilogue itself can be divided into three parts (or should, at least contain them): an enumeration of important items, an application to the actual reality, and an effective conclusion.

[2] See Chapter 2-2; 2-2-1, pp. 20ff.

[3] See Chapter 2-2-2, pp. 23ff.

different cultures and religions as their background, in order to live together in harmony.

The "being Christians," according to the author of Ephesians, means
more than denominations of Christian churches. From his deepened view
of humankind and from his experience of "being in Christ", he discerned
who was a believer in Christ and who was a heathen. From his insight,
he comprehended which manner of life was really the "being heathen"
and what was the hindrance to accepting the message of the unity which
Christ brought to the community of Ephesians. In deepening Pauline
conceptions of the earlier letters, he relativized the clear-cut Jewish
"discriminating" word "heathen" (i.e. *ethnē*) from his "status quo" of
"being in Christ." [4]

Clarifying what it meant to be heathen, we tried to understand a
right disposition for the unity which the author of Eph wanted to transmit
to his readers.

"Being heathen" creates an obstacle to two groups seeking to live
together in harmony and to become united. The manner and way of
"being heathen," according to the texts, originates in a disposition for
acknowledging the truth.[5] It is a condition and manner of life by which
man is enslaved by any thing to which he attaches himself, because of
his distorted heart and mind,[6] refusing to respond to a grace-full call of
God which is heard in his consciousness. This kind of man never opens
and cannot open his eyes towards the value of the community of Christ.
He is blind to the reality of God in Christ, and consequently cannot join
a community in Christ. His situation could become hopeless and
desperate.[7]

The characteristics of "being heathen" which we indicated above,[8]
teach us Christians to-day where lies the obstacle to living together in
harmonious accord and to unity among us.

The Opposition and Enmity

The opposition and enmity between the (former) Jewish people and
the (former) gentile were an instance drawn from the actual situation
of the community of Ephesians to whom the author of Ephesians spoke.[9]
By applying that "proto-pattern" of enmity between the Jews and the
non-Jews,[10] the author taught the recipients (i.e. "you") what caused disunity and enmity between the former Jews and the former gentiles (or,
between the Jewish Christians and the gentile Christians). Positively

---

4 See Chapter 2-2-1, pp. 20ff. and 2-2-3, pp. 29ff.
5 See Chapter 2-2-3, 1, pp. 30ff.
6 See pages 36ff.
7 See Chapter 2-2-3, esp., p. 30.
8 See Chapter 2-2-3, pp. 36ff.
9 See Chapter 2-2-3, 5, pp. 52ff.
10 See Chapter 2-3, pp. 56ff. esp. pp. 60f. and pp. 69f.

speaking, he instructed them (i.e. the readers) in what constituted the gospel of peace Christ brought to them and what was the message of reconciliation between those who hated one another, because of their difference in culture and religion. He went on to explain where lay the root and reason of enmity. The reason and root originate from an inner attitude of man. A community which does not accept equality of human-kind in the eyes of God, because of a consciousness of privilege and its superior feeling over others, such a community easily falls into a sectarian mentality, and consequently into enmity as happens when other groups do not follow its own ideology, its way of thinking and manner of life.

To create a real unity among men, therefore, Christ abolished the law (of the commandments in regulations),[11] which caused divisions and enmities, by the *Hingabe* (self-surrender) of his whole life, especially, by his whole dedication of life on the cross. To our way of thinking, this means that he abolished any form of doctrine, article, belief and a manner or custom of conduct of life which, causing division, is absolutized by a community or by a group (also by an individual), by its fixed way of comprehension without inner freedom and love of outsiders.[12] This kind of comprehension forms an introverted and self-righteous group or ghetto.

According to the text Eph 2,14ff., Christ himself is our peace, who made a bridge between both groups, unifying them into one community, thereby making peace.[13]

Profound unity with God presupposes the unity between members of a community; therefore, the author of Ephesians concludes the unit of Eph 2,14-18, with verse 2,18, describing the present condition of his community. "For through him (Christ) we both have access in one spirit to the Father."

The fact of unity between the members of the community, precisely, between the "us" and the "you," was itself a dynamically indispensable condition in order to draw near to God the Father. The community had intimate relations amongst the members and between God and themselves, God was to become their Father, and both of "us," namely both groups, who were reconciled in one community (i.e. "in one body") to God, were coming near to Him, God, in one spirit.[14]

The Somatic Comprehension of the Unity

If we Christians were to comprehend this unity and conduct our life according to this intimate unity with God, we should perceive that

---

11 See Chapter 2-3, pp. 56ff., esp. pp. 61ff.
12 See Chapter 2-3, pp. 62ff.
13 See pp. 68f.
14 See pp. 69f.

ideological unity or uniformity, by itself especially if it is superimposed by force, does not constitute the unity of Christians.

The orthopraxis in Christ promises us an end to ideology even in conventional religions, to the extent that they cause schism, disunion, and hatred between groups.

The first thing that Christian communities have to do is neither to seek for a "common" intellectual and "doctrinal" comprehension, nor to prescribe for their members a fixed law for every action and moment of life, nor to distinguish their communities from other groups and communities by signs and characteristics whether racial, cultural or religious.

The primary requirement of Christian communities is, in the words of the letter to the Ephesians, "to walk in love," as Christ loved his community and gave up his life totally for the members (cf. Eph 5,2), and to conduct life with all lowliness and meekness, with patience, forbearing with one another in love, eager to maintain the unity of the spirit in the bond of peace (cf. Eph 4,1ff.). We Christians are called to lead a life worthy of the calling to which we have been called. We have the inner impact of hope.[15] Our task is to permeate the message of reconciliation and unity into our daily life by letting it penetrate our life more and more. By this means the message can permeate the whole world.

The author of Ephesians encourages us: "Be kind to one another, tenderhearted, forgiving one another, as God in Christ forgave you" (Eph 4,32). Because we are parts of one Body (cf. Eph 4,25; 5,30).

We have to show to the world our fruits in the conduct of life which God wants us to bear (cf. Eph 5,5ff.).[16] Then, the world will believe what we are and what we believe.

In our Chapter 3, we have studied and deepened further the sense of unity of the letter which we already had explained in Chapter 2, and we found that it had a special feature. The unity of Ephesians formed the community and drew together the apostle, his collaborators and disciples (i.e. "we" group of people i.e. the sender[s]).

As we have indicated in chapter 2-3,[17] the primary concern of the author of Ephesians was the unity between the "we" group of people and the "you" group of people in one community. We repeat that we cannot simply identify the "we" people with Jewish Christians and the "you" with gentile Christians. The author of Ephesians had his deeper motif of integrating the "you" group of people into the community of Christ, more thoroughly and at a deeper level in which the apostle and his disciples (i.e. the "we" group of people) enjoyed the unity.

---

[15] See Chapter 4-2, pp. 154ff.

[16] Cf. H. Riesenfeld, "Le language parabolique dans les Epîtres de Saint Paul" in: *Littérature et Théologie Paulinienne*, (Recherches Bibliques publiées sous le patronagie du Colloquium biblicum Lovaniense V; 1960) 47-71, esp. 56f.

[17] See Chapter 2-2-3, pp. 52ff. and 2-3, pp. 56ff., esp. pp. 60f.

The unity in the community of Ephesians is dynamic. We found the dynamism by which the "new" Christians (i.e. "you") were united and integrated into the "old" but "new" community of Christ.[18] This dynamism has something to do with the literary genre of the letter to the Ephesians. The peculiarity of the language and of its style, and the current thought of the text, testify to a special literary genre. We have proposed it as "Christ-agogical"[19] literary genre in a sense of Christian "Mystagogy."

We believe that in the letter there existed already a "consensus" between the writer(s) and the recipients (namely in the text, the "we" group of people and the "you" group of people), so that the latter were ready to be guided by the former and introduced into the deeper comprehension of the divine mystery of God for unification.[20] The form of the letter has to be understood as an effective way of communication to the readers. The author of Ephesians wanted to communicate to his readers a deeper awareness and realization of the divine mystery of will.[21] On this same dynamism the changes of personal pronouns ("we" and "you" styles) are based. The author wanted to guide the recipients (i.e. "you") into the awareness of the divine mystery of will which the "we" group of people had in part actualized in their life and conduct. This is the reason why, even in the hymnic beginning (Eph 1,3-14), the author juxtaposes the "we" style and the "you" style in 1,12f.[22] and explicitly by the central section 1,7-10, especially 1,8b-10.[23] And even the usages of prepositions and verbal tenses confirm this dynamism of integrating the "new" Christians into the community of Christ fully.[24]

The Body, Image of the Divine Dynamism

The notion of "Body" (*sōma*) in our letter retains its position in this literary genre and in the intention of integration and unification. The whole complexity of the divine act which happened in Christ (according to the schema of the author of Ephesians)[25] and its dynamism are explained by using the image "Head - Body."[26]

The Body of Christ in our letter is very concrete. It is the intensified and somatized (i.e. actualized) dynamism of God. It shows a profound unity of the members in Christ with God and among the members them-

---

[18] See especially, Chapter 3-5-3, pp. 104ff.
[19] See Chapter 3, esp. pp. 75ff.
[20] See pp. 75f., 85f., and Chapter 3-6, pp. 112ff. (3-6-1; 3-6-2; 3-6-3) and Chapter 4, pp. 150ff.
[21] See Chapter 3-6: 3-6-1; 3-6-2; 3-6-3.
[22] See Chapter 3-5-3, pp. 107, 90f.
[23] See Chapter 3-6, pp. 112ff.
[24] See Chapter 3-5, especially 3-5-3, pp. 104ff.
[25] See Chapter 3-5-2, pp. 98ff.
[26] See Chapter 3-6-3 and 3-7-1; 3-7-2; 3-7-3.

selves. The Body, that is, the community of Christ, exists not for its own sake, but for the glory of God and the sake of the world. It includes a dynamism in the shape of going out and serving others, instituting a dialogue and inviting men into the profound unity which is found in the Body of Christ. It absorbs differences in humankind (whichever form they may take) into the Body itself, into its unity in Christ. The Body of Christ, the "somatized" unity, integrates all kinds of peoples to one community of Christ. Thus it grows and expands.[27] The Body, growing in the world and filling the world with itself, absorbs other peoples into its unity, and by doing so, its unity expands. It is a core of dynamism of God who is at work in Christ. It "synthonizes" with the divine dynamism and synthesizes with the dynamic of human groups which may grow in the deeper unity with Christ.

One of the main concerns of the letter is to "somatize" this awareness of the dynamism[28] and to make it visual and credible to the world.

Therefore, the apostle, playing the role of transmitting the mystery,[29] interceded for the gift of comprehension of the unity and its somatization on the part of the readers. They had still a way to traverse toward a goal. The divine execution for unity has still room for the readers (i.e. "you"). The mystery of God's will which had been made known to "us" (cf. Eph 1,9) has not yet been fully executed by the recipients. This is the reason why the apostle prayed for them twice in the letter (Eph 1,15ff.; 3,14ff.) in order to that they might attain to the fullness of God.[30]

This approach to religious reality has great value in the eyes of people who know their way to God through "Bodily" comprehension in their human and religious experiences in the Far East.

5-2: Role of Christian Community

The message of unity which Ephesians brings must permeate our life and our society where we live. Our Christian communities must be a witness to the inner intimacy of God and the unity of humankind. Now, picking up some actual problems in the world, we apply the message to them.

Sense of Life

We live and repeat our life of routine. And our life seemingly becomes dull and lifeless. However, Christian life which aims at the unity of mankind is really worth living. The real meaning of our routine life comes from the unity among the members of the community in Christ.

---

[27] See Chapter 3-7-2; 3-7-3.
[28] See especially Chapter 4-2; 4-3.
[29] See Chapter 4-1.
[30] See Chapter 4-3; especially, pp. 178f.

It leads to the intimate relation with God himself who gives a sense of life and joy and hope.

In the community, a man is evaluated as a unique person who can contribute his priceless gift to the members. By building up the community of Christ, we can vivify the world and give a hope to those who are lonely and distressed.

Message for Youth

And youth rarely find themselves in a position to choose their future professions, looking for a life worth living, in the "seemingly empty" world. One of the remarkable things in the letter is that it contains no perspective of future death. The author of Eph says in Eph 2,4ff., that we have already risen together with the "old" members of the community of Christ here and now. Death does not mean a threat to these people who lived in harmonious unity in the Body of Christ. Death cannot destroy the unity and relation between them and Christ, and their unity with each other. Christians are not looking forward to death, but for them death lies behind them. Our past does not affect us any longer, and preoccupation for the future and anxiety do not make sense for those who enjoy the real unity which Christ brought.

We Christians can give a real sense of life to youth who are seeking a life worthy of self-commitment. It is the message of unity and cooperation which is now making an "inner revolution" in this world.

The message of unity must permeate not only our small Christian world but the societies surrounding us. It challenges us and pushes us to promote the unity of Christ.

Christian Society

In our christian societies, where they exist, there should be neither class fighting nor hatred and conflict between oppressors and oppressed (cf. Eph 6,5-9).

Each man, each race, each religion, each culture has a function complementary one to the other. Mutual respect and subjection of one to another is the sign of "being Christian." The author of Eph says: "Be subject to one another out of reverence for Christ" (Eph 5,21).

To the Pan-sexual Societies

This principle of life, respect and mutual subjection, is applicable to married life.[31] Unity between man and woman, between wife and husband, reflects this divine mystery of the unity which has appeared

---

[31] We take the verse Eph 5,21 as the theme sentence of the following passages. With Gnilka, *Komm.*, 273f.; M. Barth, *Comm.*, 609ff.

in the community of Christ. Therefore, the strong attraction of both sexes does not produce an object of fear nor a menace to social life in the family, but it can even become a symbol of the mystery of the unity between Christ and his Church. It is not married life in itself that shows the unity and relation between Christ and his church, but the intimacy between Christ and the members of His body which supplies a base for a better understanding of the unity between man and woman.[32]

For centuries and centuries people have married. A man falls in love with a girl, the girl loves him. They are married, leaving their fathers and mothers and their aging families, together to share their life. Creating their new family and a unity of life with their newly born children they renew family unity. Thus the circle of unity (cf. Eph 5,31ff.) extends and grows.

This process of life receives its solid base from the mystery of Christ's unity with His church. Unity of married life grows, just as the community of Christ grows absorbing a diversity of peoples into its unity.[33]

Celibacy for the Kingdom of God

In speaking of married life, we must mention those who dedicate their life to the service of community in Christ and humankind. Especially do priests and religious in churches witness to the mystery of the unity of Christ who, loving others concretely, gave himself up for the church. Those who maintain a celibate life show that their entire dedication (i.e. whole life) is to serve and promote the growth of the Body of Christ in its full sense. These dedicated people are themselves the living witness of the somatic comprehension of the divine mystery of unification. The somatic comprehension of the divine mystery needs a whole person and whole body. This exceptional manner of christian life always warns and encourages man that married life is not by itself a real sign of the unity between Christ and His church, but, vice versa; namely, the unity of Christ with His church should be reflected in married life. Christian families therefore must be open to another wider and bigger unity of the Christ-mysterion.

The Christian Community Itself is a Mission of Unity

As a result of our study of Ephesians, we must touch on the motif of "going as a missionary." It does not mean to go to a "primitive"

---

[32] See R. Schnackenburg, "Die Ehe nach dem Neuen Testament," in: *Theologie der Ehe*, edited by G. Krems and R. Mumm (Regensburg-Göttingen 1969) 28f. and in the same book, H. Greeven, "Ehe nach dem Neuen Testament", 77ff. Cf. Mt 18,20. Married life in itself does not show the mystery of God. It shows it only in so far as both are gathered together and united in the Lord Christ. Cf. also J. Duss-von Werdt, "Theologie der Ehe. Der Sakramentale Charakter der Ehe", in: *Mysterium Salutis*, IV/2 (Einsiedeln 1973) 422-49, esp. 440f.

[33] See Chapter 3-7-3, pp. 142ff.

country to teach "Christian doctrine" and culture with "good will" and with "zeal of saving barbarians and pagans." Sometimes missionaries have tried to "indoctrinate" "pagans" and "barbarians" and to integrate them into their own mentalities and to their own customs and philosophies.

On the contrary, the mission of the church is rather, to see the multiform wisdom of God everywhere among men. In Eph 3,8ff., this task is well described: "To me (Paul), though I am the very least of all the saints, this grace was given, to proclaim to the gentiles the unsearchable riches of Christ, and to make all men aware of what is the plan of the mystery hidden for ages in God who created all things; so that through the church the manifold wisdom of God might now be made known to the principalities and powers in the heavenly places."

Consequently, the propagation of the mystery of Christ as the Lord of the whole world will take the form of a proposal to unify the good aspirations, the great efforts, at every corner of the world already going on. In deep and full respect of the diversity, the apostle announces his insight into the mystery of the world, revealed to him — according to his faith and conviction — not as means to dominate others and to overwhelm them with knowledge and power, but to serve them and to make them aware of the fact that God is working among them, to fulfill the work of Christ. As marriage and every other community among men can become the image of Christ's unity with the church, so the apostle sees in every human value and in every authentic communion between men the radiance of God's splendor. He preaches this good news amongst the nations and indicates *their riches in God.*

His conviction of this fact and his preaching is a gift of God to the world. In the same way, he knows that this ministry is a humble one and must be executed in the spirit of Christ. In this light, the apostles of Christ see themselves as bridges between differences, disunities and so many other imperfect realizations of the will of God. All men are destined to enter into the Body of Christ. All nations, all cultures, all groups of men are potential extensions of this Body. We have a joyous role in the world to encourage their unities which may be elevated to the unity of Christ, that is open to the unity with God Himself.

Our Battle Against Evil Spirits

At the end, we close our epilogue, paraphrasing the words of Ephesians 6,10ff. The author of Ephesians encouraged the readers to fight against evil spirits and powers in the heavenly places. The enemies are not humankind but transcendental powers who try to destroy our endeavour to become united. They enslave us by their power of money, sex, by fame and in one word, by the desire to rule over others.

How can we in our days describe the influence of such transcendental powers at work in the world?

Mass Media

The mass media often create hostility between people of different nations, because they only know and report a part of the truth; they very often give slanted, false or even fabricated information from a politico-economic motive, in order to protect the power and interest of a small number of men. Consequently, people fed with false information conceive enmity against other peoples who are unknown save through the manipulations of the mass media. Let the oppressed and voiceless billions of people speak out. They have a right to relate a history of humankind. Mass media has the duty to inform truthfully (cf Eph 4,25) in so far as lies in their power and to deepen mutual understanding among nations and peoples. Its role is that of uniting peoples in the Body of Christ.

Manipulation in Education of Children

A system of education and school curriculums very often create "self-righteous" attitudes towards other groups or communities, closing children's hearts to greater unities, in order to keep a group or nation or cultural group introverted. And children are very often left in ignorance of the relativity of their culture and religion.

History is normally written by those victorious in wars, condemning defeated nations and races to justify their (the victor's) injustice. One has only look at the genocides of the world. We must also learn a history from the mouths of the defeated, conquered and abandoned peoples. Let us educate our children to become members of the Body of Christ.

Existing Sin

The destiny of humankind rests in the hands of a few people. Innocent people are killed without a word. Sin exists not only as inter-personal, but also as supra-personal and inter-structural of groups. Sciences and even theologies become "official" doctrines to "serve" not humans but structures of groups and to profit and to protect evil structures of societies. To the extent that we are not aware of the real unity of Christ, we Christians may stand on the evil side of exploiters and manipulators without being conscious of it.

According to the epistle even in those days at Ephesus, the author warned his readers: "Look carefully then how you walk, not as unwise men but as wise, making the most of the time, because the days are evil" (Eph 5,15-16). But he was not pessimistic about the situation.

Similarly, our situation in the midst of the malice of "transcendental" powers at work is not desperate. The last image of the letter to Eph encourages us: Christ has already won the battle, we are victorious fighters.

As a well-known classical book about a strategy of a battlefield in ancient China, Suendz [34] says that a general never enters a battlefield unless he is sure to win.

Christ as the Head of the Body, the real *Mystagōgos* and *Stratēgikos* had already won his battle. What we Christians must do is simply to follow him as our guide. Through the existence of the community of Christ in the midst of this world, we know that we have conquered the evil powers in the heavenly places. Because Christ is our Head and we are the same Body of Christ.

---

[34] Suendz (343 B.C.?), IV, 2 (*Sōshi*, IV, 2) (Tokyo, 1974⁵) 27f.

Bibliography

Only works cited in this study are included.

Bible: Texts and Versions (including Apocrypha)

Biblia Hebraica, edited by R. Kittel (Stuttgart 1937, 1973).
R. H. Charles, *The Apocrypha and Pseudepigrapha of the Old Testament,* vol. II (Oxford 1913).
Epistula ad Colossenses, Vetus Latina, edited by H. J. Frede (Freiburg, 1966-1971).
The Greek New Testament, edited by K. Aland, M. Black, C. M. Martini, B. M. Metzger, and A. Wikgren (1975[3]).
The Holy Bible, the Revised Standard Version (1973).
The New American Bible (New York 1970).
The New English Bible (Oxford 1970[2]).
Septuaginta, edited by A. Rahlfs, (Stuttgart 1949[3]) vols. I. II.
Shinyakuseisho, kyodoyaku [The Ecumenical Translation of the New Testament] (Tokyo 1978).

Commentaries on the Letter to the Ephesians

Abbott, T. K., *The Epistles to the Ephesians and to the Colossians* (Edinburgh 1909).
Allan, J. A., *The Epistle to the Ephesians* (London 1959).
Barth, M., *Ephesians,* 2 vols. (Anchor Bible; Garden City, N. Y. 1974).
Belser, J., *Der Epheserbrief des Apostels Paulus* (Freiburg 1908).
Candisch, R. S., *Paul's Epistle to the Ephesians* (Edinburgh 1875).
Conzelmann, H., *Der Brief an die Epheser* (NTD 8; Göttingen 1976).
Ernst, J., *Die Briefe an die Philipper an Philemon an die Kolosser an die Epheser* (Regensburg 1974).
Gaugler, E., *Der Brief des Paulus an die Epheser* (Wuppertal 1961).
——, *Der Epheserbrief* (Zürich 1966).
Gnilka, J., *Der Epheserbrief* (Herders Theologischer Komm. X/2; Freiburg-Basel-Wien 1971).
Haupt, E., *Die Gefangensschaftsbriefe* (Göttingen 1902).
Houlden, J. H., *Paul's Letters from Prison* (Penguin Books 1970).
Knabenbauer, I., *Commentarii in S. Pauli Epistolas ad Ephesios, Philippenses et Colossenses* (Paris 1912).
Mayer, H. A. W., *Handbuch über den Brief an die Epheser* (Göttingen 1965).
Moule, H. G. G., *The Epistle of Paul the Apostle to the Ephesians* (Cambridge 1910).
Rienecker, F., *Der Brief des Paulus an die Epheser* (Wuppertal 1961).
Robinson, J. A., *St. Paul's Epistle to the Ephesians* (London 1914[4]).
Sadler, M. F., *The Epistles of St. Paul to the Galatians, Ephesians and Philippians* (London 1892).
Scott, E. F., *The Epistles of Paul to the Colossians, to Philemon and to the Ephesians* (London 1930).

Schlier, H., *Der Brief an die Epheser. Ein Kommentar* (Düsseldorf 1963³).

von Soden, H., *Die Briefe an die Epheser, Kolosser, Philemon, die Pastoralbriefe* (Handkomm. zum NT 3; Freiburg 1893²).

Vosté, J.-M., *Commentarius in Epistolam ad Ephesios* (Rome-Paris 1932).

Westcott, B. F., *Saint Paul's Epistle to the Ephesians* (London 1906).

Zerwick, M., *Der Brief an die Epheser* (Düsseldorf 1961).

Monographs and Articles on the Letter to the Ephesians

Allan, J. A., "The 'in Christ' Formula in Ephesians": *NTS* 5 (1958-1959) 54-62.

Batey, R., "The Destination of Ephesians": *JBL* 82 (1963) 101.

Bedale, S. F. B., "The Theology of the Church," in: *Studies in Ephesians* (1956) 64-75.

Benoit, P., "Rapports littéraires entre les épîtres aux Colossiens et aux Éphésiens', in: *Ntl. Aufsätze* (Festschrift J. Schmid; Regensburg 1963) 11-12.

———, "L'unité de l'Eglise selon l'Epitre aux Éphésiens": *Stud. Paul. Congressus 1961* (AnBib 17; Roma 1963).

Bowen, C. R., "The place of 'Ephesians' among the letters of Paul": *AngThR* 15 (1933) 279-99.

Burger, C., *Schöpfung und Versönung. Studien zum liturgischen Gut im Kolosser- und Epheserbrief* (WMANT 446); (Neukirchen 1975).

Cadbury, H. J., "The dilemma of Ephesians": *NTS* 5 (1958-1959) 91-102.

Cambier, J., "La Benediction d'Eph 1,3-14": *ZNW* 54 (1963) 58-104.

Caragounis, C. C., *The Ephesian Mysterion. Meaning and Content* (Coniectanea Biblica, NT Ser 8; Lund 1977).

Colpe, C., "Zur Leib-Christi-Vorstellung im Epheserbrief", in: *Judentum-Urchristentum-Kirche*, Festschrift für J. Jeremias: BZW 26, 172-87.

Coutts, J., "Ephesians 1,3-14 and 1 Peter 1,3-12": *NTS* 3 (1956-1957) 115-27.

———, "The Relationship of Ephesians and Colossians": *NTS* 4 (1957-1958) 201-07.

Dahl, N. A., "Adresse und Proömium des Epheserbriefes": *TZ* 7 (1951) 241-64.

———, "Cosmic dimensions and Religious knowledge," in: *Jesus und Paulus* (Festschrift für W. Kümmel); (1975) 57-75.

de la Potterie, I., "Le Christ, Plérôme de l'Église (Ep 1,22-23)": *Bib* 58 (1977) 500-24.

Feuillet, A., "L'Eglise 'plerôme' du Christ d'après Eph 1,23": *NRTh* 78 (1956) 449-472; 593-610.

Fischer, K. M., *Tendenz und Absicht des Epheserbriefes* (FRLANT 111; Göttingen 1973).

Fowler, R., "Ephesians 1.23": *Exp* 76 (1965) 294.

Gewiess, J., "Die Begriffe *plēroun* und *plērōma* im Kolosser- und Epheserbrief," in: *Vom Wort des Lebens* (Festschrift für M. Meinerz; Münster/Westf. 1950) 128-41.

Giavini, G., "La Structure litteraire d'Eph II. 11-22": *NTS* 16 (1969-1970) 209-11.

Gnilka, J., "Paränetische Tradition im Epheserbrief," in: *Mélanges bibliques en hommage au B. Rigaux* (Gembloux 1970) 397-410.

———, "Christus unserer Friede-ein Friedens-Erlöserlied in Eph 2,14-17", in: *Die Zeit Jesu* (Festschrift für H. Schlier; Freiburg-Basel-Wien 1970) 190-207.

———, "Kirchenmodell des Epheserbriefe": *BZ* 15 (1971) 161-84.

Hanson, S., *The Unity of the Church in the New Testament. Colossians and Ephesians* (ASNU 14; Uppsala-Kobenhavn 1946).

Harrison, P. N., "The Author of Ephesians": *Studia Evangelica*, vol. II (Berlin 1964) 595-604.

Hitchcock, F. R. M., "The Pleroma as the Medium of the Self-realisation of Christ" : *Exp* 48 (1922) 135-50.

Innizer, T., "Der Hymnus in Eph 1,3-14," in: *ZKT* 28 (1904) 612-21.

Jayne, D., "'We' and 'you' in Ephesians 1,3-14": *Exp* 85 (1974) 151-52.

Joüon, P., "Notes philologiques sur quelques versets de l'Épître aux Éphésiens (1, 12; 2,1-3; 2,15; 3,13.15; 4,28; 5,18.19; 6,9.19-20)": *RSR* 26 (1936) 455-56.

Krämer, H., "Zur sprachlichen Form der Eulogie Eph 1,3-14": *Wort und Dienst, Jahrbuch der Theologischen Schule Bethel* (Bethel bei Bielefeld 1967) 34-46.

Kuhn, K. G., "Der Epheserbrief im Lichte der Qumrantexte": *NTS* 7 (1960-1961) 334-46.

Lindemann, A., *Die Aufhebung der Zeit*. Geschichtsverständnis und Eschatologie im Epheserbrief (StNT 12; Gütersloh 1975).

——, "Bemerkungen zu den Adressaten und zum Anlaß des Epheserbriefes," in: *ZNW* 67 (1976) 225-35.

Lohmeyer, E., "Das Proömium des Epheserbriefes," in: *Theologische Blätter* 5 (1926) col. 120-25.

Lyonnet, S., "La bénédiction de Eph 1,3-14 et son arrière-plan judaïque," in: *A la rencontre de Dieu* (Memorial A. Gelin) (Le Puy 1961) 341-52.

Maurer, C., "Der Hymnus von Epheser 1 als Schlüssel zum ganzen Briefe": *EvTh* 11 (1951-1952) 151-72.

McGlashan, A. R., "Ephesians 1,23": *Exp* 76 4 (1965) 132-33.

Mehlmann, J., *Natura filii irae, Historia interpretationis Eph 2,3 eiusque cum doctrina de Peccato Originale nexus* (AnBib 6; Romae 1957).

Merklein, H., *Christus und die Kirche* (SBS 66; Stuttgart 1973).

——, "Zur Tradition und Komposition von Eph 2,14-18": *BZ* 17 (1973) 79-102.

——, *Das kirchliche Amt nach dem Epheserbrief* (StANT 33; München 1973).

Meyer, R. P., *Kirche und Mission im Epheserbrief* (StudBiblStuttgart 86; Stuttgart 1977).

Mitton, C.L., "Unsolved New Testament Problems". "Goodspeed's Theory regarding the origin of Ephesians": *Exp.* 59 (1947-1948) 323-27.

——, "Important hypotheses reconsidered," VII, The Authorship of the Epistle to the Ephesians: *Exp.* 67 (1955-1956) 195-98.

Montagnini, F., "Christological features in EP 1,3-14," in: *Paul de Tarse Apôtre du notre temps* (La communauté monastique de S. Paul en mémoire de Pape Paul VI) (Rome 1979) 529-39.

Montgomery-Hitchcock, F. R., "The Plerom of Christ": *ChQ* 125 (1937-1938) 1-18.

Mussner, F., *Christus, das All und die Kirche*. Studien zur Theologie des Epheserbriefes (TrThSt 5; Trier 1968[2]).

——, "Beitäge aus Qumran zum Verständnis des Epheserbriefes," in: *Ntl. Aufsätze* (Festschrift für J. Schmid) (Regensburg 1963).

Norden, E., *Agnostos Theos. Untersuchungen zur Formen-Geschichte Religiöser Rede* (Darmstadt 1971[5]).

Percy, E., *Die Probleme der Kolosser- und Epheserbriefe* (Lund 1946).

Pokorny, P., "Epheserbrief und gnostische Mysterien": *ZNW* 53 (1962) 160-94.

——, *Der Epheserbrief und die Gnosis* (Berlin, 1965).

Rader, W., *The Church and racial hostility. A History of Interpretation of Ephesians 2,11-22* (Tübingen 1978).

Ramarson, L., "Une lecture de Éphésiens 1,15 - 2,10": *Bib* 58 (1977).

Sampley, J. P., *"And the two shall become one flesh". A Study of Traditions in Ephesians 5,21-33* (Cambridge 1977).

Sanders, J. T., "Hymnic elements in Ephesians 1-3": *ZNW* 56 (1965) 213-32.

Schille, G., *Liturgisches Gut im Epheserbrief* (Göttingen 1953).

Schlier, H., *Christus und die Kirche im Epheserbrief* (Tübingen 1930).

Schnackenburg, R., "Die große Eulogie Eph 1,3-14, Analyse unter textlinguistischen Aspekt": *BZ* 21 (1977) 67-87.

Stuhlmacher, P., "Er ist unser Friede" (Eph 2,14), in: *Neues Testament und kirche* (Für R. Schnackenburg) (Freiburg 1974) 337-58.

Vanhoye, A., "L'épître aux Éphésiens, et l'épître aux Hébreux": *Bib* 59 (1978) 198-230.

Virgulin, S., "L'origine del concetto di pleroma in Ef 1,23": (AnBib 17-18), vol. II (1961) 39-43.

Wilson, R. A., "'We' and 'you' in the Epistle to the Ephesians": *StEv* (TU 87; Berlin 1964).

Yates, R., "A Re-examination of Ephesians 1,23": *Exp* 83 (1972) 146-51.

Other Books and Articles Quoted

Aland, K., *Vollständige Konkordanz zum Griechischen Neuen Testament*, vol. 1 (Berlin-New York 1977).

——, "Falsche Verfasserangaben? Zur Pseudonymität im frühchristlichen Schriftum," in: *ThRe* 75 (1979) 1-10.

Aletti, J.-N., *Colossiens 1,15-20. Genre et exégèse du texte Fonction de la thématique sapientielle* (AnBib 91; Rome 1981).

Alonso Schökel L., *Estudios de poética hebrea* (Barcelona 1963).

Alzinger W., "*Ephesos*", in: *RE*, Suppl., vol. XII, 1588-704.

Alzinger, W. - Karwiesse, S. - Knibbe, D., "*Ephesos*", in: *RE*, Suppl., vol. XII, 248-364.

Arai, S., "Zur Definition der Gnosis in Rücksicht auf die Frage nach ihrem Ursprung" (1967), in: ed. by Rudolph, K., *Gnosis und Gnostizismus* (Wege der Forschung 262; Darmstadt 1975) 646-53.

Bartchy, S. S., *First-century Slavery and 1 Corinthians 7,21* (SBL Dissertation Series 11; 1973).

[Bauer, W.] - Arndt, W. F. - Gingrich, F. W., *A Greek-English Lexicon of the New Testament and Other Early Christian Literature* (Chicago 1957, 1973[14]).

Bauer, K.-A., *Leiblichkeit das Ende aller Werke Gottes* (Gütersloh 1971).

Bauernfeind, O., "*Mataiotēs*", etc., in: *TDNT* IV, 519-24.

Baumgärtel, F., "*Kardia*", in: *TDNT* III, 605-07.

Bayer, F. W., "*Anatomie*", in: *RE*, vol. I (Stuttgart 1950).

Beasley-Murray, G. R., "The Second Chapter of Colossians": *RevExp* 70 (1973) 469-79.

Berger, K., "Apostelbrief und apostlolische Rede zum Formular frühchristlicher Briefe": *ZNW* 65 (1974) 190-231.

Bertram, G., "*anastrephō*", etc., in: *TDNT*, VII, 714-29.

——, "*strephō*", etc., in: *TDNT*, VII, 714-29.

Betz, H. D., "The Literary Composition and Function of Paul's Letter to the Galatians": *NTS* 21 (1975), 357-79.

Boman, T., *Das hebräische Denken im vergleich mit dem griechischen* (Göttingen 1952, 1965[4]).

Bornkamm, G., "*mysterion*", in: *TDNT*, IV, 802-17.

Bradley, D. G., "The Topos as a Form in the Pauline Paraenesis": *JBL* 72 (1953) 283-46.

Braun, H., "*poieō*", etc., in: *TDNT*, VI, 458-84.

Brokelmann, C., *Grundriss der vergleichenden Grammatik der semitischen Sprache*, II Band (Hildesheim 1961).

Brox, N., *Falsche Verfasserangaben. Zur Erklärung der frühchristliche Pseudepigraphie* (SBS 79; Stuttgart 1975).

Bedale, S., "The meaning of 'kephalē' in the Pauline Epistles": *JThS* 5 (1954) 211-15.

Behm, J., "*esō*", in: *TDNT*, II, 575-76.

———, "*exō*", in: *TDNT*, II, 698-99.

———, "*kardia*", in: *TDNT*, III, 608-13.

Benoit, P., *Exegese et Theologie* (Paris 1961) vol. II.

———, "Leib, Haupt und Pleroma in den Gefangenschaftsbriefen," in: *Exegese und Theologie* (Düsseldorf 1965).

Best, E. C., *An Historical Study of the Exegesis of Colossians 2,14* (Rome 1956).

Bjerkelund, C. J., *Form, Funktion und Sinn der Parakalo-Sätze in den paulinischen Briefen* (Oslo 1967).

[Blass, F.-Debrunner, A.-Funk, R. W.], *A Greek Grammar of the New Testament and Other Early Christian Literature* (Cambridge 1961).

Blass, F.-Debrunner, A.-Rehkopf, F., *Grammatik des Neutestamentlichen Griechisch* (Göttingen 1976).

Brox, N., "Zum Problemstand in der Erforschung der altchristlichen Pseudepigraphie," in: N. Brox (ed.), *Pseudepigraphie in der heidnischen und jüdisch-christlichen Antike* (Darmstadt 1977) 311-34.

Buck, C. D., *Introduction to the Study of the Greek Dialects* (Boston 1910).

Bujard, W., *Stilanalytische Untersuchungen zum Kolosserbrief, als Beitrag zur Methodik von Sprachvergleichen* (StUNT 11; Göttingen 1973).

Bultmann, R., "*nekros*", etc., in: *TDNT*, IV, 892-95.

———, *Theologie des Neuen Testaments* (Tübingen 1977[7]).

Büchsel, F., "'*In Christus*' bei Paulus": *ZNW* 42 (1949) 141-58.

———, "*thymos*", "*epithymia*", in: *TDNT* III, 167-72.

Bürchner, L., "*Ephesos*", in: *RE*, V, 2773-822.

Chrysostomos, Dio, *The Twelfth or Olympic discourse* (Loeb Class. Library, II) (translated by J. W. Cohoon), (reprint, 1977).

———, *The Fortieth Discourse: Delivered in his native city on concord with the Apameans* (Loeb Class. Library, IV; translated by H. L. Crosby) (1956; reprint, 1962).

Chrysostom, Dio, *The Thirty-First Discourse*: The Rhodian oration, (Loeb Class. Library, III; translated by J. W. Cohoon; 1951; reprint, 1961).

Conzelmann, H., *Die Apostelgeschichte* (Tübingen 1963)

———, *Der erste Brief an die Korinther* (Göttingen 1969).

———, "*phōs*", "*phōtizō*", etc., in: *TDNT*, IX, 310-58.

Cullmann, O., *Christ and Time* (London 1962, 1967).

———, *Heil als Geschichte. Heilsgeschichtliche Existenz im Neuen Testament* (Göttingen 1965).

de la Potterie, I., *La Verite dans Saint Jean*, tome II (AnBib 74; Rome 1977).

Deichgräber, R., *Gottes hymnus und Christus hymnus in der frühen Christenheit* (StUNT 5; Göttingen 1967).

Deidun, T. J., *New Covenant Morality in Paul* (AnBib 89; Rome 1981).

Deismann, G. A., *Die neutestamentliche Formel "in Christo Iesou"* (Marburg 1892).

Delling, G., "*archō*", "*archē*" etc., in: *TDNT* I, 478-89.

———, "*chronos*" in: *TDNT* IX, 581-93.

———, "*kairos*" in: *TDNT* III, 455-62.

———, "*plērēs*", "*plērōma*" etc., in: *TDNT* VI, 283-311.

———, "*stoicheō*" etc., in: *TDNT* VII, 666-87.

———, "*symbibazō*" in: *TDNT* VII, 763-66.

Dillon, J., *The Middle Platonists* (London 1977).

Dornseiff, F., *Antike und alter Orient* (Leipzig 1952).

Dotty, W. G., *Letters in primitive Christianity* (Philadelphia 1973).

Dupont, J., *Gnosis. La connaissance religieuse dans les Épîtres de Saint Paul* (Bruges-Paris 1949).

Duss-von Werdt, J., "'Theologie der Ehe.'" *Der Sakramentale Character der Ehe*, in: *Mysterium Salutis*, IV/2 (Einsiedeln 1973) 422-49.

Eltester, F.-W., *Eikon im Neuen Testament* (Berlin 1958).

Epstein, I. (ed.), *The Babylonian Talmud, seder Zeraᵓim* (London 1948).

Ernst, J., *Pleroma und Pleroma Christi. Geschichte und Deutung eines Begriffs der paulinischen Antilegomena* (BU 5; Regensburg 1970).

Feuillet, A., *Le Christ sagesse de Dieu* (Paris 1966).

Foester, W., "*aēr*", in: *TDNT* I, 165-66.

———, "*eirēnē*", etc., in: *TDNT* II, 406-20.

———, "*exestin*", "*exousia*", etc., in: *TDNT* II, 560-75.

———, "*klēronomos*", "*klēronomia*", etc., in: *TDNT* III, 776-85.

Fitzmyer, J. A., "To know Him and the power of his resurrection (Phil 3,10)", in: *Mél. B. Rigaux* (Gembloux 1970) 411-25.

Fleischer, R., *Artemis von Ephesos und verwandte Kultstaten aus Anatolien und Syrien* (Leiden 1973).

Gabathuler, H. J., *Jesus Christus, Haupt der Kirche Haupt der Welt*. Der Christushymnus Colosser 1,15-20 (AThANT 45; 1965).

Galen, *Sieben Bücher Anatomie des Galen*, in Deutsche übertragen und kommentiert von M. Simon, vol. II (Leipzig 1906).

Galen, *On the Natural Faculties* (translated by A. J. Brock (Loeb Class. Library; London reprint, 1963).

Gärtner, B., *The Temple and the Community in Qumran and the New Testament* (Cambridge 1965).

Gesenius, N. A., *Hebrew and English Lexicon of the Old Testament* (translated by E. Robinson; Oxford 1906).

Greeven, H., "Ehe nach dem Neuen Testament," in: *Theologie der Ehe*, herausgegeben von G. Krems und R. Mumm (Regensburg-Göttingen 1969).

Greshake, G., *Auferstehung der Toten*. Ein Beitrag zur gegenwärtigen theologischen diskussion über die Zukunft der Geschichte (Essen 1969).

Grossouw, W., *In Christ* (Westminster, Maryland 1952).

Gribomont, J., "De la notion de 'Faux' en litterature populare," in: *Bib* 54 (1973) 434-36.

Grundmann, W., "*hamartanō*", in: *TDNT*, I, 302-16.

———, "*syn*", "*meta*", etc., in: *TDNT*, VII, 766-97.

Gundry, R. H., *SOMA in Biblical Theology with Emphasis on Pauline Anthropology* (Cambridge 1976).

Gutbrod, W., "*Israel*", etc. in: *TDNT*, III, 356-91.

Guthrie, W. K. G., *A History of Greek Philosophy*, vol. II (Cambridge 1965).

Haardt, R., *Die Gnosis. Wesen und Zeugnisse* (Salzburg 1967).

Hesiod, *The Homeric hymns and Homerica*, (translated by H. G. Evelyn-White) (Loeb Class. Library); (Cambridge reprint, 1974).

Hay, D. M., *Glory at the Right Hand; Psalm 110 in Early Christianity* (Nashville-New York 1973).

Hengel, M., *Judaism and Hellenism. Studies in Their Encounter in Palestine during the Early Hellenistic period*, 2 vols. (Philadelphia 1974).

Honda, W., "*Eki*" (Asahishinbunsha, Chinese Classic 1; Tokyo 1978).

Hommel, P., "'Melie', Geschichte aufgrund der Quellen und des Grabungsbefunden," in: *Jahrbuch des Deutschen Archäologischen Instituts*, 23. Erg. Heft (Berlin 1967).

Haenchen, E., *Die Apostelgeschichte* (Göttingen 1965⁵).

Israelstam, J., (translated), *The Babylonian Talmud, Seder NEZIKIN: SHEBUᵓ OTH MAKKOTH EDUYYOTH ABOTH* (London 1935).

Jaeger, W., *The Theology of the Early Greek Philosophers* (Oxford 1947).
Jeremias, J., *"gōnia", "akrogōniaios", "kephalē gōnias",* in: *TDNT*, I, 791-93.
Jervell, J., *Imago Dei* (Göttingen 1960).
Jessen, O., *"Ephesia",* art. in: *RE*, V, 2753-71.
Jewett, R., *Paul's Anthropological Terms,* A Study of Their Use in Conflict Settings (Leiden 1971).
Joly, R., *Le thème philosophique des genres de vie dans l'antiquité classique* (Bruxelles 1956).
Kittel, G., *"dogma",* etc., in: *TDNT* II, 230-32.
Der Kleine Pauly, Lexikon der Antike, auf der Grundlage von Pauly's Realency-clopädie der classischen Altertumswissenschaft unter Mitwirkung Zahlreicher Fachgelehrter bearbeitet und herausgegeben von K. Ziegler und W. Sonthei-mer (Stuttgart 1967).
Kleiner, G., *"Panionion", Geschichte aufgrund der Quellen und Bodenforschung,* in: Jahrbuch des Deutschen Archäologischen Instituts, 23. Erg. Heft (Berlin 1967).
Kleinknecht, H., *"orgē",* in: *TDNT* V, 382-92.
Knibbe, D., *"Ephesos,"* in: *E,,* Suppl. XII, 248-97.
Köster, H., *"physis",* etc. in: *TDNT* IX, 251-77.
Kuhn, H. W., *Enderwartung und gegenwärtiges Heil* (Göttingen 1966).
Kuhnert, *"Ephesia grammata",* in: *RE*, V, 2771-73.
Kümmel, W. G., "Die literarische Fälschung ...", in: *ThR* 38 (1973) 64-65.
Lampe, W. H., *A Patristic Greek Lexicon* (Oxford 1961).
Laoz,, (translated and explained by Fukunaga, K.) (Asahishinbunsha, Chinese Classic 10-11; Tokyo 1978).
Lausberg, H., *Handbuch der Literarischen Rhetorik* (München 1973[2]).
Lenschau, T., *Die Gründung Ioniens und der Bund am Panionion,* in: *Klio* 36 (N.F. 18) (1944) 201-37.
Lentzen-Denis, F., "Methodische Überlegungen zur Bestimmung literarischer Gattungen im Neuen Testament": *Bib* 62 (1981).
———, in: *Theologie und Philosophie* 46 (1971) 285-89, and in: *Bib* 60 (1979) 286-91.
Levy, J., *Wörterbuch über die Talmudim und Midrachim,* Band I (Berlin-Wien 1924).
Liddell, H. G. - Scott, R., A *Greek-English Lexicon,* vols. I, II (Oxford, reprint 1948).
Lightfoot, J. B., *Saint Paul's Epistles to the Colossians and to Philemon* (London 1879).
Lindemann, A., *Paulus im ältesten Christentum. Das Bild des Apostels und die Rezeption der paulinischen Theologie in der frühchristlichen Literatur bis Marcion* (Beitr. Hist. Theol. 58; Tübingen 1979).
Lohse, E., *Der Briefe an die Kolosser und an Philemon* (Göttingen 1968).
———, *Colossians and Philemon* (translated by W. R. Poehlmann and R. J. Karris; Philadelphia 1971).
Lührmann, D., *Das Offenbarungsverständnis bei Paulus und in Paulinischen Ge-meinde* (Neukirchen-Vluyn 1965).
Lyall, F., "Roman Law in the Writing of Paul—Slaves and the Freedman": *NTS* 17 (1970) 75.
Lyonnet, S. - Sabourin, L., *Sin, Redemption and Sacrifice* (AnBib 48; Rome 1970).
Magie, D., *Roman Rule in Asia Minor,* vol. I, text (Princeton 1950).
Malatesta, E., *Interiority and covenant,* (AnBib 69; Rome 1978).
Maurer, C., *"praxis",* in: *TDNT* VI, 642-44.
McNamara, M., *The New Testament and the Palestinian Targum to the Pen-tateuch* (AnBib 27A; Rome 1978).
Metzger, B. M., *A Textual Commentary on the Greek New Testament* (1971[3]).
Michaelis, W., *"hodos",* etc., in: *TDNT* V, 42-114.
———, *"horaō",* etc., in: *TDNT* V, 315-68.

Michel, O., *"philosophia"* in: *TDNT* IX, 172-88.
———, *"oikos"* etc., in: *TDNT* V 119-59.
Momigliano, A., *Alien Wisdom, the Limits of Hellenisation* (Cambridge 1975).
Moule, C. F. D., "'Fullness' and 'fill' in the New Testament": *SJTh* 4 (1951) 79-86.
Moulton, J. H. - Milligan, E., *The Vocabulary of the Greek Testament, Illustrated from the Papyri and Other Non-literary Sources* (London 1930).
Moulton, J. H., *A Grammar of New Testament*, vol. III; *Syntax*, by N. Turner (Edinburgh 1963).
Mullins, T. Y., "Disclosure: A literary form in the New Testament": *NT* 4 (1964) 44-50.
Muszynski, H., *Fundament, Bild und Metapher in den Handschriften aus Qumran* (AnBib 61; Rome 1975).
Neugebauer, F., "Das Paulinische 'in Christo'": *NTS* 4 (1957-1958) 124-38.
Neusner, J., *A Life of Rabban Yohanan Ben Zakkai (ca. 1-80 C.E.)* (Leiden 1962).
Nötscher, F., *Gotteswege und Menschenwege in der Bibel und in Qumran* (Bonn 1958).
O'Brien, P. T., *Introductory Thanksgiving in the Letters of Paul* (Leiden 1977).
Oepke, A., *"En"*, in: *TDNT*, 537-43.
———, *"Apokalypsis"*, *"apokalyptō"*, in: *TDNT*, III, 563-92.
Olbright, T. H., "Colossians and Gnostic Theology": *RestQ* 14 (1971) 65-79.
Ollrog, W.-H., *Paulus und seine Mitarbeiter. Untersuchungen zu Theologie und Praxis der paulinischen Mission* (WMANT 50; Neukirchen 1979).
Ono, S., *Nihongo o sakanoboru* ["To Trace Back the Japanese Language"] Tokyo, 1974).
———, *Nihongo no bunpo o kangaeru* ["To Consider Japanese Grammar"] (Tokyo 1978).
Oster, R., "The Ephesian Artemis as an opponent of early Christianity": *JAC* 19 (1976) 24-44.
Pagels, E. H., *The Gnostic Paul. Gnostic Exegesis of the Pauline letters* (Philadelphia 1975).
Parisius, H. L., "Über die forensische Deutungsmöglichkeit des paulinische 'en Christō₁'": *ZNW* 49 (1958) 285-88.
Pfammatter, J., *Die Kirche als Bau. Eine exegetisch-theologische Studie zur Ekklesiologie der Paulusbriefe* (Analecta Gregoriana 110; Romae 1960).
Penna, R., *Il "mysterion" paolino* (Brescia 1978).
Percy, E., *Der Leib Christi in den paulinischen Homolegumena und Antilegomena* (Lund 1942).
———, *Die Probleme der Kolosser- und Epheserbriefe* (Lund 1946).
Picard, C., *Ephèse et claros* (Paris 1922).
Prümm, K., *"Mystères"*, art. in: *Supplément au dictionnaire de la Bible*, VI (Paris 1960) col. 1-225.
Quecke, H., Book review in: *Bib* 58 (1977) 292ff.
von Rad, G., *"Eirēnē"* etc., in: *TDNT* II, 400-06.
Ramsay, W. M., *The Church in the Roman Empire before A.D. 170* (London 1892).
Reid, J. K. S., "The phrase 'in Christ'": *ThTo* 17 (1960-1961) 353-65.
Reumann, J., "'Oikonomia'-terms in Paul in Comparison with Lucan Heilsgeschichte": *NTS* 13 (1966-1967) 147-67.
Riesenfeld, H., "Le language parabolique dans les épîtres de saint Paul", in: *Littérature et Théologie paulinienne* (Recherches Bibliques publiées sous le patronage du colloquium biblicum Lovaniense, V; 1960) 47-71.
Rigaux, B., *Saint Paul. Les épîtres aux Thessaloniciens* (Paris 1956).
———, "Révélation des mystères et perfection à Qumran dans le Nouveau Testament": *NTS* 4 (1957-1958), 237-62.

Robertson, A. T., *Kurzgefasste Grammatik des Neutestamentlichen Griechisch* (Leipzig 1911).

Robinson, J. A. T., *The Body* (London 1952).

Robinson, J. A., *"Pōrōsis" and "pērōsis"*, in: *JThS* 3 (1901-1902) 81-93.

Rossberg, C., *Praepositionum Graecarum in chartiis Ptolemaerum aetatis usu* (Jena 1908).

Rouffiac, J., *Recherches sur les caractères du grec dans le Nouveau Testament d'après les inscriptions de Prien* (Paris 1911).

Rudolf, K., "'Gnosis und Gnostizismus'. Ein Forschungsbericht", in: *ThR* 38 (1974) 1-25.

Rudolf, K., *Die Gnosis. Wesen und Geschichte einer spätiker Religion* (Leipzig 1977).

Russell, D. S., *The Method and Message of Jewish Apocalyptic* (London 1964).

Sanchez Bosch, J., *"Gloriarse" según San Pablo* (AnBib 40; Rome 1970).

Sand, A., *Der Begriff "Fleisch" in den paulinischen Hauptbriefen* (Biblische Untersuchungen, 2; Regensburg 1967).

Sanders, J. T., "The Transition from Opening Epistolary Thanksgiving to Body in the Letters of the Pauline Corpus": *JBL* 81 (1962) 348-62.

Sasse, H., *"Aiōn"*, etc. in: *TDNT* I, 197-209.

——, *"kosmeō", "kosmos"*, etc., in: *TDNT* III, 867-98.

Schattenmann, J., *Studien zum neutestamentlichen Prosahymnus* (Göttingen 1965).

Schille, G., *Frühchristliche Hymnen* (Berlin 1965).

Schlier, H., *"Anakephalaiōomai"*, in: *TDNT* III, 681-82.

——, *"Kephalē"*, in: *TDNT* III, 673-81.

——, *"Kamptō"*, in: *TDNT* III, 599-600.

——, *Mächte und Gewalten im Neuen Testament* (Questiones disputatae, 3; Freiburg 1958).

Schlier, H., *Der Römerbrief* (Freiburg 1977).

Schmauch, W., *In Christus* (Gütersloh 1935).

Schmidt, K. L., *"Ethnos"*, in: *TDNT* II, 369-72.

——, *"Kaleō", "klēsis", "eklegō"*, etc., in: *TDNT* III, 487-536.

Schnackenburg, R., "Die Ehe nach dem Neuen Testament", in: *Theologie der Ehe*, herausgegeben von G. Krems und R. Mumm (Regensburg-Göttingen 1969) 9-36.

Schneider, J., *"Meros"*, in: *TDNT*, IV, 594-95.

Schneider, C., *Kulturgeschichte des Hellenismus*, vols. I-II (München 1967/1969).

Schniewind, J., Friedrich, G. *"epaggellō", "epaggelia"*, etc., in: *TDNT* II, 576-86.

Schrenk, G. - Quelle, G., *"Patēr"*, etc., in: *TDNT*, V, 945-1022.

Schrenk, G., *"Patria"*, in: *TDNT* V, 1015-19.

——, *"Thelēma"*, in: *TDNT* III, 56-62.

——, *"Eudokeō"*, in: *TDNT* II, 738-51.

Schubert, P., *Form and Function of the Pauline Thanksgivings* (Berlin 1939).

Schweitzer, A., *Die Mystik des Apostels Paulus* (Tübingen 1930).

Schweizer, E., *"Sarx"*, in: *TDNT* VII, 119-51.

——, *"Sōma"*, in: *TDNT* VII, 1024-094.

Schweizer, E., *Grammatik der Pergamenischen Inschriften* (Berlin 1898).

Seesemann, H. - Bertram, G., *"Pateō"*, etc., in: *TDNT* V, 940-45.

——, *"Ptripatein"*, in: *TDNT* V, 944-45.

Shan tze translated and explained by K. Fukunaga (Tokyo 1978).

Sint, J. A., *Pseudonymität im Altertum. Ihre Formen und ihre Gründe* (Innsbruck 1960).

Suendz (Tokyo 1974⁵).

Speyer, W., *Handbuch der Altertumswissenschaften*, 1. Abteilung, 2. Teil (München 1971).

Stadelmann, L.I.J., *The Hebrew Conception of the World* (AnBib 39; Rome 1970).

Staab, K., *Die Thessalonicherbriefe, die Gefangenschaftbriefe* (Regensburg NT; 1969[5]).

Stauffer, E., "*Atheos*", in: *TDNT* III, 120-21.

Stählin, G., "*Orgē*", in: *TDNT* V, 419-47.

Steinmetz, F. J., *Protologische Heils-Zuversicht. Die Struktur des soteriologischen und christologischen Denkens im Kolosser- und Epheserbrief* (Frankfurt Th. St. 2. Frankfurt/M 1969).

Stewart, J. S., "A First-Century Heresy and its Modern Counterpart": *SJTh* 23 (1970) 420-36.

Strathmann, H., "*Polis*", etc., in: *TDNT* VI, 516-35.

Strack, H. - Billerbeck, P., *Kommentar zum Neuen Testament aus Talmud und Midrasch* (München 1926; reprint 1951) vol. I.

Tabachovitz, D., *Die Septuaginta und das Neue Testament* (Lund 1956).

Tischendorf, C., *Novum Testamentum Graece* (Leipzig 1859[7]).

Thumb, A., *Die Griechische Sprache im Zeitalter des Hellenismus* (Strassburg 1901).

———, *Handbuch der Griechischen Dialekte* (Heidelberg 1909).

Turner, N., *Grammatical Insights into the New Testament* (Edinburgh 1965).

Urban, A. - Mateos, J. - Alepuz, M., *Cuestiones de grammatica y lexico* (Madrid 1977).

Usami, K., "*How are the dead raised?*": *Bib* 57 (1967) 468-93.

van Roon, A., *The Authenticity of Ephesians* (Leiden 1974).

Vanhoye, A., *La structure littéraire de l'épître aux Hébreux* (Paris 1976[2]).

Vogt, E., "'Mysteria' in textibus Qumran": *Blb* 37 (1956) 247-57.

Wagner, G. (ed.), *An Exegetical Bibliography on the Letter to the Ephesians* (Zürich 1977).

Walcott, P., *Hesiod and the Near East* (Cardiff 1966).

Weinrich, H., *Sprache im Texten* (Stuttgart 1976).

Weinrich, H., *Besprochene und erzählte Welt* (Stuttgart 1977[3]).

West, M. L., *Early Greek Philosophy and the Orient* (Oxford 1971).

Westermann, C., *Isaiah 40-66*, (London 1969).

Widmann, H., "*Die literarische Fälschung im Altertum*. Bemerkungen zu w. Speyers Monographie", in: *Antiquariat* (Wien 1973) 169-74.

Wikenhauser, A., *Die Kirche als der mystische Leib Christi nach dem Apostel Paulus* (Münster 1940[2]).

Wiles, G. P., *Paul's intercessory prayers* (Cambridge 1974).

Wilson, R. McL., *Gnosis and the New Testament* (Oxford 1968).

Xenophon, *Memorabilia IV*, translated by E. C. Marchaud and O. J. Todd, (Loeb Class. Library; London 1968).

Zeilinger, F., *Der Erstegeborene der Schöpfung. Untersuchungen zur Formalstruktur und Theologie des Kolosserbriefes* (Wien 1974).

Zerwick, M., *Graecitas Biblica* (Rome 1960).

———, *Analysis philologica Novi Testamenti graeci* (Rome 1966).

Ziehen, L., "*Panionia*", in: *RE* XVIII, 601-05.

Zimmermann, G. A., "Ephesus im 1 christlichen Jahrhundert" (Diss. Leipzig, 1874).

Indices

Index of Biblical and Other Ancient Sources

Index of Greek Words

Index of Authors